Corporate T

If Taxable Income Is		The Tax Payable Is		
Over	But Not Over	Amount	Plus (Percent)	Of the Amount Over
$ -0-	$ 50,000	-0-	15%	$ -0-
50,000	75,000	$ 7,500	+25	50,000
75,000	100,000	13,750	+34	75,000
100,000	335,000	22,250	+39	100,000
335,000	10,000,000	113,900	+34	335,000
10,000,000	15,000,000	3,400,000	+35	10,000,000
15,000,000	18,333,333	5,150,000	+38	15,000,000
18,333,333	—	6,416,666	+35	18,333,333

Federal Taxes and Management Decisions

1997-98 edition

Update for the Small Business, Health Insurance, and Welfare Reform Acts of 1996 (unless otherwise noted, the following changes are effective for tax years beginning after 1996)

Page 26

The exclusion for life insurance proceeds is expanded to apply to accelerated benefits received by terminally or chronically ill individuals. The exclusion also applies to the proceeds of sales or assignments of life insurance contracts to viatical settlement providers, which are companies that purchase contracts from people with terminal illnesses.

The exclusion for personal injury awards is narrowed so that it does not apply to punitive damages, regardless of the nature of the legal claim giving rise to the damages. The only exception to this rule applies to punitive damages awarded under certain state wrongful death statutes; all other types of punitive damages must be included in the recipient's gross income.

Page 72

Congress has enacted a new, scaled-down Work Opportunity Tax Credit equal to 35 percent of the first $6,000 of wages paid to each first-year employee who belongs to a targeted group.

Page 97

Subchapter S corporations may own an 80 percent or more equity interest in a C corporation. S corporations may also own a "qualified subchapter S subsidiary." These subsidiaries must be 100 percent owned by a parent S corporation and must meet all other requirements for subchapter S status.

The limit on the number of S corporation shareholders is increased from 35 to 75.

Page 116

The maximum Section 179 annual deduction is gradually increased from $17,500 in 1996 to $25,000 over the following phase-in schedule:

For tax years beginning in-	*Maximum deduction*
1997	$18,000
1998	18,500
1999	19,000
2000	20,000
2001	24,000
2002	24,000

For tax years beginning after 2002, the maximum deduction is $25,000.

Page 191

Congress repealed the exclusion for $5,000 of employer-provided death benefits.

Page 197

Congress eliminated the 5-year averaging method for lump-sum distributions from qualified plans for tax years beginning after 1999.

Page 199

The tax law now provides for still another type of defined contribution plan: the Savings Incentive Match Plan for Employees, nicknamed a SIMPLE plan. This plan can be established by an employer with 100 or fewer employees if that employer does not maintain any other type of qualified retirement plan. Under a SIMPLE plan, employees can elect to make tax-deductible contributions of a limited percentage of their current compensation to a retirement account and employers can deduct matching contributions to these accounts.

Page 204

The percentage of annual health insurance costs that a self-employed individual may claim as an above-the-line deduction is gradually increased from 30 percent in 1996 to 80 percent over the following phase-in period:

For tax years beginning in-	*Deductible percentage*
1997	40%
1998 through 2002	45%
2003	50%
2004	60%
2005	70%

For tax years beginning after 2005, the deductible percentage is 80 percent.

Page 205

The limit on the annual contribution to a spousal IRAs is increased from $250 to $2,000. However, the aggregate contributions to the spouses' IRAs can't exceed the combined amount of compensation earned by the spouses during the year.

FEDERAL TAXES AND MANAGEMENT DECISIONS

1997–98 EDITION

The Irwin Graduate Accounting Series

Anthony, Reece and Hertenstein
Accounting: Text and Cases
Ninth Edition, ©1995

Anthony and Govindarajan
Management Control Systems
Eighth Edition, ©1995

Anthony and Reece
Accounting Principles
Seventh Edition, © 1995

Anthony and Young
Management Control in Nonprofit Organizations
Fifth Edition, ©1994

Bernstein
Financial Statement Analysis: Theory, Application and Interpretation
Sixth Edition, ©1997

Bernstein and Maksy
Cases in Financial Statement Reporting and Analysis
Second Edition, ©1994

Brownlee, Ferris and Haskins
Corporate Financial Reporting: Text and Cases
Third Edition, ©1997

Coffman, Tondkar and Previts
Historical Perspectives of Selected Financial Accounting Topics, *©1993*

Epstein and Spalding
The Accountant's Guide to Legal Liability and Ethics *©1993*

Ferris
Financial Accounting and Corporate Reporting: A Casebook
Fourth Edition, ©1996

Haskins, Ferris, Sack and Allen
Financial Accounting and Reporting, *©1993*

Haskins, Ferris, and Selling
International Financial Reporting and Analysis: A Contextual Emphasis,
©1996

Hawkins
Corporate Financial Reporting and Analysis: Text and Cases
Fourth Edition, ©1997

Van Breda
Accounting Theory
Sixth Edition, ©1997

Jones
Federal Taxes and Management Decisions,
1997–98 Edition, Eleventh Edition, ©1997

Marshall and McManus
Accounting: What The Numbers Mean
Third Edition, ©1996

Miller, Redding and Bahnson
The FASB: The People, The Process and The Politics
Fourth Edition, ©1997

Mueller, Gernon and Meek
Accounting: An International Perspective
Fourth Edition, ©1997

Shank and Govindarajan
Strategic Cost Analysis: The Evolution From Managerial To Strategic Accounting, *©1989*

Zimmerman
Accounting for Decision Making and Control
Second Edition, ©1997

FEDERAL TAXES AND MANAGEMENT DECISIONS

1997–98 EDITION

Sally M. Jones
The KPMG Peat Marwick Professor of Professional Accounting
The University of Virginia

IRWIN

Chicago • Bogotá • Boston • Buenos Aires • Caracas
London • Madrid • Mexico City • Sydney • Toronto

Irwin Book Team

Publisher:	Michael W. Junior
Sponsoring editor:	Mark Pfaltzgraff
Editorial assistant:	Mark Chernoff
Marketing manager:	Heather L. Woods
Senior project supervisor:	Rebecca Dodson
Production supervisor:	Dina L. Genovese
Art director:	Keith McPherson
Prepress Buyer:	Charlene R. Perez
Compositor:	Weimer Graphics, Inc., Division of Shepard Poorman Communications Corp.
Typeface:	10/12 Palatino
Printer:	R.R. Donnelley & Sons Company

Times Mirror
Higher Education Group

ISBN 0-256-16947-0
ISSN 1051-3523

Printed in the United States of America
1 2 3 4 5 6 7 8 9 0 DO 3 2 1 0 9 8 7 6

Dedicated to the memory of Ray M. Sommerfeld

PREFACE

Federal Taxes and Management Decisions is written as an introductory text for anyone with an interest in federal taxation. The goal of this book is to provide a conceptual overview of an extremely complex subject. The book focuses on the broad structure of the income tax law and how that law interfaces with many business, investment, and even personal activities. Basic tax policy issues are incorporated into the text, and readers are challenged to consider many social and political implications of our current tax system.

This book is pragmatic in that it concentrates on the tax consequences of transactions. Readers will be alerted to both the financial opportunities and dangers represented by these consequences. The emphasis throughout the text is on tax planning, rather than tax compliance. Consequently, *Federal Taxes and Management Decisions* is ideally suited for all business students who need to understand how taxation affects the economic environment, but who have no interest in the technical details of the law. Because the book provides a solid theoretical foundation, it is also an excellent first text for accounting and law students who intend to specialize in the tax area.

Federal Taxes and Management Decisions teaches fundamental tax concepts that tend to be quite stable over time. The author has tried to avoid in-depth discussions of details of the law that change with each new revenue bill enacted by Congress. As a result, this book does not become outdated as quickly as textbooks with a stronger compliance orientation. As a general rule, revised editions will be prepared every other year; supplements that highlight important developments will be provided to adopters of the text on an as-needed basis. The 1997–98 edition reflects current law as of March 1996.

This textbook is organized so that instructors can adapt it to the pedagogical needs of their particular course. Chapter 1 is an introduction to the role of taxes in society and the various types of taxes governments enact to raise revenues. This preliminary chapter raises important policy issues concerning the efficiency and equity of the U.S. tax system. Chapters 2 through 5 present the framework of the income tax and should be covered in sequence. Chapter 2 is a discussion of the concept of gross income for federal tax purposes. Chapter 3 deals with the general rules governing the deductibility of expenses and losses by individual taxpayers. Chapter 4 focuses on business deductions and credits. Chapter 5 distinguishes between the three types of taxable entities (individuals, corporations, and fiduciaries) and describes how each type computes its annual tax liability. This chapter also explains how the income earned by passthrough entities (partnerships and S corporations) is taxed directly to the owners of the entity. Basic tax planning ideas are interwoven into each of these four chapters, and the reader is continually reminded to consider the technical material in the larger context of business and financial decision making.

Chapters 6, 7, and 8 deal with the tax consequences of property acquisitions and dispositions. Chapter 6 describes how taxpayers may recover the cost of income-producing assets over time through depreciation, amortization, and depletion deductions.

Chapter 7 explains how gains or losses realized on the disposition of assets are taxed and looks at the unique characteristics of capital gains and losses. Chapter 8 acquaints the reader with the various nontaxable exchange provisions that play such an important role in the tax planning process.

Chapters 9 through 14 contain discussions of more advanced topics, and adopters of this text may pick and choose those topics relevant to them and their students. Even though the text is much less technical, and consequently much shorter, than any other tax textbook on the market, it still may contain more material than most students can master in one semester. Instructors who want to emphasize individual income taxation and family tax planning can omit Chapters 12 and 13 ("Corporate Acquisitions, Mergers, Divisions, and Liquidations" and "Jurisdictional Issues in International and Interstate Taxation") from their course content. Instructors who want to focus on corporate tax planning can omit Chapters 9 and 14 ("Special Limitations on Business and Passive-Activity Losses" and "Family Tax Planning").

Newly written Chapter 15, "The Tax Compliance Process" should be of great interest to every student who is, or will become, a taxpayer. The chapter opens with a discussion of the procedural rules we all must follow in paying our taxes and filing our returns. The Internal Revenue Service's audit process and the rights of taxpayers to contest the results of an audit are examined. In the last part of the chapter, the author revisits several of the important tax policy issues introduced in Chapter 1 and gives a status report on the current condition of the U.S. income tax system. The chapter closes with a look at several alternatives to an income tax that have captured the imaginations of politicians and the American public.

This is the first edition of *Federal Taxes and Management Decisions* that was prepared without the expert guidance of Professor Ray M. Sommerfeld. Ray wrote the original version of this book in 1973 when he realized that the business world needed a conceptual, planning-oriented tax text. He remained actively involved with the book until his death this past year in a boating accident. With Ray's passing, the tax community lost one of its most creative minds, and his academic colleagues lost a beloved mentor and friend. Although Ray can no longer help in solving the mysteries of the tax law, his passion for that law will always remain the inspiration behind this book.

I encourage those instructors who adopt this edition to contact me with any suggestions for improvements as well as to point out any errors. I want to acknowledge the invaluable contributions of Michael Cates, College for Financial Planning; Brian Cloyd, University of Texas-Austin; Patrick Wilkie, George Mason University; and Judy Swingen, Rochester Institute of Technology, who reviewed the previous edition of this text and offered many insightful comments that were incorporated into this edition. Finally, the opinions expressed in this text are mine alone and in no way represent an official opinion of the University of Virginia.

Sally M. Jones

CONTENTS

CHAPTER 1
An Introduction

Tax planning is a complex subject. This does not mean the average person cannot understand the fundamental concepts on which successful tax plans are based. It does mean, however, that laypeople must be satisfied with appreciating general rules and must rely on professionals in the field of taxation to implement a specific plan. Stated in another way, the average citizen must be content with a symptom-recognition level of tax knowledge.

The increasing dependence on symptom recognition combined with expert assistance is by no means restricted to the realm of taxation. In the last few decades, virtually all Americans have put their faith in specialists in fields as diverse as automobile mechanics and medicine. What is unusual in the field of taxation is the relative scarcity of published materials that can be used as a basic guide to overall tax planning. Hundreds of technical books and articles are published each year on tax subjects. Yet most of these are written by experts for other experts and are of no interest to the public. The authors believe this book is different and, in many respects, unique. Instead of dwelling on esoteric details of the law or providing line-by-line instruction as to the preparation of a Form 1040, the book attempts to present the reader with the broadest possible perspective on the U.S. tax system. The author's primary objective is to sensitize the reader to tax planning opportunities and problems. Because of its focus on symptom recognition, *Federal Taxes and Management Decisions* can be described as the tax equivalent of Dr. Spock's famous book on pediatric medicine for parents.

Usually around April 15 of each year, the popular press reports the number of individual taxpayers who earned incomes of $200,000 or more in the preceding year but who paid no federal income tax. This seasonal announcement tends to trigger two conflicting emotions: disgust for a tax system so flawed as to permit such an outrage and curiosity about how to achieve such an enviable result for oneself! This book can help you reduce your annual tax liability, but the author can't promise miracles. In reality, those taxpayers who are grist for the tabloid mill may have made some very foolish investment or business decisions that led to their current tax situation. As we will discuss in later chapters, successful tax planning rarely results in the dramatic avoidance of any and all taxes and may not even result in the payment of the minimum amount of tax in the current year.

TAX AVOIDANCE VERSUS TAX EVASION

The contents of this book are restricted to legal tax planning techniques. Legitimate attempts to reduce taxes are known as *tax avoidance;* illegal means to the same end constitute *tax evasion.* Tax evasion is a federal crime—a felony offense punishable by severe monetary fines and imprisonment. Unfortunately, the qualitative difference between avoidance and evasion is in the eye of the beholder. Many aggressive tax plans involve major questions of judgment; a taxpayer eager to implement these plans runs the risk that an IRS agent will conclude the taxpayer's behavior crossed the line between a good faith effort to minimize tax and a willful attempt to defraud the U.S. government. Individuals should always exercise extreme caution and consult a tax professional before engaging in any transaction or activity with profound tax consequences. When in doubt, they should take one simple maxim to heart: if a tax avoidance scheme seems too good to be true, it isn't true.

No socially conscious reader can escape some measure of doubt about the morality of deliberate tax avoidance. After all, taxes are theoretically collected and expended for the greatest common good. In 1947, Supreme Court Justice Learned Hand addressed this issue in his famous dissenting opinion in the case of *Commissioner* v. *Newman.* Justice Hand wrote:

> Over and over again courts have said that there is nothing sinister in so arranging one's affairs as to keep taxes as low as possible. Everybody does so, rich or poor; and all do right, for nobody owes any public duty to pay more than the law demands: taxes are enforced exactions, not voluntary contributions. To demand more in the name of morals is mere cant.

This celebrated defense of the tax planning process makes the point that each of us must pay the legally required amount of tax and not a penny more nor a penny less. This book is designed to help the average businessperson meet this precise objective by explaining and analyzing the tax law in the most straightforward, user-friendly manner possible.

THE OMNIPRESENCE OF TAXES

Taxes always have been, and probably always will be, a fact of civilized life. Many forms of taxation can be traced back to ancient times. While the Romans had no excise tax on gasoline or cigarettes, they were assessed taxes based on the number of wheels on their chariots and the salt they purchased to flavor and preserve their food.[1] Certainly our modern financial and economic life is permeated by the phenomenon of taxation. While this book focuses primarily on the federal income tax, the business manager must consider the impact of other types of taxes levied by the U.S. government. The pie chart in Figure 1–1 shows the percentage of total tax receipts generated by the major federal taxes. Note that the individual and corporate income taxes account for well over 50 percent of tax receipts, while excise and transfer taxes account for a relatively insignificant 4 percent. Federal excise taxes are imposed on the sale of a few specific items, such as airline tickets; liquor, wine, and beer; and telephone service. The two major components of the federal transfer tax, the estate tax and the gift tax, and their role in family financial planning are discussed in detail in Chapter 14. The inclusion of the

---

[1]Harold M. Groves, *Tax Philosophers—Two Hundred Years of Thought in Great Britain and the United States* (Madison, WI: The University of Wisconsin Press, 1974), p. 13.

Figure 1–1 Federal Tax Receipts (fiscal year 1994)

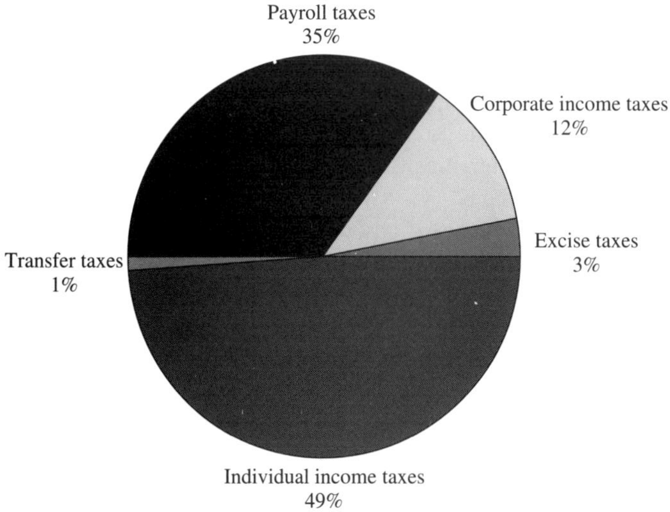

federal payroll (FICA) tax in Figure 1–1 is somewhat misleading. The revenues raised by this tax are earmarked for a single purpose—funding the nation's Social Security and Medicare systems. Consequently, the 35 percent of tax receipts attributable to the FICA tax are not available to finance any other governmental programs.

Of course, the federal government does not have exclusive jurisdiction to levy taxes. Almost every state imposes an income tax on individuals who reside or are employed in the state and on corporations doing business within the state. In addition, states rely heavily on general sales and use taxes as a source of revenue. Local governments have traditionally depended on both real and personal property taxes as the primary means to finance their programs. Over the last decade, perennial budgetary crises have forced state and local governments to aggressively apply their existing tax laws and to seek new sources of revenue. In 1992, Philadelphia decided to apply its 4.3 percent city income tax to visiting professional athletes; the city sent out 4,500 tax notices to football, basketball, baseball, and hockey players who had competed against Philadelphia teams during the year. This so-called jock tax is expected to raise an additional $7 to $10 million of annual revenue for the City of Brotherly Love.

As businesses expand their scope of activities beyond our national borders, they may become subject to the taxing jurisdiction of a foreign government. For these businesses, tax planning takes on an international dimension. Every industrialized nation levies some type of income tax on business activities conducted within its territorial boundaries. In today's global economy, multinational corporations seeking to maximize their after-tax profits must consider the impact and interaction of dozens of complex tax systems. The jurisdictional tax problems and opportunities that arise when multiple governments claim the right to tax a single stream of income are addressed in Chapter 13.

What Is a Tax?

A tax is the price paid by a citizen to support a government. A tax differs from a governmentally imposed fine or penalty because its imposition is not intended to punish unacceptable behavior. A tax differs from a user's fee charged by a government (such as a $5 admission to a national park or a 32 cent postage stamp) because the payment of a tax does not entitle the payor to any specific governmental benefit or service. One obvious characteristic of a tax is that it is compulsory; citizens are not free to choose whether or not to pay.

The calculation of most taxes is based on an extremely simple equation: a tax (T) equals a tax base (B) multiplied by a tax rate (r), which is usually expressed as a percentage. A *tax base* is some item or transaction that causes the imposition of a particular tax. A tax base is typically expressed in monetary terms. For example, a tax may be levied on the ownership of real property; the dollar value of the property is the tax base. A tax may be imposed on every retail sale; the dollar value of the consumer good purchased is the tax base. For an income tax, the base is the amount of annual taxable income. A tax base should be one that taxpayers cannot easily avoid or conceal. If a government levies a tax on the consumption of ice cream, even people who adore this particular dessert could escape taxation by ordering frozen yogurt. In contrast, if a tax were levied on the consumption of insulin, people who depend on the drug for survival would have no choice but to pay the tax.

In the equation $T = r(B)$, the amount of tax is a function of both the rate and base. This mathematical relationship suggests that a government can increase the revenues generated by an income tax by increasing either of these two variables. Politicians understand that increasing the rate is the more obvious strategy and therefore is more likely to anger the greatest number of voters. A tax increase accomplished by holding tax rates constant but expanding the definition of taxable income is more subtle and less likely to attract the public's attention. It is hardly surprising that many of the significant tax increases of the past several years have taken the form of increases in the amount and types of income subject to tax.

Behavioral Responses to Taxes

The conclusion that an increase in either the tax rate or the tax base will increase government revenues by an arithmetically determinable amount ignores the human element in the equation. People may modify their behavior in response to a change in the tax laws, thereby confounding the predicted impact on the fisc. Suppose Mr. Smith currently earns $25,000 a year as a high school teacher and pays 20 percent of that income ($5,000) in tax. Suppose also that Mr. Smith spends every penny of his $20,000 after-tax income to make ends meet. How might Mr. Smith modify his behavior if the government increased the tax rate to 30 percent, so his disposable income would fall to $17,500? One possibility is that our taxpayer would find a second job to increase his before-tax income to at least $28,600. Mr. Smith would pay $8,580 of tax on this income, leaving him with $20,020 and the same standard of living he enjoyed before the tax hike.

If Mr. Smith responds to the tax increase by working extra hours to generate more income, the government will enjoy a revenue windfall. Ignoring the possibility of a behavioral reaction, the government could anticipate collecting an additional $2,500 of tax from Mr. Smith because of the 10 percent rate increase. However, if Mr. Smith reacts by increasing his taxable income from $25,000 to $28,600, the government will actually collect $3,580 of additional tax ($8,580 tax on increased base less $5,000 tax on original base). Mr. Smith's reaction (akin to running faster in order to stay in the same place) has been labeled the *income effect* of a tax increase.

If we change the financial circumstances of our hypothetical taxpayer, might we expect a different type of behavioral response to a tax increase? Assume Ms. Harris works 50 hours a week as a self-employed management consultant, earning an annual income of $350,000. At the current 20 percent tax rate, her after-tax income is $280,000—more than enough to support her comfortable lifestyle. If the government proposes to become a 30 percent rather than a 20 percent silent partner in her business, Ms. Harris might decide to devote less time and effort to that business. Such a reaction makes sense if the after-tax value of an hour of additional labor is now worth less to Ms. Harris than an additional hour of leisure. If Ms. Harris responds to the tax hike by playing more golf and generating less taxable income, the government will suffer a revenue shortfall. Without a behavioral reaction, the government could count on an additional $35,000 of tax from Ms. Harris. But if her business income falls to $325,000 because the tax increase has dampened her entrepreneurial spirit, the incremental tax from Ms. Harris will be only $27,500 ($97,500 tax on decreased base less $70,000 tax on original base). This very different type of behavioral reaction to a tax increase is called the *substitution effect.*

The possibility of a substitution effect varies enormously across taxpayers. The degree of personal control that an individual exercises over her career influences the extent to which an hour of work can be replaced with an hour of relaxation. The substitution effect is more potent for the self-employed taxpayer than for the salaried employee with a rigid 9 A.M. to 5 P.M. schedule. The financial flexibility necessary to curtail work effort is more characteristic of a family's secondary wage earner than the primary wage earner. Finally, ambitious career-oriented individuals who are highly motivated by nonmonetary incentives such as prestige and power may be impervious to the substitution effect.

Whether a tax increase will goad a person to extra effort or whether it will be a disincentive to the work ethic depends heavily on that person's economic circumstances. Theoretically, the income effect is most powerful for lower income taxpayers, who may already be at a subsistence standard of living and do not have the luxury of choosing leisure rather than income-generating labor. The substitution effect becomes more compelling as an individual's disposable income rises and the financial significance of each additional dollar declines. From a macroeconomic viewpoint, these contradictory behavioral reactions have important tax policy implications. Conventional wisdom suggests that a government requiring additional revenues should increase the tax rate on those taxpayers with the greatest tax base, that is, the highest incomes. But if the rates climb too high, the substitution effect may become so strong that the projected revenues never materialize as more and more people are discouraged from working to subsidize the government rather than to benefit themselves.

Behavioral responses to tax rate increases are highly unpredictable and vary widely across individuals. It is hardly surprising that economists cannot agree on how to incorporate this human factor into their revenue and budget forecasts. When politicians pledge that this or that tweak in the income tax rate structure will produce the exact amount of money required to fund this or that government project, their rhetoric reflects wishful thinking rather than mathematical precision. A prime example of a tax that triggered unforeseen consequences was the 10 percent excise tax on the purchase of expensive jewelry, furs, airplanes, boats, and automobiles that Congress enacted in 1990. This *luxury tax* was intended to force high-income individuals to shoulder a major portion of the cost of that year's deficit reduction legislation. However, these individuals reacted to the obnoxious new tariff by changing their consumption habits and buying fewer luxury goods. Congress had estimated the excise tax on private airplane sales alone would raise $6 million in new revenues for fiscal year 1991. Instead, Uncle Sam's take was a disappointing $53,000. The real victims of the tax were the manufacturing companies that lost millions of dollars in sales because of reduced consumer demand and employees who lost their jobs because of resulting production cutbacks. By 1993, the chorus of anguish and anger from the boat-building, aircraft, and automobile industries convinced Congress to largely repeal the ill-fated luxury tax.

CHARACTERISTICS OF A GOOD TAX

Not even the most patriotic citizen would claim to enjoy paying taxes, and many people would consider the notion of a good tax as a contradiction in terms. But given that taxes are a necessary component of organized government, social scientists have struggled to define a set of standards by which to judge the merit of a tax. Perhaps the most objective and obvious standard is that a tax should be *sufficient* to raise the revenues necessary to allow the government to balance its budget. Critics of the current U.S. tax system who harangue that taxes are too high are ignoring the inescapable linkage between government funding and government spending. The tax burden levied on a citizenry should be dictated by the amount of money the government wishes to spend. An amount of tax in and of itself can't be described as too high or too low—it is merely sufficient or insufficient to finance the current level of government activity. Given the chronic annual budget deficits generated by the federal government and the staggering national debt resulting from such profligacy, the U.S. tax system must be given very poor marks based on the criterion of sufficiency.

A secondary problem created by an insufficient tax system is that legislators tend to fixate on the revenue impact of any proposed change in the system. Even if there is wholehearted agreement that a proposal would improve the system, benefiting the national economy and the taxpaying public alike, that proposal is doomed if it might decrease the amount of current year tax receipts and thereby exacerbate the deficit problem. In recent years, Congress has been severely hampered in its efforts at tax reform by a self-imposed constraint of *budget neutrality;* no amendment to the Internal Revenue Code that represents a potential loss of revenue can be considered unless an accompanying amendment will compensate for the projected loss.

Many economists insist that a good tax should be *neutral* so its imposition does not distort the normal decision-making processes of those individuals and institutions subject to the tax. These advocates of tax neutrality believe a competitive market results in the optimal allocation of resources within an economy. If the government interferes with the free market for goods and services through its tax system, the resulting disruption in the market may cause suboptimal or inefficient allocations. A conflicting school of thought holds that a tax system should not be neutral, but should be deliberately employed by the government as a tool of *fiscal policy.* In other words, the tax system should be designed to influence taxpayer behavior in ways that will improve on the free market allocation of resources and thereby enhance the nation's economy. Over the past several decades, Congress has favored this activist view and has continually attempted to fine-tune the economy through special incentives in the Internal Revenue Code. In subsequent chapters of this text, we will identify many of these motivational provisions and discuss their intended impact on the business environment.

Adam Smith's Canons of Taxation

In 1776, economist Adam Smith published *The Wealth of Nations,* in which he formulated his celebrated canons of taxation as guidelines for the design of a tax system. According to Smith, a good tax should be *certain.* Certainty exists to the extent that the tax is based on a predetermined set of rules, is neither arbitrary nor subjective in its application, and is collected on a recurring and regular basis. The fact that the federal income tax is based on statutory law and has been collected every year for the past eight decades suggests it meets this criterion. Unfortunately, at least two features of the tax system undermine the certainty of its application. First, the law is so lengthy and complicated that many of its provisions are understood by only a handful of experts. Because of such technical difficulty, 10 tax practitioners might reach 10 different conclusions as to how the law applies to a specific fact pattern. Second, Congress is continually revising the tax law with each new revenue bill it enacts. Taxpayers and their advisers hardly have time to understand and adapt to one set of tax rules before a new set becomes effective. This combination of complexity and unpredictability over time taints the federal income tax with a high degree of uncertainty.

Adam Smith advised that taxes should be *convenient* in the time and manner of their levy on the population and *economical* to the government to collect. For those millions of individual taxpayers who automatically pay their federal income and payroll tax liabilities through employer withholding from their paychecks and who engage a professional to prepare and file their annual returns, the tax system is reasonably convenient. For self-employed individuals, small-business owners, and corporate taxpayers, payment and filing are much more onerous tasks.

From the government's perspective, collection of the various federal taxes is very economical. The annual budget of the Internal Revenue Service averages less than 1 percent of the annual revenues collected by that government agency. (In 1994, the cost of collecting $100 of tax was only 58 cents.) This statistic, however, fails to capture the cost of the federal tax system to society as a whole. Recent research into the compliance costs of the federal individual income tax indicates an astonishing 51 percent of American households engage a tax adviser to help them file their Form 1040. The average household spends $343 per year in time and money preparing this return.[2] At the other end of the taxpaying spectrum, 1,300 large corporations participating in a recent survey revealed they paid an average of $1.6 million per year just to comply with the tax law. This national dependence on professional help has created a multibillion-dollar industry of attorneys, accountants, and tax return preparation services such as H&R Block that devote their collective intellectual resources to interpreting and applying tax laws.

Smith's final and most famous canon is that taxes should be *equitable* in that the burden of payment should be fairly apportioned among the citizenry. While no tax theorist would argue with the sentiment of this canon, there is precious little agreement as to the exact nature of a fair apportionment of the federal tax burden. Many people harbor a firm, albeit irrational, belief that their tax burden is unfairly high, while everyone else's tax burden is inexcusably low. As former U.S. Senator Russell Long expressed it, the attitude of the man on the street concerning tax equity is "Don't tax you, and don't tax me; just tax that fellow behind the tree." Clearly, any meaningful discussion of equity must rise above this type of rhetoric.

Horizontal Equity

One characteristic of a fair tax is *horizontal equity,* which means that people with the same economic *ability to pay* a tax are assessed the same amount of tax. In our federal income tax system, each person's ability to pay is quantified as his or her annual taxable income, the base on which the tax is levied. Accordingly, the system is horizontally equitable only to the extent that taxable income accurately reflects a person's ability to pay. Let's take a moment to explore this idea in more depth by comparing two people, Susan and Stan, both single, both earning a $40,000 annual salary. Neither has any additional source of income for the current year. Do Susan and Stan have an equal ability to pay a tax to the federal government? If based on these few facts, we are willing to answer yes; the implication is straightforward—Susan and Stan should report equal taxable incomes and pay identical amounts of tax for the year.

But what additional facts might be considered in measuring ability to pay? Suppose Susan suffers from a chronic illness and has $7,000 of uninsured medical expenses for the year, while Stan is in perfect health. And suppose Stan pays $4,500 of alimony to a former spouse during the year, while Susan has no such legal obligation. Based on these two new pieces of information, should we still conclude that Susan and Stan have the same ability to pay an income tax? Putting the question another way, should medical expenses and alimony somehow be incorporated into the calculation of taxable income? Certainly Susan and Stan would argue that it is only fair to consider these variables.

The equity of an income tax system can be enhanced by refining the definition of taxable income to include the many variables that significantly affect a person's financial circumstances. Such perfecting of the tax base has its price; every refinement must be enacted as an additional sentence or paragraph in the Internal Revenue Code.

[2]Blumenthal and Slemrod, "The Compliance Cost of the U.S. Individual Income Tax System: A Second Look after Tax Reform," *National Tax Journal,* June 1992, pp. 185–202.

Increased precision in the measurement of ability to pay may improve the horizontal equity of our tax system, but it also increase the complexity of the law.

Vertical Equity

The concept of *vertical equity* suggests that individuals with a greater ability to pay tax should bear a greater share of the total tax burden than individuals with a lesser ability to pay. While horizontal equity focuses on a fair measure of the tax base, vertical equity is concerned with a fair *rate structure* by which to calculate the tax on different amounts of base. To discuss some different possible rate structures, consider four individuals A, B, C, and D whose respective taxable incomes are $20,000, $20,000, $45,000, and $100,000. Under a *proportionate* rate structure, each individual would pay the same percentage of taxable income. A 10 percent proportionate tax would result in the following tax liabilities:

	Taxable Income	*Tax Liability*
Taxpayer A	$ 20,000	$ 2,000
Taxpayer B	20,000	2,000
Taxpayer C	45,000	4,500
Taxpayer D	100,000	10,000
		$18,500

Note that this rate structure results in vertical equity in the sense that D, who has the greatest ability to pay (i.e., taxable income) owes the greatest amount of tax, while C, who has more income than A or B, owes more tax than they do. Despite this result, many tax theorists believe a proportionate income tax fails to fairly apportion the tax burden among people with different amounts of income. They would argue that the 10 percent tax levied on D is much less of a hardship than the 10 percent tax levied on A, B, or C, and although the tax rate is proportionate, the economic sacrifice demanded of each taxpayer is disproportionate.

This argument is based on the theory of the *declining marginal utility of income.* This theory presumes the importance associated with each dollar of income diminishes as the amount of income increases. In other words, the minimum amount of income needed to provide the necessities of life, such as food and shelter, is relatively more important to a person than incremental amounts of income spent on luxury items. Consequently, a *progressive* tax rate structure under which the rates increase as income increases results in an equality of sacrifice across taxpayers. Referring again to taxpayers A, B, C, and D, a progressive tax consisting of a 5 percent rate on the first $20,000 of income, a 10 percent rate on the next $30,000 of income, and an 18 percent rate on income in excess of $50,000 would result in the following:

	Taxable Income	*Tax Liability*
Taxpayer A	$ 20,000	$ 1,000
Taxpayer B	20,000	1,000
Taxpayer C	45,000	3,500
Taxpayer D	100,000	13,000
		$18,500

Note that this tax structure raises the same amount of revenue for the government as the 10 percent proportionate rate structure. However, A, B, and C are paying fewer dollars of tax, while D's tax liability has increased by $3,000.

A second argument in defense of progressive taxation is that it improves the distribution of wealth across citizens and mitigates the extremes of poverty and affluence that seem an unavoidable by-product of capitalism. Tax philosopher Henry Simon eloquently summarized this argument in his oft-quoted statement: "The case for drastic progression in taxation must be rested on the case against inequality—on the ethical or aesthetic judgment that the prevailing distribution of wealth and income reveals a degree (and/or kind) of inequality that is distinctly evil or unlovely."[3]

Even though academics continue a spirited debate over the scientific and philosophic rationales for progressive taxation, the concept undoubtedly has a great deal of intuitive appeal.

> The majority of citizens and legislators in the United States and other democratic countries appear to accept ability to pay as a guiding principle of taxation and to interpret it as justifying progressivity. They talk and act as if they believe that progressive taxation is needed both to maintain a proper relation between the sacrifices of individual taxpayers and to give recognition to social priorities in the use of income and wealth.[4]

Even those opponents of progressivity who advocate a flat tax based on a proportionate rate structure usually agree that some subsistence amount of income should be exempt from any tax. But despite the general consensus that a progressive rate structure is necessary to achieve vertical equity, there is no objective means by which to determine the degree of progressivity that maximizes that equity. Refer back to the progressive rate structure under which taxpayer A paid $1,000 of tax, while taxpayer D paid $13,000 of tax. Admittedly, the government officials who designed this rate structure have no idea how either individual feels about paying tax or if the economic sacrifices represented by their tax liabilities are even remotely comparable. In the final analysis, the degree of progressivity in any income tax system is a value judgment—a matter of political taste rather than of mathematical logic or natural law.

A *regressive* tax rate structure is one under which the rates decrease as income increases. To illustrate, a regressive tax consisting of a 15 percent rate on the first $10,000 of income, a 10 percent rate on the next $25,000 of income, and a 7.3 percent rate on income in excess of $35,000 would result in the following for taxpayers A, B, C, and D:

	Taxable Income	*Tax Liability*
Taxpayer A	$ 20,000	$ 2,500
Taxpayer B	20,000	2,500
Taxpayer C	45,000	4,733
Taxpayer D	100,000	8,767
		$18,500

[3]Henry Simons, *Personal Income Taxation* (Chicago: University of Chicago Press, 1938), pp. 18–19.
[4]Richard Goode, *The Individual Income Tax* (Washington, DC: The Brookings Institution, 1976), p. 19.

The above data show that a regressive rate structure can be designed to extract the same amount of revenue from a group of taxpayers as either a proportionate or a progressive rate structure. Moreover, even under a regressive system of taxation, D is paying a greater absolute amount of tax than A, B, or C, and C is paying more tax than A or B. Nonetheless, theorists unanimously condemn regressive taxes as inherently unfair and oppressive because they impose a proportionately larger tax burden on those individuals with the smallest tax base. Even if a particular tax system is not explicitly regressive in design, it may be implicitly regressive in operation. For example, a 5 percent sales tax imposed on the purchase of consumer goods technically qualifies as a proportionate tax. However, the fact that poor people must spend a higher percentage of their incomes on consumption than the well-to-do who are able to save and invest some portion of their incomes makes a tax on consumption fall most heavily on the segment of the population with the least ability to pay.

Marginal versus Average Tax Rates

Before we leave the subject of tax rate structures, we must distinguish between marginal and average tax rates. The *marginal rate* is the rate that applies to the next dollar of base. Let's again consider the progressive rate structure described earlier in this chapter. Remember that this rate structure consisted of three *rate brackets:* 5 percent on the first $20,000 of income, 10 percent on the next $30,000 of income, and 18 percent on all income in excess of $50,000. Under this rate structure, taxpayer D with $100,000 of taxable income owes $13,000 of tax. If D earns one more dollar of income, that dollar is subject to an 18 percent rate. Nevertheless, the fact that D is in the 18 percent marginal tax bracket does not mean she is paying 18 percent of her taxable income to Uncle Sam. Her $13,000 tax liability divided by $100,000 of taxable income results in an *average tax rate* of only 13 percent. Note that under a progressive rate structure, the marginal rate is always greater than the average rate.

Individuals making tax planning decisions that involve incremental changes in taxable income should usually focus on their marginal tax rates. For example, if D is considering a new investment that will yield $10,000 of current year before-tax income, she should evaluate the investment based on an after-tax return of only $8,200 (before-tax income multiplied by 1 minus her 18 percent marginal tax rate). In contrast, meaningful discussions of vertical equity should be based on average tax rates. If we are trying to compare the tax burdens of A, B, C, and D under our progressive rate structure, the relevant comparison is between their respective average tax rates of 5 percent (A and B's $1,000 tax bill divided by $20,000), 7.8 percent (C's $3,500 tax bill divided by $45,000), and 13 percent (D's $13,000 tax bill divided by $100,000).

WHO DOES BEAR THE INCOME TAX BURDEN?

The French philosopher Colbert observed, "The art of taxation consists in so plucking the goose as to obtain the largest amount of feathers with the least amount of hissing." Human nature being what it is, people in every income level of society vociferously complain that their taxes are unreasonably high because some segment of society is not bearing their fair share of the total tax burden. Many taxpayers who consider themselves as middle class are convinced the "rich" routinely employ high-priced tax advisers to exploit exotic legal loopholes—loopholes that unfairly reduce the tax burden on the most prosperous members of society.

Before a student of taxation can make any normative judgments concerning the distribution of a particular tax burden across citizens, the incidence of the tax must be determined. *Incidence* refers to the ultimate economic burden imposed by a tax. The reader might jump to the conclusion that the incidence of a tax is on the person or organization writing the check in payment to the government. But in many cases, the payor can shift the incidence of the tax to a third party. For example, if the government imposes a tax on a business with a monopoly on a product that is in great demand by the public, the business may respond by raising its selling price by the amount of the tax. Although the business technically is the taxpayer, the incidence of the tax is on the thousands of consumers who are willing to purchase the product at the inflated price. In a complex economy, it may be extremely difficult to pinpoint the incidence of a seemingly straightforward tax.

Tax Payments by Population Segments

The Internal Revenue Service's quarterly publication, the *Statistics of Income (SOI) Bulletin,* provides valuable insight into the incidence of the individual income tax with regards to various income groups. Figure 1–2, derived from SOI data for the 1993 taxable year, divides the approximately 115 million Form 1040s filed for that year into four categories: returns reporting adjusted gross income[5] ranging from a negative amount to $19,999; returns reporting adjusted gross income of $20,000 to $49,999; returns reporting adjusted gross income of $50,000 to $199,999; and returns reporting adjusted gross income of $200,000 or more. For each of these four categories, the chart provides three bits of information: the percentage of total returns falling into each category, the percentage of aggregate adjusted gross income reported by each, and the percentage of the total amount of individual income tax paid by each.

Slightly under half the Form 1040s filed for 1993 reported adjusted gross incomes of less than $20,000. These returns accounted for 13 percent of total adjusted gross income, but only 4 percent of total individual income tax paid. In contrast, less than 1 percent of 1993 returns reported adjusted gross income of $200,000 or more. However, this sliver of the taxpaying population accounted for 13 percent of total adjusted gross income and 28 percent of total individual income tax paid. The chart also highlights the pivotal role of what we might label the great middle class of taxpayers—return filers with $20,000 to $199,000 of income who account for a 74 percent of aggregate adjusted gross income and 68 percent of the federal government's individual income tax revenues. This type of comparative data leads most political economists to

[5]Adjusted gross income is taxable income before subtracting itemized deductions, standard deductions, and personal exemptions.

Figure 1–2 Adjusted Gross Income and Income Tax Burden per Income Class, 1993

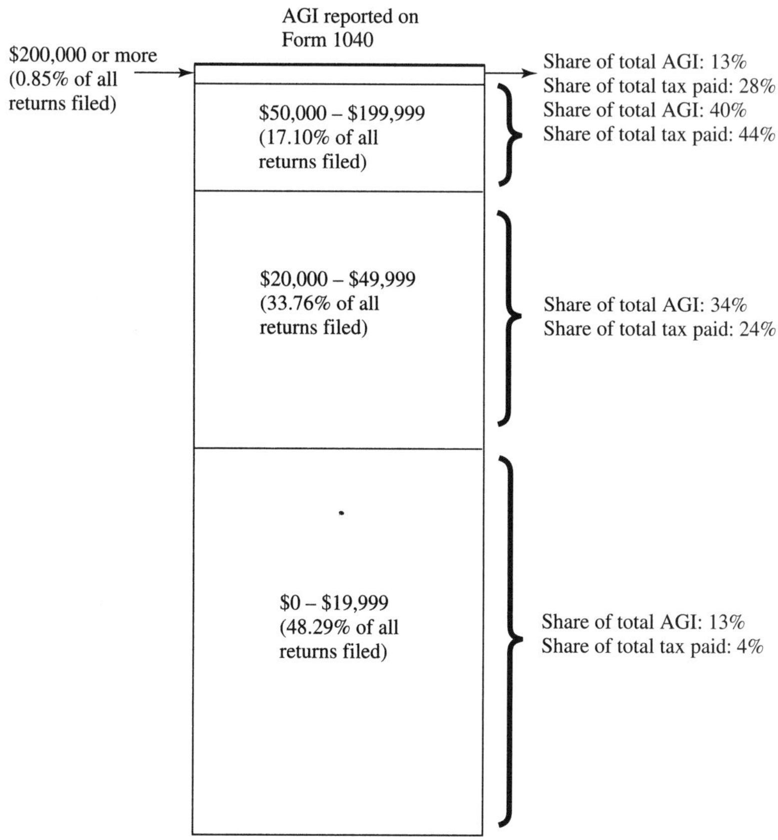

conclude that increasing the income tax burden on the rich, in whatever way that term is defined, is not a viable solution to this country's current budget woes. There are simply too few rich people to tax. A tax increase that applies to a broadly defined middle class is the sensible (albeit politically damnable) choice for raising any significant amount of new revenues.

The data reflected in Figure 1–2 don't provide any blinding insights into the vertical equity of the current federal income tax system. One reader might view the data as compelling evidence that the most affluent class of taxpayers is not, in fact, paying its fair share of the total tax burden. Another reader might decide the very same data support her belief that our progressive rate structure poisons the entrepreneurial spirit and subverts economic incentive. Once more, we are left with the conclusion that tax equity is an abstract, and therefore an elusive, goal that will be hotly debated in the political arena for as long as taxation remains a necessary by-product of organized society.

SOURCES OF THE FEDERAL TAX LAW

Statutory Authority

Throughout the remainder of this book, the author will refer to the federal tax law. Technically, this term refers to the *Internal Revenue Code,* the voluminous compilation of statutory rules written and enacted by Congress and signed into law by the president of the United States. The Internal Revenue Code is anything but a static document; virtually every year, Congress passes a revenue act that adds to, deletes from, or modifies its provisions. The code consists of numerically ordered *sections,* beginning with Section 1 and ending with Section 9602. These section numbers are used to identify specific tax rules, and tax practitioners have incorporated many of them into their professional jargon (Bob, I'm afraid our client may have a real Section 469 problem this year . . .).

Administrative Authority

In reality, the body of tax law encompasses much more than just statutory authority. The Department of the Treasury has the responsibility to write regulations that interpret and explain the often difficult (if not incomprehensible) language of the Internal Revenue Code. These *Treasury regulations* carry great weight and provide a tremendous amount of guidance to taxpayers and their advisers as to the proper application of the code. The *Internal Revenue Service* (IRS), the subdivision of the Treasury responsible for the enforcement of the law and collection of the tax, provides additional guidance in the form of published *revenue rulings* and *revenue procedures.* These pronouncements explain how the IRS believes the law pertains to a particular set of facts and circumstances.

Judicial Authority

The final major source of tax law is the *federal judicial system.* Taxpayers who disagree with the IRS's interpretation of the law as it applies to their own situation may take their case to federal court—perhaps all the way to the Supreme Court. The thousands of legal decisions handed down over the decades provide clarification and insight into the correct implementation of the tax law. Chapter 15 includes a thorough discussion of the process by which a dispute between taxpayers and the IRS is resolved by a federal judge or jury.

CONCLUSION

In this first chapter, you have been introduced to many definitions and tax policy considerations. While the discussion has focused on the federal income tax, readers should understand that, for the most part, the material covered in this chapter pertains to any existing type of tax levied by any jurisdiction, or to any new tax proposed by a revenue-hungry government. In the chapters to follow, we leave the pleasant realm of tax theory to explore the actual design and operation of the federal income tax. Nevertheless, the author would like to encourage every reader to continually apply the standards for a good tax to each new element of the system introduced in subsequent chapters. By making such an evaluation, you can reach your own conclusions as to whether that element enhances or detracts from the overall quality of the federal tax system.

PROBLEMS

1. During the current year, Ben Little performed minor construction work for a number of individuals and asked each of them to pay him in cash. Because Ben knew there was almost no chance the IRS would learn of these payments, he decided to report only half the payments as income on his current year tax return. Is Ben engaging in tax avoidance or tax evasion? Explain briefly.
2. Which of the following types of tax are not levied by the U.S. government?
   a. An estate tax.
   b. A tax on the value of personal property.
   c. A general sales tax.
   d. Excise tax on the sale of specific goods and services.
   e. A gift tax.
   f. A tax on the value of real property.
3. Gotham City recently increased its municipal sales tax on all retail goods purchased within the city limits from 2 percent to 4 percent. However, sales tax revenues increased only 15 percent because of this doubling of tax rates. What factors might account for this result?
4. Differentiate between the income effect and the substitution effect of a tax increase. Which effect is more likely to occur for individuals with meager amounts of taxable income? Which effect is more likely to occur for individuals with high incomes?
5. Both the federal government and many states impose "sin taxes"—excise taxes levied on the retail sale of liquor and cigarettes. Discuss the various reasons these particular items make a good tax base.
6. Many individuals complain that the federal income tax system is both inequitable and overly complicated. Explain why tax equity and tax simplicity can be considered conflicting goals of the income tax system.
7. Define and contrast the concepts of horizontal and vertical equity as characteristics of a good tax system.
8. The federal income tax system is based on a detailed set of statutory rules that apply uniformly to every taxpayer. Despite its apparent objectivity, the system is criticized for being very uncertain in its application. What factors account for this criticism?
9. In 1996, individuals who earn a salary or wage must pay a federal payroll tax equal to 7.65 percent of compensation up to $62,700 and 1.45 percent of any compensation in excess of this amount.
   a. In 1996, Mr. Boyd earned a salary of $40,000. Compute Mr. Boyd's payroll tax liability and his average payroll tax rate for the year.

b. In 1996, Mrs. Chen earned a salary of $90,000. Compute Mrs. Chen's payroll tax liability and her average payroll tax rate for the year.

c. In 1996, Mr. Washington earned a salary of $150,000. Compute Mr. Washington's payroll tax liability and his average payroll tax rate for the year.

d. Based on your answers to the above, on what type of rate structure is the federal payroll tax system based?

10. Mary Stuart is trying to decide whether to invest a portion of her savings in a newly organized business. In calculating her after-tax return from the investment, should Mary consider her projected marginal or average income tax rate over the life of the investment? Explain briefly.

11. During the current year, the government imposed a new 3 percent tax on corporate gross business receipts. In response to the tax, Acme Inc., a manufacturer of candy bars, decided to reduce the size of its bars by 10 percent and use a cheaper grade of chocolate in its manufacturing process. By making these changes in its products, Acme was able to maintain its pre-tax level of profitability. Analyze the incidence of the gross receipts tax paid by Acme Inc.

CHAPTER 2

The Gross Income Concept

In 1913, the 16th Amendment was added to the U.S. Constitution, giving Congress "the power to lay and collect taxes on incomes from whatever source derived, without apportionment among the several States, and without regard to any census or enumeration." This amendment established a new base for the imposition of federal taxes, while leaving to Congress the task of writing statutes to define the term *income* and the methods whereby the tax on such income should be computed.

The Internal Revenue Code defines *taxable income* as "gross income minus the deductions allowed." Consequently, the computation of taxable income involves two fundamental steps. The first step is an analysis of economic gains and benefits received to determine the extent to which these gains and benefits represent gross income. The second step is an analysis of expenses and losses incurred to determine which, if any, qualify as deductions. From a business perspective, this statutory definition ensures that the federal income tax is not imposed on gross receipts from operations, but only on business profits—the excess of gross receipts over the various deductible expenses incurred in the business activity.

Ideally, each taxpayer should be able to identify and measure taxable income in a reasonably objective manner so that the tax on the income can be computed and paid to the government on a regular basis. Of course, some period of time over which income is measured must be specified. Congress could arbitrarily specify a one-month tax reporting period or a six-month period or a two-year period. However, federal law has always based the measurement of taxable income on the familiar 12-month year.

Most individuals who do not operate their own business use a calendar year for income tax purposes without giving the decision a conscious thought. Many businesses find a *fiscal year* (any 12-month period ending on the last day of any month except December) to be a more convenient time frame over which to calculate their annual income. For example, a corporation that owns a ski resort may have an operating cycle during which business activity is at a frenetic peak during the winter months, begins to quickly decline during April, and all but ceases during the summer. The obvious time for this corporation to close its books and compute its annual income is late spring or early summer—certainly not December 31. In acknowledgment of this logic, the law allows any taxpayer operating a business to adopt a fiscal year for tax purposes if the Internal Revenue Service agrees the fiscal year corresponds to the natural operating cycle of the business.

Once a taxpayer has established a taxable year, any income *recognized* during that year must be included in the computation of current taxable income. The term *recognition* is used very precisely in the tax law; recognition of a particular item of income means that such item must be taken into account for tax purposes. Any income item not recognized in the taxable year by virtue of a specific statutory or judicial rule escapes current taxation. The concept of income recognition will be more fully developed a bit later in this chapter.

Chapter 2 concentrates on the basic concepts involved in the identification and measurement of *gross income,* the sum total of the various types of economic inflows recognized by a taxpayer during the year. The more significant statutory *exclusions* from gross income will be examined, and the important topic of *methods of accounting* will be introduced. The tax consequences of economic outflows, commonly referred to as expenses and losses, will be discussed in Chapters 3 and 4, which focus on the concept of deductibility.

THE GROSS INCOME CONCEPT

Section 61 of the Internal Revenue Code defines gross income as "all income from whatever source derived, including (but not limited to) the following items." The list of gross income items provided in the section contains some familiar entries. All payments received as compensation for services rendered represent gross income; this general category of *earned income* includes salaries, wages, fees, commissions, tips, and employee fringe benefits. Revenues generated by an active trade or business certainly constitute gross income, as do payments received by the owners of capital for the use of such capital. This latter category includes rents received by a lessor of property, interest received by a lender of money, dividends received by a corporate shareholder, and royalties received by a holder of mineral rights. Finally, when a taxpayer sells any asset at a profit, such profit is included in the definition of gross income for tax purposes.

Although the list of specific types of gross income provided in Section 61 is instructive, the more important lesson to be learned about this list is that it is not all-inclusive. The concept of gross income goes far beyond the 15 listed items and includes any and all financial gains or accessions to wealth. Because of the expansive nature of the gross income concept, taxpayers should always assume that any economic benefit they receive is includable in gross income unless an explicit statutory or judicial exception applies to the benefit.

Form of Payment

The form in which a taxpayer receives an economic benefit is wholly immaterial to the tax consequences of the receipt. A wage must be included in gross income whether it is received in the form of cash, a share of corporate stock, or a case of good scotch. If one individual performs a service for a second individual and is compensated by services performed in return, both individuals have earned income even though no cash payment changes hands. For example, if a dentist provides regular checkups for his neighbor and family and, in return, the neighbor does the accounting work for the dentist's practice, both the dentist and accountant should recognize gross income equal to the value of the services received.

Taxpayers may recognize gross income in the subtle form of the benefit created by a *discharge of indebtedness.* Assume a corporate taxpayer has an overdue account payable of $80,000 to one of its major suppliers. The supplier knows the corporation is having severe cash flow problems and consequently is eager to settle the account as quickly and as advantageously as possible. After some negotiation, both parties agree the corporation will pay $60,000 cash in full satisfaction of the account payable. Because the corporation has extinguished an $80,000 liability with only $60,000 of assets, its net worth has increased by $20,000, an accession to wealth that the corporation must recognize as gross income.

The receipt of a noncash item of income necessitates determining a *fair market value* for the item. Fair market value is the price at which an item would change hands between a willing buyer and seller in an arm's-length transaction. If an established market for a particular item exists, valuation may be relatively straightforward. An employee who receives compensation in the form of publicly traded stock in his corporate employer needs only to open his daily newspaper to determine the price at which the stock is currently trading. If no established market exists, valuation is more difficult. If our employee receives stock in a closely held corporation, the value of the stock can only be estimated by reference to the net value of the underlying corporate business. Obviously, valuation can be very subjective, often leading to disputes between taxpayers and the IRS. If a taxpayer receives property or services that must be included in gross income, typically the taxpayer tends to undervalue the item while the IRS tends to overvalue it. A reasonable compromise can usually be agreed on during the administrative or judicial proceedings accompanying the tax dispute.

Any benefit received must be susceptible to valuation in monetary terms before it can be recognized as gross income. Consider the case of a young business student who has received offers of employment from two rival firms located in the same city. The positions offered are identical in terms of job description, salary, and fringe benefits. However, the title of one position is executive vice president in training, while the title of the other is junior manager. If the student accepts the first position because it offers him greater noncash compensation in the form of prestige, does the prestige represent gross income? Luckily for our student, prestige is an example of *psychic income,* an essentially noneconomic benefit that simply cannot be valued in any reasonably objective manner and therefore escapes recognition for tax purposes.

Income can be received in the form of an indirect benefit. Suppose, for example, a physician performed services for a patient and charged the patient her normal fee. However, the physician instructed the patient to remit the fee directly to the physician's grandchild. Even though the physician never received a direct payment for the professional services rendered, she must include the indirect benefit in her gross income. The tax consequences are exactly the same as if the physician had received the fee from her patient and then made a gift of that fee to her grandchild.

Source of Payment

While people usually think of income in a business or investment context, gross income for tax purposes is not limited to gains derived from labor or capital. Gross income can arise in a purely personal context. One good example is alimony received from a former spouse, an economic benefit not obtained from either labor or capital but which must be included in the recipient's gross income. Income can also be generated by a fortuitous event. A scuba diver who accidentally finds a cache of gold doubloons under 100 feet of water must recognize income to the extent of the value of her discovery. A game show contestant who wins a trip to Jamaica will pay income tax on the value of the trip. And the gambler in Las Vegas or the winner of the Illinois state lottery may be chagrined to learn the federal government has a stake in his jackpot.

The tax law makes no qualitative judgments concerning the nature of gross income. There is no distinction in the Internal Revenue Code between income generated by activities considered socially desirable (the Nobel Peace Prize) and income from activities of more dubious societal value (earnings of a heavy metal rock star). Profits obtained from illegal activities are just as taxable as those earned from legitimate activities. In fact, income tax evasion has been the basis for legal prosecution of notorious criminals (Al Capone, for example) in cases where the government was unable to obtain a conviction on other grounds.

Finally, the status of the person or organization from which an economic benefit is derived generally does not affect gross income recognition. A salary paid by a tax-exempt organization, such as a church, a university, or a charity, must be included in the gross income of the recipient. Income received from a foreign entity is similarly includable. The United States has a *global* system of taxation applying to all income regardless of its geographic source. Under this system, the earnings of a U.S. citizen residing in Paris and working for a French corporation are taxed in the same manner as the earnings of a resident of Cincinnati who works for a business incorporated in Ohio.

THE REALIZATION CRITERION

Under generally accepted accounting principles, income is accounted for only when it is realized. *Realization* occurs when the earnings process is complete and an external transaction takes place that facilitates an objective measurement of the income. A mere increase in the value of an asset over time does not represent income in an accounting sense because the income has not been realized. If and when the asset is sold to a third party, such increase in value is considered severed from the property itself and can be measured and reported as income.

Section 1001 of the Internal Revenue Code provides that an increase in the value of an asset is not recognized as taxable income until a sale or exchange of the asset triggers income realization. Assume a taxpayer purchased marketable securities in 1980 for $25,000. Over the years, the market value of the securities has been steadily climbing. As a result, our happy taxpayer has become increasingly wealthy, although none of the increase in wealth has ever been recognized as gross income. In the current year, the securities are sold for $100,000. Finally, the taxpayer has realized $75,000 of income, the difference between his original investment and the amount realized on sale, and must settle with the federal government by recognizing the $75,000 as gross income for tax purposes.

Integration of the realization criterion into the tax law gives property owners the ability to control the timing of income recognition. The owner of property that has increased in value during the current year can defer paying tax on such increase by simply not selling the property before year-end. Alternatively, the owner of an appreciated asset who determines his marginal tax rate for the current year will be unusually low may deliberately generate income by selling the asset. Consequently, the increase in the value of the asset economically accrued in prior years (in which the owner's tax rate may have been much higher) is taxed at the current low rate.

Students of taxation quickly learn that every general rule of law is riddled with exceptions. Even though we have just established the basic premise that the realization of income for accounting purposes results in the recognition of that income for tax purposes, there are many instances in which this correlation does not hold. Later in this chapter, we will explore a specialized method of accounting for certain installment sales, the application of which causes income realized in one year to be recognized in a later year or years. In Chapter 8, we will examine a wide variety of transactions in which income realization and recognition are severed by operation of a specific statutory provision. The existence of these exceptions doesn't diminish the significance of the fact that, in most cases, the realization of income causes the simultaneous recognition of that income.

Sales and Exchanges

Realization of income and its recognition for tax purposes are triggered by the sale or exchange of property. The term *sale* implies that the amount realized is received in cash or a promise to pay cash at some future date. The term *exchange* implies the amount realized is in the form of a noncash asset. In the latter case, the amount realized is deemed to equal the fair market value of the asset received. For example, a taxpayer owning investment land with an original cost of $200,000 might be willing to exchange the land for stock in a closely held corporation. To compute the gain realized on the exchange, the corporate stock must be valued; if such value is determined to be $245,000, the taxpayer has realized (and must recognize) a $45,000 gain.

The point was made earlier in the chapter that valuation is always a tricky business, and legitimate differences in opinion frequently arise. If the IRS concludes the corporate stock exchanged for the land in the above example is actually worth $275,000, our taxpayer may be assessed the tax liability on an additional $30,000 of income. To minimize exposure to this type of dispute, taxpayers should obtain one or more independent appraisals when the computation of income depends on the value of any type of property or property right.

The Value-for-Value Presumption

Despite the uncertainty inherent in the valuation process, one presumption must be made about the value of assets involved in an exchange: the total value of assets received must equal the total value of assets surrendered. In an economic world, no rational party would agree to sell property for less than its fair market value, nor would any purchaser be willing to pay more for property than its value. This *value-for-value* presumption is at the heart of every business or investment transaction. If an individual who owns marketable securities for which she paid $12,000, but which are worth $30,000 on the current market, agrees to exchange those securities for an interest in a partnership, the exchange makes economic sense only if the owner of the securities presumes that the partnership interest is also worth $30,000. Because of this presumption, there is no need for an independent determination of the value of the partnership interest; generally the taxpayer and the IRS will agree that the amount realized on the exchange is $30,000. Therefore, the taxpayer should recognize $18,000 of gross income, the appreciation in the value of the marketable securities immediately before the exchange.

The value-for-value presumption holds only if the parties involved in a transaction are dealing at arm's length and are negotiating with only their respective self-interests in mind. If the parties are in some way related, they can no longer be realistically viewed as economic adversaries. As a result, the IRS tends to scrutinize the tax consequences of *related-party transactions* with suspicion. Let's return to the example in the previous paragraph in which our taxpayer exchanged marketable securities worth $30,000 for a partnership interest. If the other partners in the partnership are the taxpayer's children, the exchange may not be "strictly business"; the taxpayer may be transferring some part of the value of the securities to her children as a gift. Because of this possibility, the IRS cannot depend on the value-for-value presumption and may demand an independent appraisal of the value of the partnership interest to determine the amount realized on the exchange.

Consider the implications of a related-party transaction in the context of a sale of property by an individual to a corporate purchaser for $500,000. If the seller and purchaser are unrelated and are clearly dealing at arm's length, the IRS should be quite comfortable in assuming the property is worth $500,000— no more and no less. But what if the individual owns 100 percent of the corporation's outstanding stock? Now the seller and purchaser are related, and, in this extreme case, are essentially the same person. The fair market value of the property could conceivably be less than $500,000, in which case our sole shareholder might be trying to sneak a dividend out of his corporation, disguised as an amount realized on the sale of property. As we will discuss in Chapters 5 and 10, the IRS is very adroit in dealing with this type of subterfuge on the part of shareholders and their controlled corporations.

NONTAXABLE RETURNS OF CAPITAL

Many of the examples used in this chapter implicitly illustrate that a return of a taxpayer's investment in property is not gross income. Consider an individual who lends a business associate $10,000 at an 8 percent annual interest rate and receives the associate's promissory note in return. Our creditor now has a $10,000 investment represented by that note. One year later when the debtor pays $10,800 in complete satisfaction of the debt, the $10,000 repayment of principal is nothing more than a return of investment. Only the $800 interest payment is recognized as income.

If an individual pays $25,000 for a painting by a prominent local artist and sells that painting six years later for $30,000, the first $25,000 of the amount realized on the sale is a return of the original capital outlay. Only the additional $5,000 received represents a return on the initial investment recognized as gross income. The serious flaw in this example is that any change in the value of the dollar occurring between the date of purchase and date of sale is ignored. In a period of inflation, $30,000 received in the current year may have exactly the same purchasing power as the $25,000 expended six years earlier. In this case, our individual has recognized no real income at all! The failure of the federal income tax system to account for changes in the purchasing power of the dollar can result in the recognition of taxable income that economically is nothing more than a return of investment.

Many of the complex rules governing the tax consequences of business and investment transactions have been designed to distinguish between nontaxable returns of investment and taxable returns on those investments. In tax jargon, the amount of investment in any asset is called *basis*— the measure of the owner's *unrecovered after-tax dollars* represented by the asset. The important function of tax basis is illustrated in the following example. Assume that Mrs. Conway performed consulting services for ASD Inc., and the corporation issued 1,000 shares of ASD common stock with a current value of $17,500 to her in payment. Mrs. Conway must include the $17,500 value of the stock in her current year gross income and will take a $17,500 basis in the 1,000 shares. This basis prevents the same dollar amount of income from being taxed a second time when Mrs. Conway disposes of the stock. If she eventually sells the stock for $19,000 cash, only the $1,500 excess of the sales price over her basis in the shares represents additional gross income. The computation of tax basis is discussed in greater detail in Chapters 6 and 7.

EXCLUSIONS FROM GROSS INCOME

Early in this chapter, we established the basic premise that the value of any economic benefit received during the year must be recognized as gross income unless an explicit statutory or judicial exception applies to the benefit. The next section will examine the more common of these exceptions, or to use the correct technical term, these *exclusions* from gross income. Remember that each of the statutory exclusions is a deliberate creation of Congress and was enacted to accomplish a particular political, economic, or social purpose. And remember as well that what Congress gives, Congress may as easily take away! There is no guarantee that any gross income exclusion included in today's version of the law will be available to taxpayers in the years to come.

Exclusions as Government Subsidies

Certain exclusions can be explained as indirect subsidies by the federal government. One example is the exclusion for scholarship and fellowship payments under Section 117. The economic benefit of a scholarship to the recipient student may be increased because the student does not have to report the scholarship as income subject to tax. As a result, the institution granting the scholarship can provide a greater benefit for fewer dollars because the government is willing to forgo the tax on those dollars.

The scholarship exclusion is available to any individual who is a candidate for a degree from an educational institution and is strictly limited to the amount of the scholarship used to pay for tuition, fees, books, supplies, and equipment. If any portion of a scholarship represents payment for teaching, research, or other services the student is required to provide, that portion is not eligible for exclusion, but must be included in the student's gross income.

The statutory exclusion for the rental value of a home or a housing allowance furnished to "a minister of the gospel" can be viewed as an indirect subsidy to religious organizations. Traditionally, the compensation package that churches offer to their clergy includes use of a parsonage or manse. Because the value of this housing escapes taxation, the compensation package can consist of fewer dollars but represent the same economic incentive as a greater amount of salary, all of which would be includable in gross income.

State and Municipal Bond Interest

Interest paid on bonds issued by state and municipal governments is excluded from the recipient's gross income under Section 103. Accordingly, governmental units are able to sell *tax-exempt bonds* in the competitive capital markets at an interest rate lower than the market rate paid on taxable bond issues. The savings attributable to this interest rate differential represent an indirect subsidy from the federal government to local governments; if Section 103 were to be repealed, states and municipalities would be forced to pay the higher market rate of interest to raise capital.

Tax-exempt bonds are an example of a *tax-favored investment,* one for which the economic return is enhanced because of its tax characteristics. To illustrate this point, consider an individual in a 31 percent marginal tax bracket who is considering investing $50,000 in the bond market. Taxable bonds are currently paying a 10 percent return, while tax-exempt bonds (of identical risk) pay only 7 percent. If our investor purchases taxable bonds, she must recognize her $5,000 return as gross income, and her after-tax return will drop to 6.9 percent ($3,450 after-tax income divided by $50,000). If she buys tax-exempt bonds, her pretax and posttax returns are the same 7 percent; the tax characteristics of the bonds have made them the superior investment.

What if our investor were in a 15 percent rather than a 31 percent marginal tax bracket? Her after-tax return on an investment in taxable bonds would jump to 8.5 percent ($4,250 after-tax income divided by $50,000), making the taxable bond the better buy. This change in result should help the reader appreciate a very important planning point concerning tax-favored investments. The value of a tax-favored investment can be determined only with reference to the particular tax situation of each investor.

Other lessons can be learned from the above example. Even though our investor will not pay a penny of federal income tax on her tax-exempt bond interest, she must consider the impact of any state income tax before making a final decision. Typically, state tax statutes do not provide exclusions from gross income for interest paid on bonds issued outside the state. Our investor should also be aware that when she sells her tax-exempt bonds, any gain realized on the sale must be recognized as gross income; the tax-exempt label applies only to the interest paid on the bond.

Note also that the economic benefit of the tax-favored status of state and municipal bonds does not really flow to the owner. If our investor in the 31 percent tax bracket purchases tax-exempt bonds, the return on her investment will be only slightly better than if she had purchased taxable bonds. Even though she is avoiding the payment of an *explicit tax* on her investment income, she is paying an *implicit tax* in the form of a lower rate of return on that investment. If she were in a 15 percent tax bracket and misguidedly made the investment in tax-exempt bonds, she would avoid an explicit tax of $750 ($5,000 taxable interest multiplied by 15 percent), but would be paying an implicit tax of $1,500 (the excess of the interest earned on a $50,000 investment in taxable bonds over the interest earned on the same investment in tax-exempt bonds). This analysis emphasizes that at least some portion of the exclusion for tax-exempt bond interest is really an indirect subsidy to state and municipal governments—not to the investors in the bonds.

Exclusions as Incentives

Another way to explain certain statutory exclusions from gross income is to view them as incentives for taxpayers to behave in a certain way. In 1988, Congress enacted Section 135, which provides an exclusion for the income earned upon the redemption of U.S. Series EE savings bonds. The exclusion is limited to the amount of *qualified higher education expenses* incurred by the taxpayer in the year of redemption. Such expenses are defined as tuition and fees required to enroll any member of the taxpayer's immediate family in an eligible educational institution. Although there are a number of definitional and computational complexities in Section 135, the purpose of the provision is obvious: Congress wants to provide an incentive for taxpayers to save for their children's future college educations.

A wide variety of employer-provided fringe benefits are statutorily excluded from the employee's gross income. Chapter 10 contains a detailed description of the more important of these exclusions. Federal taxing authorities are willing to look the other way while employers compensate their employees with such valuable benefits as life, health, and accident insurance coverage and dependent care assistance programs because the government wants to encourage the corporate sector to provide privately funded insurance coverage and child care for as many citizens as possible.

Exclusions Based on Social Considerations

Section 102 of the Internal Revenue Code excludes the value of property received as a gift, bequest, or inheritance from gross income. The grandchild who inherits $500,000 cash and the family jewels from a deceased grandparent clearly has realized a significant economic benefit. Yet this benefit completely escapes income taxation! One possible rationale is that such intrafamily transfers don't increase the wealth of the family as a social unit. A second rationale is that gifts and inheritances represent after-tax income of the donor or decedent, and their inclusion in the recipient's gross income would actually result in double taxation. Or perhaps Congress simply believes it isn't worth the administrative hassle to attempt to capture the value of millions of small private gifts and bequests in the recipients' gross income.

A gift can be defined as a transfer motivated by detached generosity, affection, respect, or admiration. Of course, the motivation for a particular transfer is not always simple to determine. To illustrate this difficulty, consider the case of football great Paul Hornung, who was given an automobile by a publishing company in recognition of his athletic prowess. Could Mr. Hornung exclude the value of the automobile from his gross income under the authority of Section 102? The court trying the case answered in the negative, concluding the transfer was not gratuitous on the part of the publishing company, but was made in the hope that it would provide a good story and boost magazine sales.

Proceeds of life insurance contracts paid on the death of the insured are excluded from income by Section 101. This exclusion is undoubtedly attributable in part to the skill of the Washington lobbyists representing the insurance industry. Nonetheless, the exclusion also maximizes the value of life insurance proceeds to widows, widowers, and orphaned children, who may be in financial distress following the death of the family breadwinner.

It is important to understand that the Section 101 exclusion does not extend to any investment income generated by life insurance policies surrendered before death. Many types of insurance contracts (commonly referred to as whole life or universal life policies) offer an investment element as well as protection against premature death. Taxpayers who no longer need such protection (senior citizens whose children are self-sufficient and who have no financial obligations) frequently cash in their life insurance policies. Any amount of the cash surrender value received in excess of the taxpayer's investment in the insurance contract must be recognized as gross income.

Various types of payments received by individual taxpayers on account of personal injuries or illness (medical insurance payments, workmen's compensation, legal damages, etc.) are excludable from the gross income. The linkage between such compensatory payments and the plight of the disadvantaged recipient provides both a social and an economic justification for these exclusions. In contrast, a taxpayer who is awarded punitive legal damages unrelated to any physical ailment suffered by the taxpayer must include the damages in gross income. Similarly, damages awarded to a plaintiff as payment for any lost income or profit are includable under the theory that they are a substitute for taxable income.

Government Transfer Payments

Public assistance payments based on the need of the recipient, such as food stamps, welfare payments to families with dependent children, and payments to foster parents, are excludable from gross income. On the other hand, government transfer payments made irrespective of financial need generally are subject to tax. Unemployment benefits, for example, are fully taxable. Some portion of Social Security benefits may also be subject to federal income tax; the portion varies according to the income level of the recipient. For single individuals with annual incomes of less than $25,000 and married couples filing a joint return with annual incomes of less than $32,000, no amount of Social Security is included in gross income. For single individuals with annual incomes between $25,000 and $34,000 and married couples filing jointly with annual incomes between $32,000 and $44,000, 50 percent of Social Security is included in gross income. For single individuals with annual incomes in excess of $34,000 and married couples filing jointly with annual incomes in excess of $44,000, 85 percent of Social Security is includable.

ACCOUNTING METHODS

Every taxpayer must adopt a *method of accounting* by which to compute income recognized during the taxable year. Because taxable income must be reported on an annual basis, the particular accounting method adopted by a taxpayer will determine how the continuous income stream generated by that taxpayer's activities will be artificially divided into 12-month segments. Section 446 of the Internal Revenue Code grants taxpayers considerable flexibility in choosing an accounting method. However, the statute cautions that any method chosen must "clearly reflect" income; if upon audit the IRS determines an accounting method fails to provide a clear reflection of income, the taxpayer may be required to adopt a more satisfactory method for tax purposes.

Section 446(c) lists four permissible accounting methods: the cash receipts and disbursements method, the accrual method, a hybrid method combining elements of the cash and accrual methods, and any other accounting method permitted under a specific provision of the law. In this chapter, we will look at these various methods, emphasizing the relationship of the method to the recognition of gross income. In Chapter 4, we will return to the topic of accounting methods and their effect on the computation of deductible expenses and losses.

The Cash Receipts and Disbursements Method

The vast majority of individual taxpayers report their taxable income using the *cash receipts and disbursements* method of accounting. Under the cash method, gross income is recognized only when payment is received, regardless of when the income is earned, and expenses are deductible only when payment is made, regardless of when the expense is incurred. The only financial records typically maintained by cash basis taxpayers are a checkbook and an odd collection of canceled checks, "paid" vouchers, sales receipts, and some miscellaneous notes and diary-type records. These documents, along with any Form W-2 (the "Wage and Tax Statement" prepared by the taxpayer's employer) and Form 1099s ("U.S. Information Returns" prepared by banks, savings and loans, dividend paying corporations, and other payors of miscellaneous income) provide the information necessary to complete an individual tax return (Form 1040, 1040A, or 1040EZ) by April 15 each year.

The term *cash method* should not be taken too literally; the receipt of noncash forms of payment certainly triggers recognition of income to the extent of the value of the payment. The fact that no currency changes hands does not exempt a transaction from application of the cash method. Conversely, not every cash receipt represents income. For instance, a taxpayer who receives $3,000 cash in repayment of a $3,000 loan has not realized any income at all. The reader should clearly understand that the terms *income* and *cash* are not synonymous, even for a cash basis taxpayer.

Under the cash method of accounting, income is considered received when a person has unrestricted access to and control of the income, even if it is not in the person's actual possession. Treasury regulations state that this doctrine of *constructive receipt* applies when income is credited to a taxpayer's account, set apart for him, or otherwise made available so the taxpayer could draw upon it during the taxable year. For example, interest accumulating in a savings account is constructively received by the owner of the account on the day she has the right to withdraw the interest; the owner doesn't avoid income recognition merely because she declines to do so.

The courts have generally concluded that a taxpayer is in constructive receipt of an item of gross income if no substantial barrier to the taxpayer's control and possession of that income exists. Obviously, a taxpayer cannot ward off income recognition by refusing to walk to his mailbox to pick up a dividend check. But consider the case of Albert Baxter, a calendar-year taxpayer, who was notified on Saturday, December 30, 1978, that he could pick up a commission check for $13,095 from a client's office. Knowing this office was 40 miles from his home and realizing he could not deposit the check in his bank until Tuesday, January 2, Baxter decided to delay the trip until the following week. He also decided not to report the income until 1979. Not surprisingly, the IRS decided Baxter was in constructive receipt in 1978. The Ninth Circuit Court of Appeals, in what should be considered an extremely pro-taxpayer decision, concluded that the futility of the trip to collect the check was a substantial barrier to Baxter's control of the income so constructive receipt did not exist.

From the taxpayer's perspective, the cash method of accounting has the advantage of being both simple and objective; it also is readily subject to manipulation. Suppose the owner of a consulting business, a cash basis taxpayer, completes all the work required on a major engagement by the end of November of the current year. Although the $75,000 fee he expects to collect from his client was earned over the past several months, the recognition of $75,000 of income can be deferred until the next taxable year by the simple expedient of billing the client after December 31. By controlling the cash flow from his business, our consultant can also control the timing of income recognition.

The Accrual Method

Under the accrual method of accounting, income must be recognized in the period during which it is earned, regardless of when payment is received, and expenses must be deducted in the period during which they are incurred, regardless of when payment is made. If our consultant in the above scenario were using the accrual method, we would have to recognize $75,000 of gross income in the current year—the year he earned the income—even if he did not receive a check from his client until the next year.

Generally accepted accounting principles hold that only the accrual method of accounting results in a proper matching of gross income and expenses over time and a meaningful computation of net income. While the accrual method may provide a more precise and theoretically accurate measurement of income, it also requires more extensive record keeping on the part of the taxpayer.

Accounting for Business Income

As a very general rule, a business must compute its taxable income under the method of accounting used in keeping the business books and records. If a taxpayer operates more than one business, a different method of accounting may be adopted for each. At this point, it is probably worthwhile to remind the reader of the caveat mentioned at the beginning of our discussion of accounting methods: no method of accounting is acceptable for tax purposes unless, in the opinion of the IRS, that method clearly reflects income.

Most service businesses, including the professions of medicine, dentistry, law, and accountancy, keep their records and compute their taxable incomes on a cash basis. Similarly, many service-oriented businesses such as restaurants, gas stations, and specialty retail outlets prefer the simplicity of the cash method. Treasury regulations require any business maintaining inventories that are an income-producing factor to use the accrual method to account for the cost of inventories sold during the year. Because of this requirement, many small businesses use a hybrid method of accounting under which transactions related to inventories are accounted for an accrual basis, while all other items of income and expense are accounted for on a cash basis. Chapter 4 contains a more thorough look at the inventory accounting rules.

Because the cash method of accounting can be rather easily manipulated, Congress decided to limit its use by large corporate taxpayers. Section 448 prohibits regular corporations (corporations for which a subchapter S election is not in effect) and partnerships with a regular corporation as a partner from using the cash method for tax purposes. There are two important exceptions to this prohibition: personal services corporations and corporations and partnerships meeting a *de minimis* test.

A *personal service corporation* is any corporation in which substantially all the activities involve the performance of services in the fields of health, law, engineering, architecture, accounting, actuarial science, performing arts, or consulting. In addition, the stock of a personal service corporation must be owned by the professionals who perform the services for the corporate clientele. Any regular corporation meeting these definitional criteria may use the cash method to compute its taxable income.

Any corporate or partnership business that meets a statutory *de minimis* test is exempt from the application of Section 448. This test is met if the business has averaged annual gross receipts of $5 million or less for its three most recent taxable years. Corporations and partnerships falling within this exception may continue to use the cash method of accounting until their average gross receipts exceed $5 million, at which point they must convert to the accrual method.

Differences in Book/Tax Income

Virtually all major corporate taxpayers use the accrual method of accounting for both financial statement and tax return purposes. Despite this apparent consistency in the calculation of book income and taxable income, there are a surprising number of differences in the particulars of each calculation.

These differences can be primarily attributed to the fact that corporate managers have conflicting attitudes toward the measurement of income for financial statement purposes and the measurement of income for tax purposes. It is usually in management's best interest to maximize the amount of current book income reported to existing and potential investors in the corporate business. The public accounting profession, which is responsible for auditing corporate financial statements, is aware of management's natural proclivity to overstate book income. Accordingly, generally accepted accounting principles tend to be extremely conservative in determining if income has been realized during the current year. On the other hand, managers prefer to minimize the amount of taxable income (and resultant tax liability) reported to Uncle Sam for the current year. Because of this bias, the tax law and the IRS take particular pains to prevent businesses from understating current taxable income. The conflicting perspectives on income measurement reflected by accounting principles and the income tax law lead to the many *book/tax differences* discussed in later chapters of this text.

One important difference specific to the subject of this chapter involves the timing of the recognition of *prepaid income*. Under a strict accrual method of accounting, income generated by the performance of services or sale of products is not realized until the period in which those services or products are actually provided to customers, even if customers pay for them in an earlier period. For financial statement purposes, such prepayments are not includable in current income. The Treasury is unwilling to be so patient and insists that most types of prepaid income be recognized as gross income, even if the taxpayer reports on the accrual basis. For example, an accrual basis lessor who receives a $90,000 prepayment of three years' rent from a tenant should report only $30,000 of current income on its financial statements. The remaining $60,000 payment will be recorded in a deferred income account. For tax purposes, the lessor must recognize the entire $90,000 currently. Of course, this book/tax difference will reverse over the next two years as the lessor reports $30,000 of financial statement income each year without any corresponding recognition of taxable income.

THE INSTALLMENT SALE METHOD

The Internal Revenue Code provides a host of specialized accounting methods that may be used by a limited number of taxpayers. While the proper tax accounting methods that apply to such esoteric items as prepaid subscription income, solid waste reclamation costs, and nuclear decommissioning costs may be fascinating in their own right, the authors feel comfortable in omitting any discussion of these methods from this text. The statutory accounting method applicable to installment sales of property is a different matter. The *installment sale method* is routinely used by many taxpayers, and the tax consequences of its application are an important element in many business and investment decisions.

An installment sale is defined in Section 453(b) as a disposition of property where at least one payment is to be received after the close of the taxable year in which the disposition occurs. As a simple illustration, suppose Bendix Inc. sells a tract of land with a tax basis of $700,000 for a $1.2 million contract price. Under the terms of the contract, only $200,000 cash is paid at closing; Bendix receives the buyer's note for the $1 million balance. The note provides for equal principal payments over the next 10 years plus 9 percent annual interest on the unpaid balance.

Because of this completed external transaction, Bendix has realized a $500,000 gain on the sale—gain that must be included in financial statement income. For tax purposes, however, the installment sale method allows the corporation to link the recognition of this gain to the receipt of cash over the next 10 years. This linkage is accomplished through a very simple computation. The gain realized on sale is divided by the total contract price to result in a *gross profit percentage*. Cash payments received by the seller each year are multiplied by the gross profit percentage to calculate the recognized taxable gain for the year. In the Bendix example, the gross profit percentage is 41.67 ($500,000 divided by $1.2 million); in the year of sale, Bendix will recognize taxable income of only $83,333 ($200,000 multiplied by 41.67 percent). In each of the next 10 years, Bendix will recognize taxable income of $41,667 ($100,000 annual principal payment multiplied by 41.67 percent).

The reader should appreciate the fact that the installment sale method results only in the deferral of income; all of the gain realized on the sale will eventually be recognized over the life of the installment note. The benefit of such tax deferral should not be underestimated; the longer the payment of a tax liability is delayed, the smaller the real economic cost of the tax. Also note that the interest payments made under the contract in no way enter into the installment sale computation; the recognition of interest income by the seller is a separate taxable event. The installment sale method applies only to gain transactions. Any loss realized on a sale of property must be accounted for in the year of sale. And finally, this method applies automatically to any qualifying sale unless the seller formally elects out of installment sale treatment. If a seller has other losses to offset a current taxable gain, or if a seller believes current tax rates are considerably lower than the rates that will apply in future years, he has the option of recognizing his gain on sale in the current year rather than deferring such gain under the installment sale method.

Limitation on the Installment Sale Method

Ever since the enactment of the installment sale rules in 1926, Congress has been concerned that taxpayers would exploit the income deferral opportunity inherent in this accounting method. Over the years, Congress has added a series of limitations on the method's usage that have progressively narrowed its scope. One set of limitations applies to the type of property eligible for installment sale treatment. Stocks or securities traded on an established market are ineligible. Real or personal property held as inventory for sale to customers in the regular course of a taxpayer's business is also ineligible. Consequently, retailers that normally sell to their customers on a credit basis (Sears, J. C. Penney, etc.) cannot use the installment method to report their routine source of income.

A second set of limitations applies if a taxpayer attempts to convert an installment obligation into cash. Let's refer back to the Bendix installment sale. Immediately after the sale, Bendix owns a note with a principal amount of $1 million. Remember Bendix must eventually recognize $416,667 of income as note payments are received; only $583,333 of the principal collected will be a tax-free return of investment. Stating this idea in another way, Bendix has a tax basis in the installment obligation of only $583,333. If Bendix sells the installment obligation to a third party for its $1 million value, the disposition will trigger $416,667 of immediate income recognition.

What if Bendix tries the more subtle technique of pledging the note as collateral for a $1 million loan? In this case, Bendix still legally owns the installment obligation and has only used it indirectly to obtain cash. Unfortunately for Bendix, the drafters of tax legislation are not fooled by such financial sleight of hand. The installment sale rules provide that a pledge of an installment obligation is tantamount to a conversion of the obligation to cash, which will immediately accelerate recognition of the deferred income inherent in the obligation.

TAX PLANNING FOR INCOME RECOGNITION

In this final section of the chapter, we can begin to discuss basic tax planning techniques relating directly to the concept of income recognition. Many tax textbooks relegate planning to a separate chapter, usually placed somewhere near the end of the book. In a textbook such as this one, the goal of which is to familiarize readers with a broad spectrum of tax opportunities and dangers, such isolation of planning techniques from technical material would be counterproductive. In fact, the rules and regulations explained in this and subsequent chapters can be regarded as background necessary to appreciate the planning process, which is the primary focus of this book. Readers will note that many of the concepts analyzed in this section were mentioned or alluded to earlier in the chapter. In such instances, this last section both emphasizes and summarizes the planning implications of the gross income recognition process.

Tax planning can be defined as the structuring of business, financial, investment, and personal transactions to minimize the federal, state, and local tax costs in order to maximize the rate of return or the economic benefit of the transaction. More succinctly, tax planning is based on maximizing the *present value of after-tax cash flows.* Never lose sight of the crucial fact that tax planning is only one facet of the larger topic of economic planning. Tax minimization for its own sake is never the goal of the tax planning process. Taxpayers should always be willing to structure transactions in such a way as to maximize their economic rate of return, even if that structure involves a higher tax cost than alternative structures. Individuals should never make a bad economic decision simply to save tax dollars.

A corollary of this principle is that the recognition of taxable income is always better than no income recognition at all! The lament that a person can't afford to make any more money because she will be thrown into a higher tax bracket is worse than a cliché—it is nonsense. Under our federal income tax system, even the most highly compensated individual can pocket roughly 60 cents out of every additional dollar of income recognized during the taxable year. Anyone who earns enough income to boost himself or herself into the highest marginal tax bracket should be congratulated, not consoled.

Planning for Nontaxable Income

As a general rule, taxpayers favor nontaxable income over taxable income. Because of the expansive statutory presumption that any economic benefit received during the year is includable in the recipient's gross income, opportunities to earn sizable amounts of nontaxable income are limited. Nevertheless, exclusions from gross income do exist. An individual who deliberately arranges to receive a benefit eligible for a particular statutory exclusion is engaging in a tax planning strategy.

The choice of nontaxable over taxable income is optimal only if the value of the nontaxable income exceeds the after-tax value of the taxable income. In our discussion of the exclusion for municipal bond interest, we made the point that an investor will prefer taxable bonds to tax-exempt bonds if his after-tax rate of return on the former exceeds the rate of return offered by the latter. Let's expand on this idea in a slightly different context. Assume Mrs. Barker has been presented with a choice by her employer: she can either accept a $5,000 annual salary increase or enroll her two children in the employer's on-site day care center. The value of the employer-provided child care would be excludable from Mrs. Barker's gross income under Section 129. How does Mrs. Barker decide between the two options?

Her first step must be to determine the monetary value of the noncash option. If Mrs. Barker is currently spending $4,000 a year on nursery school tuition, she can easily extrapolate a $4,000 value for the employer-provided child care. The second step is to compare this value to the after-tax value of the salary increase. If Mrs. Barker is in a 31 percent marginal tax bracket, $5,000 of additional salary would shrink to $3,450 of disposable income. (This analysis ignores the impact of any payroll and state taxes.) With this combination of facts, Mrs. Barker should choose the nontaxable fringe benefit (the child care) rather than the salary increase. Note that a change in either Mrs. Barker's perceived value of the fringe benefit or her marginal tax rate could lead to the opposite conclusion. If Mrs. Barker could purchase satisfactory child care for only $3,000 a year, she should choose the taxable income. Similarly, if her marginal tax rate were only 15 percent, she would prefer the $4,250 after-tax value of the salary increase to the $4,000 value of the child care.

Deferral of Income Recognition

One of the simplest and most versatile tax planning strategies is to postpone the payment of tax for as long as the law will allow. The benefit of tax deferral is a function of the financial concept of the *time value of money.* This concept is based on the simple premise that a dollar spent today costs more than a dollar spent one year hence. The difference in cost depends on the *discount rate,* the rate of return earned on invested capital over a specified time period. As a simple illustration, consider the case of an individual who invests $1,000 at the beginning of the year at a 10 percent annual rate of return. By the end of the year, the investment will be worth $1,100. Under these economic circumstances, our investor should be indifferent between $1,000 available today or $1,100 available one year hence. Stating the same conclusion in a different way, a $1,100 payment deferred for one year costs only $1,000 in *present value* terms. Observe that the present cost of a future payment has an inverse relationship with the discount rate; the higher the rate, the smaller the present cost of the deferred payment.

The time value of money concept leads to the important conclusion that the amount of a tax in present-value terms can be reduced by deferring payment until a future period. Suppose a taxpayer in a 36 percent marginal bracket has the opportunity to make an investment early in the current year. By the end of the year, the investment has increased in value by $50,000 so that in economic terms our taxpayer has $50,000 of income. We learned in this chapter that this unrealized gain is not recognized for tax purposes. Consequently, the investor has avoided the payment of $18,000 of tax on her income. If she sells the investment in the next year, she must recognize the $50,000 increase in value as income and pay the $18,000 tax. But at a 7 percent discount rate, the present cost of an $18,000 tax payment postponed for a year is only $16,822! If the payment can be postponed for two years, the present cost of the tax drops to $15,722. If the investor has no plans to sell the investment, so that the $18,000 payment is deferred indefinitely, the present cost of the future tax payment is negligible.

Many types of life insurance and annuity contracts are considered tax-favored investments because the owners are not taxed currently on the annual increase in the value of the contracts. Taxation of this increase, referred to as the *inside buildup,* is deferred until the owner receives distributions under the terms of the contract. To illustrate, consider the case of Mr. Thomas, age 43, who purchases a single-premium annuity contract for $30,000. Under the terms of the contract, Mr. Thomas will receive a monthly payment of $500 for the rest of his life, beginning in the month he reaches age 65. The annuity company will accumulate the annual earnings on Mr. Thomas's initial $30,000 investment to fund the future annuity. Mr. Thomas will not recognize any of this income until he reaches age 65 and receives his first $500 payment, some part of which will be a tax-free return of his initial investment and the remainder of which will be taxable income.

Owners of life insurance policies with an investment element enjoy the same type of deferral. Every year the value of the policy grows without triggering income recognition to the owner. The owner will pay tax on this inside buildup only in the year she liquidates the policy for its cash surrender value. If the owner holds the policy until it matures (i.e., the insured individual dies), the inside buildup escapes taxation completely because of the Section 101 exclusion for life insurance proceeds.

Constraints on Deferral

Our federal income tax system offers numerous opportunities for tax deferral, many of which are analyzed in later chapters. However, readers should be aware of certain constraints on the deferral process. One practical problem is that the deferral of income recognition usually goes hand in hand with the postponement of the use or enjoyment of the income. Individuals who must spend every dollar of their current salaries just to make ends meet can't take advantage of most tax-deferral opportunities. And if income deferral means that a taxpayer does not have access to cash that he could reinvest in a profitable activity, the economic benefit of the deferred tax payment is reduced by the *opportunity cost* of the delayed reinvestment.

A second constraint is the enhanced degree of risk characteristic of deferral opportunities. An investor who postpones an asset sale in order to defer recognition of the unrealized gain inherent in that asset risks losing some or all of the gain if the value of the asset declines. The adage that a bird in hand is worth two in the bush has no doubt influenced many conservative investors to take their gains in the current year rather than to defer them into the uncertain future. In addition to market risk, investors must also accept the risk that deferred income may be taxed at a higher rate in the year it is finally recognized. This unfortunate result could occur if the investor's total income has increased enough to boost him or her into a higher marginal tax bracket, or if Congress decides to increase tax rates for everyone.

Tax-deferred investments often have higher transaction costs and lower before-tax rates of return than investments that are not tax-favored. For example, tax-deferred annuity contracts routinely charge all investors an annual fee, and impose a significant monetary penalty on investors who liquidate their investment in the contract within seven or so years of its purchase. Similarly, life insurance policies have the highest commissions of all financial products on the market—typically more than 50 percent of the first-year premium paid by the investor. These types of charges can overwhelm the benefits of tax deferral, especially if unexpected financial circumstances force a taxpayer to liquidate the investment after only a few years.

Finally, the tandem deferral of income recognition and tax liability is limited by the method of accounting adopted by the taxpayer. Under the accrual method, a taxpayer must recognize income in the period during which it is earned. For most routine business transactions, this requirement leaves no room for deferral maneuvers. Even taxpayers using the more flexible cash method of accounting don't have unbridled control over the timing of income recognition. In a recent pronouncement, the IRS reminded taxpayers that the doctrine of constructive receipt applies "when a cash basis taxpayer is presently entitled to money that is made immediately available to him and his failure to receive it is due entirely to his own volition. A taxpayer may not deliberately turn his back upon income and thus select the year in which he will report."

PROBLEMS AND CASES

1. Test your understanding of the gross income concept by determining the amount of income (if any) recognized by taxpayer A in each of the following situations.

    a. Taxpayer A washes B's windows and is given, in return, a bottle of Beefeater gin that retails for $20 and wholesales for $8. (Assume B operates a liquor store.)
    b. Taxpayer A washes B's windows in return for B's promise to play tennis with A at least once a week.
    c. Taxpayer A sells B a watch for $2,500; A paid $2,500 for the watch one week earlier.
    d. Taxpayer A sells B a watch for $2,500; A paid $2,300 for the watch one week earlier.
    e. Taxpayer A embezzles $16,000 from his employer.
    f. Taxpayer A finds buried Spanish coins, valued at $400, on his land.
    g. Taxpayer A purchases 200 shares of XYZ common stock for $50 per share. At the end of A's taxable year, XYZ common is selling for $62 per share on the New York Stock Exchange.
    h. Taxpayer A borrows $1,000 from B, giving B his 90-day, 10 percent note.
    i. Taxpayer A inherits $25,000 cash from his grandfather.

2. Two years ago, Mark Mullins borrowed $3,000 from his aunt to help pay for his college expenses. During the current year, Mark tried to repay the loan, but his aunt refused to accept the money, telling Mark that her pride in his completion of his degree was payment enough. Does Mark recognize gross income because of his aunt's generous act?
3. Carol Garcia was recently promoted to a vice presidency in her firm. She received a substantial increase in her salary and moved from a windowless cubicle into a spacious, newly redecorated office with a lovely view. The cost of the redecorating to Carol's firm was $6,300. Does Carol recognize gross income attributable to her new location?
4. Don Davis is three years behind on his child support payments to his ex-wife, Lois. During the current year, the court orders Don's employer to pay one third of Don's monthly salary directly to Lois until the full amount of the back payments is satisfied. Must Don include the monthly payments to Lois in his current year gross income?
5. Sam Larkin recently served as a contestant on a local game show and won a case of laundry detergent with a retail value of $200. Three months later, Sam sold the detergent at a garage sale for $130. Does either transaction cause gross income recognition for Sam?
6. Sharon Anderson, a real estate broker, just negotiated the sale of a home for a wealthy client. Two days after the sale closed, Sharon received a beautiful hand-tooled leather briefcase from the client with a card reading, "In grateful appreciation of your efforts over the past year." Should Sharon include the value of the briefcase in her current year gross income?
7. In 1992, Mel Davis paid $100 to a junk dealer for an oil painting. While cleaning the painting during the current year, Mel discovered an older painting hidden beneath the top coat of pigment. Much to his amazement, the older painting was by a well-known 19th century artist and was valued by two different appraisers at $75,000. Must mark recognize any current year gross income because of his discovery?
8. The pilots of Skyways Airlines Inc. have been on strike for four months. Barney Garland, a senior pilot participating in the strike, recently received a $7,200 strike benefit from his union, the Airline Pilots Association International. The union funded the benefits paid to Barney and other striking pilots by charges imposed on union members flying for other airlines. May Barney exclude the strike benefit from his gross income as a gift from his fellow union members?
9. Candance Muir's job requires her to travel internationally several times each month. As a result, Candance has amassed 131,590 frequent flyer miles during the current year. Even though her employer pays for her airfares, Candance may use her frequent flyer miles for personal travel. In December, Candance used 100,000 miles to acquire two first-class tickets to New Zealand for herself and her mother. The cost of these two tickets would have been $18,960. Should

Candance recognize gross income attributable to either her receipt or usage of the frequent flyer miles during the current year?

10. Dale Luccio has $10,000 to invest. He is undecided about putting the money into City of Los Angeles municipal bonds paying 6 percent annual interest or publicly traded corporate bonds paying 8.5 percent annual interest. These two investments both have the same element of risk. Dale's best guess is that his marginal tax rate for the year will be 31 percent.

    a. Based on this guess, explain to Dale which investment option is superior.
    b. Explain the implications to Dale if his guess is wrong and he ends up in only a 28 percent marginal tax bracket for the current year.

11. Ellen O'Hare is the owner and sole beneficiary of a $200,000 insurance policy on the life of her mother, who is age 82 and in poor health. The policy is fully paid for (i.e., Ellen owes no more premiums). Ellen's tax basis in the policy is $90,000. Ellen currently needs funds and is considering cashing in the policy for its $175,000 cash surrender value. She also has the option of borrowing the full cash surrender value at an annual interest rate of 4 percent. Analyze Ellen's two options from a tax planning perspective, assuming she is in a 36 percent marginal tax bracket.

12. David Chan was recently injured while performing his duties as an employee of Barton Chemical Company, Inc. During the three months David was unable to work, he received $2,000 of workmen's compensation from the state of Idaho, $4,800 of insurance payments reimbursing him for his medical expenses, and $6,300 of sick pay from his employer. Must David recognize any of these receipts as gross income on his current year tax return?

13. Liz Santos, a bartender and aspiring actress, recently won a statewide beauty pageant. As the winner, Liz was awarded a $15,000 cash scholarship to be used in any way she saw fit to further her education. Liz used the money for private acting lessons. May Liz exclude the scholarship from her current year gross income?

14. Rayburn Inc. is a calendar year corporate taxpayer. On December 12 of the current year, Rayburn billed a customer $20,000 for services rendered during October and November. The corporation had not received the payment by year-end. On December 19, Rayburn received a $4,000 check from a tenant that leases office space from the corporation. The payment was for the following year's January and February rent.

    a. If Rayburn Inc. uses the cash receipts and disbursements method of accounting, how much current year gross income should the corporation recognize because of the above transactions?
    b. Would your answer change if Rayburn Inc. were an accrual basis taxpayer?

15. Raj Sharma, a calendar year taxpayer using the cash receipts and disbursements method of accounting, billed a client for $12,000 of services performed during October of the current year. By mid-December, Raj had not received payment and called the client to demand an explanation. The embarrassed client promised

to telephone Raj as soon as a check for the full amount could be cut. Raj left his business office on December 23 and did not return until January 4. On his telephone answering machine was a message from the client that Raj could collect his $12,000 check from the client's secretary at Raj's convenience; the message was dated December 29. Must Raj recognize the $12,000 of income in the current year?

16. During the current year, Lamex Inc., an accrual basis taxpayer, sells a tract of investment land with a tax basis of $60,000 for $100,000. Payment consists of $10,000 cash at closing and a $90,000 five-year note, the first payment on which is not due until the following year.
    a. How much current year accounting income does Lamex Inc. realize on the sale?
    b. How much current year taxable income does Lamex Inc. recognize on the sale?
    c. Would your answers to *a* and *b* change if Lamex Inc. were a cash basis taxpayer?
17. Refer to the facts in problem 16. In the next year, Lamex Inc. receives its first $18,000 principal payment on the note plus $7,500 interest on the unpaid balance. How much income must Lamex recognize because of these receipts?
18. Refer to the facts in problem 16. Three years after the sale of the land, Lamex Inc. pledges the installment note as partial collateral for a $60,000 bank loan. The principal amount of the note at the date of pledge is $54,000. What are the tax consequences to the corporation of this pledge?
19. Comstat Inc. has a group legal services plan under which any employee can elect to receive up to $5,000 of his or her annual compensation in the form of nontaxable legal services. During the year, Carol Smith elects to receive the maximum amount of legal services, while Susan Parker elects to receive no legal services at all, preferring to receive her entire compensation in the form of taxable salary. From a tax planning perspective, both Carol and Susan made the correct decision. Explain this apparent contradiction.
20. Jamie Lewis is a successful attorney with enough annual income to put her into the highest federal income tax bracket. During the past several years, Jamie has performed a number of legal services for her great uncle, who is 78 years old and in failing health. Although the uncle offered to pay Jamie for her work, she refused any compensation, requesting instead that her uncle "remember her appropriately" in his will. Just this past week the uncle added a codicil to his will that provided for a $200,000 cash bequest to Jamie. The remainder of his considerable estate will pass to his two children and seven grandchildren.
    a. What tax planning objective may Jamie have accomplished through her request of her uncle?
    b. Do you see any risk inherent in Jamie's tax plan?
21. John Rayos has a choice between two stock investments. Investment A will yield a 10 percent annual rate of return in the form of quarterly cash dividends.

Investment B offers the same 10 percent rate of return. However, investment B will pay no dividends so all of the return will be reflected in the annual increase in the market value of the stock.

a. Do these two investments offer the same after-tax rate of return? Briefly explain your conclusion.
b. What tax factor should John consider before making his choice between the two investments?
c. What nontax factors should John consider before making his choice between the two investments?

Case 2–1

Sylvia O'Donnell, age 74, currently has $60,000 in a certificate of deposit paying 6 percent interest annually. In addition to the income generated by this investment, Sylvia receives Social Security and a modest pension from her former employer. The marginal rate on her taxable income has been just 15 percent for the last several years. Although Sylvia is currently in reasonable health and is capable of living independently, she anticipates that in several years she will want to liquidate the certificate of deposit and use the proceeds to buy into an assisted-living retirement home.

Sylvia recently read a magazine article on the wisdom of purchasing tax-deferred annuities. Sylvia knows that the interest income generated by her certificate of deposit is fully taxable each year, and she is wondering if she might be wise to transfer her capital into this type of tax-favored investment. Discuss briefly whether this tax planning strategy would be effective for Sylvia.

CHAPTER 3

Deductions in General

As we discussed in Chapter 2, taxable income is defined as gross income recognized during the year less any allowable deductions. A deduction may arise because a taxpayer has incurred an *expense* (a payment in money or money's worth to a third party) or a *loss* (a disposition of property for an amount less than the taxpayer's investment in the property). This chapter analyzes the general rules for determining when a particular expense or loss can be elevated to the status of a deduction, the ultimate result of which is a reduction in tax liability for the year. The bulk of the chapter is devoted to a discussion of the bewildering variety of deductions available to individual taxpayers. Corporate taxpayers typically incur expenses and losses directly relating to the corporate business; the topic of business deductions will be covered in detail in Chapter 4.

A basic premise of our federal income tax system is that no expense or loss is deductible unless a specific statutory provision authorizes the deduction. This premise is exactly the inverse of the premise that any item of income must be recognized as gross income unless authority exists for its exclusion! For tax law purposes, it is simply a fact of life that the term *income* is very broadly defined, while the term *deduction* is very narrowly defined. Tax deductions have been described as a "matter of legislative grace," meaning Congress can decide from year to year which expenses and losses should be allowed as deductions and which should have no impact on the computation of current year taxable income.

Accountants and attorneys (as well as textbook authors) involved in the tax planning process continually emphasize the desirability of deductible as compared to nondeductible expenses. As a result, individual taxpayers are too often mesmerized by the lure of tax deductions and make foolish expenditures or investments for the sole purpose of obtaining a deduction. Beginning students of taxation should never overlook the obvious: the best strategy for maximizing after-tax wealth is to avoid expenses and losses in the first place. If an expense is desirable, necessary, or unavoidable, then explore every possibility for making the expense tax deductible. To paraphrase Benjamin Franklin, a dollar saved is a dollar earned, but a dollar spent as a tax deduction can save no more than 40 cents in federal taxes.

Substantiation

Section 6001 of the Internal Revenue Code requires taxpayers to maintain records sufficient to establish the amount of gross income and deductions reported on their annual tax returns. Certainly, no taxpayer who claims large dollar amounts of deductible expenses or losses can hope to emerge unscathed from an Internal Revenue Service audit unless he or she can produce written substantiation of the expenses or losses. Substantiation may consist of a canceled check, a credit card receipt, an invoice for a product or service marked paid in full, a contract or other legal document, or a complete set of accounting records. Ideally, such substantiation should be *contemporaneous*— generated at the same time the expense or loss is incurred.

Occasionally, the IRS may allow a taxpayer to make a good faith estimate of the amount of a deductible expense for which no substantiation of the exact amount is available. In a landmark decision, the Second Circuit Court of Appeals allowed Broadway impresario George M. Cohan to deduct an impressive amount of estimated business expenses for which he had no written documentation. This case resulted in the *Cohan rule,* which provides that substantiation is not an absolute requirement for deductibility if the amount of an expense can be estimated with reasonable accuracy. In the years subsequent to the Second Circuit's decision, Congress has steadily eroded the scope of the Cohan rule by enacting rigorous requirements for substantiation of many important deductions. And even for those deductions to which the Cohan rule still applies, the prudent taxpayer should keep the most accurate records possible to minimize the potential for dispute with the IRS.

AN OVERVIEW OF DEDUCTIONS FOR INDIVIDUALS

All deductions allowable to individual taxpayers must be classified as either (1) deductions allowable in computing adjusted gross income or (2) itemized deductions. The first class of deductions are those subtracted directly from the gross income without the imposition of any overall limitation. Gross income minus these *above-the-line* deductions equals the taxpayer's *adjusted gross income* (AGI). While AGI represents an intermediate step in the computation of taxable income, it is an extremely important number in its own right. As we shall see in this and subsequent chapters, many calculations required for various and sundry purposes throughout the Internal Revenue Code are based on AGI. Unfortunately, it is impossible to define the term in any meaningful way other than to say that AGI equals gross income minus those particular deductions favored by Congress with above-the-line status.

Itemized and Standard Deductions

Itemized deductions are truly second-class deductions in the sense that they may result in limited or even no benefit to the taxpayer. These deductions are reported on Schedule A of an individual's Form 1040 and are subtracted from AGI in the taxable income computation. Later in this chapter, we will discuss certain specific itemized deductions. At this point, however, we need to consider two overall limitations on itemized deductions as a class that diminish their potential for reducing taxable income.

Every individual taxpayer is entitled to reduce AGI by the greater of itemized deductions or a *standard deduction*. Theoretically, a standard deduction can be equated to a base amount of income not subject to taxation; if every taxpayer were allowed a standard deduction of $10,000, only gross income in excess of $10,000 would end up as taxable income. The standard deduction is based on filing status; in 1996, married couples filing a joint return may claim a standard deduction of $6,700, while married individuals filing separate return may claim a standard deduction of only half that amount. The 1996 standard deductions for heads of households (a special filing status discussed in Chapter 5) and single individuals are $5,900 and $4,000, respectively. If a taxpayer is over age 65 before the end of the tax year, he may claim an additional standard deduction—$800 if he is married, $1,000 if he is single. A taxpayer who is legally blind may claim an additional standard deduction of these same amounts. All of the various standard deduction amounts are indexed to inflation and change every year.

In a year in which an individual's total itemized deductions are less than the standard deduction, the individual will not even bother to file a Schedule A with her return, and the itemized deductions will have yielded no tax benefit. In a year in which itemized deductions exceed the standard deduction, only the excess amount has a differential impact on taxable income. To illustrate this point, assume Mr. Clark, a single gentleman who is age 73 and blind, has AGI of $30,000 and itemized deductions of $7,350 in 1996. Because his itemized deductions exceed his $6,000 standard deduction ($4,000 plus two additional $1,000 deductions), he will subtract the full $7,350 of itemized deductions from his AGI. If he had not bothered to keep track of his itemized deductions, he could still claim the standard deduction, thereby reducing his AGI by $6,000.

High-income taxpayers face a limitation on the total amount of itemized deductions they may claim. If the AGI reported on a tax return exceeds an inflation-adjusted threshold amount, the total itemized deductions claimed on the return must be reduced by 3 percent of the AGI in excess of the threshold. In 1996, the threshold amount is $117,950 ($58,975 for a separate return filed by a married individual). Two additional rules complicate this rather straightforward provision. First, the itemized deductions for medical expenses, investment interest expense, gambling losses, and personal casualty losses are not subject to reduction. Second, the reduction can never exceed 80 percent of the total remaining itemized deductions; in other words, every taxpayer, regardless of income level, may claim at least 20 percent of these deductions.

Personal and Dependency Exemptions

As we discussed in the preceding paragraphs, the standard deduction is not keyed directly to any actual expense or loss, but instead represents a base amount of income on which no federal tax is levied. The tax law expands upon this concept by providing for a second type of artificial deduction based on the number of people in the taxpayer's family. Generally, every taxpayer who files a return (both husband and wife on a joint return) is entitled to an inflation-adjusted *personal exemption* (the 1996 exemption amount is $2,550). Each additional dependent a taxpayer may claim on his return yields an additional *dependency exemption.*

This exemption mechanism ensures that the greater the number of people being supported by the income reported on a return, the less of that income will be taxed. Suppose Mr. and Mrs. Green file a joint return on which they report adjusted gross income (AGI) of $50,000 and a standard deduction of $6,700. The Greens have no children or other dependents, so they may deduct a total exemption amount of $5,100, resulting in taxable income of $38,200. Mr. and Mrs. Brown report the same AGI and standard deduction amounts as their neighbors, the Greens. The Browns, though, have five children who can be claimed as dependents on their tax return. Consequently, the Browns' total exemption amount is $17,850, and their taxable income is only $25,450.

A taxpayer may claim another person as a dependent only if a three-pronged test is net with respect to that person. First, the person must either have a familial relationship with the taxpayer (lineal ancestor or descendant, sibling, aunt or uncle, niece or nephew, or in-law) or reside in the taxpayer's home. Second, the taxpayer must provide at least 50 percent of the financial support of the person for the taxable year. Finally, the person's gross income for the year must be less than the exemption amount; this third requirement is waived for any child of the taxpayer who is (1) under the age of 19 or (2) a full-time student under the age of 24.

It is not unusual for an individual who qualifies as another person's dependent to earn sufficient income during a year to require the filing of a tax return. An individual claimed as a dependent on another taxpayer's return may not claim a personal exemption on his own return. Moreover, the standard deduction on the return is limited to the greater of the taxpayer's earned income or $650. Consider the situation of Billy Smith, the 15-year-old son of Jack and Sandy Smith. Billy's income from his paper route during the school year and a summer job as a lifeguard totals $2,200. If Billy's parents claim him as a dependent on their return for the year, Billy's tax return on which he reports his $2,200 of earned income will reflect a standard deduction of only $2,200 and no personal exemption. If Billy's earned income for the year were $5,000, his standard deduction would be $4,000 (the full standard deduction for a single taxpayer) and his taxable income would be $1,000. If Billy's $2,200 of income consisted of unearned income, such as interest and dividends, his standard deduction would be only $650 and his taxable income would be $1,550.

The standard deduction and personal and dependency exemptions can be viewed in combination as a subsistence amount of income the federal government chooses not to tax. Millions of low-income individuals pay no tax because their gross incomes are less than the total amount of their standard deductions and exemptions. Congress has decided the tax shelter provided by personal and dependency exemptions should be available only to low- and middle-income taxpayers. Accordingly, the shelter is phased out for individuals with high incomes. The total exemption amount claimed on a return must be reduced by 2 percent for each $2,500 (or fraction thereof) by which AGI exceeds an inflation-adjusted threshold amount. The 1996 thresholds are:

Filing Status	*Phaseout Applies to AGI in Excess of*
Single persons	$117,950
Married persons filing jointly	176,950
Heads of households	147,450
Married persons filing separately	88,475

To illustrate the effect of the exemption phaseout, assume Mr. and Mrs. Rogers file a 1996 joint return on which they claim five exemptions, resulting in a total exemption amount of $12,750. If the Rogers's AGI for the year is $192,000, their exemption

Figure 3–1 Activities of an Individual Taxpayer

amount must be reduced by 14 percent (2 percent multiplied by seven, which is $15,050 excess AGI divided by $2,500 and rounded up to the nearest whole number). Therefore, the Rogers's exemption amount is reduced from $12,750 to $10,965. If the Rogers's AGI exceeds $299,450, their exemption amount will be phased out completely; 2 percent multiplied by the excess AGI divided by $2,500 will equal a 100 percent reduction in the total exemption amount.

The Taxable Income Calculation

Before turning to a discussion of specific tax deductions, we can summarize the relationship of above-the-line deductions, itemized deductions, the standard deduction, and exemptions in the following formula for the computation of the taxable income of an individual.

	Gross income recognized
less:	Above-the-line deduction
	Adjusted gross income (AGI)
less:	The greater of itemized deductions or standard deduction
less:	Personal and dependency exemptions
	Taxable income

A FRAMEWORK OF INDIVIDUAL TAX DEDUCTIONS

Over a single year, an individual can engage in thousands of activities resulting in expenses or losses. Deductibility of each expense or loss depends on the unique facts and circumstances of each particular activity. The first step toward a general understanding of the complex web of tax rules determining deductibility is the development of a framework by which to organize these thousands of activities into a manageable number of general categories.

For federal income tax purposes, every activity in which a person is involved can be described generically as a business activity, an investment activity, or a personal activity. Thus, Figure 3–1 represents the entire realm of possible activities in which an individual might incur an expense or loss.

This trisected circle provides a basic framework for analyzing the deductibility of individual expenses and losses. A different fundamental assumption as to deductibility applies to the activities in each category. By mastering these simple assumptions, the student of taxation can begin to make some sense of this chaotic area of the law.

BUSINESS ACTIVITIES

The general assumption applying to business activities is that related expenses and losses are above-the-line deductions (i.e., fully deductible in computing the taxpayer's AGI). Two sections of the Internal Revenue Code confer this highly desirable status. Section 162(a) permits a deduction for all routine expenses paid or incurred during the year in operating a business. Section 165(c)(1) echoes this theme by providing that uninsured losses incurred in a trade or business are fully deductible. Because of these two statutory provisions, our federal income tax is imposed only on net business profits rather than on the gross receipts of the business.

Chapter 4 is devoted to a thorough discussion of business deductions and losses. At this point, we need only to discuss what type of activity qualifies as a trade or business for tax purposes. Although the term *trade or business* is used over 60 times in the Internal Revenue Code, it is never precisely defined. As a result, the determination of trade or business status depends on the facts and circumstances of each activity. Over the years, several criteria have emerged from the hundreds of court cases in which this determination was the subject of litigation. The primary criterion is that the individual must have entered into the activity to make money; the existence of a *profit motive* is critical. (Interestingly, the courts have held that a taxpayer's expectation of profit doesn't necessarily have to be reasonable, as long as the taxpayer has a bona fide intent to generate profit.) The individual must also have committed his time, talent, and energy to the activity on a regular, extensive, and continuous basis. This active and ongoing involvement is the second major criterion distinguishing a trade or business activity from the other pursuits.

For most people, their business activity is obvious—it is the labor in which they engage to earn a living for themselves and their families. An employee is in the trade or business of being an employee, reporting both his salary or wages earned and any employment-related expenses on his Form 1040. A self-employed individual who owns and operates a business as a sole proprietor reports gross revenues and deducts all related business expenses on Schedule C of Form 1040. The management of even a single piece of rental real estate is generally treated as a trade or business for tax purposes.[1] Gross rents received and all deductions relating to the rental activity

[1]Purists might be offended by the classification of actively managed rental real estate as a business because Section 212, rather than Section 162, authorizes the deduction of rental expenses. See Reg. Sec. 1.212-1(b). However, these expenses are deductible above-the-line and are much more functionally related to business expenses than to other types of Section 212 investment expenses.

are reported on Schedule E of the lessor's Form 1040. One person can have several business activities; many energetic taxpayers work as salaried employees during the day, while managing their own businesses during the evenings and on weekends.

INVESTMENT ACTIVITIES

If a taxpayer enters into an activity with the intention of making a profit, but does not expend the entrepreneurial effort required to elevate the activity to trade or business status, the activity will fall into the investment segment of Figure 3–1. Investment activities consist of the ownership of income-producing assets or assets held for long-term appreciation in value. Generally, owners play a rather passive role with respect to their investments, and it is this passivity that distinguishes an investment activity from a business activity.

Individuals may devote a substantial amount of time to managing their investments. Consider the case of Joseph and Dorothy Moller, a retired couple who derived virtually all their considerable income from four portfolios of marketable securities. During the taxable year in question, the Mollers each spent approximately 40 hours a week managing these portfolios. This industrious couple did not purchase and sell securities for speculative purposes; instead, they were primarily interested in payment of interest and dividends as well as the long-term growth potential of their various holdings. The Mollers attempted to deduct certain expenses related to the home office in which they did all their work. Because the Internal Revenue Code permits this particular deduction only if the activity conducted in the home office is a business, the Mollers argued that their active and constant exercise of managerial and decision-making functions transformed their investment activities into a business. Although the trial court was persuaded by this argument and allowed the deductions, the appellate court reversed the lower court's decision by concluding: "A taxpayer who merely manages his investments seeking long-term gain is not carrying on a trade or business. This is so, irrespective of the extent or continuity of the transactions or the work required in managing the portfolio. The fact that the Mollers spent much time managing a large amount of money is not determinative."

Investment-Related Expenses

Section 212 allows as a deduction all the ordinary and necessary expenses paid or incurred during the taxable year (1) for the production or collection of income; (2) for the management, conservation, or maintenance of property held for the production of income; or (3) in connection with the determination, collection, or refund of any tax. If an investor in marketable securities subscribes to *The Wall Street Journal* to monitor the general investment climate as well as the performance of specific publicly traded stocks, the subscription cost is deductible under Section 212. If that same investor rents a safety deposit box in which to keep stock certificates and other investment-related documents or pays a fee to an investment counselor for advice, these expenses are also deductible. Finally, if any taxpayer uses the services of an accountant or attorney, the professional fee attributable to tax compliance or tax-planning advice is deductible.

Although Section 212 applies to a relatively few types of expenditures, it does provide the basic authority for deducting expenses related to investment activities. Actually, the Internal Revenue Code is extremely grudging concerning the deductibility of such expenses. While Section 212 represents the general rule, other statutory provisions impose various restrictions that seriously undermine this generalization. For example, Section 212 expenses can be claimed only as itemized deductions; if a taxpayer fails to generate a critical mass of itemized deductions (i.e., itemized deductions in excess of the standard deduction to which the taxpayer is entitled), any investment expenses for the year will not affect the computation of taxable income.

A second restriction is that Section 212 expenses fall into the unfortunate category of *miscellaneous itemized deductions,* which are deductible only to the extent their total amount exceeds 2 percent of the taxpayer's AGI for the year. Because of the severity of this limitation, few individuals actually receive any tax benefit from Section 212 expenses. To quickly illustrate this point, assume that a person with AGI of $75,000 incurs $800 of investment expenses during the year, which happen to be his only miscellaneous itemized deduction. This $800 amount falls far short of his $1,500 threshold (2 percent of $75,000), and none of the expenses can be included in his total amount of itemized deductions.

Investment Interest Expense

The most significant investment expense incurred by most individuals is the interest they pay on borrowed funds used to purchase investment property. If the investment property happens to be tax-exempt state or municipal bonds, no deduction is allowed for interest paid on the borrowed funds. The logic of this rule is readily apparent: Congress does not want to subsidize the acquisition of investments that generate nontaxable income. If the investment property has the potential to yield taxable income, the interest paid on the borrowed funds is deductible, but only to the extent the borrower recognizes any type of investment income for the year.

Suppose an investor borrows $50,000 at 9 percent and invests the money in a mutual fund yielding 12 percent for the year. The investor's $6,000 of dividend income from the fund exceeds his $4,500 interest expense, so the entire $4,500 may be claimed as an itemized deduction. What if, instead, our investor uses the $50,000 to purchase an interest in undeveloped land, which is expected to appreciate in value over the year but which will not be sold before year-end? If we assume our taxpayer has no investment income from other sources, he will have no recognized investment income in the current year, and none of his investment interest expenses can be deducted. Luckily, the law allows his $4,500 of disallowed interest expense to be carried forward into future taxable years. If our investor receives any type of investment income in a subsequent year, he may then deduct his investment interest expense to the extent of such income.

Investment Losses

Section 165(c)(2) permits individuals to deduct "losses incurred in any transaction entered into for profit, though not connected with a trade or business." Here again is a general rule that seems to allow a tax deduction when a taxpayer sells or otherwise disposes of an investment asset and the amount realized on the disposition is less than the tax basis in the asset. Unfortunately for those thousands of stock market aficionados who always manage to buy high and sell low, the permissiveness of this general rule is an illusion. As we will discover in Chapter 7, specialized restrictions on the deductibility of *capital losses* render the general rule of deductibility almost meaningless.

Individuals may claim a capital loss if a loan made to a third party in any nonbusiness capacity proves to be uncollectible. A taxpayer claiming a loss for a *nonbusiness bad debt* should be prepared to offer evidence that the loan was a bona fide investment originally made with the expectation of repayment. When a person lends money to a family member or friend and the facts of the transaction indicate the creditor had no real intention of enforcing the obligation, the IRS often concludes the purported loan was really a gift. As a result, the creditor cannot claim a bad debt loss upon default by the relative or friend.

PERSONAL ACTIVITIES

When an individual engages in a personal activity, the basic assumption is that all related expenses and losses are nondeductible. Most individual taxpayers understand that the everyday expenses incurred in managing a household, raising a family, pursuing social or civic interests, and enjoying leisure time cannot be claimed as tax deductions. However, individuals are often surprised and dismayed to learn that a loss realized on the sale of a personal asset is also nondeductible. Because of the depressed state of the residential real estate market in certain regions of the country, it is not unusual for families to sell their homes for considerably less than they originally paid for them. Although this economic loss can be financially devastating, it is nondeductible under the theory that ownership of a family dwelling is a personal activity rather than a transaction entered into for profit.

Of course, it is not always easy to distinguish between a personal activity and a profit-motivated activity. An individual who buys a painting to display on the wall above the fireplace in her home may be motivated both by her aesthetic appreciation of fine art and her belief that the value of the painting will appreciate significantly over time. Is the ownership of the painting a personal activity or an investment activity? The answer to this question may have important tax implications.

If our individual borrowed money to finance her purchase, the interest paid on the debt is a nondeductible expense if the painting is primarily a personal asset. If the painting can be considered an investment, the interest should be classified as investment interest and is deductible to the extent our art lover has investment income for the year. What if the individual carries a special insurance policy on the painting? Are the annual premiums she pays a nondeductible personal expense or a potentially deductible expense incurred for the protection of investment property? The answers to the above questions depend on the facts and circumstances surrounding the purchase of the painting; certainly the IRS will be looking for any facts suggesting a personal activity, while our taxpayer will emphasize any facts tending to substantiate her investment motive.

The same type of uncertainty surrounds the classification of expenses with a business flavor, although they are not directly incurred in the active conduct of a trade or business. Many college students who spend their undergraduate years dressed in sweatshirts and blue jeans reluctantly spend a significant amount of money on their first professional wardrobe. For these young adults, the prospect of wearing a conservative business suit may hold absolutely no element of personal enjoyment. Nonetheless, both the IRS and the courts have consistently ruled that the cost of clothing suitable for general wear is a personal rather than a business expense. This same logic dictates that expenses related to personal appearance (hair styling, manicures, cosmetics, health spas, etc.) are nondeductible, even if the taxpayer can demonstrate that good grooming is essential to his or her success in the business world.

The Hobby Loss Rule

Many enjoyable activities have the potential, at least, to generate revenue. Such activities seem to straddle the line between the personal and business segments of Figure 3–1. Let's analyze the situation of Mr. Conroe, a partner in a prosperous firm of attorneys. During his evening hours and on weekends, Mr. Conroe breeds Labrador retrievers. Not only does he show his own animals in local and regional competitions, but he also sells puppies and trains and shows dogs owned by others. This secondary activity generates a modest amount of revenue (at this point, the reader should understand that the recognition of these revenues as gross income is a foregone conclusion). But are the expenses related to the dog breeding activity deductible business expenses or nondeductible personal expenses?

Section 183 adopts a middle ground between this harsh all-or-nothing approach. Even if the dog breeding activity really should be considered Mr. Conroe's *hobby* (i.e., a personal activity not engaged in for profit), this section graciously allows a deduction for the related expenses to the extent of the gross income generated by the hobby. If Mr. Conroe's revenues from puppy sales and training sessions total $10,000 in the current year, he may offset this income with $10,000 of his feed bills, veterinary fees, and other canine expenses. If his expenses for the year exceed $10,000, the excess amount (his operating loss from the dog breeding activity) is a nondeductible personal expense.

Very few taxpayers who engage in secondary activities resulting in operating losses are willing (at least initially) to concede that such activities are hobbies rather than legitimate businesses. Most taxpayers report these activities as business operations on Schedule C and deduct any net loss against other sources of income reported on their Form 1040. If a taxpayer with a questionable business loss is challenged by the IRS, he may stoutly contend he has every intention of someday making a profit from the activity. But if the taxpayer expects to successfully resist the challenge and preserve the deductibility of his current year loss, he must present evidence to support his contention.

Such evidence usually stems from the businesslike manner in which the taxpayer has conducted his activity. A taxpayer who maintains a proper set of accounting records and a separate bank account for the activity and advertises his service or product (or puppies) in appropriate trade journals is more likely to win his case than a taxpayer who does none of these things. Of course, the best way for a person to prove a profit motive exists is to actually make a profit. Section 183 provides a *presumption* that if an activity has shown a profit in three out of five consecutive years, it is a legitimate business rather than a hobby. In such cases, the burden of proof shifts to the IRS to gather sufficient evidence indicating such activity is not a business; the IRS rarely, if ever, attempts to do so.

Many people are surprised to learn that the tax law treats gambling activities in very much the same manner as it treats hobbies: gambling losses are deductible only to the extent of gambling winnings for the year. In other words, those lucky few who show a net profit from their gambling activities should report the profit as taxable income. The vast majority of gamblers who bet on more losers than winners over the course of a year cannot deduct their net gambling loss against any other source of income.

Business Use of a Personal Residence

As we mentioned earlier, ownership of a residence is a personal activity, so the expenses of maintaining the residence are nondeductible. Nevertheless, when a homeowner uses a portion of his residence as an office out of which to conduct a business activity, the expenses allocable to the *home office* may qualify as business deductions. To illustrate, assume a self-employed consultant uses one room of his home as his business office. If the room represents 15 percent of the home's square footage, the consultant can claim 15 percent of his monthly utilities, homeowner's insurance, and any general repair and maintenance costs on his home as business expenses. He can also compute a depreciation deduction based on 15 percent of the cost of the home. (Depreciation deductions are the subject of Chapter 6.)

The possibility of transforming some percentage of monthly household expenditures into tax deductions might prompt the conversion of many a spare bedroom into a home office—even if such office has little to do with the successful conduct of the taxpayer's trade or business. To prevent this obvious potential for abuse, Congress designed a remarkably strict set of rules regarding deductions for a home office. Essentially, the office must be used *exclusively* on a regular basis as the *principal place of any business* operated by the taxpayer or as a place to meet with patients, clients, or customers of the business. If the taxpayer is an employee, the use of a home office must be for the *convenience of the taxpayer's employer.* Thus, if an employer routinely provides adequate office space for its work force, an employee who chooses to work during evenings and on weekends at her personal residence is precluded from claiming a home office deduction.

A second situation in which a personal residence can be used in a business activity is when the owner rents the residence to third parties for some portion of the year. This situation typically arises when the residence is a vacation home, rather than the family's principal residence. While the Internal Revenue Code does allow a deduction for the expenses of maintaining the residence (utilities, insurance, repairs, depreciation, etc.) properly allocable to any rental period, the total amount of these deductions is limited to the amount of the rental income generated by the residence. This tough *vacation home rule* makes it impossible for an individual to create a loss to be deducted against other sources of income by temporarily converting personal property (a vacation home) into rental property.

Personal Expenses and Losses as Itemized Deductions

The list of exceptions to the rule that personal expenses and losses are nondeductible is very short. Moreover, with one major exception, all the tax deductions attributable to purely personal activities must be claimed as itemized deductions. The exception is the deduction for alimony paid to a former spouse. Perhaps because every dollar of alimony paid by one individual can be directly traced to the gross income reported by another individual, Congress was willing to designate alimony payments as above-the-line deductions reducing the payor's AGI for the year. In the next few pages of this chapter, we will look at the list of personal deductions. Because the focus of this text is on the role of taxation in business decisions, our discussion of these nonbusiness deductions will be in summary form only.

Individuals may deduct the amount of cash or the fair market value of property given to any not-for-profit organization granted tax-exempt status by the IRS. The rationale for this *charitable contribution deduction* is that it encourages private citizens to redistribute their wealth to public institutions benefiting our society as a whole. By allowing a deduction for charitable giving, the federal government is providing an indirect subsidy for thousands of social, civic, cultural, religious, and educational organizations located throughout the country. (The subsidy is not available for political contributions, which are completely nondeductible.) The role of charitable giving in family tax planning and the various limitations on the amount of this deduction are discussed in Chapter 14.

Any expenses paid for medical treatment for taxpayers and their families are deductible to the extent such expenses are not reimbursed by insurance. Deductible medical expenses include payments to health care professionals and facilities, medical insurance premiums, and prescription drugs. The *medical expense deduction* provides a measure of relief to families who must bear extraordinary health care costs. To ensure that such relief is available only to those taxpayers who really need it, the deduction is limited to the amount by which medical expenses for the year exceed 7.5 percent of the taxpayer's AGI.

The tax law is also sympathetic to families who have suffered uninsured personal losses attributable to theft or to natural disasters such as floods, fires, or storms. Taxpayers may claim a deduction for the decline in value of personal property stolen, damaged, or destroyed as a result of such occurrences. This *casualty loss deduction* is limited to the total of such losses for the year in excess of 10 percent of the taxpayer's AGI.

Any income or property taxes paid by individuals to a local, state, or foreign government are deductible for federal income tax purposes. Keep in mind this *personal tax deduction* is rather limited in scope since it applies only to income taxes or taxes levied on the value of real or personal property. Consequently, state and local sales taxes, gift and inheritance taxes, employee payroll (FICA) taxes, and employment taxes paid with respect to household employees are considered nondeductible personal expenses.

The final—and certainly the most controversial—item on our list of deductible personal expenses is the deduction for *qualified residence interest.* Qualified residence interest is defined as interest paid on any acquisition debt (a mortgage incurred to purchase, construct, or substantially improve a personal residence) or home equity debt (typically a second mortgage on a residence the proceeds of which may be used for any purpose). Both acquisition debt and home equity debt must be secured by the personal residence.

The deduction for qualified residence interest clearly represents an important subsidy to the American homeowner. Proponents of the deduction claim it encourages home ownership, thereby strengthening the construction and housing industries and indirectly benefiting state and local governments dependent on real estate as a property tax base. However, as home ownership becomes less affordable to middle-class citizens, this subsidy becomes more difficult to justify. The difficulty is compounded by the fact that the deduction is available for interest paid with respect to two personal residences owned by a taxpayer.

In 1986, Congress tried to dissipate some of the political controversy over the deduction by limiting the amount of a taxpayer's acquisition debt and home equity debt to $1 million and $100,000, respectively. As a result, a taxpayer who takes out a $1.5 million mortgage to buy a home may deduct only two thirds of the interest she will pay. The interest attributable to the $500,000 portion of the mortgage not considered acquisition debt is nondeductible personal interest.

Summary

The preceding discussion of the tax consequences of expenses and losses incurred by individuals can be quickly summarized by reference to Figure 3–2, which depicts the three categories of individual activities. At this point in the chapter, the reader can appreciate that this trisected circle presents the most simplistic overview of a tremendously complicated subject. The general rule of deductibility for each category is riddled with exceptions, and the lines between the categories are often blurred. Nevertheless, as this textbook examines the more important of these exceptions in subsequent chapters, the reader can maintain his or her perspective by referring back to Figure 3–2.

PLANNING FOR TAX DEDUCTIONS

The best way to introduce any discussion of tax planning strategies involving the concept of deductibility is to repeat the pragmatic advice offered at the beginning of this chapter. The most effective way to maximize the after-tax cash flow from any activity is to minimize the costs associated with that activity. As a general rule, tax deductions are a by-product of economic costs. When a taxpayer reduces or eliminates a cost, he or she may also lose a tax deduction. An astute tax planner never mourns this loss.

Most people understand that the economic cost of any expense or loss is reduced if some portion of the expense or loss is tax deductible. If an individual in a 36 percent marginal tax bracket incurs a $1,000 expense that is fully deductible on her current year return, her tax bill for the year will decrease by $360. Accordingly, her after-tax cost of the expense is only $640. If only half the expense is deductible, its after-tax cost is $820. Of course, if the expense is not deductible at all, its after-tax cost equals its $1,000 before-tax cost. This simple analysis leads to an equally simple conclusion: taxpayers should always prefer a deductible to a nondeductible expense.

Substituting Deductible Expenses for Nondeductible Expenses

Individuals have few realistic opportunities to shift their expenses from the nondeductible to the deductible category. Most expenses in the two categories are not interchangeable. Obviously, a family can't decide to stop buying groceries because

Figure 3–2 Deductibility of Individual Expenses and Losses

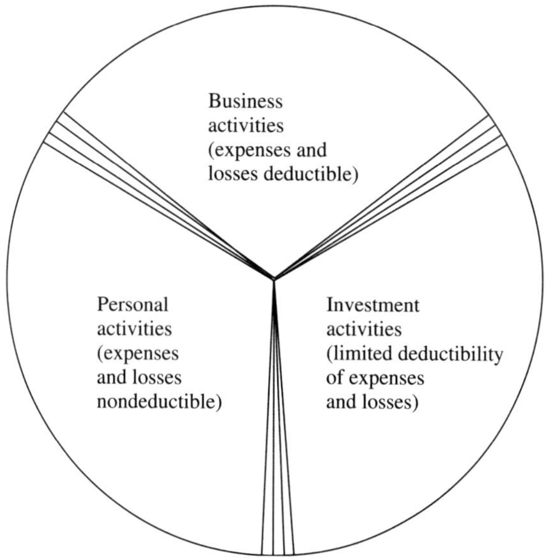

the cost is nondeductible, nor is there any type of deductible expense that results in food on the dinner table. Even in those few cases in which substitution is possible, serious nontax constraints may exist. For example, individuals can provide housing for their families by making nondeductible rent payments or by making payments on a home mortgage, the interest element of which is an itemized deduction. Unfortunately, this theoretical choice is meaningless to taxpayers who are financially unable to purchase a home.

As part of the Tax Reform Act of 1986, Congress repealed the deduction for personal interest expense, with an important exception for qualified residence interest. Taxpayers whose homes were worth more than the mortgage incurred to purchase the home were quick to realize these new rules could be used to their advantage. Specificially, these taxpayers could take out a second mortgage, a home equity loan, and use the proceeds to pay off other personal debts. Because the interest on the first $100,000 of home and equity debt qualifies as an itemized deduction, this conversion of personal debt into home equity debt shifted the interest payment on the debt from the nondeductible to the deductible category. Thousands of homeowners responded enthusiastically to this planning technique. Between 1987 and the end of 1990, outstanding second mortgage debt in the United States nearly doubled to a total of $330 billion. Only about a third of the money borrowed was used for home improvements; another third went to pay off existing consumer debt, while the remaining third was used to finance new consumption, such as automobiles. According to a recent study, approximately 20 percent of U.S. homeowners now have home equity loans or lines of credit.

Controlling the Timing of Deductions

Individuals who keep careful records of their occasional expenses qualifying as itemized deductions may be frustrated to discover that the total of these deductions for the year is about equal to the available standard deduction. A person in this situation who resigns himself to claiming the standard deduction every year may be missing a planning opportunity. Remember cash basis taxpayers can often accelerate or postpone the payment of a tax-deductible expense and thereby control the year in which the deduction is recognized. Consequently, these taxpayers can plan to bunch two years' worth of itemized deductions into a single year.

Suppose Chuck Lewis, an unmarried taxpayer in a 36 percent marginal tax bracket, makes a number of routine charitable contributions, the yearly total of which averages $2,900. Chuck also pays annual state and local property taxes of $1,200. The sum of these itemized deductions is $4,100, just $100 more than Chuck's $4,000 standard deduction. The tax savings attributable to itemizing is a paltry $36 (36 percent of the $100 excess of itemized deductions over the standard deduction). If Chuck would plan to make two years of charitable contributions in the current year and prepay his next year's property tax liability, his current year itemized deductions would total $8,200, and his tax savings from itemizing would jump to $1,512 (36 percent of the $4,200 excess itemized deductions). In the following year, Chuck could not itemize but would simply claim his standard deduction. Through nothing more than careful timing, Chuck has decreased his tax liability over the two-year period.

As a general proposition, taxpayers should accelerate the recognition of a deduction into the earliest taxable year. Because of the time value of money, the value of the tax savings attributable to a deduction is maximized when the deduction is recognized currently. Consider the case of a calendar year individual in a 36 percent tax bracket who anticipates incurring $10,000 of deductible medical expenses in January of the next year. This expense will yield a $3,600 tax savings, but not until next year's tax return is filed. At a 7 percent discount rate, the present value of the savings is only $3,364. But if this individual can reschedule her medical treatment for December and pay the $10,000 cost before year-end, the deduction will be reported on this year's return, and the tax savings will be worth a full $3,600 in present value terms.

Many people are unable to accelerate or prepay deductible expenses because they simply don't have enough extra money in the bank. Think back to our earlier example involving Chuck Lewis. The notion that Chuck should bunch his itemized deductions into one year is theoretically sound. Yet to do so, Chuck must budget two years' worth of expenses to be paid out of one year's income. If his cash flow constraints are too restrictive, the bunching strategy may have to be abandoned as impractical.

Losses between Related Taxpayers

Ever since Congress defined taxable income as gross income net of allowable deductions, taxpayers and their advisers have searched for ways to create artificial *paper deductions* bearing no relationship to cash outflows or declines in wealth. Throughout this text, we will encounter many rules and regulations drafted to ensure that a taxpayer's deductions are not totally divorced from at least some risk of economic loss to that taxpayer. Let's close this chapter by examining one of the most widely applicable of these rules.

Section 267(a), which disallows the recognition of any loss realized on sales of assets between related parties, is based on the theory that such losses may be devoid of economic consequences. A taxpayer who owns a business or investment asset with a tax basis in excess of the asset's fair market value can certainly trigger a legitimate tax loss by selling the asset to an unrelated third party. In such cases the tax loss mirrors a true economic loss; any future increase in the value of the asset will benefit only the unrelated purchaser. But if the sale is to a related party, such as a member of the taxpayer's immediate family, a future increase in value will indirectly belong to the taxpayer, negating the purported economic loss realized on the sale.

Section 267(b) contains a long list of related parties to whom the loss disallowance rule applies. This list includes members of the same family, a corporation and its controlling (more than 50 percent) individual shareholder, and two corporations, controlled by the same shareholders. One interesting feature of Section 267(a) is that it applies to sales between family members regardless of the emotional relationship between buyer and seller. For example, if a brother sells an asset at a loss to his sister, the loss is automatically disallowed for tax purposes, even if the brother can prove that the siblings have been bitterly estranged for years and the transaction between them was strictly business.

CONCLUSION

In this chapter, we have developed a framework of the tax law governing the deductibility of expenses and losses. The chapter makes no attempt to examine even a fraction of the myriad definitional and operational rules, exceptions to these rules, and exceptions to the exceptions that are the bane of the tax return preparer's existence but are of little interest to the business executive. Instead, our focus has been conceptual, and our goal has been to provide a broad perspective on the topic of deductibility. In Chapter 4, we will build on this perspective as we examine in greater detail the topic of business deductions and losses.

PROBLEMS AND CASES

1. Larry Lopiano, a single taxpayer, has AGI of $22,000 and has incurred only $1,100 of itemized deductions through December 26 of the current taxable year. On December 28, Larry incurs a $2,000 expense.
   a. What is the effect on Larry's taxable income if the expense qualifies as an above-the-line deduction?
   b. What is the effect on Larry's taxable income if the expense qualifies as an itemized deduction?
   c. How would your answer to *b* change if the amount of the expense were $5,000?
2. Kelly Jarrett has AGI of $147,000 for the current taxable year. In November, Kelly incurs a $6,300 expense.

a. What is the effect on Kelly's taxable income if the expense qualifies as an above-the-line tax deduction?
b. How would your answer change if the expense qualifies as an itemized deduction and Kelly has incurred $7,200 of other itemized deductions during the current year? (Assume Kelly incurred no medical expenses, investment interest expense, gambling losses, or personal casualty losses during the year.)
c. How would your answer to *b* change if Kelly's AGI for the year is $500,000?

3. Donald Blaine and Donna Blake are both unmarried taxpayers who each earn an annual salary of $20,000 and have no other sources of income and no deductible expenses. However, for the current year Donald has taxable income of $13,450, while Donna has taxable income of only $2,900. Can you explain this apparent inconsistency?
4. While checking the computations on his 1996 tax return, Greg Loan realized he had misclassified a $2,700 itemized deduction as an above-the-line business deduction. Greg decided not to correct the error because he assumed such correction (i.e., increasing his $173,390 AGI by $2,700 and claiming an additional $2,700 itemized deduction) would have no impact on his taxable income. Is Greg correct in his assumption?
5. Mr. and Mrs. Luis Munoz recently celebrated the birth of their first child. What will be the impact of the blessed event on the taxable income of the Munoz family if the AGI reported on their current year jointly filed tax return is $94,000?

   a. How would your answer change if the Munoz family's AGI is $200,000?
   b. How would your answer change if the Munoz family's AGI is $300,000?
6. During the current year, Sharon Bee and Tom Evans, single individuals, both earned $5,000 of dividend and interest income. Neither Sharon nor Tom had any other source of income or any deductible expenses. Sharon Bee was required to file a federal tax return on which she correctly reported $4,350 of taxable income. Tom Evans, however, was not even required to file a return for the current year. How can two taxpayers in such apparently similar economic circumstances be in such dramatically different tax situations?
7. Determine which of the following expenses incurred by an individual is nondeductible, an itemized deduction, or an above-the-line deduction for federal tax purposes.

   a. Alimony paid to a former spouse.
   b. Child support paid to that same former spouse.
   c. College tuition.
   d. A cash donation to the American Cancer Society.
   e. A cash handout to a homeless vagrant.
   f. Salary paid to the taxpayer's business secretary.
   g. Salary paid to the nanny who takes care of the taxpayer's children.
   h. Income tax paid to the state of Connecticut.

i. Premiums paid for family medical and dental insurance.
j. Premiums paid for life insurance for the taxpayer and spouse.

8. In the current year, Randy Meeks paid the following amounts of interest to various creditors. In each case, determine if the interest payment is nondeductible, an itemized deduction, or an above-the-line deduction.

   a. \$21,000 interest on a \$280,000 first mortgage incurred for the construction of Randy's personal residence.
   b. \$3,000 interest on a \$30,000 second mortgage on the residence. The loan proceeds were used to pay off a number of personal debts to various members of Randy's family.
   c. \$15,000 interest expense on a \$190,000 bank loan incurred to purchase equipment used in Randy's business.
   d. \$4,000 interest expense on a \$40,000 bank loan incurred to purchase a new automobile for Randy's 16-year-old son, Chris.
   e. \$1,700 interest incurred to purchase shares in a new mutual fund. Randy earned \$2,300 of taxable income from this investment in the current year.
   f. \$890 of interest on credit cards.

9. Lily Mariko, a resident of Seattle, owns a tract of investment land in Oregon. During the current year, Lily paid \$2,100 of property taxes on the land. She made one trip to visit the property to make sure the fences and no-trespassing signs were in good repair and that no trash had been dumped on the land. Her total expense for the trip was \$780. Lily also paid \$1,800 for a legal opinion concerning the effect of certain local zoning restrictions on her plans to develop the land in the future.

   a. If Lily's AGI for the current year is \$40,000, determine to what extent the above expenses will reduce her current year taxable income. You may assume that Lily itemizes deductions for the year.
   b. How would your answer change if Lily's AGI were \$150,000?

10. Maggie Clark is a self-employed architect who earns in excess of \$100,000 a year. She also is an enthusiastic artist. During the current year, she spent \$4,900 on oil paints, canvasses, supplies, and lessons at the local community college. She also made several trips to the National Gallery in Washington, D.C., to attend lectures on painting technique. The total cost of these trips was \$3,350.

    a. During the current year, Maggie earned \$12,000 from the sale of her paintings. May she deduct any amount of her expenses associated with her activities as a painter?
    b. Would your answer change if Maggie earned only \$2,000 from the sale of her paintings during the current year?

11. Denise Carter recently held a garage sale in which she disposed of a number of used household goods, old furniture and clothing, and paperback books. In hopes of ridding herself of what she considered junk, she put a very low price on every item. Denise's strategy was successful; she pocketed over \$1,200 in cash and

sold almost everything. Denise donated the few unsold items to Goodwill Industries. What are the tax consequences of the garage sale to Denise?

12. Clara Matsumoko is the director of advertising for a large multinational corporation. Clara has a staff of 14 people who work under her direct supervision. In order to promote a collegial work atmosphere for her group, she always remembers each person's birthday with a card and an expensive bottle of wine or similar gift. Clara gives these presents regardless of her personal like or dislike of the recipient because she believes the gesture greatly enhances her staff's productivity. During the current year, Clara spent $733 on cards and gifts. May she report this amount as a business expense on her tax return for the year?
13. In December of the current year, Stuart Blake paid a legal fee of $15,800. The itemized bill from Stuart's attorney showed the following:

Consultation concerning contested guardianship of Mr. Blake's nine-year-old orphaned nephew	$ 3,800
Defense of a patent infringement suit against Mr. Blake's business	12,000
	$15,800

Can Stuart deduct any portion of this $15,800 expense on his current year individual tax return? Explain briefly.

14. During the current year, both the Morgan family and the Logan family incurred $8,100 of unreimbursed medical expenses. The Morgans were able to deduct $6,000 of the expenses on their current year tax return, while the Logans were unable to deduct any of the medical expenses. How do you explain this apparently inequitable result?
15. Samuel Epstein owns a home that he used as his personal residence until February 1 of the prior year. Although Sam originally paid $200,000 for the home, its appraised value on February 1 was only $140,000. On this date, Samuel moved out of the home and converted it to rental property. The home has been leased to the current tenants ever since. In December of the current year, Samuel sells the property for $125,000. Apply the general principles concerning the deductibility of losses to this situation to determine how much of this loss should be deductible on Samuel's current year tax return. (Ignore any amount of depreciation on the residence allowable since its conversion to rental property.)
16. John Burns works full time as a financial analyst for a corporate employer. He has an office at corporate headquarters where he works during the week. However, John frequently takes work home over the weekend and uses one room of his five-room apartment as an office in which to perform this work. May John claim 20 percent of his apartment rent as a business expense?
17. During the current year, Mike Stone had a run of bad luck. While he was on a fishing trip, his Rolex watch, which had cost him $8,000, fell off his wrist into the lake. The watch was uninsured. Later in the year, a fire destroyed his new

Ford Taurus for which he had just paid $21,000. The reimbursement from his insurance company was only $15,000.

a. Do either of these sad events give rise to a potential tax deduction for Mike?
b. Compute the amount of the deduction assuming Mike's AGI for the year is $75,000.

18. During the current year, Cal Cisneros paid a $600 state sales tax on the purchase of a new personal automobile. He also paid a federal gift tax of $300, $700 of federal employer payroll taxes on the salary paid to his housekeeper, and $150 of personal property taxes. May Cal claim any amount of these tax payments as itemized deductions?

19. During the current year, Samantha Cole paid a $2,000 tax return preparation fee to her CPA. The CPA's bill showed that $1,200 of the fee related to the preparation of Samantha's Schedule C, which reflected the gross income and deductions generated by Samantha's sole proprietorship for the year. May Samantha deduct the entire $2,000 fee in computing her current year taxable income?

20. Yoon Sun Han owns marketable securities with a tax basis of $11,000. During the current year, she sold these securities to her brother.

a. What are the tax consequences to Yoon Sun if the amount realized on the sale was $15,500?
b. How would your answer change if the amount realized were only $9,000?
c. Would your answer to *b* change if the sale were to Yoon Sun's best friend rather than to her brother?

Case 3–1

Mr. and Mrs. Jamieson, ages 68 and 66, are a married couple who always claim the standard deduction when filing their joint tax return. The Jamiesons own and operate a local restaurant, the Shoreline Grill, as a sole proprietorship. The Jamiesons are both graduates of State University and make regular donations to their alma mater. Their method for doing so is a bit unusual. At the beginning and during halftime of each State University home football game, the public address system informs the crowd that The Shoreline Grill will contribute $50 to the University's athletic scholarship fund for every first down the State University team makes during the game. As a result of this commitment, Mr. and Mrs. Jamieson contributed a total of $4,950 to State University during the current year.

What tax planning objective may the Jamiesons have accomplished by structuring their donation to State University in this manner?

CHAPTER 4

Business Deductions and Credits

In the previous chapter, we developed a conceptual framework for determining the deductibility of expenses and losses incurred by individuals. In Chapter 4, we continue our discussion of deductions by looking more closely at the tax consequences of expenses and losses incurred in the operation of a trade or business, and the impact of the taxpayer's method of accounting on those consequences. The principles discussed in the chapter apply to any and all businesses, whether operated by one individual as a sole proprietorship, by a group of individuals in partnership, or by a corporation. Corporate taxpayers, unlike individual taxpayers, are presumed to engage solely in business (as opposed to personal or investment) activities. As a result, any discussion of business tax deductions is basically synonymous with a discussion of corporate tax deductions. The few special rules uniquely applicable to businesses operated in the corporate form will be explained in Chapter 5.

ORDINARY AND NECESSARY BUSINESS EXPENSES

Section 162 of the Internal Revenue Code provides a generic deduction for "all the ordinary and necessary expenses paid or incurred during the taxable year in carrying on any trade or business." The term *ordinary* implies that an expense incurred by a particular business is deductible only if it is common or customary in that type of business. An ordinary expense does not have to occur with any regularity of frequency during the life of a single business. For example, a medical practice that incurs legal expenses to defend itself against a malpractice suit may be lucky enough to face such litigation only once during its existence. Even so, the legal expense is considered ordinary because it is common to medical practices everywhere.

The term *necessary* implies that an expense must be helpful and appropriate to the production of business revenues. Note that an expense must be both ordinary and necessary if it is to meet the definition of a Section 162 deduction.

Finally, any expense related to the production of nontaxable income cannot be deducted. A common example is the annual premium paid by a business to insure the lives of its officers and chief employees. Such *key-man life insurance* is intended to compensate the business for the unanticipated loss of essential personnel; consequently, the business itself (rather than the insured employees' families) is named as beneficiary under the policy. Although the insurance premiums are both ordinary and necessary, they are nondeductible because life insurance proceeds are excludable from the business's gross income.

A list of the common Section 162 deductions would include most operating expenses from a business income statement. Nevertheless, some current accounting expenses are not deductible in computing taxable income, and some tax deductions cannot be expensed under generally accepted accounting principles. In dealing with this inconsistency, remember that the word *deduction* tends to be a narrower, more legalistic term than the word *expense.*

Start-up Costs

Section 162 authorizes the deduction of expenses incurred *in the active conduct* of an operational business. The operational phase of a new business doesn't begin until the business has matured to the point that it can generate revenues. Any ordinary and necessary expenses incurred before this point must be considered preoperating *start-up expenditures* to which Section 162 is inapplicable. Consider the case of Mr. Adams, a retired schoolteacher, who has decided to open a day care center. Before any children can be enrolled, our entrepreneur must locate and rent a suitable location, hire and train staff, and apply for the operating license required under state law. The day care center cannot legally open its doors to students, and consequently is not in a position to generate revenues, until this license is granted. As a result, the rent paid for the location, the salaries paid to the staff, and any other expenses incurred before receipt of the license are nondeductible and must be capitalized to an asset account.

Luckily, our taxpayer can mitigate this harsh result by making a tax election to amortize these start-up expenditures over 60 months, starting with the month in which the active business begins. Start-up expenditures include all ordinary and necessary expenses incurred in the preoperational phase of a new business, as well as the costs of investigating either the creation or acquisition of a business. Returning to our example, assume Mr. Adams incurred $4,800 of start-up expenditures before his day care center began operations on September 1 of the current year. If Mr. Adams properly files an election statement with his tax return for the calendar year, he may deduct $320 of these expenditures ($4,800 multiplied by 4/60) on that return. The $4,480 unamortized balance will be deductible over the next 56 months of the center's operation.

The obvious follow-up question to this example is: "What happens if Mr. Adams fails to make the election to amortize his start-up expenditures?" Unless Mr. Adams has engaged a competent tax adviser, he will probably deduct his $4,800 start-up expenditures along with his other ordinary and necessary operating expenses on his current year tax return. While this deduction is improper, it is certainly not fraudulent; Mr. Adams is simply unaware of this particular complexity in the tax law. If the return is audited and the agent assigned to the case discovers the error, Mr. Adams will lose his $4,800 deduction. And because he failed to make a proper election, he forfeited the opportunity to amortize the capitalized expenditures. In that case, the start-up expenditures will not yield any tax benefit to Mr. Adams until they are written off at some future date when he closes or sells his business.

Although Section 162 is inapplicable to start-up expenditures associated with a new business, the section's general rule of deductibility encompasses the *expansion costs* of an existing business. Once Mr. Adams is operating his first day care center, he has established an active trade or business. If he decides to open a second center at a different location, he will repeat the process of renting a suitable facility, hiring and training additional staff, and incurring expenses before the opening of the new center. Although the distinction between these preoperating expenses and the initial $4,800 associated with the first center is admittedly subtle, these expenses are currently deductible because they are incurred in carrying on Mr. Adams's existing business.

Public Policy Considerations

Despite its lenient attitude concerning the deductibility of most business expenses, Congress has drawn the line with respect to several types of expenses for which deductibility might frustrate or contravene public policy. No deduction is allowed for fines or penalties paid to a government for the violation of any law. In 1991, Exxon Corporation paid $25 million in criminal fines in connection with the *Valdez* oil spill. Because the corporation's taxable income and corresponding tax liability were not reduced by this payment, Exxon was forced to absorb the full financial impact of the fines. Illegal bribes, kickbacks, or other payments made in consideration of a referral of a client, patient, or other customer are nondeductible. Although this general prohibition applies only to illegal payments, the law specifies that even a legal kickback or rebate made by a provider of services under Medicare or Medicaid cannot be deducted. Finally, Section 280E denies a deduction for any and all expenses connected with illegal trafficking in drugs.

While it is common for businesses to make contributions to political campaigns, such contributions are nondeductible. The law also denies any deduction for *lobbying expenses* incurred in communicating with federal and state government officials or employees for the purpose of influencing legislation. This prohibition does not extend to efforts to influence local laws; lobbying costs with respect to county and city governments are fully deductible as ordinary and necessary business expenses.

The Revenue Reconciliation Act of 1993 amended Section 162 by limiting the deduction for annual compensation paid to a publicly traded corporation's chief executive officer and the four other most highly compensated corporate officers to $1 million each. The details of this limitation are discussed in Chapter 10. At this point, suffice it to say that Congress imposed this limitation in response to public outrage over the huge salaries paid to corporate executives and the belief that corporate boards of directors were not acting in the shareholders' best interests by authorizing such salaries.

Capitalized Expenditures

When a business incurs an expense resulting in the creation of an asset with a useful life extending substantially beyond the close of the current year, the expense must be capitalized to an appropriate fixed asset account. If the asset is of a type that will diminish in value because of physical wear and tear or technical obsolescence, the capitalized cost may be deducted over the estimated useful life of the asset or an arbitrary recovery period specified by statute. The various methods for recovery of capitalized costs through depreciation, amortization, or depletion deductions are the subject of Chapter 6.

The organizational costs of forming a corporation or a partnership are not deductible in the year incurred because they create an intangible business asset (i.e., the organization form) that will last as long as the business is in operation. Therefore, legal and accounting fees attributable to the formation of the business entity and any filing or registration fees paid to the state in which business will be conducted must be capitalized. However, newly formed corporations and partnerships may elect to amortize their organizational costs over a 60-month period, starting with the month in which business begins.

Two types of business expenses arguably result in a long-term benefit but are nonetheless fully deductible in the year paid or incurred. Research and experimental costs are currently deductible, even if the research leads to the development of an identifiable business asset with an extended useful life. This lenient treatment reflects our government's belief that industrial research and experimentation are crucial to the nation's economic well-being and should be encouraged. Advertising costs are also currently deductible as ordinary and necessary business expenses, even though a successful advertising campaign can improve a company's competitive position for years to come. In past years, both Congress and the Treasury have publicly expressed their concern over the huge advertising budgets of many companies and the corresponding loss of federal revenues attributable to deductible advertising expenses. To date, lobbyists for the advertising industry have successfully quashed any legislative attempt to change the status quo.

OTHER STATUTORY BUSINESS DEDUCTIONS

The Internal Revenue Code contains a number of sections that elaborate on the basic theme of Section 162 by providing more intricate rules governing the deductibility of certain categories of business expenses and losses. In this portion of the chapter, we will examine the more important of these statutory deductions.

Interest Expense

All interest paid or accrued on debt incurred in connection with a trade or business (other than the business of performing services as an employee) is fully deductible. The deductibility of business interest has particular significance for individual taxpayers who cannot deduct interest expense associated with personal activities and who can deduct investment interest expense only to the extent of net investment income. For tax purposes, interest expense is characterized by reference to the use of the proceeds of the underlying debt. This *tracing rule* (while enormously complex in its application) creates significant tax planning opportunities for individuals savvy enough to structure their debt so as to maximize the deductibility of the interest they must pay.

Assume Mrs. Sharp determines she will need $25,000 to contribute to a business in which she is a general partner. The partnership will use the contributed funds to purchase a new telephone system. Mrs. Sharp also anticipates spending $25,000 to purchase a new power boat for the personal use and enjoyment of her family. To finance these projected expenditures, Mrs. Sharp plans to borrow $20,000 from her credit union and to withdraw $30,000 from a savings account. Does it make any difference which dollars are funneled into the partnership and which dollars buy the boat? If Mrs. Sharp is careful to structure her transactions so the borrowed funds can be traced to the partnership contribution, the entire amount of interest paid to the credit union can be characterized as business interest and will result in an above-the-line deduction on Mrs. Sharp's tax return for the year. If Mrs. Sharp ignores the tax implications of her transactions and uses the borrowed funds for the boat purchase, the interest she will pay won't be deductible.

Taxes Paid in Connection with a Business

You may recall from Chapter 3 that state and local income and property taxes are deductible, regardless of the context in which the taxes are incurred. The statute also confers deductibility on other types of taxes—such as franchise, excise, transfer, or occupancy taxes—paid or accrued in carrying on a trade or business. The federal income tax itself is not a deductible business expense.

One important category of business-related taxes consists of the various employment taxes levied by the federal and state governments. Employers must pay both a federal and state unemployment tax based on the salaries and wages paid to their employees; the revenues from these taxes fund the unemployment benefit programs of the respective governments. Employers also must pay the tax authorized under the Federal Insurance Contribution Act (FICA), which funds our national Social Security and Medicare systems. This *employer payroll tax* equals 7.65 percent of a base amount of compensation paid to each employee (the 1996 base amount is $62,700) plus an additional 1.45 percent of compensation in excess of the base. In 1996, the employer payroll tax with respect to a $100,000 salary is $5,337 (7.65 percent of $62,700 plus 1.45 percent of $37,300). Even as a deductible business expense, this FICA tax represents a significant cost of hiring personnel!

The employer payroll tax is only half the story. A tax of exactly the same amount is imposed on employees who receive salaries or wages, so the total payroll tax burden doubles to 15.3 percent of base compensation plus 2.9 percent of any excess compensation. (As we mentioned in Chapter 3, the *employee payroll tax* is considered a nondeductible personal expense.) Employers are required by law to withhold the employee's portion of the FICA tax from the wage or salary paid; the withholding, along with the employer's portion of the tax, is remitted to the Treasury by the employer.

Individuals who go into business for themselves quickly learn they can't escape the heavy burden of the payroll tax. Such individuals must pay the federal *self-employment tax* on any net earnings generated by their business activities. The self-employment tax rate is 15.3 percent on the current year base amount of earned income ($62,700 in 1996) plus 2.9 percent of any earned income in excess of the base. If the reader is experiencing a sense of *deja vu*, it is because this rate is exactly the same as the combined employer/employee payroll tax rate. To complete the analogy between the two taxes, individual taxpayers are allowed to claim *half* of any self-employment tax paid (the equivalent of the deductible employer payroll tax) as an above-the-line deduction in computing adjusted gross income. A final reassuring comment: If an individual receives employee compensation and also generates self-employment income, the amount of FICA tax paid with respect to the compensation is taken into account in the computation of the self-employment tax the individual must pay.

Business Bad Debts

When a business concludes that the full or partial amount of an account receivable or other debt owed to the business cannot be collected, the worthless (uncollectible) portion can be recognized as a *bad debt deduction.* For accounting purposes, many companies establish a reserve for bad debts and expense the annual addition to this reserve on their income statements. For tax purposes, a bad debt deduction is available only for debts actually written off during the current year. To illustrate this common difference between the computations of book income and taxable income, assume Supra Inc., an accrual basis corporate taxpayer, begins the current year with a $298,000 balance in its bad debt reserve. During the year, $155,000 of accounts receivable are deemed worthless and are written off against this reserve. Based on the year-end balance in accounts receivable, Supra's accountants determine that a $173,000 addition to the reserve is necessary, and as a result, the year-end balance in the reserve increases to $316,000. Supra's financial statements for the current year will show a bad debt expense of $173,000; the company's tax return will show a bad debt deduction of $155,000.

Meals, Entertainment, and Travel Expenses

While many travel and entertainment expenses can be legitimately classified as ordinary and necessary business expenses, it is no coincidence that business conventions are more frequently held in San Francisco or New Orleans than in Des Moines, Iowa. No one can dispute that business activities involving travel or entertainment have a tremendous potential to yield personal enjoyment and, consequently, hold the same potential for taxpayer manipulation and abuse. In an attempt to curb the worst excesses in this area, Congress has woven a remarkably complicated web of restrictions and limitations on the deductibility of business meal, entertainment, and travel expenses.

Section 274 contains dozens of special requirements relating to the deduction of expenses incurred in any activity "generally considered to constitute entertainment, amusement, or recreation." The section applies to a tantalizing variety of expenditures; the deductibility of theater tickets, cocktail receptions, admissions to athletic events, hunting and fishing trips, maintenance of company-owned yachts and airplanes, business gifts, and meals with clients or customers depends on the successful negotiation of the Section 274 maze. While a detailed exploration of this topic is well beyond the scope of our text, a brief look at some basic rules in the context of two taxpayer scenarios should give the reader a sense of its forbidding complexity.

Bill Bates, a self-employed businessman, knows that the best way to finalize some sensitive details of a contract with a major customer is informally on the golf course. Pursuant to this plan, Bill spends $150 for green fees and carts and another $80 on drinks and dinner after the round. If these entertainment expenses are to be tax deductible, they must be *directly related* to the conduct of Bill's business (i.e., the activity in which the expenses were incurred must be principally characterized as business rather than pleasure, and business must have actually been discussed or engaged in during the activity). Bill must maintain some type of written documentation describing the relationship of the entertainment to his business, as well as the amount, date, and place of the expenses; without *substantiation* no deduction is permitted. Let's assume that Bill and his customer did, in fact, successfully complete their business while traversing the fairways, and that Bill kept meticulous records concerning this activity. Nonetheless, the statute provides that only 50 percent of the cost of business meals and entertainment ($115 in Bill's case) is deductible; the disallowed 50 percent is a crude measure of the personal benefit implicit in the expenditure.

Now let's turn to the case of Louise Cates, an attorney who wants to attend a legal convention in New York City. Since she has never visited the Big Apple, Louise decides to extend her trip by several days to do some sightseeing and shopping. What portion of her travel expenses may she deduct? Section 162 warns that deductible travel expenses must not be "lavish or extravagant under the circumstances." In this scenario, let's assume away this nebulous requirement. If the primary purpose of Louise's trip is business, the entire substantiated cost of her round-trip transportation is deductible, even if some of her time in Manhattan is devoted to personal enjoyment. For those days during which she attends the convention, Louise's substantiated living expenses for lodging, cab fares, laundry, telephone, and so forth, as well as 50 percent of her meal costs, are deductible. However, the incremental living expenses for the extra days she spends just for fun are totally nondeductible. This framework for the deductibility of travel expenses applies only to domestic travel; the rules concerning foreign travel take a quantum leap in both rigor and complexity. In this area more than any other, an ounce of prevention is worth a pound of cure, so see your tax adviser at the same time you apply for your passport!

No doubt at this point the more cynical of our readers are asking: who is to know if Bill Bates and his customer really discussed any business over those 18 holes? And did any other attorney actually see Louise Cates attend even a single technical session of the legal convention? Despite Section 274, the area of business entertainment and travel continues to be one in which taxpayers can easily bend or even break the rules of the game. For this reason, IRS agents pay particular attention to these deductions, scrutinizing a taxpayer's records for suspicious or unsubstantiated expenditures. While there is no law that business activities have to be all work and no play, the prudent businessperson should always refrain from conspicuous excesses.

Employee Business Expenses

You may remember from Chapter 3 that every employee is considered to be in the business of rendering services as an employee. People frequently incur out-of-pocket expenses related to their employment; common examples of *employee business expenses* include subscriptions to professional or trade journals, union dues, uniforms, and continuing education courses. Many employee business expenses are routinely reimbursed by the employer. The tax treatment of reimbursed expenses reflects the fact that the economic burden of such expenses falls entirely on the employer. The employee neither reports the reimbursement as gross income nor claims the expenses as a deduction; hence, the whole transaction has no impact on the employee's tax return for the year.

The tax consequences of *unreimbursed* employee business expenses are much less benign. Congress has expressed its belief that a deduction for such expenses is generally inappropriate on the theory that if an expense is really necessary to the successful performance of an employee's duties, the employer should provide reimbursement. Acting on this belief, Congress demoted unreimbursed employee business expenses to the ignominious category of *miscellaneous itemized deductions*, which are deductible only to the extent they exceed 2 percent of an individual's adjusted gross income. The tax planning implication of all this should be obvious: An employee who is expected to pay any significant amount of out-of-pocket business expenses should always negotiate with his or her employer for specific reimbursement of such expenses.

Both employees and self-employed individuals may claim a deduction for unreimbursed expenses of a household move necessitated by a change in the geographic location of their employment. This *moving expense deduction* is subject to a host of complicated requirements and limitations. On a more positive note, this deduction escapes classification as an itemized deduction and is deductible above-the-line.

TRANSACTIONAL AND NET OPERATING LOSSES

During the course of the taxable year, a business may incur a loss on a transaction involving the disposition of property that is not part of the inventory of the business. If property is damaged or destroyed as a result of casualty or theft, any amount of uninsured loss is fully deductible. If property is sold, exchanged, or abandoned, any realized loss will be either a fully deductible *ordinary loss* or a *capital loss*; the distinction depends on the type of asset involved in the transaction. Chapter 7 includes a thorough discussion of the tax consequences of dispositions of various types of property used in a trade or business. At this juncture, suffice it to say that as a very general rule, losses incurred on the disposition of tangible assets used in the actual operation of a business are fully deductible. In contrast, losses incurred on the disposition of intangible assets or assets held by the business for investment purposes (as opposed to operational purposes) are considered capital losses, the deductibility of which is quite limited.

If business operations for the entire taxable year result in an excess of allowable deductions over gross income, the excess is labeled a *net operating loss* (NOL). For the year in which an NOL is generated, a business obviously has no taxable income and no tax liability. But a more subtle fact is that an amount of current deductions equal to the NOL has yielded no tax benefit at all; the business would have the same zero tax bill with or without these excess deductions. For any business with an operating cycle exceeding 12 months, this fact could lead to a real distortion in the effective rate of tax assessed on net business income.

Let's look at a simple theoretical model of this potential problem. The manufacturing business run by Theta Inc., a calendar year taxpayer, has an operating cycle of 24 months. In the taxable year in which a cycle begins, Theta has very little gross income but considerable deductible expenses, the result of which is a $200,000 NOL for the year. In the second taxable year during which the operating cycle is completed,

Theta recognizes the bulk of its gross income attributable to that cycle and reports $500,000 of net income. If Theta had to pay tax on this annual amount of income, the corporation's tax bill would be $170,000. Although the statutory corporate tax rate is only 34 percent, Theta's effective rate on its $300,000 of economic income earned over one operating cycle would be 57 percent!

To prevent the tax rate distortion that could result from an artificial 12-month reporting period, the law allows a business to average its income by offsetting losses incurred in one year against income recognized in another. Specifically, Section 172 states that a current year NOL is carried back as a deduction against any taxable income reported in the three years immediately before the current year. Any amount of NOL in excess of such previous years' income may be carried forward as a deduction to the next 15 taxable years. In the case of an *NOL carryback*, the taxpayer will fill out a simple form showing (1) the amount of the current year NOL deducted against prior year income and (2) the recomputed amount of prior year tax liability. After the form is properly filed with the IRS, the taxpayer has nothing more to do than watch the mail for the refund check. In the case of an *NOL carryforward*, the NOL will be reported as a deduction on each future tax return filed by the business until it has been totally absorbed against gross income or until it expires.

Two additional features of the NOL deduction deserve mention. First, the deduction is available to both corporate and individual taxpayers. The computation of a corporation's NOL requires little more than a straightforward comparison of gross income and deductible business expenses. The computation of an individual NOL is much more difficult. Because the Form 1040 is such a hodgepodge of personal, investment, and business-related items, calculation of the precise amount of any net loss attributable solely to excess business deductions becomes a complicated process.

A second interesting feature is that the taxpayer can elect to give up the carryback of a current year NOL to prior years and keep the entire loss as a prospective deduction for future years. In most cases, businesses are eager to use an NOL carryback deduction to create immediate cash flow in the form of a tax refund. However, if a business determines that its marginal tax rate during the three-year carryback period was significantly lower than its projected marginal tax rate in future years, a decision to forgo the carryback may maximize the economic value of the NOL deduction.

METHODS OF ACCOUNTING AND DEDUCTIBILITY

Every business must adopt a method of accounting by which to compute its annual taxable income. In Chapter 2, we compared the cash and accrual methods and identified the business characteristics that usually dictate the choice of accounting method. In this section, we will examine how the choice of a particular accounting method affects the deductibility of business expenses. While the method generally has no effect on the *fact* of a deduction, it has everything to do with the *timing* of the deduction. Congress understands that it is in the best interest of a business to claim a deduction in the earliest possible taxable year. Consequently, much of the subsequent discussion concerns the statutory and regulatory restrictions on the use of various accounting methods to accelerate the deduction of business expenditures.

Expense Prepayments by Cash Basis Taxpayers

Under the cash method of accounting, an expense is deductible in the year payment is made. Consequently, a cash basis business can create a current deduction by paying an expense before the year in which that expense contributes to the generation of revenues. This strategy is hampered by Treasury regulations warning that any expense creating an asset with a useful life extending "substantially beyond the close of the taxable year" is not currently deductible, but must be capitalized and amortized over its useful life. Both the courts and the IRS agree that, as a rule of thumb, payments for an asset to be consumed by the close of the following year are fully deductible in the year of payment. For instance, a calendar year cash basis firm could buy four months' worth of office supplies on December 29 and take a current deduction for the entire cost. If, however, the firm purchased two years' worth of supplies, the cost must be capitalized to an asset account and deducted over the next two taxable years.

For many years, cash basis businesses with a bit of excess liquidity toward the end of their taxable years could generate current deductions by making prepayments of interest expense to cooperative creditors. Congress forestalled this popular tax planning technique by enacting a statutory requirement that all *prepaid interest* be capitalized and amortized over the life of the underlying debt.

Deduction Requirements for Accrued Expenses

Under the accrual method of accounting, a business liability attributable to current operations should result in a current expense even if payment of the liability is postponed until some future year. Consider the example of a company providing a medical reimbursement plan for its work force. At year-end, the company routinely estimates the amount of reimbursable expenses incurred by its employees over the past 12 months for which claims have not yet been filed. Under generally accepted accounting principles, this company must accrue both a current expense and a liability for the estimated amount. Because of the general presumption that a business uses the same method of accounting for tax purposes as it uses for financial statement purposes, it would seem this company could claim the accrued expense as a deduction on its current year tax return. The Internal Revenue Service, however, is deeply suspicious of tax deductions based on nothing more than the taxpayer's expectation of a future economic cost. Consequently, the law holds that an accrued expense cannot be deducted currently unless it passes the *all events test*.

For most routine year-end accruals that result in a proper matching of the accrued expense against current revenues, this test has just two requirements: all events must have occurred to establish the fact of the taxpayer's liability for the expense, and the amount of the liability must be determinable with reasonable accuracy. In a major victory for the IRS, the Supreme Court held that an accrual for estimated medical reimbursement costs (such as those described in the preceding paragraph) failed the all events test because the corporate employer's liability for the reimbursement was not absolutely established until its employees actually filed their completed claim forms.

In the case of certain nonrecurring, extraordinary accruals, the all events test has a third requirement; *economic performance* with respect to the liability must occur before a deduction is allowed. Since a complete analysis of the concept of economic performance would require at least a dozen additional pages, let's content ourselves with two examples illustrating the severity of this requirement.

Suppose that in the current year an accrual basis partnership enters into a binding contract with a legal firm under which the firm agrees to provide future professional services for a flat fee of $500,000. The partnership will not pay the fee until the services are completed. At the end of the year, the partnership accrues a $500,000 liability. Can this accrual trigger a $500,000 current tax deduction? Since both the legal fact and the amount of the liability are certain, the accrual meets the first two requirements of the all events test. Nevertheless, in this example, the law stipulates that economic performance will not occur (and the partnership will not get its $500,000 tax deduction) until the year in which the services are actually performed for the partnership by the legal firm.

As a second example, consider the situation in which an employee is gravely injured due to the alleged negligence of his corporate employer. The corporation's independent auditors insist the firm accrue its contingent liability for legal damages and show the corresponding expense on its current year income statement. For tax purposes, the accrued expense cannot be deducted because the fact of the liability has not yet been established. Two years later, the employee has his day in court and the jury awards him $1.2 million in damages. At this point, the first two requirements of the all events test are finally satisfied. But in the case of a liability arising out of any tort, economic performance is not deemed to occur until the corporation actually makes a $1.2 million payment to the employee.

The lesson to be learned from these two examples is that the government's concern over so-called *premature accruals* has resulted in a rule of law delaying a tax deduction for many business expenses properly accrued for financial statement purposes. The all events test for deductibility can force an accrual basis business to adopt the cash method of accounting for many estimated or contingent expenses.

Accounting for Inventories

Any business maintaining inventories of goods to be sold to customers is required to account for the inventories using the accrual method. This requirement means a business cannot simply deduct the total cost incurred in the manufacture or purchase of inventory, but must capitalize the portion of this cost attributable to any inventory on hand at the end of the year. Only the portion of the cost attributable to inventory sold during the year is currently deductible. The *cost of goods sold* is based on the following formula:

	Cost of inventory on hand at the beginning of year
+	Cost of new inventory manufactured or purchased
	Cost of inventory available for sale
−	Cost of inventory on hand at end of year
	Tax-deductible cost of inventory sold

This formula is based on two assumptions: (1) all the various costs associated with the manufacture or purchase of new inventory are properly included on line two, and (2) the total of these costs is properly allocated between ending inventory on line four and inventory sold on line five.

With regards to the first assumption, businesses naturally prefer to treat any expenditure as a currently deductible *period cost* rather than a *product cost* capitalized to inventory. Not surprisingly, the tax law contains explicit rules concerning the types of expenditures that must be capitalized. These *uniform capitalization* (unicap) *rules*, which are as strict as they are complicated, consign a variety of direct and indirect costs to inventory. The second assumption is a function of the method of accounting adopted by a business to account for the flow of products through inventory. In the unusual case in which the exact cost of each inventory item can be determined, a business can use the *specific identification method* to value ending inventory and compute cost of goods sold. When specific identification is impossible, the business must choose a costing convention that has nothing to do with the physical movement of goods through the system. The two most familiar costing conventions are *FIFO* (first-in, first-out) and *LIFO* (last-in, first-out).

The selection of an inventory costing convention may have a substantial impact on the amount of taxable income recognized in the current year. During a period of rising prices, it is generally to a firm's advantage to adopt LIFO because, as the name implies, the LIFO convention assumes that the last goods manufactured or purchased were the first goods sold. In an inflationary economy, the most recently acquired goods are the most expensive. If a firm assumes these goods are the first to be sold, it maximizes the dollar amount allocable to deductible cost of goods sold and minimizes the amount capitalized to ending inventory. While the tax advantage of the LIFO convention is apparent, its popularity in the corporate sector has been diminished by the fact that any firm electing LIFO for tax purposes must also use it to prepare the firm's financial income statements. As a result of such forced conformity, any reduction in taxable income attributable to LIFO is mirrored by a reduction in accounting income and earnings per share reported to creditors and shareholders.

BUSINESS TAX CREDITS

In this section, we take our first in-depth look at tax credits. A *tax credit* is a direct reduction in tax liability. As such, the value of a credit is much greater than the value of a deduction of the same dollar amount. Consider the case of a corporation in a 34 percent marginal tax bracket that is entitled to a \$50,000 deduction. The tax savings resulting from the deduction is only \$17,000 (\$50,000 multiplied by the marginal tax rate). If the corporation were entitled to a \$50,000 credit against its current year tax bill, the tax savings attributable to the credit would be a full \$50,000. A second difference between a deduction and a credit is that a deduction usually results from an expense or loss incurred by a taxpayer. A credit is an artificial creation of Congress. The majority of tax credits are *nonrefundable*—they can reduce tax liability to zero, but any amount of excess credit will not generate a refund from the Treasury.

Credits are enacted to foster social or economic goals, the nature of which is usually obvious from the structure of the credit. Over the past decades, Congress has experimented with a variety of credits designed to encourage businesses to engage in socially or economically desirable transactions. Certain credits have proven to be powerful incentives—others have been embarrassing failures. The role of credits as behavioral inducements can be illustrated by a quick look at two of the business credits available today. The amount of the *targeted jobs credit* equals 40 percent of the first $6,000 of first-year wages paid to individuals who are members of economically disadvantaged target groups. This credit is clearly intended as an indirect government subsidy to any employer willing to give an ex-convict, a Vietnam veteran, or a ghetto youth a chance at gainful employment.[1]

The *rehabilitation investment credit* is based on a percentage of the rehabilitation costs of (1) commercial buildings originally placed in service before 1936 and (2) all certified historic structures. This credit encourages businesses to undertake urban renewal projects that might be financially unfeasible without the tax savings represented by the credit. Other business credits are linked to the clinical testing of orphan drugs, nonconventional fuel production, research and experimentation activities, construction of low-income housing, and the provision of access to disabled individuals. The list should give the reader a sense of the variety of "carrots" Congress dangles in front of the business community's nose. A final point is that Congress is continually fiddling with its list of business credits. Because tax credits bear no relationship to any accepted definition of economic income, Congress is rather casual about enacting new ones and repealing those that have outlived their usefulness as an instrument of fiscal policy.

BUSINESS TAX PLANNING

At the end of Chapter 3, we discussed the basic planning concepts relating to the deductibility of expenses and losses. In the tax environment, the majority of deductions arise from business transactions; as a result, opportunities for meaningful tax planning are most frequently encountered by individuals who operate their own sole proprietorships or by corporations and partnerships engaging in trade or business activities. The Internal Revenue Service is aware that the stakes in the tax planning game are the highest when businesses engage in complex transactions involving millions of dollars, and it concentrates its audit efforts accordingly. For the calendar year 1993, about 1 percent of the approximately 114 million individual tax returns filed were eventually audited by the IRS. However, the audit percentage nearly quadrupled to 3.57 percent for those individual returns reflecting gross business receipts in excess of $100,000. During 1993, corporations filed 2.7 million tax returns. Although only 2.31 percent of total returns filed were audited, 25 percent of all corporations with assets worth between $50 million and $100 million were examined, while 55 percent of all corporations with assets worth over $250 million were subjected to IRS scrutiny.

The history of the federal income tax reflects the ongoing struggle between taxpayers structuring business transactions to minimize their tax burdens and the IRS policing

[1]The targeted jobs credit expired on December 31, 1994. Congress is currently considering reinstating it in modified form as the "work opportunity tax credit."

those transactions to make sure taxpayers play by the rules as written by Congress and interpreted by the Treasury. When a taxpayer and the IRS can't agree on how the rules should apply to a particular transaction, a federal court may have to settle the controversy. Many taxpayers are unpleasantly surprised to learn they usually bear the burden of proof in the litigation process. In other words, the IRS is presumed to be correct in its interpretation of the law, and the taxpayer must be prepared to present sufficient evidence to overturn this presumption.

Judicial Tax Traps

Over the years, both the IRS and the federal courts have tried to ensure that taxpayers adhere not only to the letter but also to the spirit of the law. Consequently, three important judicial doctrines have evolved in the tax area; by invoking these doctrines, the IRS can cry foul when a taxpayer seems to be manipulating or bending the rules to secure an unwarranted advantage. The *business purpose* doctrine holds that a transaction will not be given effect for tax purposes unless it is intended to achieve a valid and independent business purpose. The lack of any business motive on the part of the participants can render a transaction meaningless, at least from the perspective of the IRS, even if the transaction is in literal compliance with the tax law.

The *substance-over-form* doctrine holds that the IRS is entitled to look through the legal formalities to determine the true economic substance (if any) of a transaction. If the substance differs from the form, the tax consequences of the transaction will be based on the reality rather than the illusion. For example, consider the situation in which the owner and president of a closely held corporation negotiates a leasing arrangement with a local businessman. Under the terms of a binding contract, the corporation agrees to pay annual rental of $35,000 for the use of certain business equipment. The form of this transaction certainly indicates the corporation should be entitled to deduct the rental payment as an ordinary and necessary business expense. Unfortunately, the IRS agent who audits the corporation's tax return uncovers two interesting facts: the local businessman who is the lessor in the transaction is a candidate for a state political office, and the corporation has no apparent need for the type of business equipment described in the contract. If the agent concludes the substance of the transaction is a political contribution, the corporation may lose its annual $35,000 deduction.

The *step-transaction* doctrine allows the IRS to collapse a series of intermediate transactions into a single transaction to determine the tax consequences of the arrangement. This tax trap is usually sprung when the intermediate transactions are obviously interdependent, so the taxpayers involved would not have consummated the first transaction without believing the whole series of transactions would occur.

Consider the case of Mr. Cox, who wants to sell an investment asset to his closely held corporation, but who understands that the loss realized on the sale to this related party is nondeductible. Mr. Cox might be tempted to sell the asset to an unrelated third party who just happens to be a close business associate eager to please. Just a few days after the first sale, the business associate sells the asset to the closely held corporation. Except for the fact that Mr. Cox apparently can recognize his realized loss on the intermediate sale, the end result of the two steps is identical to that of a straightforward sale by Mr. Cox to his corporation. IRS application of the step-transaction doctrine would collapse the two steps into a single sale by Mr. Cox to a related party.

The courts have not been consistent in their acceptance of the IRS's application of the step-transaction doctrine. On some occasions the courts have given full recognition to each carefully orchestrated movement in a complicated tax minuet; on other occasions the courts have refused to see the beauty of it all. In a recent decision in which the Tax Court held against the government, the judge observed, "Overall plans and integrated transactions do not, without more, justify application of the step transaction doctrine. Foresight and planning do not transform a nontaxable event into one that is taxable."

There is considerable overlap in the scope of the three judicial doctrines described in the preceding paragraphs; the IRS frequently uses them in combination to challenge an offending transaction. A second pertinent observation is that the doctrines seem to be the exclusive property of the government. Taxpayers have rarely been successful when they have tried to undo the undesirable outcome of a botched transaction by arguing that the form of the transaction, a form deliberately selected by the taxpayer, should be ignored. Finally, the IRS's application of these judicial doctrines is extremely subjective. Given the omnipresent threat of the doctrines, a taxpayer can never be certain that a particularly creative tax plan will work, even if it seems to comply with the letter of the law.

CONCLUSION

This chapter has introduced the important tax issues relating to the operation of an active trade or business and has focused on the treatment of common business expenditures. Many expenditures are currently deductible, in which case the business's before-tax cost of the expenditure is reduced by the tax savings attributable to the deduction. A few business expenditures are completely nondeductible so that the before-tax cost and after-tax cost are equal. Expenditures that result in a long-term benefit to the business usually cannot be deducted currently but must be capitalized to an asset account. In such case, the expenditure becomes the business's tax basis in the asset. Figure 4–1 provides a simple diagram that should help the reader in reviewing these different results.

Figure 4–1 Tax Treatment of Business Expenditures

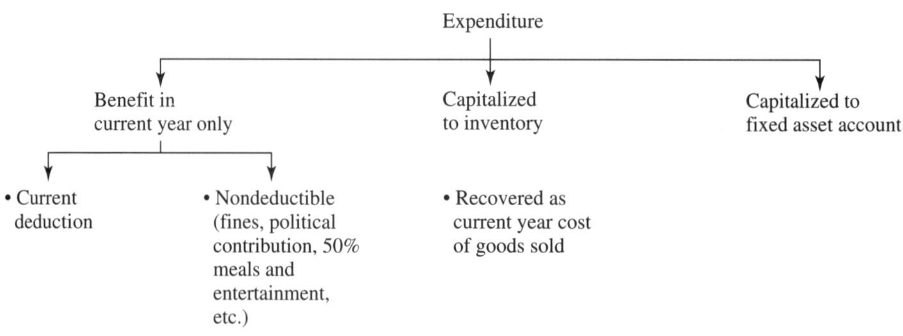

PROBLEMS AND CASES

1. William Schultz is the sole proprietor of Schultz's German Bakery, which has three retail outlets in Nashville, Tennessee. During the current year, William decided to try his hand at the restaurant business and opened a German restaurant adjacent to one of his bakeries. Before the restaurant's grand opening, William incurred $18,000 of related ordinary and necessary expenses (staff training, advertising, rent, etc.). What is the proper tax treatment of these expenses on William's current year tax return?
2. Ellen Ortega owns and operates a landscaping and yard maintenance business as a sole proprietorship. She is considering hiring a new employee for a starting annual salary of $20,000. If Ellen is in a 31 percent marginal tax bracket, what is the annual after-tax cost of adding this employee to her payroll? (Include the effect on Ellen's self-employment tax but ignore the impact of any federal or state unemployment taxes in making your calculation.)
3. Jerry Clark recently graduated from veterinary school and opened his own practice in Sante Fe, New Mexico. For the current year, his net earnings from self-employment were $32,000. If Jerry has sufficient investment income so that his earned income is subject to a 36 percent marginal income tax rate, compute the amount of this income available to Jerry after he pays both his self-employment and income tax liabilities.
4. During the current year, Betsy Adams decided she will never be able to collect a $5,000 two-year-old debt from Ned Nickols. Describe the tax consequences of this decision under each of the following assumptions.
   a. The $5,000 was a business account receivable, attributable to Ned's purchase of goods from Betsy's sole proprietorship.
   b. Betsy lent the $5,000 to Ned as an investment in a new motion picture he was filming.
   c. Betsy lent the $5,000 to Ned because he was a valuable employee (as well as a good friend) whose work for Betsy was suffering because of his preoccupation with personal financial problems.
5. Steve Okamoto, a fashion designer, put on his first major show in Paris during the current year. Steve flew his proud parents from their home in New York City to Paris so they could see the show and share in his success. A canny businessman, Steve made sure all the trade journals and newspapers learned of this act of filial devotion. As a result, Steve received an enormous amount of positive publicity for his show. Do you think Steve can deduct the cost of his parents' trip as a business expense?
6. Louis Lincoln is the president and sole shareholder of Lincoln Industries Inc. Louis is a student of Eastern philosophies and is a great believer in the value of transcendental meditation. In fact, Lincoln Industries Inc. employs a religious consultant who leads all the Lincoln employees in 15 minutes of daily meditation and relaxation techniques. Since the corporation began this program, employee absenteeism has declined by 13 percent. Does the religious

consultant's $20,000 annual salary represent a current tax deduction for Lincoln Industries Inc.?

7. During the current year, Branden Inc. and Cortell Inc. formed a partnership to construct a shopping mall in Houston, Texas. The partners paid $24,000 of fees to the law firm that drafted the partnership agreement and $17,500 to the CPA firm that set up an accounting system for the partnership. The partnership began business in October of the current year and elected a fiscal year ending June 30 for tax purposes. To what extent are the $41,500 of professional fees deductible in the partnership's first taxable year?
8. Early in the current taxable year, Myantis Inc. purchased certain commercial real estate for use in its business. Shortly after the transaction closed, a dispute over the property's boundary developed. Myantis incurred $12,000 of legal fees in the successful resolution of the dispute. Can the corporation deduct the legal fees on its current year tax return?
9. Marion Lee is the financial vice president of Trandex Inc. During the current year, Marion traveled to Washington, D.C., to testify before a congressional committee concerning legislation that would have a direct and major impact on Trandex Inc.'s overseas operations. Marion also attended a fund-raising dinner for a senator sympathetic to the corporation's position on the legislation. The cost of Marion's trip was $1,300, while the cost of the dinner was $1,500. What are the tax consequences of these expenses to Trandex Inc.?
10. In December of the current year, Drexel Inc., a calendar year cash basis taxpayer, made a $4,500 payment to an independent consultant who will spend the next six months designing a new marketing plan for one of the corporation's major products. Drexel also paid $1,800 of interest on a $10,000 bank loan, which was made in January of the current year. The payment represented 24 months of interest. To what extent may Drexel deduct these two payments in the current year?
11. Reardon Manufacturing Inc. is an accrual basis taxpayer. At the beginning of the year, the cost of Reardon's inventory on hand (1,000 units) was $100,000. The total cost of the inventory manufactured during the year (2,000 units) was $400,000. At the end of the year, Reardon had only 1,200 units remaining in inventory.
    a. What is Reardon's current year deduction for cost of goods sold if it uses the FIFO method of accounting for inventories?
    b. What is Reardon's current year deduction for cost of goods sold if it uses the LIFO method of accounting for inventories?
    c. Which method of accounting would Reardon prefer to use for tax purposes? For financial accounting purposes? May Reardon use different methods of accounting for income for these two purposes?
12. Ted Carola, a single taxpayer, is an executive vice president of Acme Inc. During the current year, Ted spent $18,000 on business meals and entertainment with various Acme clients. His company fully expects Ted to perform this function on its behalf.
    a. Assume that Acme Inc. makes no formal reimbursement to Ted for the $18,000 of out-of-pocket expenses. If Ted's current year adjusted gross

income is $250,000 and he is in a 36 percent marginal tax bracket, what is his after-tax cost of these business expenses?

b. Assume that Acme reimburses Ted for every dollar of substantiated business meal and entertainment expense. How does this change affect your answer to *a*?

13. Ashley Ferguson is an English professor employed by the University of Maryland. During the year, Ashley subscribes to a number of professional and literary journals. The university does not reimburse Ashley for her subscription costs, which average $700 per year.

    a. To what extent may Ashley deduct this $700 business expense on her current year tax return?

    b. Would your answer change if Ashley is also a published author and earns $30,000 a year in royalties from her books?

14. Jansen Inc. is a calendar year accrual basis corporation. At the end of the year, Jansen accrued a $280,000 current year expense and corresponding liability for the annual bonuses to its executives; these bonuses were approved at the December board of directors meeting and will be paid to the executives on February 15 of the next year. During the year, Jansen Inc. was sued by a business competitor for libel. The corporation's auditors insisted the corporation accrue $400,000 of estimated settlement expense in the current year, even though Jansen does not expect the suit to go to court for at least three years. In what year may Jansen claim a tax deduction for these accrued expenses?

15. For the current taxable year, Alpha Corporation's marginal tax rate is 15 percent, while Zeta Corporation's marginal tax rate is 35 percent.

    a. If both Alpha and Zeta are entitled to an additional current year deduction of $2,000, what amount of tax savings will the deduction generate for each corporation?

    b. If both Alpha and Zeta are entitled to a current year tax credit of $2,000, what amount of tax savings will the credit generate for each corporation? (Assume that each corporation's precredit current year tax liability exceeds $2,000.)

Case 4–1

Assume Congress recently enacted a nonrefundable business credit based on the cost of any qualifying alcohol and drug counseling programs provided by any corporate employer to its employees. The credit is limited to 50 percent of the total cost of the qualifying program. If a corporation elects to take the credit, none of the program costs may be claimed as a current year business deduction. Any amount of unused credit (the amount of credit in excess of current year tax liability) may not be carried back or forward to another taxable year.

a. Barker Inc. spends $80,000 for a qualifying counseling program during the current year. If Barker Inc. has $500,000 of taxable income before any consideration of the cost of the qualifying counseling program and is in a 34 percent tax bracket, should it elect the new credit or should it deduct the program's cost as an ordinary and necessary business expense?

b. Would your answer change if Barker Inc. had taxable income of only $50,000 before any consideration of the cost of the qualifying counseling program? The corporation's tax liability on $50,000 of taxable income would be $7,500.

Case 4–2

Twenty years ago, the Belmona Corporation developed, manufactured, and marketed Kepone, a highly poisonous chemical pesticide. As a result of manufacturing processes that violated state environmental standards, harmful quantities of Kepone were discharged into the soil and groundwater. The state of Arkansas recently sued Belmona for damages and the corporation was indicted for criminal negligence with respect to the unlawful discharge of toxic waste. The judge in the case imposed a $13 million fine on Belmona.

After extensive meetings with the judge and prosecutors, Belmona created the Central Arkansas Environmental Foundation, the stated objectives of which are to alleviate the effects of Kepone waste and to generally enhance the environment. Belmona contributed $8 million to this nonprofit organization and the judge promptly reduced the fine payable to Arkansas to $5 million. Can Belmona deduct the $8 million payment to the Foundation as an ordinary and necessary business expense?

CHAPTER 5

The Taxable Entities

In the preceding chapters, we studied the generic rules governing the computation of taxable income that are common to all taxpayers. Before we can calculate the federal tax liability imposed on a given amount of income, we must identify the type of taxpayer that earned the income. Fortunately, this task is relatively easy because the federal system provides for only three types of taxpaying entities: *individuals, corporations,* and *fiduciaries.* The distinction among these taxable entities is important for two reasons. First, a different rate schedule must be used by each to compute the tax payable for the year. Second, the Internal Revenue Code contains specialized rules unique to the computation of the taxable incomes of the three types of entities.

In this chapter, we will examine the rate schedules, the specialized tax rules, and the nontax characteristics distinguishing individual, corporate, and fiduciary taxpayers. We will also consider the tax consequences of conducting business in the *partnership* or the *S corporation* form. Partnerships and S corporations are not taxable entities; consequently, their net business income must be taxed directly to the partners or shareholders who own the entity. The final section of the chapter focuses on the concept of income shifting among taxable entities to minimize the tax burden on the income. As we will learn, the current tax environment offers minimal opportunity for this particular tax planning strategy.

INDIVIDUAL TAXPAYERS

Theoretically, every living person is a separate and distinct taxable entity. Age is of no significance; a six-year-old child who earns income by appearing in a television production is as much a taxable entity as her parents. As such, this little prodigy will have her own tax return for the year, reflecting both the gross income she received and any deductible expenses incurred in connection with her employment. Obviously, the child's parents or legal guardians are responsible for filing the return and paying any tax liability. The important point is that the individual, rather than the family unit, is the taxable entity.

Filing Status and Tax Rates

The law contains four different rate schedules for the computation of individual tax liability. (The 1996 rate schedules are reproduced on page 83.) Every person must determine his or her *filing status* in order to choose the appropriate rate schedule. An individual who is married at the close of the taxable year typically files a joint tax return with his or her spouse on which the rate schedule for *married filing jointly* is used in the tax calculation. Widows or widowers (described as *surviving spouses* for tax purposes) with dependent children may qualify to use this schedule for two years after the death of their marital partners. Married couples have the option of filing two separate tax returns on which the rate schedule for *married filing separately* is used. In a limited number of situations, a married couple can derive some tax benefit by filing separately. However, most couples that file separate returns do so for nontax, personal reasons. An unmarried individual who maintains a home for a child or other dependent family member is eligible to use the rate schedule for *heads of households*. Finally, any unmarried individual who fails to qualify as a head of household will file his or her tax return using the rate schedule for *single taxpayers*.

All four of the individual rate schedules are based on five brackets of taxable income. The first four brackets are taxed at 15 percent, 28 percent, 31 percent, and 36 percent, respectively, and the open-ended fifth bracket is taxed at 39.6 percent. The ranges of the brackets vary across schedules. A comparison of the schedules reveals that the married filing jointly schedule has the widest brackets, and therefore results in the smallest tax liability for any given amount of income. This fact suggests the rate structure is biased in favor of married taxpayers; for example, in 1996 a married couple with $50,000 of taxable income had a tax bill of $8,787, while an unmarried individual with a $50,000 income paid $10,880 in tax. Based on these numbers, our bachelor could easily argue that he is paying a $2,093 penalty for being single! But now let's suppose the married couple in this example are both employed and earn identical salaries so that each had a taxable income of $25,000 before they married. As single taxpayers, each had a tax liability of $3,880, and the combined tax burden on their incomes was only $7,760. By saying "I do," our couple incurred a marriage penalty in the form of $1,027 of additional federal tax.

The preceding computations show that our federal income tax system is not marriage neutral. The lack of such neutrality is not the result of congressional ineptitude, but is the unavoidable by-product of a progressive income tax system under which married couples may file a joint tax return. To illustrate, assume that four people, A, B, C, and D, are taxed under a rate schedule imposing a 10 percent tax on income up to $50,000 and a 15 percent tax on any income in excess of this amount. The following table presents the relevant information if A, B, C, and D all file returns as single taxpayers.

Taxpayer	*Taxable Income*	*Tax*
A	$50,000	$5,000
B	50,000	5,000
C	25,000	2,500
D	75,000	8,750

What happens if A marries B and C marries D? Now there are two married couples, each with a combined income of $100,000. Under a tax system that is strictly marriage neutral, couple AB should pay only $10,000 of tax, while couple CD should pay $11,250. However, under a tax system permitting joint filing, married couples such as AB and CD who have equal incomes should pay equal amounts of tax. The federal income tax system is designed to achieve the latter result; married couples who file joint returns all use the same rate schedule to compute their tax liabilities, so couples with the same amount of taxable income will bear identical tax burdens. As a result, the marriage of two single taxpayers invariably results in a change, for better or for worse, in the twosome's tax bill.

Individual Tax Credits

In Chapter 4, we discussed the variety of tax credits generated by business operations. The law also provides for several nonbusiness tax credits available only to individual taxpayers. Congress designed these credits to enhance the equity of the tax system as it applies to people in particular economic circumstances. For example, taxpayers who must pay for child care in order to be gainfully employed may claim a *dependent care credit* based on a percentage of the cost of the care. The precise amount of the credit is a function of the number of dependents and the adjusted gross income reported on the taxpayer's return. While the dollar amount of this credit is relatively small (the maximum credit available is $1,440), it can represent a substantial tax savings to low-income families for whom decent child care is a major household expenditure.

Individuals who have reached the age of 65 or are permanently and totally disabled may be eligible for a modest *credit for the elderly and disabled.* This credit equals 15 percent of a limited amount of retirement income, a credit base that must be reduced by any Social Security or other retirement benefits received by the retiree. Because the computation of the precise amount of the credit is so complicated, eligible individuals may file their returns with a request that the IRS compute their credit for them.

The Earned Income Credit. In Chapter 3, we discussed the fact that many low-income families pay no income tax because of the availability of personal and dependency exemptions and the standard deduction in computing taxable income. However, poor families are not sheltered from the employee payroll tax, which is levied on the first dollar of wages or salary earned during the year. In 1975, Congress enacted the *earned income credit* (EIC) to offset the impact of the payroll tax on low-income workers and to encourage individuals to seek employment rather than to depend on welfare. The dollar amount of the EIC is a percentage of earned income (wages, salary, or self-employment income) reported on the Form 1040. The credit amount varies with the number of children in the family and decreases as the family's earned income increases. For 1996, the maximum EIC available to a family with two or more children and earned income of $11,610 or less is $3,556. If the family's earned income exceeds the $11,610 threshold, the EIC gradually phases out and is eliminated when earned income reaches $28,495. The government estimates that more than 15 million families, the poorest fifth of this country's work force, will qualify for the EIC in 1996. The IRS will compute the credit for taxpayers who request such assistance when filing their income tax returns.

The EIC is our first and only example of a *refundable* credit: a person may receive a refund equal to the full amount of the credit even if such refund exceeds the amount of tax paid during the year. Suppose the Barney family's Form 1040 shows that $550 of income tax was withheld from Mr. Barney's wages during the year, but that the family's current year tax liability is only $300. If the Barneys do not qualify for an earned income credit, they are entitled to a $250 refund. Assume that the Barneys do qualify for a $2,000 earned income credit. If the credit were nonrefundable, it would reduce their tax liability to zero and increase their refund to $550. In this case, the $1,700 of credit in excess of the tax liability would yield no benefit to the Barneys. Because the EIC is refundable, the Barneys will receive such excess as an additional refund, bringing their total refund for the year to $2,250.

Payment and Filing Requirements

At this point in the text, we have discussed each step involved in the computation of an individual's annual federal tax liability. These steps are reflected in the following formula:

	Gross income recognized
less:	Above-the-line deductions
	Adjusted gross income
less:	The greater of itemized deductions or standard deduction
less:	Personal and dependency exemptions
	Taxable income
multiplied by:	Tax rates based on filing status
	Tax liability
less:	Credits
	Tax payable

The U.S. Individual Income Tax Return Form 1040, on which all the above data are compiled, must be filed with the Internal Revenue Service by the 15th day of the fourth month following the close of the taxable year. (For calendar year taxpayers, this is the familiar April 15 due date.) Any individual who is not ready to file his return by this date may simply request an *automatic extension* of the deadline for four months (until August 15 for calendar year taxpayers). If the four-month extension isn't enough extra time, an individual may request a second extension for two more months (until October 15). This second extension is not automatic, and the IRS will grant approval only if the taxpayer can show unusual circumstances justifying further delay.

These generous extensions of time to file a tax return do not postpone the payment of tax owed for the year. In fact, individuals remit their taxes to the federal government on a pay-as-you-go basis (i.e., periodically over the course of the year). For employees, these periodic tax payments are withheld from every salary or wage check received; employers have the responsibility of depositing their employees' income tax withholding with the Treasury. Individuals with investment income or earnings from self-employment must make quarterly payments of the estimated tax on such income to

Filing Status	*1996 Taxable Income Subject to 15% Rate*	*1996 Taxable Income Subject to 28% Rate*	*1996 Taxable Income Subject to 31% Rate*	*1996 Taxable Income Subject to 36% Rate*	*1996 Taxable Income Subject to 39.6% Rate*
Single persons	0–$24,000	$24,001–$58,150	$58,151–$121,300	$121,301–$263,750	over $263,750
Married persons filing jointly	0–$40,100	$40,101–$96,900	$96,901–$147,700	$147,701–$263,750	over $263,750
Heads of households	0–$32,150	$32,151–$83,050	$83,051–$134,500	$134,501–$263,750	over $263,750
Married persons filing separately	0–$20,050	$20,051–$48,450	$48,451–$73,850	$73,851–$131,875	over $131,875

the Treasury. Taxpayers who fail to make timely payments of at least 90 percent of their current year tax liability in the form of *withholding* and *quarterly estimate payments* may face a substantial underpayment penalty. Because of the uncertainty inherent in estimating the amount of tax owed for the year in progress, the law provides a *safe-harbor estimate.* Taxpayers with adjusted gross incomes of $150,000 or less in the preceding taxable year may pay current year estimated tax equal to 100 percent of the preceding year's tax liability. By doing so, such taxpayers avoid any underpayment penalty, regardless of the amount of their actual current tax liability The safe-harbor estimate for individuals with adjusted gross incomes in excess of $150,000 in the preceding year jumps to 110 percent of the preceding year's tax liability.

If a person somehow managed to fine-tune her withholding and quarterly estimate payments so these prepayments equaled the actual tax liability computed on her Form 1040, she would have no additional tax to pay when the return is filed. Realistically, taxpayers either underestimate or overestimate their current liabilities. In the former case, the unpaid balance should be remitted to the Treasury by the *unextended* filing date for the tax return; if a taxpayer requests an extension of time to file, the estimated balance due should be remitted with the extension request. If a taxpayer's prepayments exceed the actual tax liability, the Treasury will refund the excess once the return has been filed.

For some psychological reason, people seem to take an inordinate amount of pleasure when they discover that Uncle Sam owes them a tax refund. But from a strict financial perspective, a tax refund is equivalent to an interest-free loan made to the federal government. The best tax planning strategy is to prepay the minimum amount of current year tax required in order to avoid any underpayment penalty. Even if this strategy results in a sizable amount of additional tax due when the return is filed, the taxpayer has enjoyed the use of the cash required to pay this tax for the maximum length of time.

CORPORATE TAXPAYERS

A corporation is a legal entity formed under state law to conduct a business operation. Ownership of the entity is embodied in the outstanding shares of the corporation's stock. *Closely held* corporations are privately owned by relatively few shareholders; *publicly held* corporations, the stock of which is traded on an established securities market, may have thousands of shareholders.

Many entrepreneurs choose to operate in the corporate form because of the advantageous legal characteristics of a corporation. Perhaps the most important characteristic is the *limited liability* of the shareholders for corporate debt. If a corporate business gets into financial trouble and doesn't have sufficient funds to pay its creditors, those creditors can't look to the personal assets of the owners of the corporation for satisfaction. Consequently, a shareholder's business risk is limited to the amount of his investment in the corporation's stock. A second attractive characteristic is the *unlimited life* of a corporation. In the eyes of the law, a corporation is a person separate and distinct from its owners, so its identity is not affected by changes in the composition of its shareholders. This characteristic gives corporations the vitality and stability so conducive to the operation of a successful business.

Figure 5–1 Tax Rates for Most Corporate Taxpayers

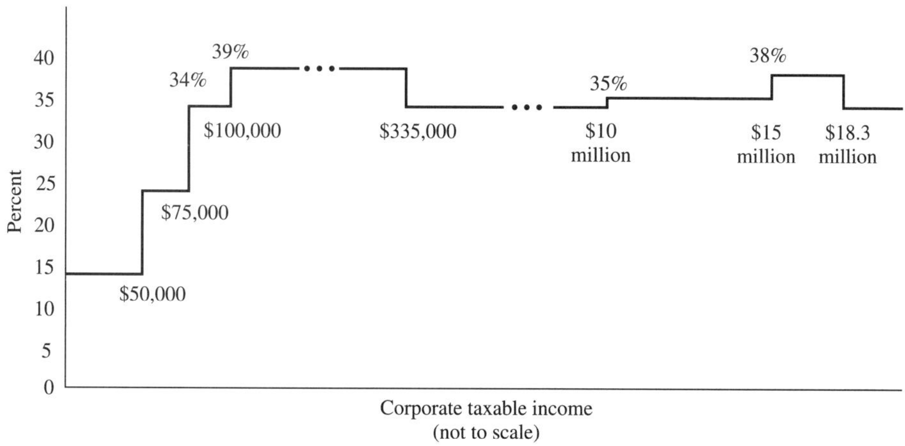

Corporate Tax Rates

The fact that domestic corporations are taxable entities in their own right is one of the cornerstones of our federal income tax system. Corporations compute their own taxable income and pay tax based on their own rate schedule, as shown in Figure 5–1: 15 percent of the first $50,000 of taxable income, 25 percent of the next $25,000 of taxable income, and 34 percent of any taxable income in excess of $75,000. Corporations must also pay an additional 5 percent of taxable income from $100,000 to $335,000. The purpose of this surtax is to recoup the tax savings represented by the 15 and 25 percent rates. Note the maximum amount of the surtax is $11,570, an amount equaling the difference between the $13,750 tax imposed on the first $75,000 of income and 34 percent of $75,000. The significance of the surtax is that corporations with incomes in excess of $335,000 (but less than $10 million) effectively pay a flat-rate federal income tax of 34 percent.

The corporate tax rate increases to 35 percent on taxable income in excess of $10 million. Corporations with taxable incomes in excess of $15 million must pay a second surtax of 3 percent on the first $3,333,333 of such excess. The maximum second surtax of $100,000 recaptures the benefit of the 34 percent rate on the first $10 million of taxable income. Consequently, corporations with incomes in excess of $18.3 million effectively pay a flat-rate tax of 35 percent on their total taxable income.

Corporations owned and operated by individuals performing certain professional services for the corporation's clientele are denied even the minimal progressivity of the corporate tax rate schedule. Any amount of taxable income earned by these *personal service corporations* is taxed at a flat 35 percent rate. Personal services include those performed in the fields of health, law, engineering, architecture, accounting, actuarial services, performing arts, and consulting.

Corporations organized exclusively for "religious, charitable, scientific, testing for public safety, literary, or educational purposes, or to foster national or international amateur sports competition" are not subject to federal income taxation. The tax law is quite generous in granting tax-exempt status to many different types of *not-for-profit* corporations. However, a tax-exempt corporation straying from its intended purpose into a profit-motivated activity may find itself subject to tax on any amount of *unrelated business income* earned for the year.

The Double Taxation of Corporate Income

Distributions of corporate earnings to shareholders (i.e., dividends) are not deductible in the computation of corporate taxable income and therefore are paid with after-tax dollars. These dividends must be included in the recipient shareholders' gross incomes and are taxed a second time at the shareholder level. This phenomenon of double taxation can result in a very high effective rate of tax on business income. One dollar of corporate earnings shrinks to 65 cents because of the corporate income tax.[1] If this 65 cents is paid as a dividend to individual shareholders in the 39.6 percent marginal tax bracket, only 39.26 cents of the original dollar survives as disposable income to the owners of the business. This double tax is illustrated in Figure 5–2.

The combination of a corporate-level income tax and the nondeductibility of dividend payments has several important consequences. Corporations have a strong incentive to avoid dividend payments and retain their after-tax dollars to finance current operations and business growth. To the extent the retention of earnings increases the value of the corporate business, stockholders enjoy a return on their investment in the form of an increase in the market price of their shares. Unlike the receipt of a cash dividend, this type of investment return is not currently taxable; income recognition is deferred until the shares are sold and the increase in value becomes a realized gain. While this gain will be taxed in the year of sale, the benefit of significant deferral cushions the economic impact of the double taxation of corporate earnings. Moreover, the gain on the sale of stock will be characterized as capital gain. As we will discover in Chapter 7, capital gains have certain unique, and very positive, characteristics prompting individual taxpayers to prefer them to other types of income.

The nondeductibility of dividend payments creates a corporate bias in favor of debt financing. A corporation that raises additional capital by borrowing can deduct the interest paid to its creditors so the after-tax cost of the interest payments is only 65 percent of the before-tax cost. If the corporation raised the capital by selling a new issue of stock, the after-tax cost of dividends paid to the new shareholders would equal the before-tax cost. Of course, the choice of debt financing has serious nontax implications, one of the more important of which is that interest and principal payments (unlike dividends paid on common stock) are not discretionary on the part of corporate management. Corporations with high debt-to-equity ratio tend to have more burdensome cash flow commitments and a greater risk of insolvency than corporations with less debt in their capital structures.

---

[1]In this and subsequent references to corporate taxpayers, a 35 percent tax rate is presumed.

Figure 5–2 Double Taxation of Corporate Income

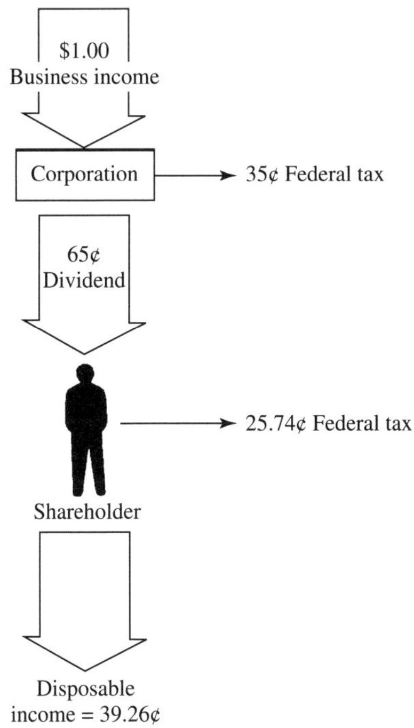

One of the more insidious repercussions of the corporate income tax is that corporations become easy political targets in any debate on tax reform. No individual enjoys paying taxes, and human nature being what it is, most people are convinced their tax bill is too high because some other taxpayer's bill is too low. Impersonal corporate taxpayers are natural scapegoats, and the hue and cry becomes "tax the giant corporations, not the hardworking middle class." This sentiment ignores the fact that a corporation is nothing more than a form in which people conduct business and that an increase in the corporate tax represents an additional cost of doing business.

In certain markets, that cost may be passed directly on to consumers in the form of higher prices for the corporation's product. If a corporation decides to respond to a tax increase by cutting back on production costs and standards, the tax is passed on to the corporation's suppliers, employees (in the form of lower wages or work force reductions), and indirectly to consumers (in the form of reduced quality). If the competitive market is such that a corporation can neither raise its prices nor cut its costs, a tax increase will be passed on to investors in the form of reduced dividends and depressed share prices. The economic incidence of the corporate tax and whether that tax falls hardest on consumers, suppliers, labor, or capital has been researched and debated for decades without definitive results. Nonetheless, one conclusion is inescapable: corporations do not pay taxes—people do.

Alternatives to Double Taxation

One alternative to the double tax inherent in the present system is the option of ignoring the corporate entity and allocating all corporate income immediately and directly to the stockholders, whether or not the corporation distributes any of its earnings as cash dividends. This alternative would be administratively cumbersome, if not impossible, for large, publicly held corporations in which the ownership changes daily. In addition, this alternative could create major hardships if a corporation earned a sizable income but made minimal cash distributions. Under these conditions, a shareholder might face a large tax liability with limited funds with which to pay the tax.

A second alternative is the allowance of a corporate deduction for dividend distributions to shareholders. During the congressional deliberations culminating in the Tax Reform Act of 1986, the Treasury (undoubtedly caught up in the excitement of the moment) proposed a deduction equal to 50 percent of dividends paid. Estimates of the enormous revenue loss inherent in this radical proposal caused the Treasury to downgrade the amount of the deduction to a more modest 10 percent. To the disappointment of many tax theorists, the final version of the act abandoned the idea.

A third alternative is a system in which shareholders are given a tax credit based on the amount of corporate tax attributable to the dividends includable in their gross incomes. For example, if a shareholder received a dividend of $65,000, representing $100,000 of business income out of which $35,000 of corporate tax had already been paid, the shareholder would include the full $100,000 (cash received grossed up by the amount of tax paid) in her income and compute her tax liability accordingly. She would then reduce the liability by a credit of $35,000. The end result is that the $100,000 of business income is taxed only once at the marginal rate of the individual shareholder. Variations of this system are currently used in Canada and several Western European countries.

Computation of Corporate Taxable Income

Those readers who recall the complexities of calculating the taxable income of an individual should be relieved to learn that, in comparison, the calculation of corporate taxable income is quite straightforward. The formula for the calculation is gross income minus allowable deductions equals taxable income. Federal tax law generally assumes that corporations have only a business persona, so all activities undertaken by corporations are business activities. Consequently, there is no artificial distinction between above-the-line and itemized deductions and no computation of adjusted gross income on a U.S. Corporation Income Tax Return Form 1120. Nor is there any differentiation between business and investment activities; as a result, the Section 163(d) limitation on deductibility of investment interest expense, so onerous to many individual taxpayers, does not apply to corporations.

The discussions of gross income in Chapter 2 and business deductions and credits in Chapter 4 provide the essential information necessary to calculate corporate taxable income. There are just a few special rules unique to this calculation, two of which are generally applicable. The first rule affects corporations making contributions to qualified charities during the taxable year. Such contributions are deductible only to the extent of 10 percent of current year taxable income. Contributions in excess of this limitation can be carried forward for five years to be deducted against future taxable income.

The second rule has a much greater economic significance. In calculating its taxable income, a corporation can deduct a percentage of the dividends received during the year from other taxable domestic (but not foreign) corporations. The amount of this *dividends received deduction* (DRD) depends on the extent of the recipient's investment in the corporation paying the dividend. The DRD is 70 percent if the recipient corporation owns less than 20 percent of the outstanding stock of the payor, 80 percent if the recipient owns 20 percent to 79 percent of the stock, and 100 percent if the recipient owns 80 percent or more of the stock. The beneficial impact of the DRD cannot be overemphasized; while corporate taxpayers must include the full amount of dividends received in their gross incomes, little if any of this amount will be taxable.

The rationale behind the DRD should be obvious if we reconsider a point made earlier in the chapter. Business income earned by a corporate entity may be subject to a double tax to the extent it is distributed as a dividend to the entity's owners. If one corporation owns another corporation's stock, will a single business income stream be subject to a triple tax? In the absence of the DRD, that would be the result and corporate ownership of another corporation's stock would be of dubious value. To avoid this serious problem inherent in the multicorporate ownership structures characteristic of a modern economy, Congress decided to grant the DRD to corporate entities.

Payment and Filing Requirements

The corporate income tax return must be filed with the Internal Revenue Service by the 15th day of the third month following the close of the corporation's taxable year. Corporations may request an automatic six-month extension of this filing date. A corporation's estimated current tax liability must be paid in four quarterly installments during the year; failure to deposit 100 percent of the actual tax due in the form of estimated payments may result in a sizable underpayment penalty. A corporation will avoid this penalty if its quarterly payments total 100 percent of the tax liability reported on its prior year return. This safe-harbor estimate may not be used by large corporations (those generating taxable income of $1 million or more during any of the three years preceding the current year). However, large corporations with highly fluctuating patterns of annual income may look to other statutory exceptions to the strict 100 percent requirement to obtain relief from any underpayment penalty.

Consolidated Corporate Returns

The tax law permits *affiliated groups* of corporations to file a single *consolidated tax return* rather than separate returns for each legal entity within the group. The decision to file a consolidated return is an elective one binding for all subsequent years unless the group is terminated or the IRS grants permission to discontinue the election. An affiliated group consists of a parent corporation owning 80 percent or more of the stock of at least one includable corporation. Once this parent-subsidiary nucleus is formed, other 80-percent-controlled includable corporations may be added to the group. The term *includable corporation* does not extend to foreign corporations, tax-exempt corporations, subchapter S corporations, insurance companies, and miscellaneous other types of corporations granted special tax treatment of one kind or another. A consolidated group may consist of just two corporations or an international organization as complex as IBM, General Motors, or any other Fortune 500 company.

The administrative ease of filing a single Form 1120 rather than any number of separate corporate tax returns is one obvious and important benefit of consolidation. Other benefits include the following:

1. The right to offset the operating losses of one corporation in the group against the operating income earned by other members.
2. The right to calculate various deduction and credit limitations on a consolidated basis.
3. The right to defer the recognition of profits or gains on intercompany transactions.

The Treasury regulations governing consolidated tax returns are both lengthy and complicated, and any further discussion of their intricacy is beyond the scope of this text. Nevertheless, the reader should be aware that the majority of affiliated corporate groups do elect to file their returns and pay their tax liabilities on a consolidated basis.

SPECIAL CONSIDERATIONS OF CLOSELY HELD CORPORATIONS

The Internal Revenue Service estimates that 95 percent of the corporations in the United States are closely held, and that as a group, they account for over 40 percent of the gross domestic product (GDP). In this section, we will examine a few of the interesting tax problems and opportunities characteristic of closely held corporations. Both the problems and opportunities stem from the fact that a corporation is nothing but a legal fiction operating for the economic benefit of its shareholders. When a small group of people, or even a single individual, owns all the shares, it is difficult to distinguish between the corporation's interests and the personal interests of its owners.

The shareholders of a closely held corporation often find it hard to understand that the business operated by the corporate entity is not their business. After all, such shareholders usually constitute both the board of directors and the management group, thereby playing an active role in day-to-day corporate operations. Nonetheless, the corporation is a taxable entity separate and distinct from its shareholders, who by definition must be regarded as investors. Any misperception concerning the relationship between a corporation and its shareholders can lead to trouble.

For example, assume a sole shareholder decides, strictly for the sake of convenience, to pay some of his corporation's bills from his own bank account. This shareholder might conclude he can simply deduct the payment on his own tax return as a business expense, rather than bothering with a reimbursement from the corporation.

However, our shareholder is not in the corporate business; his ownership of the stock is an investment activity. His payment of the corporate expense is correctly classified as a nondeductible contribution to corporate capital. If the shareholder also happens to be a corporate employee, he could argue that the payment is an unreimbursed employee business expense, qualifying as a miscellaneous itemized deduction. Because of the virtually prohibitive 2 percent AGI limitation on such deductions, this argument might or might not result in any current tax benefit to our shareholder.

Constructive Dividends

Shareholders in closely held corporate businesses tend to become acutely aware of their status as investors when they want to extract some portion of the profits from the business and realize that any such return on their investment will be a nondeductible dividend. Few shareholders are willing to tolerate the double taxation of business income inherent in dividend payments and aggressively seek alternate ways to bail cash out of the corporation. The standard technique for avoiding dividend payments requires a shareholder to assume an additional role with regard to his corporation. Quite frequently, shareholders serve as corporate officers and executives. In their roles as employees, they are entitled to salaries, the payment of which represents both positive cash flow to the recipient and a deductible corporate expense. Similarly, shareholders often assume the role of creditor by lending money to their corporations; interest paid on the shareholder debt is deductible at the corporate level. Still a third possibility is for shareholders to lease property to their corporations; the rent payments are deductible by the corporate lessee. Note that in all the above cases, the cash flow, whether in the form of dividends, salary, interest, or rent, must be recognized as ordinary income to the recipient. The important difference is at the corporate level: the after-tax cost of a $1 dividend is $1 while the after-tax cost of a dollar of salary, interest, or rent is only 65 cents.

The IRS has no quarrel with shareholders to transact with their corporations, as long as the transaction is based on reasonable terms similar to those that would be negotiated between the corporation and unrelated third parties. Unfortunately, shareholders can display an unfortunate tendency toward greed by negotiating salaries, interest, rents, and similar payments that violate this arm's-length standard. If a shareholder receives any type of payment the IRS considers unreasonable in light of all surrounding facts and circumstances, the IRS will reclassify the unreasonable portion of the payment as a *constructive dividend.*

To illustrate this concept, suppose that Mr. Charles, sole shareholder and chief executive officer of Charles Industries, Inc., receives an annual salary of $450,000. If other companies comparable in size and function to Charles Industries, Inc., pay their CEOs $400,000 to $500,000 every year, and if Mr. Charles has the talent and experience to merit such handsome compensation, the salary appears reasonable and should be fully deductible on the corporate tax return. Conversely, if the CEO salaries paid by comparable businesses average only $300,000 a year, and Mr. Charles spends more time on the golf course than at corporate headquarters, the IRS may conclude that

$150,000 or more of his salary is really just a disguised dividend, the payment of which will not reduce the corporation's current year taxable income.

Penalty Taxes on Corporate Accumulations

Shareholders in closely held corporations who have no pressing need for cash from the corporate business can circumvent the problem of double taxation by the simple expedient of never declaring a corporate dividend. Such shareholders are content to enjoy the nontaxable increase in the value of their stock attributable to the deliberate accumulation of after-tax corporate earnings. Many years ago, Congress attempted to discourage this tactic by enacting two penalty taxes aimed at corporations that fail to distribute at least some portion of their profits as shareholder dividends.

The *accumulated earnings tax* can be imposed on any corporation "formed or availed of for the purpose of avoiding the income tax with respect to its shareholders by permitting earnings and profits to accumulate instead of being divided or distributed." This tax-avoidance purpose is presumed to exist when a corporation accumulates earnings beyond the reasonable needs of its business. The tax equals 39.6 percent (the highest marginal rate for individual taxpayers) of any current year *accumulated taxable income,* defined roughly as taxable income net of income taxes and dividends paid. Theoretically, a corporation with $1 million of current taxable income that fails to pay any dividends for the year and has no financial, economic, or legal justification for retaining any of its $660,000 of after-tax earnings could be liable for an accumulated earnings tax of $261,360 (39.6 percent of $660,000).

Admittedly, the imposition of this penalty tax is a very uncertain and subjective matter. Many closely held corporations have retained millions of dollars of after-tax income without a moment's concern for the accumulated earnings tax. Such peace of mind can be attributed to the existence of compelling and undisputed business reasons justifying the accumulation.[2] On the other hand, corporations vulnerable to the tax display two common symptoms: They have a history of minimal or nonexistent dividend payments, and their balance sheets reveal an overabundance of nonbusiness liquid assets such as jumbo certificates of deposit, portfolios of marketable securities, investment properties, and most damning of all, substantial loans to shareholders.

Corporations qualifying as personal holding companies may be liable for a *personal holding company tax.* The statutory definition of a personal holding company is technically complex—suffice it to say that personal holding companies are (1) owned by a small number of individual taxpayers and (2) have taxable incomes consisting primarily of passive investment income such as dividends, interest, rent, and royalties. The personal holding company tax equals 39.6 percent of any undistributed corporate earnings. Accordingly, a personal holding company that distributes all of its after-tax earnings as dividends to its shareholders has no liability for any additional penalty tax.

---

[2]Corporations that are not personal service corporations are allowed to accumulate $250,000 of after-tax earnings without demonstrating a reasonable business need for such accumulation. Personal service corporations (as defined on page 86) may accumulate only $150,000 on this "no questions asked" basis.

FIDUCIARY TAXPAYERS

Fiduciaries, a designation including both estates and trusts, are the third type of entity subject to federal income taxation. An *estate* is a legal entity created to temporarily hold title to and manage the assets of a deceased individual until ownership of the assets can be properly transferred to the decedent's rightful heirs, legatees, or devisees. An estate must report and pay tax on any income generated by the decedent's assets during this interim period. After these assets are distributed and the estate is closed, the new owners will report the future income from the assets on their respective individual returns.

A *trust* is a contractual legal arrangement involving the ownership and management of investment property. Pursuant to the directions of the creator, or *grantor,* of the trust, a trustee will hold legal title to property in which a beneficiary or set of beneficiaries is given the equitable interest. Such an arrangement is usually designed for the protection of the beneficiary, who may be a minor child or a person incapable of competently managing the trust property. The trustee has a fiduciary responsibility to conserve and manage the property in the best interests of the beneficiaries. The position is often filled by the trust department of a financial institution; professional trustees receive an annual fee to compensate them for services rendered.

Estates and trusts are not intended to function as business entities. Estates are merely transitional property owners required by legal necessity, while trusts are created for personal and family reasons. Fiduciary taxable income is computed under the set of rules applicable to individual taxpayers. If the fiduciary distributes cash or property to any beneficiary during the taxable year, fiduciary income equal to the amount of the distribution will be taxed to the beneficiary. To illustrate this modified passthrough system of taxation, assume a trust collects $65,000 of investment income during its taxable year and incurs $10,000 of deductible expenses. During the year, the trust distributes $12,000 in cash to an individual beneficiary. As a result of the distribution, $12,000 of the $55,000 of taxable income will be allocated to the beneficiary on a Schedule K–1, and the beneficiary must include this amount of investment income on her Form 1040 for the year. The $43,000 of undistributed income will be reported on a U.S. Fiduciary Income Tax Return Form 1041 as the trust's taxable income for the year.

The fiduciary tax rate schedule consists of five brackets ranging from 15 to 39.6 percent. These brackets are extremely narrow; in 1996, all fiduciary income in excess of $7,900 is taxed at the highest marginal rate. Fiduciaries are not entitled to any standard deduction and the personal exemption amounts are a nominal $600 for an estate and $100 or $300 for a trust (depending on the particular legal structure of the trust arrangement).

NONTAXABLE BUSINESS ENTITIES

Partnerships

Entrepreneurs frequently decide to pool their respective resources by becoming co-owners of an enterprise that they will operate in partnership form. *Partnerships* are legal entities created by contractual agreement among two or more business associates.

Such associates can include individuals, corporations, fiduciaries, or even other partnerships. All 50 states have enacted statutes (generally patterned after the Uniform Partnership Act and the Uniform Limited Partnership Act) to define the characteristics of and requirements for partnerships operating within the state.

The contract creating a partnership is referred to as the *partnership agreement.* Individuals who are considering forming a partnership should seek professional help in drafting their agreement, and the final product should always be in writing. A partnership agreement defines the legal rights and responsibilities of the partners and specifies each partner's ownership interest in the capital of the business as well as the percentage of future profits and losses to be allocated to each.

The status of each partner as *general* or *limited* should be clearly established in the partnership agreement; each partnership must have at least one general partner. The distinction is critical because general partners have unlimited personal liability for debts incurred by the partnership, while limited partners are protected from the claims of partnership creditors. State law generally prohibits limited partners from active involvement in the partnership business. Limited partners who violate this prohibition may find they have forfeited the right to limited liability for the partnership's debts.

Partnerships are both legal entities (title to property can be held and conveyed in the partnership name) and accounting entities (financial books and records are maintained by the partnership). Partnerships, however, are not taxable entitles; Section 701 states that persons carrying on business as partners shall be liable for income tax only in their separate or individual capacities. Partnerships are required to file an annual return, Form 1065, with the IRS, but this return is for informational purposes only. The return shows the calculation of the partnership's net business income or loss for the taxable year and the allocation of that income or loss to the various partners. Because partnerships serve as conduits for income ultimately taxed at the partner level, they are described as *passthrough entities.*

The tax advantage of the partnership form is that business income is not subject to double taxation. One dollar of income earned by a partnership represents one dollar of business income taxed for the first and only time to the owners of the business.[3] If a dollar of partnership income is allocated to an individual partner in the 39.6 percent marginal tax bracket, that dollar results in 60.4 cents of after-tax income. This single tax regime is illustrated in Figure 5–3. Compare this result with the double tax illustrated in Figure 5–2 and the attraction of operating a business as a nontaxable passthrough entity should be clear.

Subsequent to the close of its taxable year, a partnership must issue a Schedule K–1 to each partner. This schedule provides detailed information concerning the partner's share of the various items of income, gain, loss, deduction, and credit generated by the partnership. The character of each item survives this passthrough process; therefore, any item that might affect the computation of any partner's taxable income must

[3] If partnership income is allocated to an owner that is also a passthrough entity (such as another partnership), the income is again passed through until it is finally allocated to a taxable entity (i.e., an individual or corporation).

Figure 5–3 Single Taxation of Partnership Income

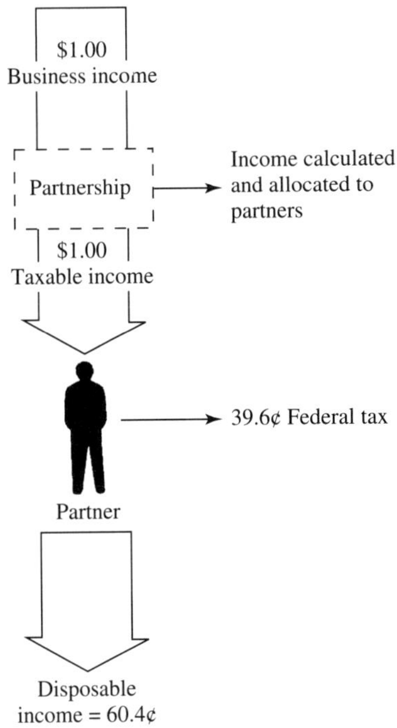

be separately listed on the Schedule K–1. For example, municipal bond interest earned by a partnership retains its tax-exempt character so that partners may exclude their allocated share from their gross incomes. Similarly, dividend income earned by a partnership retains its character as investment income, and each individual partner may use his allocated share to absorb any investment interest expense incurred during the year. If a partnership makes a donation to charity, each partner's Schedule K–1 must show a separate allocation of the donation. Partners must include their allocated share with any other charitable contributions made during the year. For corporate partners, these total contributions are subject to the 10 percent limitation discussed earlier in the chapter. For individual partners, total contributions must be reported as itemized deductions on Schedule A.

When a partnership operates a profitable business, each partner's allocated share of business income is commingled with income from all other sources on an individual partner's Form 1040, a corporate partner's Form 1120, or a fiduciary partner's Form 1041. An individual who conducts a business as a general partner is considered self-employed for tax purposes, and his allocated share of the partnership's business income is self-employment income. The fact that a partner is allocated income on a Schedule K–1 does not necessarily mean the partner received a cash distribution of a corresponding amount. If the partnership retains a sizable amount of the cash generated by current year operations to fund current or future business needs, partners may have to use cash from other sources to pay the tax liability on the partnership income. Conversely, if a partnership generates a business loss, the partners can use their shares of the loss as ordinary deductions against any other source of income recognized during the year.

Associations, Publicly Traded Partnerships, and Limited Liability Companies

The fact that a business is organized in an unincorporated form under state law does not guarantee it will escape the corporate income tax. The Internal Revenue Code, rather than local law, establishes the standards for determining the proper classification of a business entity for federal tax purposes. If a partnership displays too many of the legal and functional characteristics of a corporation, the IRS may classify it as an *association*—an unincorporated entity taxable as a corporation. Association status is a subjective determination, based on facts and circumstances, and the courts have adjudicated many a dispute between taxpayers and the IRS concerning the correct classification of a business as either a partnership or an association.

Before 1988, *publicly traded partnerships* (also known as master limited partnerships) represented the extreme case of partnerships donning the trappings of corporations. Ownership interests in these business partnerships were traded on established security markets and were virtually indistinguishable from equity stock. In the Revenue Act of 1987, Congress enacted a sweeping rule that any publicly traded partnership must be treated as a corporation for federal tax purposes. Because of the broad scope of this rule, Congress included a generous transition period; partnerships already in existence as of the enactment date of the law will not be forced to assume a corporate identity until taxable years beginning after 1997.

Many states allow businesses to be organized as *limited liability companies* (LLCs), unincorporated entities that offer investors limited liability for debts incurred by the business. The other legal characteristics of LLCs cause them to bear a greater resemblance to partnerships than corporations. As a result, the IRS has ruled that LLCs are considered partnerships for federal tax purposes, so the income or loss generated by these hybrid entities is taxed directly to the investors, based on their relative ownership interests in the LLC.

Subchapter S Corporations

Individuals trying to decide on the optimal form in which to operate a business confront a dilemma. From a legal and financial perspective, a corporation may be the best choice; from a tax perspective, the allure of a single level of taxation makes a partnership a clear favorite. Fortunately, the tax law offers a third alternative, the subchapter S corporation, which in the right set of circumstances can provide entrepreneurs with the best of both worlds. The label *S corporation* has significance only for tax purposes; S corporations have the legal characteristics of an incorporated entity under state law. For federal tax purposes, however, an S corporation is a passthrough entity, the income of which is included on the returns of each shareholder and taxed only once at the shareholder level.

An S corporation files a Form 1120S on which its annual income is measured and characterized. The various items of corporate income, gain, loss, deduction, and credit are then allocated to the shareholders based on the number of shares owned. The amount and character of each item is separately listed on a Schedule K–1 issued to every shareholder at the close of the corporate taxable year. This passthrough process is virtually identical to that used by partnerships.

A corporation is eligible for subchapter S status if it meets just a handful of statutory requirements.

1. The corporation itself must be a domestic corporation with only a single class of outstanding common stock. The shares of common stock may carry different voting rights without violating this requirement.
2. The corporation may not own a controlling (80 percent plus) interest in a subsidiary corporation.
3. Only individuals, estates, and certain trusts may be shareholders of the corporation. Nonresident aliens may not be shareholders.
4. The number of shareholders is limited to 35. A married couple is considered a single shareholder, even if both spouses own shares.

Although S corporations are technically labeled small business corporations in the Internal Revenue Code, there are no restrictions concerning the dollar amount of the corporation's net worth, sales volume, or number of employees; hence, S corporations may be very large corporate enterprises.

A corporation becomes an S corporation by the unanimous election of its shareholders. The election is permanent for the life of the corporation unless shareholders owning a majority of the stock agree to revoke the election. An S election can be lost through sheer carelessness; an election is immediately terminated upon the infraction of any of the eligibility requirements. For example, if an individual shareholder neglects to consult his tax adviser and sells some of his stock to a partnership, the subchapter S status of the corporation ends as of the day of sale.

As you might imagine, such *inadvertent terminations* can have disastrous tax consequences. Moreover, the shareholders of a corporation that has lost its S election generally cannot make a new election for five years. Because of the severity of the problem, the law provides a very generous relief measure. If upon discovery of an inadvertent termination the corporate shareholders take immediate steps to remedy the situation (i.e., reacquisition of the stock from the offending partnership in our example), the IRS may be willing to overlook the incident and allow the original S election to remain in effect.

INCOME SHIFTING AMONG TAXABLE ENTITIES

In any income tax system with either progressive rates or differential rates across taxable entities, tax liabilities can be reduced by funneling income into the entity facing the lowest marginal tax rate. This premise is both very simple and very powerful: If entity A faces a marginal rate of 50 percent while entity B faces a marginal rate of only 20 percent, every dollar of income shifted from A to B and thereby *sheltered* from A's higher rate results in a tax savings of 30 cents. Historically, taxpayers and their advisers have devoted a great deal of time and energy thinking up novel ways to achieve this highly desirable result. The IRS has been equally busy in challenging those income-shifting schemes that crossed the fine line between tax avoidance and tax evasion. In this final section of the chapter, we will discuss the many constraints on income shifting that limit the extent to which this technique can effectively be used in the tax planning process.

Nontax Constraints on Income Shifting

While the income shift described in the preceding paragraph deprived the Treasury of 30 cents of revenue, it also deprived entity A of 50 cents of after-tax wealth. Obviously, a rational person has no interest in any tax plan involving a shift of his or her wealth to a stranger. Income-shifting plans are viable only when the taxpayer from whom the income is being diverted can continue to control, enjoy, or benefit from the income in some indirect manner. For example, the income shift from A to B may make sense if A and B are father and son, and A is eager to contribute to his offspring's financial support. A second possibility is that A is the sole shareholder of corporation B so any income shifted to B remains under A's indirect control. Entity A must also consider any transactional costs of structuring and implementing a tax plan to accomplish an effective income shift to entity B. Such costs must be weighed against the tax savings to be achieved; legal and accounting fees alone can quickly turn an interesting planning idea into a losing proposition. Clearly, both economic and practical constraints limit the range of income-shifting possibilities.

Prohibitions against Assignment of Income

The federal courts have consistently supported the proposition that our income tax system cannot tolerate arbitrary assignments of income from one taxpayer to another. The 1930 Supreme Court decision in *Lucas* v. *Earl* established that income must be taxed to the person who earns it, even if another person has a legal right to the wealth represented by the income. Thus, a taxpayer who receives a $10,000 salary check from her employer can't avoid recognition of $10,000 of income by endorsing the check over to her mother. In the picturesque language of the Court, the tax law must disregard arrangements "by which the fruits are attributed to a different tree from that on which they grew."

In 1940, the Supreme Court elaborated on this theme in *Helvering* v. *Horst.* This case involved a parent who detached negotiable interest coupons from corporate bonds and gave the coupons to his son as a gift. When the coupons matured, the son collected the interest and reported it as gross income on his return. The Court concluded the interest income was taxable to the father because he continued to own the underlying asset (the bonds) that created the right to the interest payments. The holdings in these two cases have become part of the judicial bedrock of federal tax law. In literally thousands of taxpayer disputes, the IRS has been able to frustrate income-shifting schemes by invoking the doctrine that income must be taxed to the entity who renders the services or owns the capital with respect to which the income is paid.

The Kiddie Tax

Before 1986, individuals in high tax brackets routinely made gifts of investment securities to their minor children or grandchildren so the dividends and interest earned on the securities would be reported on the child's tax return and taxed at a low marginal rate. In 1986, Congress attacked this income-shifting technique by amending the law to require that any unearned income in excess of an indexed base amount ($650 in 1996) received by a child under the age of 14 be taxed at the parent's marginal rate. For example, if Mr. and Mrs. Blake made a gift of $50,000 worth of common stock to their 10-year-old dependent son Brian and the stock paid $4,000 of dividends in 1996, Brian's taxable income would be $3,350 ($4,000 gross income minus $650 standard deduction). Normally, the tax on $3,350 of income at a 15 percent rate would be only $503. But under the *kiddie tax* rules, $2,700 of Brian's income ($3,350 minus $650 base) is taxed at the marginal rate that applies to Mr. and Mrs. Blake's 1996 taxable income. If the Blakes are in the 36 percent bracket, Brian's tax bill will be $1,070 (36 percent of $2,700 + 15 percent of $650).

Corporations as Tax Shelters

The marginal rates faced by individual taxpayers are higher than the rates applicable to corporate taxpayers. Consequently, individuals can shelter income from tax by operating their businesses in corporate form. Let's consider a situation in which a consortium of individuals in the 39.6 percent marginal tax bracket undertakes a new business projected to generate $75,000 of annual income. If the business is organized as a partnership or an S corporation, the tax burden on the income stream will be $29,700 (39.6 percent of $75,000). If the business is organized as a regular corporation, the tax on the income will be only $13,750 (15 percent on the first $50,000 of income plus 25 percent on the remaining $25,000 of income). If the consortium's income projections are too conservative, so that corporate taxable income actually exceeds $75,000, each incremental dollar will be taxed at a 34 percent rate; in addition, each dollar of income between $100,000 and $335,000 will be subject to the 5 percent surtax. But even if the business generates annual income in excess of $335,000 so that the corporation is effectively paying a flat 34 percent tax, this rate is still 5.6 percentage points less than the rate that would apply if the business were operated in an unincorporated form.

At this point in the example, perceptive readers might think that if and when the annual income earned by the newly formed corporation exceeds $75,000, the consortium could easily divide the corporation into two smaller corporate entities and split the income stream between them. Shouldn't it be possible to double the shelter offered by the progressive corporate tax rates by shifting income from a single corporate taxpayer to two corporate taxpayers? Unfortunately, Congress was way ahead of our readers on this one. The Internal Revenue Code provides that in the case of *controlled groups* of corporations, the progressive rate schedule is applied to the aggregate taxable income of the group rather than the separate incomes of each member. A controlled group can be either a *brother-sister* configuration of corporations owned by the same individual shareholders or a *parent-subsidiary* configuration. In either case, any taxable income of the group in excess of $75,000 will be taxed at a 34 percent marginal rate.

Figure 5–4 Controlled Corporate Groups

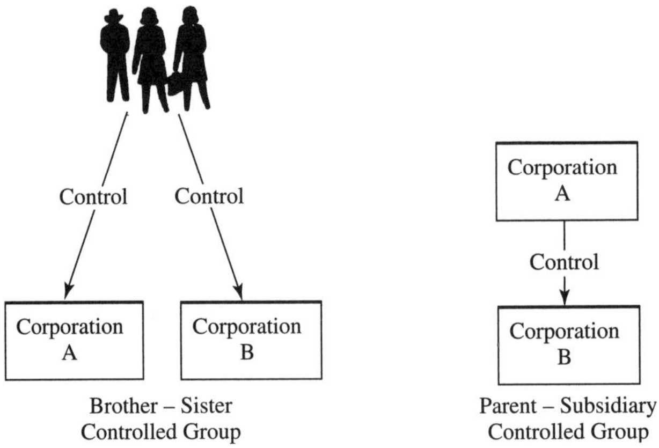

A major problem with using a corporation to shelter business income from the high individual marginal rates is that the after-tax cash generated by the business is often in the wrong bank account. The individual shareholders cannot spend the profits from their business on personal consumption unless the corporation distributes the profits to them as dividends. Of course, these dividends would be fully taxable to the shareholders, and this double taxation would negate the savings attributable to the use of the corporate form. Corporations can be viewed as tax shelters only to the extent they accumulate, rather than distribute, after-tax income. As we learned earlier in the chapter, the threat of the accumulated earnings tax prevents corporate businesses from carrying this technique to ridiculous extremes. It is no coincidence that the 39.6 percent penalty rate on unwarranted accumulations equals the highest marginal rate that could apply if the after-tax corporate income was distributed and subjected to a second round of taxation at the shareholder level.

Section 482

Taxpayers who are overzealous in their attempts to shelter income from high tax rates may initiate income-shifting schemes having no purpose other than tax avoidance. As we discussed in Chapter 4, the Internal Revenue Service has a number of powerful judicial doctrines at its disposal with which to attack pro forma transactions devoid of business purpose or economic substance. Congress has also provided the IRS with a very potent statutory weapon against abusive transactions in the form of Section 482 of the Internal Revenue Code.

Section 482 states that in the case of two or more businesses under common ownership or control, the IRS has the authority to allocate gross income or deductions between or among the businesses if such allocation is "necessary in order to prevent evasion of taxes or clearly to reflect the income" of any of the businesses. The IRS has been particularly successful in using this authority to thwart artificial shifts of income between controlled entities. To illustrate the type of situation in which Section 482 can be applied, let's assume Alpha Inc. and Beta Inc. are owned by the same group of shareholders. Alpha Inc. operates a very profitable manufacturing business; Beta Inc. is a regional wholesaler that purchases its inventory from a number of suppliers, including Alpha. Beta has generated losses for several years and as a result has substantial net operating loss carryforwards into its current taxable year.

In this situation, the owners of the two corporations have an incentive to shift income away from Alpha (and its 35 percent tax rate) to Beta (with a current year marginal tax rate of zero). Such a shift could easily be accomplished if Alpha sells its product to Beta at cost instead of the normal marked-up price charged to unrelated wholesalers. When Beta sells Alpha's product to its customers, the entire profit margin on the product will be included in Beta's income. In this rather transparent example, Alpha's preferential pricing arrangement with Beta clearly distorts the taxable incomes of both corporations. If a tax audit uncovers the distortion, the IRS will not hesitate to shift the proper amount of Beta's income back to Alpha under the mandate of Section 482.

CONCLUSION

This chapter has provided an overview of the three types of entities subject to the federal income tax. Remember that the basic rules governing the recognition of gross income and the deductibility of expenses and losses apply to all three types. As a result, the computations of taxable income for individuals, corporations, and fiduciaries are fundamentally similar.

Understand that a business entity may or may not be a taxable entity. For a business operated as a sole proprietorship, net business income is reported as a component of the individual owner's adjusted gross income and taxed at the individual rates. For a business operated in the corporate form, net business income is reported by the corporate entity and taxed at the corporate rates. The owners of the corporation are not taxed unless and until the corporation pays a dividend. For a business operated as a partnership or S corporation, net business income is not taxed to the entity but is passed through to the business's owners (partners or shareholders). The income is reported on the owners' returns and taxed at either the individual or corporate rate, whichever applies.

PROBLEMS AND CASES

1. Both Claire Bates and Max Hoen are employees of a regional accounting firm. Claire's annual salary is $95,000, while Max's salary is $50,000. Currently, Claire and Max are single individuals. If they decide to marry, will they pay a marriage penalty on their first jointly filed tax return? (A detailed calculation is not necessary in answering this question. A thoughtful look at the tax rate schedules for single taxpayers and married taxpayers filing jointly should suffice.)
2. Bob and Kim Snow have read about the marriage penalty on couples who file a joint tax return. To avoid the penalty, Bob and Kim decide to file separate tax returns for the current year. Bob's taxable income on his return is $55,000, while

Kim's is $40,000. Their taxable income on a jointly filed return would have been $95,000. How much tax will the Snows save by filing separate returns?

3. The tax law provides for both nonrefundable and refundable credits. Explain the difference between the two types.
4. When he accepted his current employment position three years ago, Marty Glass instructed his employer to withhold substantially more federal income tax from Marty's monthly paycheck than is required by law. As a result, Marty receives a sizable tax refund every spring, which he faithfully invests in a mutual fund. Marty views this strategy as an efficient means of enforced savings. Do you agree?
5. Julio Ramirez, a calendar year taxpayer, has been seriously ill since the beginning of the current year. Because Julio has been unable to attend to any financial matters, his CPA has advised him to request an automatic extension for filing his prior year's tax return. Julio is delighted with this idea because he estimates that he will owe $20,000 in tax with the return, and he wants to avoid liquidating any of his investments to pay this amount for as long as possible. By requesting an automatic extension, how long may Julio delay paying the $20,000 tax due?
6. Zeb Gray operates his own consulting business. In November of the current year, Zeb completed a major project for which he plans to charge $15,000. Without consideration of this $15,000, Zeb's current year taxable income will be about $130,000. Zeb and his wife will file a joint return for the current year. However, Zeb's wife is in the process of filing for divorce, so Zeb will file as a single taxpayer next year. Zeb estimates that his taxable income next year (without consideration of the $15,000 consulting fee) should be about $125,000. From a tax planning perspective, should Zeb try to collect the $15,000 fee before the end of the current year or should he delay billing his client until after December 31 in order to defer recognition of the income (and payment of the tax on that income) until the following year?
7. Nora White's 1996 adjusted gross income (consisting of both salary and investment income) was $176,000 and her 1996 tax liability was $47,200. For 1997, Nora estimates that her employer will withhold $30,000 from her salary. Compute the total amount of quarterly estimate payments that Nora must make during 1997 to ensure that she will not incur an underpayment penalty for the year.
8. Jemima Blake purchased 1,000 shares of Upflight Inc. for $10,000 in 1989. These shares represent a 30 percent ownership interest in the corporation. During the current year, Upflight defaulted in a $60,000 debt to one of its major creditors.
   - *a.* To what extent can the creditor demand repayment of this debt from Jemima Blake?
   - *b.* Would your answer to *a* change if Upflight Inc. were an S corporation?
   - *c.* Would your answer to *a* change if Upflight were a partnership and Jemima were a 30 percent general partner? A 30 percent limited partner?

9. Gamma Inc. averages $40,000 of taxable income a year. Because it is in need of a quick influx of cash, Gamma is considering two options: selling a new issue of nonvoting preferred stock to the public for a total offering price of $50,000 or borrowing $50,000 from a local bank. The current market dividend rate on preferred stock is only 5.6 percent, while the interest rate the bank would charge is 9 percent.

   a. Which option minimizes Gamma Inc.'s after-tax cost of capital?
   b. Would your answer change if Gamma's average taxable income is $300,000?
   c. Would your answer change if Gamma's average taxable income is $45,000?

10. Leftwich Inc. manufactures laundry detergent and other cleaning products. During the current year, Congress increases the corporate income tax rate by 2 percentage points. Leftwich's marketing department determines the corporation cannot raise its prices and hope to retain its current market share. The corporation's vice president in charge of production concludes that manufacturing costs cannot be reduced by another penny. Consequently, Leftwich's before-tax profits remain constant, while after-tax profits decline by 2 percent. The stock market reaction to this decline in earnings is a fall in Leftwich's price per share.

   a. In this scenario, who is bearing the economic cost of the increase in the corporate tax rate?
   b. How would your answer change if Leftwich had been able to hold its after-tax profits constant by cutting costs—namely shutting down the on-site day care center for its employees' preschool children?

11. During the current year, Wyona Inc. received $25,000 of dividends from Apex Inc. and $4,000 of dividends from Cromwell Inc. Wyona owns 2 percent and 60 percent respectively of these two corporations. Neither Apex nor Cromwell owns stock in any other corporate entity. Wyona Inc. distributed all of its current after-tax income to its two shareholders, Dale and Susan Wyona.

   a. Assuming that all three corporations in the problem face a flat 34 percent tax rate and that Dale and Susan are in the 39.6 percent marginal tax bracket, compute the effective tax rate on the business income represented by the Apex and Cromwell dividends.
   b. How would your answer change if Wyona Inc. is an S corporation?

12. Able Inc. owns 100 percent of the stock of Zero Inc. During the current year, Able Inc. generated $350,000 of taxable income and Zero Inc. generated a $200,000 net operating loss.

   a. How much current year tax liability can Able save by electing to file a consolidated tax return with its controlled subsidiary?
   b. Assume Zero Inc. generated $100,000 of taxable income (rather than a net operating loss) for the current year. What is the total tax liability of the two corporations if they file a consolidated tax return? How would your answer change if they file separate tax returns for the year?

13. Myra Cole serves as secretary-treasurer for Cole Products Inc., all the outstanding stock of which is owned by various members of the Cole family. Myra herself owns 10 percent of the stock. During the current year, Myra's salary is $50,000. The salary range for secretary-treasurers of other corporations similar in function and size to Cole Products Inc. is $40,000 to $50,000.

    a. Myra has an M.B.A. from UCLA and averages 55 hours a week at her job. Based on these facts, what are the tax consequences of the $50,000 salary payment to the corporation and to Myra?

    b. How would your answer to *a* change if Myra were a high school dropout who works only one hour every morning at the corporate headquarters making coffee and opening the mail?

    c. How would your answer to *b* change if Myra were not a shareholder in the family corporation? She was given her current position by the corporate president, her brother Mike, who owns 55 percent of Cole Products Inc.'s outstanding stock.

14. Mr. and Mrs. Adams own and operate four separate businesses—W, X, Y, and Z. The major characteristics of the businesses for the year can be summarized as follows:

Business	*Legal Form*	*Predistribution Taxable Income*	*Distributions to Owners*	*Taxable Income*
W	Sole Proprietorship	$30,000	$15,000	$30,000
X	Partnership	50,000*	-0-	50,000*
Y	Corporation	42,000	12,000	30,000
Z	S Corporation	(20,000)*	7,000	(27,000)*

*The Adamses' share only

The $15,000 distribution from Business W represents cash generated by the sole proprietorship used by the Adamses to pay their son's college tuition. The Adamses reinvested the remaining available cash in business equipment and inventory. The distributions from the two corporate businesses (Y and Z) were salary payments to Mrs. Adams.

a. Based on the above data, what amount of adjusted gross income must the Adamses report on their current year federal tax return?

b. Which of the four businesses added more to the Adamses' taxable income than to their personal checking account (cash) balance? Explain briefly.

c. Which of the four businesses added more to the Adamses' checking account (cash) balance than to their taxable income? Explain briefly.

15. Danny Kwak, a single taxpayer, operates a photographic studio as a sole proprietorship. His average annual income from this business is $100,000. Danny has come to you for tax advice. He wants to know how the tax liability on his business income will be affected if he incorporates the sole proprietorship. If he does incorporate, he plans to draw out a $60,000 annual salary (as corporate president) and pay no dividends.

a. How will you respond to Danny's query if the corporation will not be a personal service corporation?
b. Would your answer to *a* change if the corporation will be a personal service corporation?
c. Would your answer to *a* change if Danny makes a subchapter S selection for the corporation?

16. Lucy Trevino operates a retail hardware store as a sole proprietorship; this business generates $60,000 of annual net income. Lucy is in the 31 percent marginal tax bracket and would like to reduce the total federal tax on the income from the store by shifting some of it to her two children, ages 18 and 20. How much income tax can be saved under the following strategies? In answering this problem, assume the children are Lucy's dependents and have no other source of income during the year.
    a. Lucy hires her two children to work 20 hours a week in the store. She pays each of them a reasonable annual salary of $10,000.
    b. Lucy creates a family partnership by giving each child a one-third ownership interest in the profits and capital of the business.
    c. Lucy incorporates the business and gives each child one third of the corporation's common stock. The shareholders make a subchapter S election for the new corporation.
17. Although trusts are often used to achieve the personal financial planning goals of a family, they are ineffective for sheltering income from the highest individual marginal tax rates. Explain briefly.
18. Mr. and Mrs. Calhoun, who are in a 39.6 percent marginal tax bracket, want to make a $100,000 gift to their 11-year-old son Adam. The Calhouns could fund the gift with corporate bonds that pay interest quarterly or CVB Inc. common stock. CVB Inc. is an aggressively growth-oriented business that has not declared a dividend for the past eight years. From a tax planning perspective, which asset should the Calhouns give to Adam?
19. Mega Investment Partnership owns 100 percent of the stock of two corporations, Banner Inc. and Ramex Inc. Banner Inc. operates an architectural business; Ramex Inc. constructs and operates commercial real estate. Both corporations are very profitable and are in the 34 percent marginal tax bracket. During the current year, Banner Inc. designs several buildings and shopping centers for Ramex Inc., charging Ramex $50,000 for services rendered. The IRS determines that an arm's-length price for such services is $300,000 What are the tax consequences of this determination to the two corporations?

Case 5–1

Denton Stone, a single individual, has annual taxable income of $110,000. Denton would like to shift some income to his two adult children. Denton's tax attorney has suggested that

Denton transfer $200,000 worth of investment securities with a 10 percent annual yield to a permanent (irrevocable) trust created for the benefit of these children. The trustee fee would be $1,200 per year, and 100 percent of annual trust income net of this fee would be distributed to the children in equal shares. After 20 years the trust would terminate, and the investment securities would be divided between the children.

a. How will this plan affect the family's aggregate economic income if one of Denton's children is in the 15 percent marginal tax bracket, while the other is in the 28 percent marginal tax bracket?

b. How would your answer to *a* change if Denton's annual taxable income is $300,000?

Case 5–2

Ellen and Everett Terry have accumulated a sizable investment portfolio over the last 15 years. The Terrys have four children, ages 21 to 29, with whom they would like to share their wealth in some formalized manner. However, none of the children are particularly astute businesspeople. Consequently, the Terrys decide to transfer their investment portfolio to a newly created corporation in exchange for both voting and nonvoting stock. The nonvoting stock will be given to the Terry children. In this way, Ellen and Everett can continue to manage their investments (as corporate president and vice president), but the annual income from the investments can be distributed as dividends to all six shareholders in the family corporation.

a. If the stock in Terry Family Corporation (TFC) is owned in equal amounts by the six family members, and the corporation's gross income for the current year consists of $120,000 of dividends from corporations in which TFC owns less than a 1 percent interest, compute the total tax on this investment income if TFC distributes a $10,000 current year dividend to each shareholder. In making your calculations, assume that Ellen and Everett Terry and their two older children are in a 31 percent marginal tax bracket, while the two younger children are in only a 15 percent marginal tax bracket.

b. Would the Terry family benefit by making a subchapter S election for TFC? Explain briefly.

CHAPTER 6

Cost Recovery Deductions

In Chapter 4, we distinguished between business expenditures that result in an economic benefit in only the current year and those that result in an economic benefit extending over a number of taxable years. The former category may result in a current tax deduction, while the latter category must be capitalized to an appropriate fixed asset account. In this chapter, we will examine the variety of tax rules by which capitalized costs may be recovered over time in the form of deductions against future taxable income.

COST RECOVERY DEDUCTIONS AND THE PRESENT VALUE CONCEPT

Because of the time value of money, a current year deduction results in a greater tax savings in present value terms than the same deduction deferred until a future year. Consequently, the after-tax cost of a business expenditure is minimized when the expenditure is currently deductible. If the expenditure must be capitalized, its after-tax cost depends on the length of time over which the expenditure can be converted into a series of tax deductions. To illustrate this fundamental concept, suppose a business facing a 34 percent marginal tax rate makes a $100,000 expenditure. The table at the top of page 108 shows the computation of the after-tax cost of this expenditure under three different assumptions.

For all three assumptions, the table shows the $100,000 before-tax cost of the expenditure as a negative number. The first assumption is that the business may claim a $100,000 current deduction for the expenditure. The deduction generates a current tax savings of $34,000, which reduces the after-tax cost of the expenditure to $66,000.

The second assumption is that the business may deduct $50,000 of the expenditure in the current year but must defer the deduction for the remaining $50,000 until the following year. In both years, the deduction saves the business $17,000 in tax. However, the present value of these savings is only $33,038 ($17,000 current savings plus $16,038, the present value of $17,000 saved one year hence at an assumed 6 percent discount rate). Consequently, the after-tax cost of the expenditure is $66,962.

The third assumption is that the business must capitalize the $100,000 expenditure to a fixed asset account. In this case, the business establishes a $100,000 tax basis in the new asset. Assuming the business is allowed to *recover* this basis over 10 years in the form of a $10,000 annual deduction, it will save $3,400 of tax each year. The present value of this stream of savings at a 6 percent discount rate is $26,526 and the after-tax

	Assumption 1: $100,000 Deduction in Year 1	*Assumption 2: $50,000 Deduction in Current Year; $50,000 Deduction in Year 2*	*Assumption 3: $10,000 Deduction in Years 1 through 10*
Before-tax cost	($100,000)	($100,000)	($100,000)
Year 1 tax savings	$34,000	$17,000	$3,400
Discounted present value of tax savings in year:			
2		16,038	3,208
3			3,026
4			2,855
5			2,693
6			2,541
7			2,397
8			2,261
9			2,133
10			2,012
Discounted present value of total tax savings	$34,000	$33,038	$26,526
After-tax cost	($66,000)	($66,962)	($73,474)

cost of the expenditure is $73,474. At the end of the 10-year period, the business's tax basis (its unrecovered cost) in the asset has been reduced to zero. Note that under all three assumptions, the business has recovered its total $100,000 expenditure in the form of tax deductions. The difference in the after-tax cost under each assumption is entirely attributable to the timing of such deductions.

The analysis of the after-tax cost under the third assumption ignores the possibility that the asset created by the $100,000 expenditure may have economic value at the end of 10 years, even though the business has recovered the entire cost of the asset in the form of tax deductions. If the business can sell the asset, the present value of the after-tax amount realized on sale reduces the after-tax cost of the initial expenditure. For example, assume that the business can sell the asset in year 11 for $30,000 cash. Because the business's tax basis in the asset is zero, the gain recognized on sale is $30,000.

Cash realized on sale	$30,000
Unrecovered tax basis	-0-
Gain recognized	30,000
	34%
Tax on gain	$10,200

If the gain is taxed at 34 percent, the after-tax amount of cash realized by the business in year 11 is $19,800. The present value of this cash inflow at a 6 percent discount rate is $11,056 and the after-tax cost of the initial $100,000 expenditure drops to $62,418.

Cash realized on sale	$30,000
Tax paid on gain	(10,200)
After-tax cash in year 11	$19,800
Expenditure in year 1	($100,000)
Present value of:	
Tax savings in years 1–10	26,526
After-tax cash in year 11	11,056
After-tax cost of expenditure	($62,418)

In this example, $30,000 of the cost-recovery deductions allowed to the business in years 1 through 10 did not correspond to a decline in the value of the asset and did not reflect any economic cost to the business. Such deductions are referred to in the tax literature as *paper deductions*.

TAX BASIS OF BUSINESS ASSETS

Leveraged Asset Purchases

Most business assets are acquired through an outright purchase, and the price paid plus any costs related to getting the asset in place and into production become the initial *cost basis* of the asset. If a purchaser finances an acquisition by borrowing money and using the newly acquired property as collateral for the debt, the initial basis of the property equals its entire cost, not just the purchaser's equity. Assume Tara Inc. buys an office building for $5 million by paying $1 million cash and borrowing $4 million from a commercial lender. Tara's debt is secured by a mortgage on the building. Although Tara's current year investment in the building is only $1 million, its cost basis is the full $5 million purchase price. Regardless of the rate at which it accumulates additional equity in the building through principal repayments on the loan, Tara will enjoy an immediate stream of cost-recovery deductions with respect to this $5 million basis.

Tax planners refer to the use of borrowed funds to create tax basis as *leverage*. The use of leverage in asset acquisitions can dramatically reduce the purchaser's after-tax cost of the asset. To illustrate this important tax planning principle, refer back to the third assumption in the earlier example in which a business facing a 34 percent marginal tax rate pays $100,000 for a fixed asset and can recover the cost at a rate of $10,000 over 10 years. At the end of the recovery period, the asset can be sold for $30,000. Let's introduce leverage into this example by assuming the business paid $16,000 cash and borrowed $84,000 to finance the acquisition. The $84,000 loan is repayable in equal installments over 12 years and bears a simple 6 percent interest rate on the unpaid balance. The annual interest payments are fully deductible by the business. The annual after-tax cash flows attributable to the combination of the cost recovery deductions allowable to the business and the annual interest and principal payments on the acquisition debt are computed as follows:

Year	*Tax Savings from Cost-Recovery Deductions*	*Principal Repayment*	*Interest Payment*	*Tax Savings from Interest Deduction*	*After-Tax Cash Outflow*	*Discounted Present Value of Cash Outflow*
1	$3,400	($7,000)	($5,040)	$1,714	($6,926)	($ 6,926)
2	$3,400	(7,000)	(4,620)	1,571	(6,649)	(6,273)
3	$3,400	(7,000)	(4,200)	1,428	(6,372)	(5,671)
4	$3,400	(7,000)	(3,780)	1,285	(6,095)	(5,117)
5	$3,400	(7,000)	(3,360)	1,142	(5,818)	(4,608)
6	$3,400	(7,000)	(2,940)	1,000	(5,540)	(4,140)
7	$3,400	(7,000)	(2,520)	857	(5,263)	(3,710)
8	$3,400	(7,000)	(2,100)	714	(4,986)	(3,316)
9	$3,400	(7,000)	(1,680)	571	(4,709)	(2,954)
10	$3,400	(7,000)	(1,260)	428	(4,432)	(2,623)
						($45,338)

In the above table, the tax savings generated by the annual $10,000 cost-recovery deduction and the interest deduction are shown as positive numbers in columns 1 and 4. The annual principal and interest payments on the debt are shown as negative numbers in columns 2 and 3. The annual after-tax cash flow in column 5 is simply the sum of the numbers in the first four columns. Column 6 is the present value of each year's cash flow assuming a 6 percent discount rate.

At the end of year 10, the asset's tax basis has been reduced to zero, and the unpaid balance of the loan is $14,000. If the business sells the asset in year 11 for $30,000, the business must pay a $10,200 tax on the recognized gain and can use $14,000 of the sales proceeds to retire the debt. After these payments, the net cash realized on sale is $5,800.

Cash realized on sale	$30,000
Tax paid on gain	(10,200)
Cash paid to retire debt	(14,000)
After-tax cash in year 11	$ 5,800

The present value of this cash inflow at a 6 percent discount rate is $3,239. Consequently, the after-tax cost of the asset to the business is $58,099.

Expenditure in year 1	($16,000)
Present value of:	
Net cash outflows in years 1 through 10	(45,338)
After-tax cash in year 11	3,239
After-tax cost of expenditure	($58,099)

By leveraging the acquisition of this asset, the business in this example reduced its after-tax cost of the asset from $62,418 to $58,099. This reduction would be even greater if the business's internal rate of return on its productive assets is greater than the rate at which it can borrow money. In such case, the discount rate applied to the stream of after-tax cashflows in years 1 through 11 would be the higher internal rate, and the net present value of the stream would be a smaller number. For example, if the business's internal rate of return were 8 percent, the present values of the cash outflows in years 1 through 10 and the $5,800 cash inflow in year 11 would drop to $42,416 and $2,687, respectively. Using these new numbers, the after-tax cost of the asset is only $55,729.

Converted Personal Assets and Self-Constructed Assets

The tax law allows periodic cost-recovery deductions only with respect to property used in a trade or business or held for the production of income. An individual's tax basis in personal assets (such as a private residence, home computer, or family automobile) is not recoverable until the owner disposes of the asset. An individual who enters into a new business venture may decide to use an existing personal asset in such venture, thereby converting it to a business asset. In this case, the basis of the asset eligible for cost-recovery deductions is limited to the *lesser* of the owner's original cost basis in the asset or the asset's fair market value at date of conversion.

If a business decides to construct an asset to be used in its operations, the direct costs of construction (labor and materials) as well as a proper share of many indirect costs attributable to the construction project must be capitalized. The *uniform capitalization* (unicap) *rules,* which govern the types of indirect costs that must be capitalized to inventory and which were introduced in Chapter 4, also apply to self-constructed business assets.

Repairs or Capital Improvements?

Any business owning tangible properties must make incidental repairs and perform routine maintenance on such properties to keep them in good working order. Repair and maintenance costs that are regular and recurring in nature and that do not materially add to either the value or the useful life of an asset are currently deductible. In contrast, an expenditure that substantially increases the value or life of an asset should be capitalized and added to the basis of the asset. Such *capital improvement costs* will not yield an immediate tax benefit, but will increase the future cost-recovery deductions with respect to the asset. The distinction between a repair and a capital improvement is not always obvious. Of course, the business will always opt for the former classification, while the IRS will argue for the latter.

The business community and the IRS are presently engaged in a hot debate concerning the proper treatment of *environmental cleanup costs.* Many companies, either voluntarily or because of government mandate, are spending millions of dollars to clean up pollutants, toxic wastes, and other dangerous substances unleashed on the environment as industrial by-products. These companies are asserting that these cleanup costs should be currently deductible, while the IRS is maintaining that such costs must be capitalized. In a recent case, a business that replaced the old asbestos insulation in all its manufacturing equipment with a nonhazardous insulation took a deduction for the replacement costs. The business justified the deduction because the replacement was made to protect the health of its employees and did not improve the operating efficiency or increase the value of the equipment. Moreover, the replacement costs were incurred to remedy a historical problem and were not related to the generation of future business income. The IRS determined that the asbestos replacement did, in fact, result in a long-term benefit to the business by permanently improving its work environment; therefore, the IRS required the business to capitalize the replacement costs to the basis of the reinsulated equipment.

Current Deductions of Capital Expenditures as Subsidies

The tax law contains a number of special rules permitting businesses to claim current deductions for expenditures that clearly should be chargeable to a capital account. These preferential rules reduce the after-tax cost of the expenditure and thereby represent an indirect federal subsidy to the business. For example, a business may deduct the first $15,000 of the annual costs of removing *architectural and transportation barriers* from buildings or transportation equipment to make such facilities more accessible to handicapped or elderly people. Farmers may deduct *soil and water conservation expenditures,* which include the cost of leveling, grading, and terracing land, constructing drainage ditches and earthen dams, and planting windbreaks to inhibit soil erosion. Farmers get a second tax break in the form of an immediate deduction for the cost of fertilizers or other materials used to enrich farmland. Oil and gas producers may deduct *intangible drilling and development costs* (IDC) associated with locating and preparing wells for production. Expenses such as wages, fuel, repairs to drilling equipment, hauling, and supplies that contribute to the development of a productive well certainly result in a long-term benefit to the producer. By allowing a current deduction for such IDC, the tax law provides an incentive for producers to undertake new drilling and development projects.

DEPRECIATION OF TANGIBLE BUSINESS ASSETS

Under generally accepted accounting principles, businesses must write off or *depreciate* the capitalized cost of tangible assets over their *estimated useful lives.* Consequently, the cost of an asset is expensed over that period during which the asset is contributing to the revenue-generating activity of the business. Depreciation applies only to *wasting assets* that (1) lose value over time because of wear and tear, physical deterioration, or obsolescence and (2) have a predictable useful life. *Nonwasting* assets, such as land and works of art acquired for display, that lack these characteristics are nondepreciable. For financial statement purposes, depreciation may be calculated under a variety of methods and a business may choose the method that results in the best matching of annual depreciation expense against annual revenues.

Before 1982, depreciation for tax purposes was also based on the approximate useful life of the property in question. Because the productive life of any property is a subjective determination, businesses and the IRS were constantly wrangling over the question of asset lives. Businesses aggressively argued for the shortest life over which to recover the tax bases of their tangible assets while the IRS adopted a more conservative viewpoint. As part of the Economic Recovery Tax Act of 1981, Congress enacted the

Section 168 *Accelerated Cost Recovery System* (ACRS) to replace the existing depreciation rules. In 1986, Congress rewrote Section 168; the revised set of rules has been dubbed the *Modified Accelerated Cost Recovery System* (MACRS). Under MACRS, estimated useful life is irrelevant in the computation of tax depreciation. Accordingly, in today's business world, there is no correlation between the computation of depreciation for book purposes and for tax purposes. Annual depreciation expense on a firm's financial statements and the depreciation deduction on its current year tax return may be markedly different numbers.

The Mechanics of MACRS

In this next section, we examine the rules for calculating depreciation under MACRS. The reader should understand that Congress alters these rules almost every year. The computational rule that applies to a business asset over its entire life is the rule in effect for the taxable year in which the asset was *placed in service.* As a result, a business that places two identical assets in service in two different years may be required to use a slightly different method to compute the annual tax depreciation with respect to each asset. This congressional tinkering with the details of Section 168 causes enormous record-keeping problems to the business community and drives tax practitioners to distraction. Luckily, business managers can familiarize themselves with the structure of MACRS and its pivotal role in the tax planning process by examining only the most general current rules.

Recovery Periods. Every wasting asset eligible for depreciation under MACRS is assigned to one of nine *recovery periods.* Table 6–1 lists these periods and examples of assets assigned to each. For the most part, the MACRS recovery period for an asset is shorter than the asset's estimated useful life. The shortened time frame over which a business may deduct its investment in a depreciable asset reduces the after-tax cost of the asset and acts as an incentive for businesses to make capital acquisitions.

Depreciation Methods and Conventions. The method by which annual depreciation is calculated is a function of the recovery period. Properties with a 3-year, 5-year, 7-year, or 10-year recovery period are depreciated using a 200 percent declining-balance method. Properties with a 15-year or 20-year recovery period are depreciated using a 150 percent declining-balance method. For these six classes of property, MACRS lives up to its name—depreciation deductions are indeed accelerated into the early years of the recovery period. Such front-end loading of tax depreciation provides a further reduction in the after-tax cost of tangible personalty.

Before 1986, depreciable real property (rental and commercial buildings) could also be depreciated using an accelerated declining-balance method. Under current law, however, properties with a 27.5-year, a 39-year, or a 50-year recovery period must be depreciated using a straight-line method. For such properties, MACRS is an accelerated cost-recovery system in name only.

The depreciation computation requires some assumption as to how much depreciation may be claimed in the year of an asset's acquisition or disposition. Under MACRS,

Table 6–1 Recovery Periods for Tangible Business Assets

ACRS Recovery Period	*Assets Included*
3 years	Small manufacturing tools, racehorses and breeding hogs, special handling devices used in food manufacturing
5 years	Cars, trucks, buses, computers, typewriters, duplicating equipment, breeding and dairy cattle, and cargo containers
7 years	Office furniture and fixtures, railroad track, most machinery and equipment
10 years	Single-purpose agricultural and horticultural structures, assets used in petroleum refining, vessels, barges, and other water transportation equipment, fruit or nut bearing trees and vines
15 years	Land improvements such as fencing, roads, sidewalks, bridges, irrigation systems, and landscaping, telephone distribution plants, pipelines, billboards, and service station buildings
20 years	Municipal sewers, certain farm buildings
27.5 years	Residential rental real property (duplexes and apartments)
39 years	Nonresidential real property (office buildings, factories, and warehouses)
50 years	Railroad grading or tunnel bore

assets with recovery periods ranging from 3 to 20 years are generally assumed to be placed in service or sold exactly halfway through the year. This *midyear convention* means that in the first year of an asset's recovery period, only one-half year of depreciation may be deducted, regardless of whether the asset was placed in service on the first day or the last day of such year. The same rule applies to a year in which an asset is sold. A *midmonth convention* applies to the year in which depreciable realty (assets with recovery periods of 27.5, 39, or 50 years) is placed in service or sold. For example, a calendar year business that places a newly acquired building in service on March 2 is entitled to nine and one-half months' depreciation with respect to the building in the first year of the recovery period.

To illustrate a simple MACRS computation, assume a calendar year business purchases a computer for $38,000 and places it in service on September 19 of the current taxable year. The computer has a five-year recovery period and the taxpayer may use the 200 percent declining-balance method to compute annual depreciation. Under this method, the straight-line rate of depreciation is doubled, and the resulting rate is applied each year to the unrecovered basis of the asset. For five-year property, the straight-line rate is 20 percent, and the 200 percent declining-balance rate is 40 percent. For the first year, the depreciation deduction with respect to the computer is $7,600 (one half of 4 percent of the $38,000 cost basis). For the second year, the deduction is $12,160 (40 percent of the $30,400 unrecovered cost basis at the beginning of the year).

IRS Depreciation Tables. To allow taxpayers to avoid this cumbersome math process, the IRS publishes a set of tables that incorporate the MACRS computations rules. The tables consist of a series of annual percentages that are multiplied against the

Table 6–2 MACRS for Business Personalty

If the Recovery Year Is:	*And the Recovery Period Is:* 3-Year	5-Year	7-Year	10-Year	15-Year	20-Year
	the Depreciation Rate Is:					
1	33.33	20.00	14.29	10.00	5.00	3.750
2	44.45	32.00	24.49	18.00	9.50	7.219
3	14.81	19.20	17.49	14.40	8.55	6.677
4	7.41	11.52	12.49	11.52	7.70	6.177
5		11.52	8.93	9.22	6.93	5.713
6		5.76	8.92	7.37	6.23	5.285
7			8.93	6.55	5.90	4.888
8			4.46	6.55	5.90	4.522
9				6.56	5.91	4.462
10				6.55	5.90	4.461
11				3.28	5.91	4.462
12					5.90	4.461
13					5.91	4.462
14					5.90	4.461
15					5.91	4.462
16					2.95	4.461
17						4.462
18						4.461
19						4.462
20						4.461
21						2.231

Applicable depreciation method: 200 or 150 percent
Declining-balance switching to straight-line
Applicable recovery periods: 3, 5, 7, 10, 15, 20 years
Applicable convention: half-year

undepreciated cost basis of the asset to result in the correct amount of depreciation for the year. Table 6–2 contains the annual percentages for the six recovery periods that apply to business personalty. Our business that purchased a $38,000 computer could refer to the table to determine that in the year in which the computer was placed in service, the correct depreciation deduction is $7,600 (20 percent of $38,000). In the second year, the deduction is $12,160 (32 percent of $38,000), and so forth. Note that for each of the recovery periods, the table switches from a declining-balance method to a straight-line method in the year in which the latter method results in a greater deduction (the fourth year for five-year property). Note also that because only one-half year of depreciation is allowed in the year of acquisition, one-half year of depreciation must lag into an extra year in the recovery period. Thus, the $38,000 computer will not be fully depreciated until the sixth year, in which the final depreciation deduction will be $2,188 (5.76 percent of $38,000).

Table 6–3 provides the percentages used to compute annual depreciation for 27.5-year (residential rental properties). Because such properties (as well as properties with a 39-year or 50-year recovery period) must be depreciated on a straight-line basis, this table is of limited benefit in any year other than the year of acquisition or disposition in which the midmonth convention applies. In all other years, depreciation can be calculated by dividing the cost of the property by 27.5.

The Section 179 Election

To relieve small businesses from the burden of maintaining depreciation schedules for tangible personalty,[1] Congress enacted Section 179, which authorizes taxpayers to elect to deduct up to $17,500 of the cost of such property placed in service during the taxable year. Any amount of cost in excess of this dollar limit must be capitalized and recovered through normal MACRS depreciation. The $17,500 maximum annual deduction must be reduced dollar for dollar by the amount of the taxpayer's total cost of tangible personalty placed in service during the year in excess of $200,000. For example, assume Beta Inc. placed in service $213,000 of machinery and equipment during the current year. The corporation may elect to deduct only $4,500 of this cost ($17,500 maximum deduction reduced by $13,000 excess cost). Clearly, the Section 179 election is of no benefit to large businesses that regularly acquire more than $217,500 worth of tangible personalty each year. For small businesses, however, the Section 179 election is enormously beneficial and is made routinely. For businesses operating as partnerships or S corporations, the annual limitation on the Section 179 deduction applies at both the entity and the owner level. Thus, if five individuals are equal partners in a business that acquires $150,000 of tangible personalty in the current year, the partnership may elect to expense only $17,500 of this cost rather than five times this amount.

AMORTIZATION OF INTANGIBLE ASSETS

Businesses may own a variety of assets that have no physical substance but nonetheless represent a valuable property right or economic attribute. The tax basis in such *intangible* assets may be recoverable under some type of *amortization method* authorized by the Internal Revenue Code. As a general rule, amortization is permitted only if the intangible asset has a finite life. The tax basis in equity interests (corporate stocks, bonds, partnership interests, etc.) that have a perpetual life is not amortizable but can be recovered only when the business disposes of the interest. In contrast, the tax basis in intangibles such as self-created patents or copyrights may be deducted ratably over the duration of years that the asset confers an exclusive legal right on its owner. A property lease is another example of an intangible asset with an ascertainable life; the cost of acquiring a lease is generally amortizable over the term of the lease as stated in the lease agreement.

As part of the Revenue Reconciliation Act of 1993, Congress enacted Section 197, which allows businesses to amortize the cost of many types of *purchased* intangible assets ratably over a 15-year period, regardless of the actual length of time over which

[1]The term *personalty* refers to property other than land and permanent attachments thereto.

Table 6–3 MACRS for Residential Rental Property

If the Recovery Year Is	*And the Month in the First Recovery Year the Property Is Placed in Service Is:*											
	1	*2*	*3*	*4*	*5*	*6*	*7*	*8*	*9*	*10*	*11*	*12*
	the Depreciation Rate Is:											
1	3.485	3.182	2.879	2.576	2.273	1.970	1.667	1.364	1.061	0.758	0.455	0.152
2	3.636	3.636	3.636	3.636	3.636	3.636	3.636	3.636	3.636	3.636	3.636	3.636
3	3.636	3.636	3.636	3.636	3.636	3.636	3.636	3.636	3.636	3.636	3.636	3.636
4	3.636	3.636	3.636	3.636	3.636	3.636	3.636	3.636	3.636	3.636	3.636	3.636
5	3.636	3.636	3.636	3.636	3.636	3.636	3.636	3.636	3.636	3.636	3.636	3.636
6	3.636	3.636	3.636	3.636	3.636	3.636	3.636	3.636	3.636	3.636	3.636	3.636
7	3.636	3.636	3.636	3.636	3.636	3.636	3.636	3.636	3.636	3.636	3.636	3.636
8	3.636	3.636	3.636	3.636	3.636	3.636	3.636	3.636	3.636	3.636	3.636	3.636
9	3.636	3.636	3.636	3.636	3.636	3.636	3.636	3.636	3.636	3.636	3.636	3.636
10	3.637	3.637	3.637	3.637	3.637	3.637	3.636	3.636	3.636	3.636	3.636	3.636
11	3.636	3.636	3.636	3.636	3.636	3.636	3.637	3.637	3.637	3.637	3.637	3.637
12	3.637	3.637	3.637	3.637	3.637	3.637	3.636	3.636	3.636	3.636	3.636	3.636
13	3.636	3.636	3.636	3.636	3.636	3.636	3.637	3.637	3.637	3.637	3.637	3.637
14	3.637	3.637	3.637	3.637	3.637	3.637	3.636	3.636	3.636	3.636	3.636	3.636
15	3.636	3.636	3.636	3.636	3.636	3.636	3.637	3.637	3.637	3.637	3.637	3.637
16	3.637	3.637	3.637	3.637	3.637	3.637	3.636	3.636	3.636	3.636	3.636	3.636
17	3.636	3.636	3.636	3.636	3.636	3.636	3.637	3.637	3.637	3.637	3.637	3.637
18	3.637	3.637	3.637	3.637	3.637	3.637	3.636	3.636	3.636	3.636	3.636	3.636
19	3.636	3.636	3.636	3.636	3.636	3.636	3.637	3.637	3.637	3.637	3.637	3.637
20	3.637	3.637	3.637	3.637	3.637	3.637	3.636	3.636	3.636	3.636	3.636	3.636
21	3.636	3.636	3.636	3.636	3.636	3.636	3.637	3.637	3.637	3.637	3.637	3.637
22	3.637	3.637	3.637	3.637	3.637	3.637	3.636	3.636	3.636	3.636	3.636	3.636
23	3.636	3.636	3.636	3.636	3.636	3.636	3.637	3.637	3.637	3.637	3.637	3.637
24	3.637	3.637	3.637	3.637	3.637	3.637	3.636	3.636	3.636	3.636	3.636	3.636
25	3.636	3.636	3.636	3.636	3.636	3.636	3.637	3.637	3.637	3.637	3.637	3.637
26	3.637	3.637	3.637	3.637	3.637	3.637	3.636	3.636	3.636	3.636	3.636	3.636
27	3.636	3.636	3.636	3.636	3.636	3.636	3.637	3.637	3.637	3.637	3.637	3.637
28	1.970	2.273	2.576	2.879	3.182	3.458	3.636	3.636	3.636	3.636	3.636	3.636
29	0.000	0.000	0.000	0.000	0.000	0.000	0.152	0.455	0.758	1.061	1.364	1.667

Applicable depreciation method: straight-line
Applicable recovery period: 27.5 years
Applicable convention: midmonth

the asset is expected to yield an economic benefit to the purchaser. Amortization begins in the month in which the intangible asset is acquired. *Section 197 intangibles* include *goodwill,* defined as the portion of the value of a business attributable to the expectancy that customers will continue to patronize it, and *going concern value,* that portion of the value attributable to the synergism of business assets working in coordination. Under generally accepted accounting principles, capitalized goodwill and going concern value are typically amortizable for financial statement purposes over a 40-year period.

Section 197 also applies to the following categories of assets:

1. Information-based intangibles such as accounting records, operating systems or manuals, customer lists, and advertiser lists.
2. Customer-based or supplier-based intangibles such as favorable contracts with major customers or established relationships with key suppliers.
3. Know-how intangibles such as designs, patterns, formulas, certain patents and copyrights, and other intellectual properties.
4. Work force intangibles such as the specialized skills, education, or loyalty of company employees, or favorable employment contracts.
5. Covenants not to compete and similar arrangements with prior owners of the business.
6. Franchises, trademarks, and trade names.
7. Licenses or permits granted by a governmental unit or agency.

A number of assets are specifically excluded from the definition of Section 197 intangibles. Perhaps the most important exclusion is for computer software that can be readily purchased by the general public, is subject to a nonexclusive license, and has not been substantially modified for a particular business use. The cost of such software may be amortized over a 36-month period.

DEPLETION

As minerals are extracted from the earth and sold, taxpayers owning an economic interest in those minerals are entitled to recover their investment through a depletion deduction. For both accounting and tax purposes, the capitalized costs of locating mineral deposits and removing them from the ground may be deducted over the period during which the mine or well is productive. The annual *cost depletion* deduction is determined by multiplying the unrecovered cost basis in the mine or well by the ratio of the current year's units of production divided by estimated total units of production.

Assume a mining company spent $500,000 for geological surveys, mineral rights, and excavation costs, all of which were capitalized as the tax basis of a new copper mine. At the beginning of the first year of production, the company's engineers estimate the mine should produce 80,000 tons of copper ore. During the year, 20,000 tons of ore are extracted and sold. The company's cost depletion deduction for this year equals $125,000 ($500,000 multiplied by 20,000 tons/80,000 tons). At the beginning of the second year, the engineers revise their estimate of the mine's remaining productivity to 65,000 tons, and during this year 32,000 tons of copper ore are extracted and sold. The cost depletion deduction for the second year is $184,615 ($375,000 unrecovered basis multiplied by 32,000 tons/65,000 tons). By the year in which the mine is no longer productive, the mining company will have recovered its entire $500,000 tax basis through cost depletion deductions.

Percentage Depletion

To encourage the high-risk business activity of mineral exploration and extraction, Congress came up with the idea of *percentage depletion,* an annual deduction based on the gross income generated by a mineral property multiplied by an arbitrary statutory rate. For example, the depletion rate for sulphur and uranium is 22 percent; the rate for gold, silver, copper, iron ore, natural gas, and crude oil is 15 percent, and the rate for asbestos, coal, and lignite is 10 percent. In any year, a business may deduct the *greater* of the cost depletion or percentage depletion attributable to its mineral properties. To illustrate the relationship of percentage depletion and cost depletion, return to our example of the copper mine and add the assumption that the company can sell its ore for $40 per ton in each year of production. The following table shows the computation of the company's annual depletion deduction (the number in bold type in either the cost depletion or the percentage depletion column).

Year	*Estimated Tons of Production (Beginning of year)*	*Annual Production*	*Gross Income*	*Unrecovered Tax Basis in Mine (Beginning of year)*	*Cost Depletion*	*Percentage Depletion (15% of gross income)*
1	80,000	20,000	$ 800,000	$500,000	**$125,000**	$120,000
2	65,000	32,000	1,280,000	375,000	184,615	**192,000**
3	30,000	17,000	680,000	183,000	**103,700**	102,000
4	15,000	18,500	740,000	79,300	79,300	**111,000**
5	5,000	4,000	160,000	-0-	-0-	**24,000**
6	2,500	2,000	80,000	-0-	-0-	**12,000**

Note that in years one through four, the company deducted the greater of cost depletion or percentage depletion and reduced the tax basis in the mine accordingly. But in year four, a curious thing occurs: The company claims a $111,000 depletion deduction that exceeds its unrecovered basis in the mine by $31,700! The tax magic of the percentage depletion deduction is that it is not limited to the capitalized cost of the mineral property. Percentage depletion is available in every year in which the property generates gross income, regardless of the fact that the tax basis in the property has been reduced to zero. In such cases, percentage depletion is not a cost-recovery deduction at all, but a thinly disguised exclusion from gross income.

The availability of percentage depletion has a positive effect on the rate of return generated by investments in mining operations and represents a valuable government subsidy to the extractive industries. Not surprisingly, this highly beneficial provision is subject to a number of statutory limitations. Annual percentage depletion with respect to a mineral property may not exceed 50 percent (100 percent in the case of oil and gas properties) of that year's taxable income attributable to that property. In the oil and gas industry, only *independent producers* and *royalty owners* are entitled to percentage depletion; this tax break is denied to the large integrated companies that extract, refine, and sell oil and gas to retail customers. Furthermore, percentage depletion can be

Figure 6–1 Tax Treatment of Business Expenditures

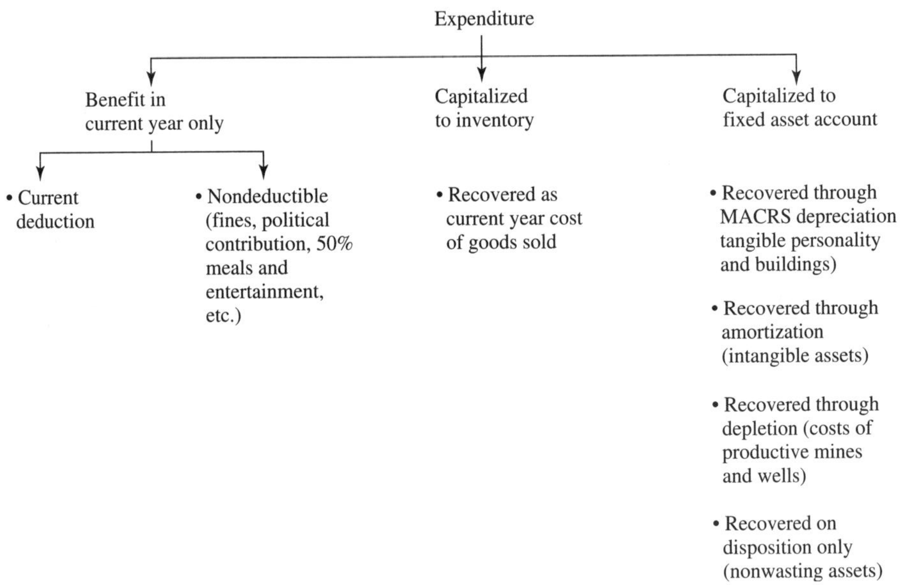

computed only with respect to a maximum average daily production of 1,000 barrels of oil or 6 million cubic feet of natural gas.

CONCLUSION

The after-tax cost of any business expenditure is a function of three key variables: (1) the time period over which the business can claim the expenditure as a deduction, (2) the marginal tax rate in the year or years of the deduction, and (3) the discount rate used to calculate the present value of the tax savings attributable to the deduction. This chapter has focused on the first of these variables by describing the different methods by which taxpayers can compute cost-recovery deductions with respect to their business assets. Figure 6–1 provides an expanded summary of the tax treatment of business expenditures and should help the business manager maintain a perspective on the key roles that depreciation, amortization, and depletion play in the tax planning process.

PROBLEMS AND CASES

1. During the current year, Dan Wright moved out of his personal residence into an apartment and rented the residence to the Myer family under a three-year lease. Dan intends to build a new home for himself and to permanently hold the old residence as rental property. Dan's cost basis in the old residence was $180,000,

and its appraised fair market value on April 6 (the date the Myers signed the lease and moved in) was $135,000 ($110,000 building value and $25,000 land value).

a. Compute Dan's current year depreciation deduction with respect to the residence.

b. How would your answer to *a* change if the original cost of the house and land had been $80,000 and $20,000, respectively?

2. For many years, Carter Chemicals Inc. disposed of its industrial waste by burying it in earthen pits on a tract of undeveloped land owned by the corporation. During the current year, the Environmental Protection Agency determined the buried chemicals were polluting the local water supply and required Carter Chemicals to begin a multiyear cleanup program. During the current year, the corporation spent $789,000 for excavating and transporting contaminated soil to a federally approved dump site and backfilling and replanting the tract of land. To what extent may Carter Chemicals deduct this $789,000 expenditure on its current year tax return?

3. Petra Lee is a professional musician. During the current year, she paid $28,000 for an antique bass viol made by famed instrument maker Francesco Ruggieri in the late 17th century. Petra insured the instrument for $30,000, paying a current year premium of $580. She uses the instrument daily for both practice and performance purposes. To what extent may Petra deduct the $28,580 cost associated with the purchase of the viol on her current year tax return?

4. The Cromwell Ltd. Partnership purchased a 15-year-old apartment complex on June 2 of the current year for $3.8 million. The partnership allocated $800,000 of the purchase price to the land and $3 million to the building. The complex had not been maintained very well by its previous owners, so the partnership spent $49,000 to replace all the carpeting, $18,000 to repaint many of the interior and exterior walls, $8,300 to clean out the gutters, and $22,000 for additional landscaping. How should the partnership treat each of the above expenditures for federal tax purposes?

5. Maria Escalona is a real estate broker who uses her Ford Taurus to show properties to her clients. She also uses the Taurus for personal reasons (grocery shopping, driving her kids to their school activities, etc.). The cost of the automobile was $25,000. During the current year, Maria kept a business journal in which she recorded 26,000 miles of business travel in the Taurus. The total mileage on the car from January 1 through December 31 of the current year was 34,918. To what extent should Maria be entitled to claim a cost-recovery deduction with respect to the Taurus in the current year?

6. Barton, Inc., a calendar year taxpayer, spent $89,000 on new machinery (with a seven-year recovery period for MACRS purposes) that was placed in service on March 9 of the current year.

   a. Assuming the machinery was the only tangible property purchased by Barton Inc. during the year, compute the maximum cost-recovery deduction with respect to the machinery that Barton may claim on its current year tax return.

b. How would your answer to *a* change if the total cost of the machinery had been $204,000?

c. How would your answer to *a* change if the total cost of the machinery had been $225,000?

7. Summa Inc. recently leased commercial office space out of which it will operate one of its business activities. The corporation spent $17,000 on built-in cabinets, bookcases, and lighting fixtures that were necessary to conform the office space to its particular needs. The MACRS recovery period for such assets is seven years. However, Summa has only a four-year lease on the property, after which time all the leasehold improvements will revert to the lessor. Briefly identify and discuss the tax issue suggested by Summa's situation.

8. Ellis Designs Inc., a calendar year taxpayer, purchased new business equipment for $80,000 and placed it in service on February 1 of the current year. The corporation determined the equipment has an estimated useful life of 144 months (12 years) and no salvage value and used a straight-line method to compute depreciation expense for financial statement purposes.

   a. Compute book depreciation expense for the current year.

   b. Assuming the property has a five-year MACRS recovery period and no Section 179 election was made, compute tax depreciation for the current year.

   c. Is the book/tax difference in depreciation a permanent difference or a timing difference? Briefly explain your answer.

9. The STV Partnership purchased a light truck for use in its business during the current year. The cost of the truck was $41,000 and it has a five-year recovery period for MACRS purposes. The truck was placed in service by the partnership on November 29. STV purchased other tangible personalty throughout the year at a total cost of $412,000.

   a. Compute the partnership's current year depreciation deduction with respect to the truck.

   b. Compute the partnership's depreciation deduction with respect to the truck for the second and third years of the recovery period.

   c. The partnership sold the truck on March 19 of the fourth year in the recovery period. How much depreciation may STV claim with respect to the truck in this year?

10. ACME Products Inc. constructed a new manufacturing plant for a total cost of $7,615,000 and placed it in service on October 29 of the current year. To finance the construction, ACME took out a $6 million, 30-year mortgage on the property. Compute ACME's depreciation deductions with respect to the manufacturing plant for the first, second, and third years of its operation.

11. In the current year, Bob Marks purchased a business from David Lennox for a lump-sum price of $750,000. The business consisted of $43,700 of accounts receivable; inventory (appraised value of $237,000); office supplies (appraised value of $31,000); furniture and fixtures (appraised value of $325,000); and a favorable lease on commercial office space with a remaining term of 39 months.

Bob determined that the value of this lease was $20,000. The purchase contract stipulated that David Lennox would refrain from engaging in a competitive business activity in the immediate geographic location for two calendar years after the year of sale. Discuss how Bob Marks will recover the cost of each of the assets acquired as part of the business purchase.

12. On May 12 of the current year, Jane Slack purchased a taxi business from Manuel Munoz for a lump-sum price of $60,000. The business consisted of a two-year-old taxi worth $19,000, Manuel's license to operate a cab in New York City, and Manuel's list of regular clients. The taxi has 175,000 miles on the odometer, and Jane estimates it should last for no more than 18 months before she will have to replace it. The cab license has no expiration date. Jane thinks the customer list will be valuable to her for only about six months, after which time she should have established her own client base. Based on these facts, compute Jane's cost-recovery deductions in the year she purchases the business, assuming she does not elect Section 179 expensing with respect to the taxi's cost.
13. Robby Thomas wants to buy the business operated by the Sloan Corporation. Ted and Margaret Sloan, the sole shareholders of the corporation, have offered to sell their stock to Robby for $250,000. They also would be willing to have their corporation sell all its operating assets to Robby for $300,000. Briefly discuss any potential differences in Robby's before-tax and after-tax costs of:

    a. A purchase of 100 percent of the stock in the Sloan Corporation.
    b. A purchase of all of Sloan's operating assets.
14. During the current year, A&Z Inc. spent $335,000 of capitalized costs to develop a uranium mine in southern Utah. At the beginning of the first year of production, the corporation's geologists estimated that 250,000 tons of ore could be extracted from the mine. During this year, 48,000 tons were mined and sold; A&Z's gross revenues from the sales totaled $575,000, and its current year operating expenses for the mine were $148,000. Based on these facts, calculate the current year taxable income generated by the uranium mine.
15. In what fundamental way does percentage depletion differ from every other cost recovery method? Explain briefly.

Case 6–1

Weems Inc. needs a new piece of equipment to be used in its manufacturing process. The corporation could purchase the equipment in the current year for $300,000. This fixed asset would have a seven-year MACRS recovery period, could be used in the manufacturing process for eight years, and could be sold as salvage in the ninth year for $15,000. As an alternative, Weems Inc. could lease the equipment for eight years at an annual rental of $50,000.

Based on these facts, which option (buy or lease) minimizes Weems Inc.'s after-tax cost of obtaining the equipment? In making your calculations, disregard any financing costs and assume

Weems is in a 35 percent marginal tax bracket and uses a 6 percent discount rate to compute the present value of its future cash flows.

Case 6–2

Bart Anderson runs a construction equipment rental yard. He owns five aging light-duty trucks that have been fully depreciated for tax purposes. Bart believes these trucks will last for five more years with $4,250 of annual maintenance each. He could sell these trucks in the current year for $4,000 each and buy five new trucks for $22,000 each. Maintenance on each new truck would be only $1,000 per year. Both the old and new trucks would generate the same amount of revenue over the five-year period (current year and four subsequent years).

Bart operates his business as a sole proprietorship and faces a 36 percent marginal tax rate. In the current year, he will not purchase any tangible business assets other than the trucks. He will use the Section 179 election in computing his current year cost-recovery deduction with respect to the trucks. At the end of the five-year period, Bart estimates he could sell the new trucks for $8,000 each. Based on these facts, would Bart minimize his after-tax costs with respect to his fleet of trucks by keeping the old trucks or selling them and buying new trucks? In making your calculations, disregard any financing costs and assume a 6 percent discount rate to compute the present value of future cash flows.

CHAPTER 7

Tax Consequences of Property Dispositions

The tax consequences of dispositions of tangible and intangible property interests are among the most complex in the Internal Revenue Code. This chapter focuses on the set of rules governing the taxation of gains and losses generated by property dispositions, as well as the tax planning dangers and opportunities created by these rules. The chapter begins with a review of the realization criterion, the concept of tax basis, and the types of realized loss that generally may be recognized for tax purposes. The limitations on the deductibility of capital losses and the taxability of net capital gains are then analyzed. The term *capital asset* is defined, and the peculiar role of Section 1231 business assets is explained. The chapter concludes with a discussion of tax planning techniques based on the unique treatment of capital gains and losses.

REALIZATION AND RECOGNITION REVISITED

From an accounting perspective, any increase or decrease in the value of property over time does not represent gain or loss until the owner converts the property into a new and different asset through an external transaction with another party and the change in value is *realized*. For tax purposes, gain or loss attributable to a fluctuation in property value must be realized before it can be *recognized*; that is, included in the computation of current year taxable income. This linkage between accounting realization and tax recognition is presumed unless explicitly severed by a specific provision of the tax law. In this chapter, we will look at dispositions of property that trigger both realization and recognition of gain or loss. In Chapter 8, we will examine a number of transactions involving dispositions in which realized gain or loss is not recognized for current tax purposes.

Relief of Debt as Amount Realized on Disposition

The amount of gain or loss realized on the disposition of property is measured by the difference between the amount realized and the owner's adjusted basis in the property. *Amount realized* equals the amount of cash plus the fair market value of any noncash assets or services received in exchange for the property. If the owner of property is relieved of debt because of the property's disposition, the relief is considered an additional amount realized on disposition. Suppose Len Jackson owns a tract of investment land for which he paid $400,000 and which is subject to a mortgage of $275,000. The mortgage is *recourse debt*, which means Len is personally liable for its repayment. In the current year, Len receives an offer from an unrelated third party to purchase the land for $500,000. The purchaser will assume Len's mortgage (with the approval of the creditor) and pay him the $225,000 balance of the purchase price in cash. Len's amount realized on sale is $500,000 and he has a realized gain of $100,000.

Amount realized:		
Cash	$225,000	
Relief of debt	275,000	
		$500,000
Tax basis in land		(400,000)
Gain realized		$100,000

Note that the inclusion of debt relief in the amount realized on the disposition of an asset is consistent with the tax rule that the cost basis of property includes any amount of debt incurred by the buyer to finance the acquisition.

Let's change the facts in the above example by assuming that the value of the land has declined severely and Len is financially unable to make interest and principal payments on the mortgage. The creditor forecloses and subsequently sells the land at auction for $245,000, applying the sales price against the unpaid mortgage. Len is legally required to pay the $30,000 balance of the debt out of his own pocket. In this case, Len's amount realized on the disposition is $245,000, and he has a realized loss of $155,000.

Amount realized:	
Sales price applied to debt	$245,000
Tax basis in land	(400,000)
Loss realized	($155,000)

What if, after the foreclosure, the creditor decides not to pursue its legal claim to an additional $30,000 from Len? In this case, Len would recognize $30,000 of forgiveness-of-indebtedness income. This last twist of the facts does not affect the tax consequences of Len's disposition of the land.

Nonrecourse Debt. The rule that relief of a liability is included in the amount realized on the disposition of property encompasses both recourse and nonrecourse debt. *Nonrecourse debt* is secured only by the specific property that serves as collateral; the debtor is not personally liable for its repayment. Consider the situation of Marco Inc., which owns depreciable real estate with a $410,000 adjusted basis ($610,000 original cost less $200,000 depreciation). The land is subject to a $500,000 nonrecourse mortgage. First let's suppose Marco sells the land for its current value of $700,000. The purchaser pays Marco $200,000 cash and takes the land subject to the mortgage. In this case, Marco realizes $700,000 on the disposition of the land and the corporation has a $290,000 gain.

Amount realized:		
Cash	$200,000	
Relief of debt	500,000	
		$700,000
Tax basis of real estate:		
Cost	$610,000	
Depreciation	(200,000)	
		(410,000)
Gain realized		$290,000

Now suppose the value of the land has fallen to $440,000. In real estate jargon, the land is now *underwater* (i.e., its value is less than the encumbering mortgage). Marco has no economic incentive to continue to service the $500,000 mortgage to maintain its ownership interest in an asset worth $440,000. Accordingly, Marco allows the creditor to foreclose on the land. Even though the land is worth only $440,000, the creditor has no legal right to any additional payment from Marco and incurs a $60,000 loss on the financing arrangement. And what of Marco? Because the corporation has been relieved of $500,000 of debt upon the disposition, Marco realizes a $90,000 gain.

Amount realized:		
Relief of debt		$500,000
Tax basis of real estate:		
Cost	$610,000	
Depreciation	(200,000)	
		(410,000)
Gain realized		$ 90,000

This certainly may seem a peculiar result—a realized gain when Marco has surrendered an asset to a creditor and has received no cash or property in return. Peculiar or not, such *phantom gain* is included in Marco's current year gross income and subject to the federal income tax.

ADDITIONAL BASIS RULES

The computation of the correct amount of gain or loss realized on the disposition of property depends on the proper determination of the owner's adjusted basis in the property. The basis of property is initially established upon its acquisition. If property is acquired by purchase, the price paid represents the owner's *cost basis*. As we learned in Chapter 6, this basis is increased by any subsequent capital improvements to the property. If the tax basis in the property is depreciable, amortizable, or depletable, the owner will recover his investment in the property over time in the form of annual cost recovery deductions. In such case, the initial cost basis is adjusted downward by the amount of the annual deductions until it is reduced to zero.

Taxpayers who own equity stocks or shares in mutual funds should pay close attention to the cost basis in these investments. If a taxpayer elects to have any dividends declared on her existing shares used to purchase more shares, the *reinvested dividends* become the taxpayer's cost basis of the new shares. Because investors make no direct cash payments for these shares, they may overlook the additional basis in computing gain or loss realized on future stock sales. In order to help their clients avoid this mistake, many brokerage houses and security firms now maintain records of the cost basis of the various securities included in their clients' investment portfolios.

The Tax Basis of Gifted Property

Taxpayers may acquire assets other than by purchase. For example, an individual may receive property in the form of a gift. In such case, the adjusted basis of the property in the hands of the *donor* (the person who made the gift) generally becomes the basis of the property in the hands of the *donee* (the recipient of the gift). To illustrate the tax implications of this *carryover basis* rule, let's suppose Mrs. Stone transfers the title in certain real estate with a cost basis of $100,000 and a recently appraised fair market value of $150,000 to her son Brian as a gift. The disposition of property by gift is not a realization event for tax purposes, and Mrs. Stone is not required to recognize the $50,000 appreciation in the real estate's value as gross income. The receipt of the gift does not trigger income recognition to Brian—gifts are a specific exclusion from gross income. However, Brian's tax basis in the gifted land is its $100,000 carryover basis from his mother, not its $150,000 fair market value. If Brian eventually sells the land for $150,000, he will recognize a $50,000 taxable gain. Consequently, although his mother's investment in the land is permanently excluded from Brian's gross income, the appreciation in the land will be taxed to Brian in the year it is realized.

While the tax law allows the potential income represented by the appreciation in the value of gifted property to be shifted from a donor to a donee, it does not permit the shifting of a loss represented by a decline in value. Assume the fair market value of the land that Mrs. Stone gave Brian was only $90,000 at date of gift. If Brian subsequently sells the property for *less than* this value, a corollary to the carryover basis rule limits his basis to the *lesser* of the donor's basis or fair market value at date of gift. To illustrate, if Brian sells the property for $85,000, his recognized loss is only $5,000, not $15,000. If, however, he eventually sells the property for more than $100,000, his gain will equal only the excess of the amount realized over this carryover basis. The end result of this rather confusing rule is that Brian can never recognize the $10,000 decline in value of the gifted land as a loss. And what if he sells the land for more than its $90,000 value at date of gift but less then the $100,000 carryover basis? In this twilight zone of the tax law, Brian recognizes neither gain nor loss on the disposition of the land.

The Tax Basis of Inherited Property

When an individual dies, all property rights owned by such individual are transferred to other individuals or institutions under the terms of the decedent's last will and testament or under state intestacy law if the decedent died without a valid will. The disposition of property at death is not a realization event for tax purposes, so any difference between the value of assets transferred at death and the decedent's adjusted basis in the assets is not recognized as gain or loss on the decedent's final income tax return. On the other side of the transaction, inherited property is specifically excluded from the gross income of the decedent's legatees, devisees, or heirs-at-law. Under one of the most controversial rules in the Internal Revenue Code, these new owners generally take a tax basis equal to the property's fair market value as of the date of the decedent's death. This *fair-market-value basis* rule means that any unrealized gain or loss inherent in the property simply disappears at death, or, in a more macabre analogy, is buried along with the decedent.

For income tax planning purposes, the significance of this basis rule can hardly be overemphasized. Reconsider the case of Mrs. Stone and her son Brian. If Mrs. Stone were to devise the land in which she had a cost basis of $100,000 to Brian on her death, and if the land's appraised value was $150,000 on that sad day, Brian's basis in the land would be *stepped up* to $150,000. He could then sell the land immediately after inheriting it, recognizing not a penny of income. From the IRS's viewpoint, $50,000 of economic gain has permanently escaped taxation. Of course, if Mrs. Stone's land had declined in value so it was worth only $90,000 on her death, the $10,000 unrealized loss would similarly expire. To prevent this undesirable tax consequence, Mrs. Stone should be advised to simply sell the land to an unrelated third party before her death, thus realizing the loss and securing the value of any resulting tax deduction.

Because of the fair-market-value basis rule, persons of substantial means have a strong incentive to retain appreciated assets until death so as to pass them on to younger-generation family members with a stepped-up tax basis; this tendency is commonly referred to as the *locked-in effect*. An in-depth discussion of the estate planning implications of this effect is included in Chapter 14. The fair-market-value basis rule has been part of the tax law since its inception and has been consistently criticized as a loophole available only to those families with accumulated wealth. The rule is costly; the revenue loss to the Treasury attributable to the step up of basis at death is estimated at over $50 billion every year. As part of the Tax Reform Act of 1976, Congress repealed the rule, replacing it with a carryover basis provision that would have resulted in the preservation of both unrealized gains and losses in property transferred at death. For a number of political and administrative reasons, the carryover basis provision was deemed unworkable and after just two years was retroactively repealed. Bruised by the failure of this reform initiative and for lack of a better alternative, Congress reestablished the familiar if theoretically flawed rule that inherited property takes a basis equal to its fair market value as of the date of the decedent's death.

Basis Adjustments to Interests in Passthrough Entities

In Chapter 5, we learned that a regular corporation is an independent taxpayer for federal income tax purposes, separate and distinct from its shareholders. In contrast, partnerships and S corporations are treated as conduits; the income or loss items generated by these passthrough entities are allocated to the various partners and shareholders and included in their current year taxable income computations. These items represent increases or decreases in the owners' after-tax investment in the passthrough entity and are recorded as positive or negative adjustments to the owners' tax bases in their equity interests. Specifically, a partner's basis in a partnership interest or a shareholder's basis in S corporation stock is increased by any pro rata share of passthrough income or gain and decreased by any pro rata share of passthrough deduction or loss. If the owner recoups a portion of his or her investment by receiving a cash or property distribution from the entity, the tax basis in the entity must be reduced accordingly.

To illustrate these basis adjustment rules, assume Dale and Mary invest $30,000 and $70,000 cash, respectively, for a 30 percent and a 70 percent interest in M&D Inc., an S corporation. Assume further that (1) both shareholders and their corporation are calendar year taxpayers, (2) M&D Inc. recognized a $60,000 business loss in its first year of operations, and (3) M&D made no distributions to its shareholders during the year. Because M&D is a passthrough entity, Dale and Mary reported and deducted respective business losses of $18,000 and $42,000 on their Form 1040s for the year. They also reduced their tax bases in their corporate stock by the decline in the amount of their investment in M&D Inc. represented by the business losses.

	Dale's Stock Basis	*Mary's Stock Basis*
Initial cash contribution	$30,000	$70,000
Year 1:		
Partner's share of:		
Business loss	(18,000)	(42,000)
Year 2:		
Partner's share of:		
Business income	10,500	24,500
Cash distributions	(3,000)	(7,000)
Tax basis at the beginning of Year 3	$19,500	$45,500

Further assume M&D earned $35,000 of business income in its second taxable year and made a $3,000 and $7,000 cash distribution respectively to Dale and Mary. In this year, the two shareholders reported and paid tax on their $10,500 and $24,500 pro rata shares of M&D's income and increased their stock bases by identical amounts. They also reduced their bases by the amount of cash withdrawn from the business. Conceptually the *net* increases in their bases for the year ($7,500 for Dale and $17,500 for Mary) represent the amount of undistributed business income that the two shareholders have recognized currently but have allowed to remain invested in the corporate enterprise. At the beginning of the third taxable year, Dale's basis in her M&D stock is $19,500 and Mary's basis is $45,500.

THE TAX TREATMENT OF CAPITAL LOSSES

When a taxpayer realizes a gain on the disposition of any type of asset, that gain must be recognized for tax purposes unless the taxpayer can find a statutory rule that exempts the gain from current taxation. In contrast, when a taxpayer realizes a loss on an asset disposition, the loss is not deductible unless the Internal Revenue Code specifically says so. As a general rule of thumb, losses realized by individual taxpayers on the disposition of personal assets are nondeductible, while losses realized on the disposition of investment or business assets are deductible. For corporate taxpayers (who have only a business persona), realized losses are generally deductible in the year incurred.

These broad rules are overlaid with an additional limitation on the deductibility of capital losses incurred by both individual and corporate taxpayers. *A capital loss can be deducted only to the extent of capital gains recognized by the taxpayer.* If a taxpayer realizes an amount of capital loss in excess of current year capital gains, the excess loss does not reduce current year taxable income.

A *capital* gain or loss is defined as the gain or loss realized on the sale or exchange of a capital asset. A gain or loss that does not fall within this definition is referred to as *ordinary* gain or loss. Note the two components of the capital gain or loss definition. First, the asset involved in the realization transaction must be a capital asset. This crucial term is defined in a subsequent segment of this chapter. Second, the gain or loss must be triggered by a sale or exchange. If a capital asset is disposed of in a transaction other than a sale or exchange, any realized gain or loss is ordinary. For instance, in the unusual case in which a taxpayer formally relinquishes his legal claim to a capital asset, the taxpayer may recognize any unrecovered tax basis in the asset as an ordinary *abandonment loss*.

Individual Capital Losses

The tax law relaxes the primary limitation on the deductibility of capital losses by allowing an individual taxpayer to deduct up to $3,000 of the excess of current year capital losses over current year capital gains against any other type of income. Any amount of nondeductible capital loss is carried forward indefinitely into the subsequent years. Consider the case of Mr. Baxter who in the current year sells two capital assets he has held for investment purposes, recognizing a $13,000 gain on the first sale and a $7,500 loss on the second. The capital loss is fully deductible above-the-line, leaving Mr. Baxter with $5,500 of net capital gain included in his current year adjusted gross income.

Capital gain	$13,000
Capital loss deductible to extent of capital gain	(7,500)
Net capital gain included in AGI	$ 5,500

If we alter the facts so that Mr. Baxter's loss on the second sale was $22,000, he may deduct $13,000 of the loss because of his current year capital gain plus another $3,000. The $6,000 nondeductible capital loss becomes a carryforward into the following year.

Capital gain	$13,000
Capital loss deductible to extent of capital gain	(13,000)
Additional deduction	(3,000)
Net capital loss included in AGI	($3,000)
Capital loss carryforward into next year ($22,000 – $16,000 current year deduction)	($6,000)

Assume that in the following year, Mr. Baxter does not sell any capital assets, but is allocated a $1,200 capital gain from a partnership in which he owns an interest. He may deduct $1,200 of his capital loss carryforward because of this gain plus another $3,000, thereby reducing the carryforward to $1,800.

Capital gain allocated from partnership	$1,200
Capital loss carryforward deductible to extent of capital gain	(1,200)
Additional deduction	(3,000)
Net capital loss included in AGI	($3,000)
Capital loss carryforward into next year ($6,000 – $4,200 current year deduction)	($1,800)

For an individual taxpayer who recognizes a significant capital loss and who has no stream of current or future capital gains against which to deduct the loss, the $3,000 exception to the capital loss limitation is small consolation. If Mr. Baxter recognized a current year capital loss of $90,000 and never recognized another capital gain, he would have to live 30 years to reap the full tax benefit of the loss!

Worthless Securities. An individual who owns a business or investment asset that has become worthless in the current year obviously cannot find an independent buyer who will pay anything for the valueless property. Because of the lack of a sale or exchange, the individual can't actually realize the economic loss inherent in the asset and may claim an ordinary abandonment loss equal to the unrecovered basis of the asset. In the case of *worthless securities*, the statute prevents this result by stipulating that the economic loss be treated as derived from a sale of the security on the last day of the taxable year. This fictitious sale (for an amount realized of zero) triggers a capital loss equal to the investor's basis in the worthless security. For purposes of this rule, securities include (1) corporate stocks and (2) bonds, debentures, or other forms of indebtedness issued by corporations or governments with interest coupons or in registered form.

Section 1244 Stock. Equity investments in new corporate entities typically involve a higher degree of risk than investments in well-established corporations with proven track records of profitability. Individuals may be dissuaded from investing in speculative, start-up businesses because of the higher probability of loss coupled with the fact that such loss will be capital in nature. To encourage the flow of capital into new corporate ventures, Congress decided to bend the rules governing the tax consequences of losses realized by individual taxpayers on the disposition of *Section 1244 stock.* Married individuals filing a joint return may deduct a maximum of $100,000 of such losses as ordinary losses each year. Unmarried taxpayers or married taxpayers filing a separate return may deduct a maximum of $50,000 annually. Any realized loss in excess of these limits retains its character as capital loss.

As a general rule, the first $1 million of common or preferred stock issued by a corporation that derives more than 50 percent of its annual gross receipts from the conduct of an active business qualifies as Section 1244 stock. This label applies only to stock issued directly by the corporation to an investor in exchange for money or property. In other words, an individual cannot obtain Section 1244 stock by purchasing it from another shareholder or receiving it as a gift or inheritance. The Section 1244 label has no downside to the investor. If the fledgling corporate venture is a success and the stock is eventually sold at a gain, that gain is capital. If the stock is sold at a loss or becomes worthless, a significant portion (if not all) of such loss will yield an immediate tax benefit in the form of a deduction against any other source of the investor's gross income for the year.

Corporate Capital Losses

The tax law cuts no slack for corporations insofar as the limitation on the deductibility of capital losses. Corporate capital losses are deductible only against corporate capital gains. However, a corporation may carry a current year net capital loss back to its three previous taxable years and forward for five taxable years, deducting the net loss against any net capital gain included in corporate taxable income for the year. To illustrate this rule, suppose that Rio Inc. sells two capital assets during the current year, recognizing a $50,000 gain on the first sale and an $85,000 loss on the second. Rio may deduct $50,000 of the capital loss against the capital gain, thereby eliminating the gain from current year taxable income. However, the $35,000 net capital loss is nondeductible and does not further affect the computation of the current year taxable income of the corporation. Rio's taxable income for its three previous years is as follows:

	19x1	*19x2*	*19x3*
Ordinary income	$600,000	$400,000	$730,000
Net capital gain	-0-	10,000	12,000
Total taxable income	$600,000	$410,000	$742,000

Because it had no net capital gain in the earliest year of the carryback period (19x1), Rio cannot deduct any portion of its capital loss carryback in that year. The corporation may deduct $10,000 and $12,000 of the carryback against the taxable income reported in the second and third years of the carryback period and file for a refund of tax based on the reduced tax liabilities for those years. The $13,000 of Rio's current year net capital loss not deducted as a carryback may be carried forward and netted against any capital gains that the corporation recognizes during its next five taxable years.

Worthless Securities in Operating Subsidiaries. Corporations owning securities that become worthless during the taxable year are subject to the same rule that applies to individuals—the securities are treated as having been sold on the last day of the taxable year. If, however, the worthless security is in an *affiliated corporation*, the security is not considered a capital asset. An affiliated corporation is any 80 percent controlled subsidiary that has always derived more than 90 percent of its annual gross receipts from the conduct of an active trade or business.

Assume Acme Inc. owns 10 percent of the outstanding stock in Beta Inc. with a basis of $4 million and 100 percent of the outstanding stock of Zeta Inc. with a basis of $15 million. During the current year, the businesses operated by Beta and Zeta fail, and the stock in both corporations becomes worthless. Acme Inc. is treated as having sold its Beta and Zeta stock on the last day of its taxable year for an amount realized of zero. The $4 million loss attributable to the Beta stock is a capital loss to Acme. But if Zeta Inc. has always been an operating subsidiary (i.e., meets the 90 percent gross receipts test), Acme may claim the $15 million loss attributable to the Zeta stock as an ordinary deduction.

THE TAXATION OF NET CAPITAL GAINS

Even the most unsophisticated businessperson has a vague perception that the tax law favors capital gains over other types of income. In the previous section, you learned that capital gains have the unique capacity to absorb capital losses, thereby producing a current tax benefit from an otherwise nondeductible loss. This characteristic in and of itself makes capital gains a very desirable type of income. And for corporate taxpayers, this is the only salutary characteristic of capital gains. Any amount of net capital gain—the excess of current year capital gain over current year capital loss—is taxed at the same rate as any other type of corporate income.

For individual taxpayers, net capital gains have an additional charm in that they are taxed at a maximum rate of 28 percent rather than at the regular rates on ordinary income, which can be as high as 39.6 percent. This preferential rate applies only to net *long-term* capital gains, which are those realized from the sale or exchange of assets that the taxpayer has held for at least 12 months. Any discussion of the technical interplay between short-term and long-term capital gains and losses is beyond the scope of this text and is of little practical interest in the tax planning process. Suffice it to say that individual investors or business managers who are aware of this favorable tax rate and who have a lick of sense make sure they hold their capital assets for at least a year before realizing their gains. Accordingly, for the remainder of this text, all references to capital gains will imply long-term gains.

As an example of the quantitative impact of this preferential tax rate, assume Ms. Samms, a single taxpayer, has taxable income for 1996 of $125,000, all of which is ordinary. Her tax liability on this income is $34,070 and her marginal rate on the income in excess of $121,300 is 36 percent. If Ms. Samms' taxable income consisted of only $95,000 of ordinary income and a $30,000 net capital gain, her tax bill would total only $32,985, $24,585 of tax at the normal rates on her ordinary income and $8,400 of tax on her capital gain at a 28 percent rate. Note that the preferential capital gains rate benefits only those individuals whose marginal tax rate exceeds 28 percent. For 1996, single individuals will not benefit unless their taxable income exceeds $58,150, married couples filing jointly or separately will not benefit unless their income exceeds $96,900 or $48,450, respectively, and heads of household will not benefit unless their income exceeds $83,050.

What is the theoretical justification for a tax rate on individual capital gains that is less than the tax rate on other types of income? This tax policy question is particularly relevant in assessing the vertical equity of the income tax system because capital gains are recognized most frequently by upper-income taxpayers who own investment assets. One argument in favor of the tax concession is that capital gains are not recognized annually over the years during which they economically accrue, but instead are bunched into the single year in which the capital asset is sold and the gain is realized. Given a progressive tax rate structure, such *bunching* could cause the gain to be taxed at a higher rate than if the gain had been taxed in increments over the years during which the capital asset was appreciating in value. A preferential rate on capital gains offsets the artificially high tax caused by the bunching phenomenon. Critics of the preferential rate are quick to point out that this argument ignores the tax benefit of the deferral of taxation of capital gains until the year of realization, a benefit that in some measure compensates for the detriment of bunching.

A second argument is that the 28 percent maximum rate on capital gains counteracts inflation. In Chapter 2, we learned that the tax basis in an asset is not adjusted for changes in the purchasing power of the dollar. If a taxpayer holds an asset for a significant time, the amount of current dollars realized on sale of the asset may exceed the asset's historic cost basis in strictly monetary terms, but some or even all the gain realized may be inflationary rather than a true increase in the economic value of the asset. While the problem of the taxation of inflationary gains is very real, a single rate that applies indiscriminately to all capital gains is a crude solution. Congress has occasionally considered the notion of indexing the tax basis of all assets to reflect changes in the value of the dollar, but has been dissuaded from this theoretically sound idea by the complexity it would add to the tax law.

Many tax theorists contend that the preferential rate on capital gains encourages the mobility of capital. Without a tax break on realized gains, taxpayers owning highly appreciated capital assets may be unduly reluctant to liquidate or convert such assets because of the tax cost. This *locked-in* effect distorts financial decision making and impinges the efficiency of the stock and bond markets. A variation on this theme is that the preferential rate mitigates the risk associated with many capital investments and thereby increases the supply of venture capital to the nation's economy. This hypothetical influx of capital spurs long-term economic growth and creates new jobs.

Qualified Small-Business Stock

In 1993, Congress acted on its belief that a preferential rate on capital gains stimulates investment in new business ventures by enacting Section 1202. This code section provides for an exclusion of 50 percent of any gain realized by a noncorporate taxpayer on the sale or exchange of *qualified small-business stock*. The amount of gain eligible for the exclusion is limited to the greater of (1) 10 times the taxpayer's basis in the stock or (2) $10 million.

Qualified stock must be acquired directly from a small-business corporation in exchange for money, property, or services provided to the corporation. An investor cannot obtain small-business stock by purchasing it from another shareholder or receiving it as a gift or inheritance. Moreover, the exclusion is available only if the taxpayer held the stock for more than five years before its sale or exchange.

The definition of a Section 1202 *small-business corporation* is quite involved. Basically, the corporation must be a regular corporation (not an S corporation), have less than $50 million of gross assets as of the date the stock is issued, and use at least 80 percent by value of its tangible and intangible assets in the active conduct of a trade or business. A corporation licensed by the Small Business Administration as a specialized small-business investment company (SSBIC) is treated as meeting this active business test. In addition, the corporation can't be involved in the performance of professional services, or in a financial, leasing, real estate, farming, mining, or hospitality business.

The combined effect of the new 50 percent Section 1202 exclusion and the 28 percent maximum rate on capital gains can reduce the effective tax rate on gains realized from the sale of qualifying small-business stock to a tempting 14 percent. Clearly, the exclusion will play an important role in the tax planning process for years to come. However, because the exclusion applies only to dispositions of stock issued after August 10, 1993, and held by the investor for at least five years after issuance, it will have no impact on individual tax liabilities until 1998.

Capital Gains as Investment Income

Readers may recall from Chapter 3 that individuals may deduct investment interest expense only to the extent of any net investment income recognized during the taxable year. When an individual recognizes a capital gain on the sale of an investment asset, the tax law offers an interesting choice. The individual may elect to treat all or any portion of such gain as investment income, thereby securing a deduction for investment interest to the extent of such gain. But in making this election, the individual must forfeit the 28 percent preferential tax rate on the gain. This rule prevents taxpayers from deriving a double benefit from their capital gains. The gains can increase the investment interest expense deduction for the year or be taxed at a 28 percent top rate, but not both.

CAPITAL ASSET DEFINED

Section 1221 of the Internal Revenue Code defines capital assets by exception when it states that all assets are capital assets unless they fall into one of the five following categories:

1. Inventory items or property held by the taxpayer primarily for sale to customers in the ordinary course of business.
2. Accounts or notes receivable acquired in the ordinary course of business (i.e., acquired on the sale of inventory or for the performance of services).
3. Real or depreciable property used in a trade or business (including rental real estate) and intangible business assets amortizable under Section 197.
4. A copyright, literary, musical, or artistic composition, a letter or memorandum, or similar property held by a taxpayer whose personal efforts created the property or a person to whom the property was gifted by the creator. Note that patents are conspicuously absent from this category.
5. Certain publications of the United States government.

Any asset that does not fit into one of these categories is, by default, capital in nature. Consequently, any asset held by an individual for personal or investment reasons is a capital asset. Any business asset owned by an individual, partnership, or corporation that is not an account receivable, an inventory item, depreciable personalty, realty, or a Section 197 intangible is a capital asset.

Capital asset status is not determined by the nature or character of the asset itself, but by the use for which the asset is held by its owner. To illustrate this crucial distinction, let's look a bit closer at the fourth category of capital asset listed above. Assume a sculptor purchases $50 worth of clay and creates a work of art that she sells for $5,000 to a corporate purchaser. The corporation uses the sculpture as decoration in the lobby of its corporate headquarters. This work of art is not a capital asset in the hands of its creator, so the sculptor's $4,950 gain realized on the sale is ordinary income. In contrast, the sculpture is a capital asset to the corporation because it is not a depreciable business asset. As a result, if the corporation were to sell the sculpture, any realized gain or loss would be capital.

Individuals who are not licensed real estate brokers but who make occasional sales of undeveloped real property often find themselves in a dispute with the IRS concerning the nature of the gain realized on the sale. The individual invariably maintains that he or she held the land as an investment (i.e., a capital asset) and that the gain on sale should properly be characterized as capital gain. The IRS counterclaims that the taxpayer is engaging in a real estate business and held the land primarily for sale to customers in the regular course of such business. As a result, the gain on sale should be ordinary income. Such disputes have frequently culminated in litigation. In cases in which the real estate sale in question was an unusual or isolated occurrence, the courts have tended to side with the taxpayer. If, however, the taxpayer engaged in similar transactions on a regular and frequent basis or improved and subdivided the land prior to sale, the courts have been willing to agree with the IRS that the taxpayer is in the business of selling real estate and that the land is a noncapital inventory asset.

Fortunately for those who play the securities markets, the IRS has not taken this combative stance with regard to investors who buy and sell publicly traded stocks and bonds. Regardless of the frequency, regularity, or magnitude of such sales, investors can rest assured that all realized gains (and losses) are capital in nature. The reason for such assurance is a matter of semantics. Because individuals sell marketable securities indirectly through a broker rather than directly to other investors, they are not deemed to be holding the securities for sale *to customers* within the meaning of Section 1221. Therefore, only professional securities dealers and underwriters recognize ordinary income from trading transactions.

Section 1231 Assets

The exclusion of business inventories and accounts receivable from the definition of capital assets is self-explanatory. Virtually every business is based on the routine rendering of services or the sale of merchandise to clients or customers. The profit derived from both these activities should be taxed as ordinary income. For consistency's sake, the sale of accounts receivable generated by these activities should also result in ordinary income. In contrast, the exclusion of real or depreciable property used in a trade or business from the capital asset definition seems counterintuitive to most businesspeople. In fact, the term *capital asset* as used in the accounting and economics literature expressly refers to tangible, long-term balance sheet properties such as office or factory buildings, machinery, equipment, computers, furniture, and fixtures.

By deliberately classifying business realty and depreciable business personalty as noncapital, Congress was not expressing any philosophic dissatisfaction with the traditional business concept of capital assets. Instead, Congress was trying to ensure that losses realized upon the sale of such assets would not be subject to the onerous limitation on the deductibility of capital losses. To achieve this result, Congress enacted Section 1231, which applies to real and depreciable assets used in a trade or business and Section 197 intangibles. The basic operating rule of this section is fairly simple. If the net result of all sales and exchanges of *Section 1231 assets* during the taxable year is a loss, such loss is treated as derived from the sale of a noncapital asset. If the net result is a gain, the gain is treated as derived from the sale of a capital asset. Note that this asymmetric rule offers the best of both worlds to the business community—ordinary loss or capital gain on the sale of most business properties.

Let's work through an example of the application of Section 1231. During the current year, the Crawford sole proprietorship sold a Section 1231 asset for a $45,000 gain and a second Section 1231 asset for a $20,000 loss. The $25,000 net gain from the two transactions is treated as a capital gain to the owner of the business. Now change the facts to assume the proprietorship made a third sale of a Section 1231 asset during the year that resulted in a $55,000 realized loss. The net result from the three Section 1231 transactions is now a $30,000 loss, which is deductible by the owner of the business as an ordinary loss.

Depreciation Recapture

The straightforward heads-I-win, tails-you-lose rule of Section 1231 is subject to a major modification when applied to the sale of *depreciable* or *amortizable* assets. This modification requires that any portion of a gain realized on the sale be characterized as ordinary income to the extent of depreciation or amortization allowed with respect to the asset. The rationale behind this *recapture* requirement can best be explained through a numeric example (presented in tabular form below). Assume a business purchased an asset several years ago for $100,000 and has claimed $40,000 of MACRS depreciation with respect to the asset through the current year. Accordingly, the asset's adjusted basis is only $60,000. If the asset could be sold for its original cost of $100,000, the business would recognize a $40,000 taxable gain. Without a recapture requirement, this gain would be Section 1231 in nature, with the potential (subsequent to the Section 1231 netting process) of ultimate capital gain treatment. However, the entire gain is attributable to the previous years' depreciation deductions, which reduced the business's ordinary taxable income in those years by $40,000.

Sales price		$100,000	$90,000	$105,000	$48,000
Initial cost	$100,000				
Depreciation	(40,000)				
Adjusted basis		(60,000)	(60,000)	(60,000)	(60,000)
Gain (loss) recognized		$ 40,000	30,000	45,000	(12,000)
Gain recaptured as ordinary income		$ 40,000	$30,000	$ 40,000	-0-
Section 1231 gain (loss)		-0-	-0-	5,000	($12,000)

The recapture requirement is intended to prevent this transformation of ordinary income into capital gain. In our example, the $40,000 gain on sale must be recaptured as ordinary income rather than classified as Section 1231 gain. If the sales price of the asset in the current year had been only $90,000, the entire $30,000 gain would be recaptured as ordinary income. If the sales price had been $105,000, only $40,000 of the $45,000 gain would be recaptured and the remaining $5,000 gain (the actual appreciation in the value of the asset) would be Section 1231 gain. Finally, if the sales price of the asset were just $48,000, the $12,000 loss would be Section 1231 in nature; the recapture requirement applies only to gains.

The above example implies that the recapture requirement extends to 100 percent of any cost-recovery deductions claimed with respect to a Section 1231 asset. This is the case with respect to depreciable personalty and Section 197 intangibles. The recapture requirement is less stringent with respect to depreciable realty (i.e., buildings and other permanent structures). Although Congress has changed the technical details of the recapture rules for real property many times over the last 30 years, the essential concept is that only the amount of *accelerated depreciation* in excess of *straight-line* is subject to recapture.[1]

To illustrate the concept of recapture with respect to business real property, suppose a business sells a commercial office building for a total price of $1 million, $200,000 of which is attributable to the value of the underlying land and $800,000 of which is attributable to the value of the building itself. The business purchased the property 15 years ago for $1,120,000 and allocated $170,000 and $950,000 of this cost basis to the land and building, respectively. The business has deducted $600,000 of accelerated depreciation with respect to the basis of the building through date of sale. Straight-line depreciation over the 15-year period would have been only $325,000; consequently, the business has deducted $275,000 of excess accelerated depreciation. The computation of the business's gain on sale is as follows:

Land		
Sales price		$200,000
Initial cost	$170,000	
Depreciation	-0-	
Adjusted basis		(170,000)
Section 1231 gain		$ 30,000
Building		
Sales price		$800,000
Initial cost	$950,000	
Depreciation	(600,000)	
Adjusted basis		(350,000)
Gain recognized		$450,000
Gain recaptured as ordinary income (excess accelerated depreciation over straight-line)		$275,000
Section 1231 gain		$175,000

[1]Taxpayers may claim only straight-line depreciation on business real estate placed in service after 1986. Consequently, buildings placed in service subsequent to that date have no recapture potential and will generate only Section 1231 gain or loss on their disposition.

TAX PLANNING FOR CAPITAL GAINS AND LOSSES

Both individual and corporate taxpayers normally prefer that any gain recognized on the disposition of property be classified as capital gain rather than ordinary income. Conversely, taxpayers who dispose of property at a loss stand to derive a greater tax benefit if the loss is ordinary rather than capital in nature. Thus, the tax planning implications of any proposed sale or exchange depend on whether the transaction is anticipated to generate a gain or loss.

Converting Ordinary Income into Capital Gain

Since 1921, when the federal tax law first granted preferential treatment to capital gains, taxpayers and their advisers have shown considerable ingenuity in devising transactions in which the economic potential for ordinary income is transformed into capital gain. This tax planning alchemy is described as *conversion*. Congress has been diligent in its attempt to forestall the most obvious or abusive of such conversion techniques; the Internal Revenue Code contains dozens of anticonversion rules. These rules apply to many different types of sophisticated business and financial transactions, and any comprehensive discussion of their application is beyond the scope of this text. Nevertheless, a brief explanation of just one anticonversion provision, the Section 1276 market discount rule, can give the reader an insight into this fascinating aspect of our federal income tax system.

Investors who purchase publicly traded corporate bonds may pay a price for a particular bond that is less than the stated redemption price of the bond at maturity. This difference, referred to as a *market discount*, is attributable to the fact that the stated interest rate on the bond is below the current interest rate available on comparable investments. For example, a bond that entitles the holder to receive $1,000 on its redemption five years hence and that will pay the holder 4 percent interest during that five-year period might sell on the market for only $930 if the current interest rate on newly issued bonds is 6 percent. From an economic perspective, the $70 discount compensates for the 2 percent differential between the bond's stated interest rate and the current rate. In other words, when the bond matures and the holder collects $1,000, the overall return on his $930 investment should equate to 6 percent.

Even though a market discount on a bond is functionally equivalent to interest, before 1984 investors could hold such bonds to maturity and report the excess of the redemption proceeds over their cost basis as capital gain. In 1984, Congress curtailed this popular conversion strategy by enacting Section 1276, which requires that gain recognized on the disposition (i.e., sale or redemption) of a market discount bond be recognized as ordinary income to the extent of the accrued market discount on such bond. The original version of Section 1276 did not apply to tax-exempt state and local bonds. In 1993, Congress expanded the scope of this anticonversion rule to include such bonds. Under current law, the stated interest payments on tax-exempt bonds are excluded from the investor's gross income, but the gain realized on redemption will be fully taxable as ordinary income.

Converting Capital Loss into Ordinary Loss

The classification of a loss realized on the sale or exchange of an asset depends on the character of the asset in the hands of the seller. As we learned earlier in this chapter, Section 1221 is very explicit about the five categories of assets that are noncapital in nature. If a particular asset does not fall into one of these well-defined exceptions, the literal language of the statute mandates that the asset be characterized as capital. Nonetheless, in 1955, the Supreme Court concluded that the literal language was not reflective of the congressional intent behind the definition of capital assets. The case was *Corn Products Refining Co.* v. *Commissioner*, and the assets under scrutiny were corn futures contracts. The plaintiff in the case was a corporate taxpayer that maintained an inventory of raw corn, which it used in the manufacture of a variety of food products. To guarantee its future supply of corn at a favorable price, the corporation routinely purchased corn futures—contracts to purchase a fixed amount of grain on a future date for a stipulated price. If the corporation decided not to take delivery on a particular contract, the contract was sold. The corporation reported its net gain from these sales as capital gain, eligible for the highly preferential tax rate on corporate capital gains then in effect. The IRS contended the net gain should be taxed as ordinary income because the futures contracts were not capital assets. While the IRS conceded the contracts did not fall into any of the noncapital asset categories specified in the law, it emphasized that the contracts had not been purchased by the corporation for speculative or investment reasons, but solely to guarantee a source of inventory. The IRS argued that because the contracts were of vital importance to the operation of the corporation's business, they should be classified as noncapital. The Supreme Court was persuaded by this argument, concluding, "Congress intended that profits and losses arising from the everyday operation of a business be considered as ordinary income or loss rather than capital gain or loss."

This relaxed judicial interpretation of the statutory definition of capital assets was an open invitation to other corporate taxpayers confronted with potentially nondeductible capital losses resulting from the sale of business assets. If a corporation could come up with a feasible story as to why the asset was an integral component of its business operation, it could invoke the *Corn Products doctrine* and claim the loss as an ordinary deduction. This subjective facts-and-circumstances method of converting capital loss into ordinary loss was part of the tax law for three decades. Finally, in 1988, the IRS challenged the application of the doctrine in the case of *Arkansas Best Corporation* v. *Commissioner*. The corporate taxpayer in this case owned a controlling interest in a subsidiary corporation. When the subsidiary encountered severe financial difficulties, its parent company purchased additional equity stock to provide much-needed capital to the subsidiary's foundering business. When the parent eventually sold this stock, it reported an ordinary loss on the grounds that the stock had been purchased "exclusively for business purposes and subsequently held for the same reasons." The IRS insisted the stock in the subsidiary was a capital asset and the loss recognized on its sale was a capital loss. In an opinion that amounted to a reversal of the *Corn Products* decision and a deathblow to the *Corn Products* doctrine, the Supreme Court held for the government, concluding that a taxpayer's motivation in purchasing an asset is irrelevant to the question of whether or not such asset is capital in nature. Because of the decision in *Arkansas Best*, the definition of capital asset is again dependent on a literal reading of Section 1221. If an asset does not fall within one of the five exclusions listed in that section, it is a capital asset—period.

PROBLEMS AND CASES

1. During the current year, Dr. Carla May performed extensive dental services for Steve Green and his family. Steve was short of cash and offered to settle his $4,900 bill with Carla by giving her 150 shares of corporate stock. Steve had purchased the stock in 1990 for $3,500.

   a. How much gain or loss does Steve recognize on the disposition of his stock?
   b. What are the tax consequences of this transaction to Carla May, and what tax basis does she have in the 150 shares of stock?

2. Several years ago, Tyro Inc. purchased a warehouse for use in its business for $645,000. To date, Tyro Inc. has claimed $63,000 of depreciation deductions with respect to the warehouse. During the current year, Tyro sold the warehouse to the XYZ Partnership and received a cash payment of $325,000. The warehouse is subject to a $400,000 nonrecourse mortgage; consequently, the bank holding the mortgage had to approve the sale before legal title could be transferred from Tyro to XYZ.

   a. How much gain or loss does Tyro Inc. recognize on the sale of the warehouse?
   b. What tax basis will the XYZ Partnership have in the warehouse?

3. In 1995, Dana Potts paid $47,600 for 3,400 shares of GKL Mutual Fund and made an election to have the fund reinvest her annual dividends in additional shares of stock. In 1995 and 1996, Dana received Form 1099s from GKL that showed the following:

	Dividends Reinvested	*Shares Purchased*	*Price per Share*	*Total Shares Owned*
1995	$5,070	312	$16.25	3,712
1996	$5,780	340	$17.00	4,052

   In both years, Dana properly included the GKL dividends in her gross income.

   a. If Dana sells her 4,052 shares for $18.00 per share in 1997, compute the gain recognized on sale.
   b. Assume that Dana sells only 800 shares of GKL stock in 1997. Identify the tax issue suggested by the sale of only a partial interest in Dana's investment in GKL.

4. In 1993, Lydia Franklin received 50 shares of Acme stock as a gift from her aunt. The aunt purchased the stock for $12,000 in 1985. The fair market value of the stock at date of gift was $16,950. During the current year, Lydia sold the stock for $20,000.

a. How much gain or loss must Lydia recognize on the sale?
b. How would your answer to *a* change if the value of the stock at date of gift had been $9,500 and Lydia sold it for $6,000? For $10,000? For $18,000?

5. On January 4, 1996, Connie Moore paid $50,000 cash to purchase 2,500 shares of stock in Summa, Inc., an S corporation. On November 10, 1996, Connie received a $13,400 cash distribution from Summa. In March 1997, Connie received a 1996 Schedule K-1 from Summa showing that her allocable share of 1996 corporate ordinary business income was $36,700, her allocable share of dividend income received by Summa was $4,900, and her allocable share of a corporate charitable contribution was $1,500. Unfortunately, Connie did not itemize deductions for 1996 so she derived no tax benefit from the allocated charitable contribution. Based on these facts, compute Connie's tax basis in her Summa stock as of January 1, 1997.

6. Jim Sedj, a self-employed engineer, owns the following assets. Determine which are capital assets.

   a. A small computer used solely in Jim's professional work.
   b. Land owned by Jim on which his office building is located.
   c. Undeveloped land directly across the street from Jim's office that he purchased as an investment.
   d. A sailboat that Jim sails on Chesapeake Bay when he needs to "get away from it all."
   e. An automobile that Jim uses 70 percent of the time for business purposes and 30 percent of the time for personal purposes.
   f. Jim's personal residence.
   g. A house that Jim leases to tenants.
   h. An oil painting that Jim received as a gift from an artist friend.
   i. A three-year note for $6,200 that Jim accepted from a client in payment of professional services rendered.
   j. A United States savings bond that Jim received as a gift from his parents when he turned age 21.
   k. Twenty shares of General Electric common stock. (Jim buys and sells stock for his own account on a regular basis. During the current year, he engaged in over 30 transactions involving publicly traded stock.)

7. On July 2 of the current year Ms. Clay sold investment securities for $58,700. She purchased these securities for $45,000 on November 28, 1990. On October 12, she sold her personal residence for $140,000. She purchased this residence on March 18, 1980, for $158,000. On December 13, she sold a diamond ring that she had worn every day for 12 years for $22,500. The original cost of the ring in 1981 was $14,000. Ms. Clay did not sell or exchange any other assets during the year. Calculate the net effect of these sales on Ms. Clay's adjusted gross income.

8. On January 28 of the current year, CCK Inc. sold land held for investment for $560,000. CCK Inc. purchased the land in 1990 for $600,000. On June 19, the corporation sold investment securities for $235,000. The securities were

purchased in 1988 for $190,000. On September 12, CCK Inc. determined that Marco Inc. long-term registered bonds that CCK had purchased in 1987 were worthless; the corporation's cost basis in these bonds was $25,000. During the current year CCK Inc. generated $398,000 of taxable income from its day-to-day business operations.

a. Assuming CCK Inc. and Marco Inc. are not affiliated corporations, compute CCK Inc.'s taxable income.

b. How would your computation change if CCK Inc. and Marco Inc. are affiliated corporations?

9. In 1989, Miles Mathis, a single taxpayer, paid $45,000 to LLP Inc. for 500 shares of newly issued LLP Inc. common stock. In 1991, Miles purchased 1,000 additional shares of LLP common from the Vestco Partnership for $70,000. In the current year, Miles sold all 1,500 shares of LLP common for a total price of only $27,000 ($18 per share). Assuming LLP Inc. has qualified as a Section 1244 small-business corporation from the date of its incorporation, describe the tax consequences of the sale.

10. In the current year, taxpayer J recognized a $70,000 long-term capital gain, a $10,000 short-term capital gain, and a $45,000 long-term capital loss.

    a. If taxpayer J is a regular corporation with $360,000 of ordinary income generated by its day-to-day business operations, compute J's regular tax liability.

    b. If taxpayer J is a single individual with taxable income of $170,000 before consideration of his capital gains and losses, compute J's regular tax liability.

    c. If taxpayer J is a single individual with taxable income of $15,000 before consideration of his capital gains and losses, compute J's regular tax liability.

11. For the current year, Mary Stuart had $890 of investment income in the form of dividends and recognized a $7,200 net long-term capital gain. She incurred $5,600 of investment interest expense during the year.

    a. If Mary's taxable income before consideration of her dividend income, capital gain, and investment interest is $300,000, compute the effect on her current year tax liability if she elects to treat $4,710 of her capital gain as investment income.

    b. Compute the effect on her current year tax liability if she does not elect to treat any of her capital gain as investment income.

12. On March 29 of the current year, Dan Curtis, a self-employed businessman, sold rental real estate for $125,000. Dan's adjusted basis in the real estate was $102,000, and he had computed depreciation with respect to the property using the straight-line method. Dan called his tax adviser to ask if the $23,000 gain recognized on the sale would be taxed as ordinary income or capital gain. Dan was upset when his adviser told him it was impossible to answer that question in March, but to call back in late December. Can you explain why the tax adviser couldn't give Dan a definitive answer to his question?

13. Pauline Andrews has decided to invest approximately $50,000 in a recently incorporated business. The corporation is selling newly issued common stock for $81.30 per share. However, a close friend of Pauline who purchased 700 shares in the corporation just seven months ago but who is in need of ready cash has offered to sell his shares to Pauline for only $80 per share. Can you give Pauline two good tax reasons why she should pay the extra $1.30 per share to buy the stock directly from the corporation?
14. On January 8 of the current year, Acme Inc. sold business equipment (original cost $20,000, adjusted basis $12,000) for $16,800. On July 1, Acme sold a second piece of business equipment (original cost $60,000, adjusted basis $44,000) for $65,000. On November 3, Acme sold marketable securities (cost basis $25,000) for $16,000. Acme made no other asset dispositions during the year. Determine the effect of these three transactions on Acme's current year taxable income.
15. During the current year, Nordo Inc. sold commercial real estate (land and building) with an adjusted basis of $490,000 for $300,000. Nordo also sold an apartment complex (land and building) with an adjusted basis of $1,200,000 for $1,275,000. Nordo used the straight-line method to compute the depreciation with respect to both buildings. Nordo made no other dispositions of assets during the year. Determine the effect of these two transactions on Nordo's current year taxable income.

Case 7–1

Things are not going well for Lake Austin Condominiums. Six years ago, units sold for $100,000; today their market value is approximately $70,000. Rita and Tom Cedillo purchased their condo six years ago for $100,000 and have lived in it ever since. They stopped making payments on their recourse mortgage when it had a principal balance of $89,200. During the current year, the mortgage company foreclosed on the unit and subsequently sold it for $68,000. Although the Cedillos are still solvent, the mortgage company decided it would be prudent to accept $10,000 in full settlement of the $21,200 unpaid balance of the mortgage.

Billy Joe Buttrick bought a condominium six years ago for business purposes and has rented the property to tenants ever since. During the current year, Billy stopped servicing an $84,000 nonrecourse mortgage on the condo. The savings and loan company that held the mortgage foreclosed; at date of foreclosure, Billy's adjusted basis in the rental unit was $77,000 ($100,000 cost less $23,000 accumulated straight-line depreciation).

a. What are the current year tax consequences of the foreclosure and the settlement of the mortgage to the Cedillos?

b. What are the current year tax consequences of the foreclosure to Billy Joe Buttrick?

c. How would your answer to *b* change if Billy's adjusted basis at date of foreclosure had been $87,500 rather than $77,000?

Case 7–2

Naomi Levy, a professional singer who earns $750,000 of income in an average year, purchased 15 acres of undeveloped ranch land for $935,000 in 1982. This year she is considering subdividing the land into one-third acre lots, improving the land by adding streets, sidewalks, and utilities, and advertising the 45 lots for sale in a local real estate journal. She anticipates the improvements will cost $275,000, and she could sell the lots for $40,000 each. She is also considering an offer from a local corporation that wants to purchase the 15-acre tract and will pay her $1.4 million for the property in its undeveloped state.

a. Assuming Naomi makes no other property dispositions during the year, which alternative (develop or sell) would maximize her after-tax cash from the property disposition?

b. Would your answer change if Naomi has a $200,000 capital loss carryforward into the current year?

CHAPTER 8

The Nontaxable Exchanges

In Chapter 7, we discussed the tax consequences of gains and losses that are realized and recognized in the same taxable year. In Chapter 8, we will analyze a number of transactions that trigger gain or loss realization but do not result in the current recognition of that gain or loss. These transactions are referred to as *nontaxable exchanges,* and each one is authorized by a special provision of the Internal Revenue Code. Congress enacted these various provisions for particular tax policy reasons, which we will consider as we look at the details of selected provisions in the second half of this chapter. In the first half of the chapter, we will identify the tax characteristics common to all nontaxable exchanges. Once the mechanics of a generic nontaxable exchange are thoroughly understood, mastering the details that differentiate and distinguish the specific exchange provisions becomes relatively easy.

The importance of the nontaxable exchange provisions derives from the fact that they permit taxpayers to convert capital from one form into another without any current tax cost. In other words, a nontaxable exchange provision makes the tax law *neutral* with respect to certain business or investment decisions. To illustrate this concept, consider the situation in which Mr. Maxwell, who is in a 39.6 percent marginal tax bracket, owns an investment asset with a tax basis of $50,000 and a fair market value of $110,000. The asset is generating $6,600 of annual income, which represents a 6 percent return on value. Mr. Maxwell is contemplating selling this investment and reinvesting the proceeds in a new business venture that promises a 7.5 percent return on capital. If the sale of the original investment results in a recognized gain of $60,000, Mr. Maxwell will have only $86,240 of after-tax proceeds ($110,000 – $23,760 tax) to reinvest. The future income generated by the new investment would be only $6,468 per year (7.5 percent of $86,240) and Mr. Maxwell would be worse off financially because of the transaction. Clearly, he should reject the new investment opportunity offering a higher pre-tax rate of return because of the front-end tax cost. On the other hand, if the conversion of the original investment into an equity interest in the new business venture could be accomplished tax-free, Mr. Maxwell could contribute his full $110,000 of capital to the venture and earn $8,250 per year. Consequently, the new investment would be superior to the old, and Mr. Maxwell could restructure his investment portfolio accordingly.

A GENERIC NONTAXABLE EXCHANGE

The features of the nontaxable exchange provisions scattered throughout the Internal Revenue Code vary substantially. Some provisions are mandatory if the prescribed conditions are met; others are elective. Some apply to realized gains only, while others apply to both realized gains and losses. Certain provisions require a direct exchange of noncash assets, and others allow the taxpayer to be in a temporary cash position. Nevertheless, all the nontaxable exchanges share several important characteristics. We will analyze these characteristics in the context of a generic nontaxable exchange. By doing so, we can focus on the fundamental structure of nontaxable exchanges and avoid needless repetition throughout the remainder of the chapter.

Exchanges of Qualifying Property Interests

Every nontaxable exchange involves the transformation of one property interest into another. The precise type of property interest that can be swapped tax-free depends on the unique qualification requirements of the operative statutory provision. But only a taxpayer's surrender and receipt of *qualifying property* can result in nonrecognition of realized gain or loss. Consider the diagram of an exchange between taxpayers A and B in Figure 8–1. Given that the exchange involves only qualifying property to both taxpayers, it is nontaxable to both. What else do we know about this exchange? Assuming A and B are unrelated parties dealing at arm's length and in their own economic self-interest, we know the qualifying properties must be of equal value. (This is the value-for-value presumption introduced in Chapter 2.) We also know that two taxpayers are involved in the exchange with independent sets of tax consequences. In other words, the transaction can be analyzed to determine the outcome to A or the outcome to B, or the outcomes to both.

Before we can determine the tax consequences of the exchange, we must know the values of the qualifying properties and A's and B's respective tax basis in the property each is surrendering. This information is presented in Figure 8–2. Because taxpayer A is surrendering property with an adjusted basis of $14,000 in return for property worth $20,000, A has a $6,000 realized gain. Because the exchange involves qualifying property and is therefore nontaxable, none of the gain is

Figure 8–1

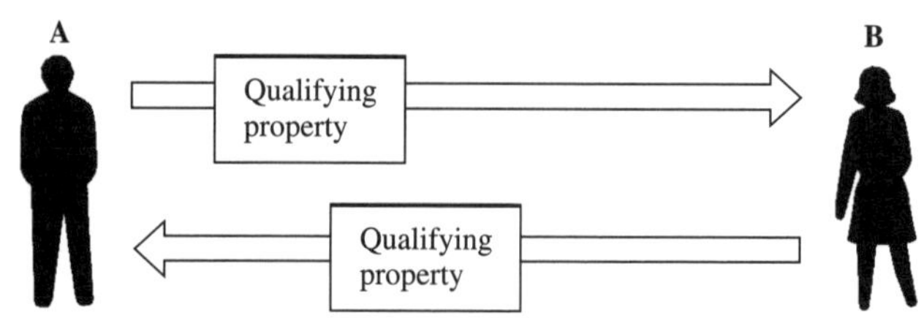

Figure 8–2

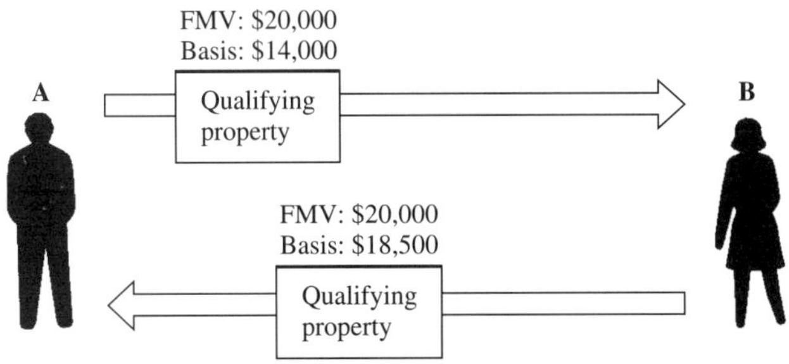

recognized. Similarly, B's surrender of qualifying property with an adjusted tax basis of $18,500 in return for qualifying property worth $20,000 results in a $1,500 realized but unrecognized gain.

The Substituted Basis Rule

The next characteristic of our generic nontaxable exchange stems from the fact that the label *nontaxable* is a misnomer. Congress never intended that the realized gains and losses triggered by nontaxable exchanges should permanently escape recognition. Instead, Congress designed the nontaxable exchange provisions to ensure that unrecognized gains and losses would merely be *deferred* until some future year in which the qualifying property received in the exchange is disposed of in a taxable transaction. This deferral of any unrecognized gain or loss is accomplished through a special rule for calculating the tax basis of the qualifying property received: The basis of this property equals the basis of the qualifying property surrendered. Note that in our generic exchange, A and B each paid $20,000 (the value of the property surrendered) to acquire their new properties. Because the exchange is nontaxable to both parties, they do not take a cost basis in their properties. Instead, A's basis in his new property is $14,000, while B's basis in her new property is $18,500.

This *substituted basis rule* causes the unrecognized gain or loss on a nontaxable exchange to be embedded in the basis of the qualifying property received. This gain or loss remains dormant for as long as the participant in the exchange continues to hold the property. If and when a participant makes a taxable disposition of the property, the deferral ends and the unrecognized gain or loss attributable to the nontaxable exchange finally comes home to roost. To illustrate this important concept, return to the facts in our generic exchange. If A and B sell the property each received in the nontaxable exchange for $20,000 cash at any time after the exchange, they will realize and recognize gain of $6,000 and $1,500 respectively, the exact amount of gain deferred in their exchange transaction. This observation suggests a second method for computing the basis of qualifying property received in a nontaxable exchange: That basis will always equal the property's fair market value minus any deferred gain or plus any deferred loss realized on the exchange.

The Effect of Boot

To this point, the facts of our generic exchange transaction are a bit contrived in that the values of the properties that A and B want to exchange are equal. A much more realistic scenario would be that the values of the properties qualifying for nontaxable exchange treatment are unequal. In such case, the party to the exchange owning the qualifying property of lesser value must agree to transfer additional value in the form of cash or nonqualifying property to make the exchange work economically.

In tax jargon, any cash or nonqualifying property included in a nontaxable exchange is called *boot.* The presence of boot does not disqualify the entire exchange. Instead, the taxpayer receiving the boot must recognize an amount of realized gain equal to the value of the boot. Refer to Figure 8–3 in which the value of the qualifying property surrendered by B is only $19,200. For A to agree to the exchange, B had to throw in $800 cash, so A receives $20,000 of total value in exchange for his asset worth $20,000. In this case, A has received $800 of boot and must recognize $800 of his $6,000 realized gain.

Because A had to recognize and pay tax on $800 of gain, he is entitled to increase his basis in the newly received property by this amount. In other words, A's investment in his new property consists of his $14,000 basis in the surrendered property plus $800 of taxable gain. However, A owns two new assets over which he must spread his $14,800 total basis—$800 cash and the qualifying property. Cash must take a basis equal to its face value. Consequently, only $14,000 of basis is allocated to the qualifying property. This $14,000 basis number can also be derived by subtracting A's $5,200 deferred gain from the $19,200 value of the qualifying property.

The fact that B paid $800 boot in our generic exchange does not cause any gain recognition to her. She surrendered property with an aggregate basis of $19,300 ($800 cash plus $18,500 basis of qualifying property) and received property worth $20,000. Therefore, she has a $700 realized gain, none of which is recognized. The basis in B's newly received property is $19,300, the aggregate substituted basis of the cash and property surrendered. This $19,300 basis number equals the $20,000 fair market value of the new property less B's $700 deferred gain on the exchange.

Figure 8–3

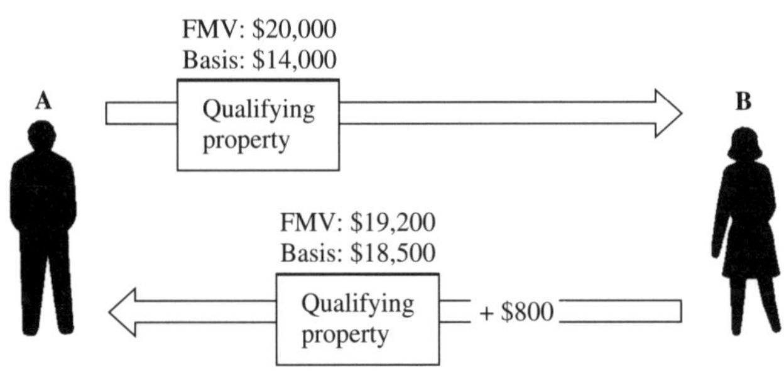

Two more facts concerning the presence of boot in a nontaxable exchange should be mentioned. First, the receipt of boot can never trigger recognition of more gain than the recipient realized on the exchange. For example, if A had received $7,000 of cash and qualifying property worth $13,000 in exchange for his property, the receipt of $7,000 of boot would trigger recognition of the entire $6,000 gain realized. (After all, A would recognize only a $6,000 gain if he had sold the property for $20,000 cash!)

Second, the receipt of boot does not trigger any recognition of realized loss. Consider the new set of facts in Figure 8–4. In this case, A surrenders qualifying property with a basis of $23,000 in exchange for $800 cash and qualifying property worth $19,200. As a result, A has a $3,000 realized loss, none of which is recognized. And what of A's basis in the newly received property? His $23,000 tax basis in the surrendered property must be spread over the $800 cash received and this new property. Because the cash must absorb $800 of the substituted basis, A's basis in the qualifying property is limited to $22,200. Remember that this basis number can also be calculated by *adding* A's $3,000 deferred loss to the $19,200 fair market value of the property.

SPECIFIC NONTAXABLE EXCHANGE PROVISIONS

The Internal Revenue Code bestows nontaxable exchange status on a wide assortment of transactions in which taxpayers realize gains and losses. Taxpayers who plan to dispose of assets that are worth less than their adjusted basis naturally want to avoid any provision that would prevent them from recognizing their losses. On the other hand, taxpayers wanting to dispose of assets that have appreciated in value deliberately seek these provisions to defer the recognition of their realized gains. In the second half of this chapter, we will survey the more important of the nontaxable exchange provisions and examine the role of each in the tax planning process.

Like-Kind Exchanges

Section 1031 provides that no gain or loss is recognized to a taxpayer who surrenders business or investment property in exchange for business or investment property of *like kind*. The policy rationale for this nontaxable provision is that taxpayers who

Figure 8–4

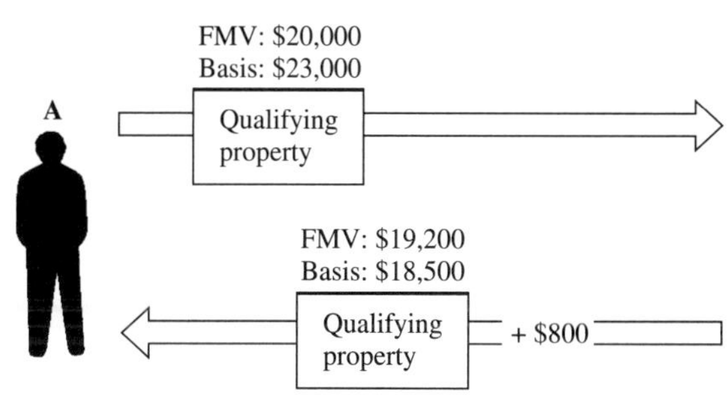

convert a business or investment asset into another asset of essentially the same nature have changed the legal form rather than the economic substance of their property interests and thus should not pay any tax on the conversion.

The definition of like-kind property as it applies to tangible personalty[1] held for business or investment purposes is determined by reference to a detailed IRS classification system. For example, automobiles and taxis constitute one class of like-kind property, while buses constitute another. Accordingly, the exchange of an automobile held for business use for another business automobile would be nontaxable, but the exchange of that automobile for a bus would be a fully taxable event. Airplanes and helicopters are like-kind properties, while airplanes and tugboats are not. Office furniture and copying equipment are like-kind properties, while copying equipment and computers are not. Livestock of the same sex are like-kind properties, while livestock of different sexes are not. If a rancher swaps a bull held for breeding purposes for another bull, he has a nontaxable like-kind exchange, but if he swaps the bull for a breeding heifer, the exchange is taxable. By now, the reader should have gotten the point: Taxpayers who want to dispose of business personalty through a nontaxable exchange should consult their tax advisers to determine exactly which types of property qualify as like-kind. One final caveat—Section 1031 does not apply to an exchange of inventory or any property held primarily for resale to customers.

In contrast to the restrictive rules defining like-kind personalty, virtually all types of business and investment real estate are considered like-kind. Therefore, any swap of realty for realty can be structured as a tax-free exchange. The owner of undeveloped investment land in Arizona can negotiate with the owner of an apartment complex in midtown Manhattan to exchange their properties, and the resulting transaction will be nontaxable to both parties. This particular like-kind exchange is diagramed in Figure 8–5. Note that the investment land has an appraised value of $800,000, while the apartment complex is worth $925,000. As a result, the Arizonan pays the New Yorker $125,000 of cash to equalize the values exchanged.

The practical question suggested by Figure 8–5 is how did the Arizonan and the New Yorker ever find each other? The likely answer is that they worked through a real estate broker who specializes in (and charges for) putting together real property like-kind exchanges. And what are the tax consequences of the exchange? The Arizonan has a realized gain of $300,000 ($925,000 value of property received less $625,000 aggregate basis of cash and property surrendered), none of which must be recognized. The Arizonan's substituted basis in his new Manhattan real estate is $625,000 (which equals the $925,000 value of the property less his $300,000 deferred gain). The New Yorker has a realized gain of $440,000 ($925,000 aggregate value of cash and property received less $485,000 basis of property surrendered). Because she received $125,000 of boot, she must recognize $125,000 of the gain currently. The New Yorker's substituted basis in the Arizona land is $485,000 (which equals the $800,000 value of the land less her $315,000 deferred gain).

---

[1]The term *personalty* refers to property other than land and permanent attachments thereto.

Figure 8–5

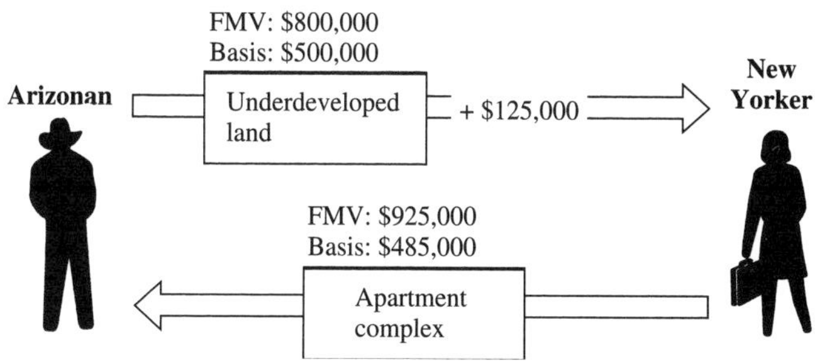

Exchanges of Mortgaged Properties. Many real property interests involved in like-kind exchanges are subject to mortgages that are transferred along with the property and become the legal responsibility of the new owner. As we learned in Chapter 7, a taxpayer who is relieved of debt on the disposition of property must treat the relief as an amount realized on disposition. In the Section 1031 context, a party that surrenders a mortgaged property is considered to have received boot equal to the amount of the relief of indebtedness. In other words, the relief of debt is treated exactly like cash received in the exchange, while the assumption of debt is treated as additional cash paid.

Figure 8–6 presents a like-kind exchange involving a Chicago shopping mall and a commercial office building in St. Louis. The net value of the shopping mall is $500,000 ($730,000 appraised value less $230,000 mortgage), while the unencumbered value of the office building is $500,000. When ABC Inc. surrenders the shopping mall in exchange for the office building, it realizes a $435,000 gain ($730,000 aggregate value of property received and debt relief less $295,000 basis in the property surrendered). Because ABC Inc. has received $230,000 of boot in the transaction (the relief of debt), the corporation must recognize $230,000 of its gain. ABC Inc.'s substituted basis in the St. Louis property is $295,000. The XYZ Partnership has an $87,000 realized gain on the exchange ($730,000 value of property received less $643,000 aggregate basis of property surrendered and debt assumed), none of which is recognized. The partnership's substituted basis in the shopping mall is $643,000.

In a Section 1031 exchange in which both properties are subject to a mortgage, so both parties are relieved of debt, only the net amount of debt is considered as boot given and boot received. For example, if party A surrenders real estate subject to a $120,000 mortgage in exchange for real estate owned by party B subject to a $100,000 mortgage, party A has enjoyed a net relief of debt of $20,000 and is considered to have received $20,000 of boot in the exchange. Party B has assumed a $20,000 net amount of additional debt and is considered to have paid $20,000 of boot in the exchange. Consequently, party A must recognize up to $20,000 of any gain realized, while party B has a totally nontaxable exchange.

Figure 8–6

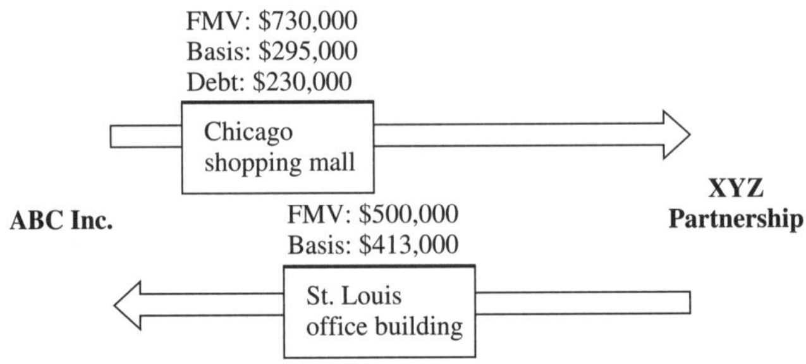

Involuntary Conversions

Generally, taxpayers control the circumstances in which they dispose of property. However, in certain situations a disposition is involuntary; property may be stolen or be destroyed by a natural disaster such as a flood or a fire. Even in these unfortunate situations, the owner may realize a gain if the property is insured and the insurance proceeds exceed the owner's basis in the property. Another example of an *involuntary conversion* is a condemnation of private property by a government agency that takes the property for public use. If a government has the right of eminent domain, it can compel a property owner to sell the property to the agency for its fair market value. If the condemnation proceeds exceed the basis of the condemned property, the owner has a realized gain.

Section 1033 provides that a taxpayer who realizes a gain on the involuntary conversion of property may elect not to recognize the gain if two conditions are met. First, the taxpayer must reinvest the amount realized on the conversion (the insurance or condemnation proceeds) in property that is *similar or related in service or use.* This condition essentially requires taxpayers to replace their original property to avoid paying tax on the realized gain. Both the IRS and the courts have been very strict in their interpretation of the concept of similar or related property. For example, the IRS has ruled that a taxpayer who owned a bowling alley that was destroyed by fire and who used the insurance proceeds to purchase a billiards parlor was ineligible for Section 1033 nonrecognition treatment because the properties were not similar in function. The second condition imposed by Section 1033 is that replacement of the involuntarily converted property must occur within the two taxable years following the year in which the conversion occurred. Taxpayers making the Section 1033 election usually have ample time to locate and acquire suitable replacement property.

If the cost of qualifying replacement property equals or exceeds the amount realized by a taxpayer on an involuntary conversion, none of the taxpayer's realized gain is recognized. If the taxpayer does not reinvest the entire amount realized in replacement property (i.e., the taxpayer uses some of the insurance or condemnation proceeds for other purposes), the amount not reinvested is treated as boot, and the taxpayer must recognize gain accordingly. In either case, the basis of the replacement property is its cost less the amount of the taxpayer's unrecognized gain. As a result, unrecognized gain is deferred until the taxpayer disposes of the replacement property in a future taxable transaction.

To illustrate the impact of the Section 1033 election, consider the case of Yates McCallum, who owned business equipment with an adjusted basis of $80,000 that was destroyed in the most recent California earthquake. Yates received $100,000 of insurance proceeds because of the destruction of his property, thereby realizing a $20,000 gain on the involuntary conversion. He purchased virtually identical equipment in the taxable year after the disaster. The following table shows the tax consequences to Yates under four different assumptions concerning the cost of the replacement property.

Insurance Proceeds	*Amount Reinvested*	*Gain Recognized*	*Gain Deferred*	*Basis of Replacement Property*
$100,000	$135,000	$ -0-	$20,000	$115,000
100,000	100,000	-0-	20,000	80,000
100,000	92,000	8,000	12,000	80,000
100,000	77,000	20,000	-0-	77,000

Section 1033 is clearly intended to provide relief to taxpayers who are deprived of property through circumstances beyond their control and who want nothing more than to return to the status quo by replacing that property. The section applies to the involuntary conversion of any type of asset—business, investment, or personal. It is elective; taxpayers may choose to invoke or ignore its nonrecognition rule, depending on their particular tax situation for the year. Finally, if a taxpayer realizes a loss on the destruction of property by casualty or theft or because of the condemnation of property by a government authority, Section 1033 does not affect the extent to which such loss may be deductible under other relevant provisions of the Internal Revenue Code.

Sales of Personal Residences

The next nonrecognition exchange provision we will examine is the one most familiar to and appreciated by individual taxpayers. Section 1034 provides that gain realized on the sale of a personal residence is not recognized if the seller reinvests the amount realized on the sale in a new residence. To secure nonrecognition, the seller must purchase a new home within a four-year period beginning two years before the date of sale of the original residence and ending two years after such date. The rule applies only to the sale of an individual's *principal* residence; gain realized on the sale of a second residence, such as a vacation home, is ineligible for nonrecognition treatment. Section 1034 does not apply to realized losses. Unfortunately, as we learned in Chapter 3, such losses are nondeductible because a residence is a personal asset.

The mechanics of Section 1034 are virtually identical to those of the involuntary conversion provision. Full nonrecognition results only if the individual reinvests the entire amount of proceeds from the sale of the original home in the new home. If the individual buys a new home that costs less than the sales proceeds, the amount of excess proceeds is treated as boot, and the individual must recognize capital gain accordingly. The basis of the new home equals its cost less the amount of any unrecognized gain.

The Section 121 Exclusion. Individuals can enjoy the deferral of gain authorized under Section 1034 every time they sell a principal residence for a profit. But with each sale, the amount of deferred gain is embedded in the basis of the new home. If an individual finally decides to sell a principal residence and not use the proceeds to buy still another home, the deferred gain will be recognized in the year of the final sale. Consider the situation of Mr. and Mrs. Erwin, who purchased their first modest home in 1955 for just $15,000. Over the next 40 years, the Erwins occupied a succession of principal residences. The information concerning the purchase and sale of these homes is shown in the following table. Each time the Erwins sold a home, they deferred the entire gain realized by reinvesting the sales proceeds in a more expensive dwelling. In each case, the tax basis of the new home equaled its cost less the gain deferred on the sale of the previous residence.

	Cost	*Tax Basis*	*Sales Proceeds*	*Gain Realized*	*Gain Deferred*
Home 1	$ 15,000	$ 15,000	$ 22,800	$ 7,800	$ 7,800
Home 2	35,000	27,200	80,000	52,800	52,800
Home 3	112,000	59,200	155,000	95,800	95,800
Home 4	200,000	104,200	—	—	—

In the current year, the Erwins reached retirement age and decided to sell their fourth home for $231,000. They invested the proceeds in high-grade investment securities and rented an apartment in Coral Gables, Florida. What's wrong with this picture? Note that the tax basis in the fourth home was only $104,200, so the Erwins realized a $126,800 capital gain on its sale. This gain represents the $95,800 cumulative amount of the gains deferred on the sales of the Erwins's first three residences plus the $31,000 appreciation in the value of their last home. In short, a lifetime of income deferral has finally caught up with the Erwins, and they are facing a potentially devastating tax bill of $35,504 (28 percent of $126,800) in the current year.

Congress was sympathetic to the plight of individuals such as the Erwins and decided to provide a "deferral escape clause" in the form of Section 121. This section permits individuals to elect to exclude the first $125,000 of gain recognized on the sale of a personal residence from gross income. This exclusion is available only if (1) the seller (or the seller's spouse on a joint return) has reached age 55 before the date of sale, and (2) during the five-year period ending with the date of sale, the residence has been the principal residence of the seller for periods aggregating at least three years. Moreover, the Section 121 exclusion can be used only once in a taxpayer's lifetime.

Readers should understand that Section 121 provides a permanent exclusion from gross income and is not a nontaxable exchange provision per se. Nonetheless, in the tax planning process, the gain deferral available under Section 1034 and the ultimate exclusion of some or all of that gain under Section 121 are inextricably bound. In the

Erwins's situation, their election to use Section 121 would reduce their taxable gain on the sale of their last home to a mere $1,800, and $125,000 of the deferred gains attributable to their principal residence sales would escape taxation forever.

Exchanges of Property for Equity Interests

In the very early days of the income tax, Congress concluded the tax law should be neutral with respect to the formation of business entities. If entrepreneurs and investors undertake a new business venture and decide to organize the business as a corporation or partnership for sound legal or financial reasons, they should not be discouraged from doing so because of any tax cost associated with the organization. In addition, taxpayers who create corporations or partnerships are usually changing only the form in which business is being conducted. Subsequent to the formation of the entity, the taxpayers continue to own the business in their roles as shareholders or partners. Because of these policy reasons, Congress enacted Sections 351 and 721, two nontaxable exchange provisions that are used every day by the business community.

Corporate Formations. Section 351 provides that no gain or loss is recognized when property is transferred to a corporation solely in exchange for that corporation's stock if the transferors of property are in control of the corporation immediately after the exchange. In this context, the term *property* is defined very broadly and includes cash and tangible and intangible assets. Personal services are not property; individuals who perform services for a corporation in exchange for that corporation's stock must recognize the value of the stock as compensation income. For Section 351 purposes, *control* is defined as ownership of at least 80 percent of the corporation's outstanding stock.

The utility of Section 351 should be readily apparent; this nontaxable exchange provision allows entrepreneurs and investors to form new corporations without any front-end tax cost. To illustrate, suppose Bob Brown and Jane Harris decide to contribute business assets used in their respective sole proprietorships to newly incorporated B&J Inc. This incorporation is diagramed in Figure 8–7. Bob's assets are worth

Figure 8–7

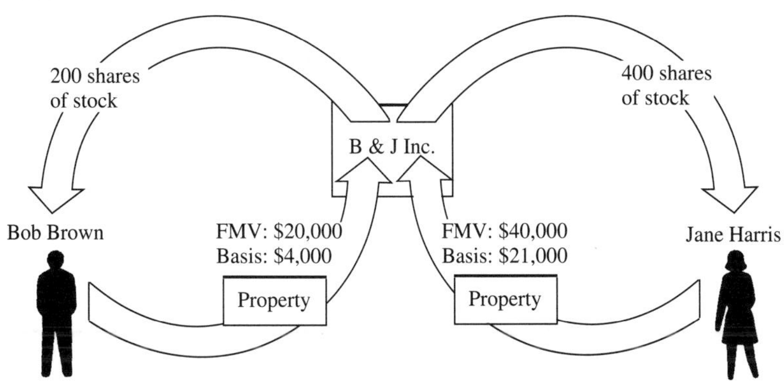

$20,000 and have an adjusted basis of $4,000, while Jane's assets are worth $40,000 and have an adjusted basis of $21,000. In exchange for these assets, the corporation issues 200 shares of voting common stock to Bob and 400 shares to Jane. These 600 shares are worth $60,000, the total value of the business assets now owned by B&J.

Bob's realized gain on the exchange is $16,000 ($20,000 value of 200 shares received less $4,000 basis of assets surrendered), while Jane's realized gain is $19,000 ($40,000 value of 400 shares received less $21,000 basis of assets surrendered). Because Bob and Jane are both transferors of property and because together they are in control of B&J Inc. immediately after the exchange, neither will recognize any gain because of the incorporation. Each will take a substituted basis in their shares of stock ($4,000 stock basis for Bob and $21,000 stock basis for Jane), so that their unrecognized gains are deferred until they dispose of the stock in a taxable transaction.

The exchange is also tax-free to B&J Inc. Section 1032 provides that no gain or loss is recognized by a corporation that exchanges its own stock for property or services. In an exchange transaction that is also tax-free to the recipients of the stock, the corporation takes a carryover basis in the property received. Thus, in the B&J example, the corporation's tax basis in the assets acquired from Bob and Jane is $4,000 and $21,000, respectively; if any of these assets are depreciable or amortizable, B&J's cost-recovery deductions will be computed with respect to the carryover basis amount. Of course for financial statement purposes, these assets are booked at their $20,000 and $40,000 fair market values, and book depreciation and amortization will be based on these numbers.

The toughest requirement in Section 351 is that the transferors of property be in control of the corporation immediately after the exchange. If this control requirement can't be met, the exchange is fully taxable to the transferors. Assume that four years after B&J's incorporation, Bob Brown decides to acquire an additional 300 shares by transferring real property worth $100,000 with an adjusted basis to Bob of $65,000. Immediately after this exchange, Bob owns 500 of the 900 shares of B&J's outstanding stock. His 55.5 percent interest falls far short of the 80 percent requisite control, and Bob must recognize and pay tax on the $35,000 gain realized on the exchange. Because the transaction is fully taxable, Bob has a $100,000 cost basis in his new 300 shares. Interestingly, this exchange does not trigger any gain recognition to B&J. Section 1032, the section granting nontaxable exchange treatment at the corporate level, is independent of Section 351 and applies regardless of the tax consequences of the exchange at the shareholder level. In this case, because Bob recognized the entire appreciation in the transferred real estate as taxable gain, B&J's tax basis in the real estate is its $100,000 fair market value.

Partnership Formations. Section 721 provides that neither the partners nor the partnership recognizes gain or loss when property is transferred to a partnership in exchange for an equity interest therein. If Bob Brown and Jane Harris in Figure 8–7 prefer to operate their business as a partnership rather than a corporation, they could transfer their appreciated assets to B&J Partnership in exchange for a one-third and a two-thirds interest in partnership capital, profits, and losses without recognizing any gain. Bob's basis in his partnership interest would be a substituted basis of $4,000, Jane's basis in her partnership interest would be a substituted basis of $21,000, and the partnership would take a carryover basis in the contributed properties of $4,000 and $21,000, respectively.

While Section 721 is clearly a first cousin to Section 351, it lacks any type of control requirement and is therefore more flexible. For example, if Bob Brown eventually contributes his appreciated real estate to the partnership in exchange for an increase in his partnership interest from 33.3 percent to 55.5 percent, the exchange will be nontaxable to Bob, and his $35,000 realized gain will be deferred. He will increase the basis in his partnership interest by the $65,000 basis of the transferred real estate, and the partnership will take a $65,000 carryover basis in the property.

Exchanges of Equity Interests

Section 1031, which provides nonrecognition treatment for like-kind exchanges of business and investment assets, does not apply to exchanges of corporate stock or partnership interests. As a result, the exchange of an equity interest in one business for an equity interest in a different business is usually a fully taxable event, with both participants in the exchange recognizing any realized gain or loss. For instance, if Meg Sloan owns a 10 percent interest in the RST Partnership with an adjusted basis of $75,350 and Barb Evans owns a 50 percent interest in the EFG Partnership with an adjusted basis of $43,000, and if both partnership interests are worth $50,000, Meg and Barb might decide to swap interests. In this case, Meg will have a $25,350 recognized capital loss, while Barb will have a $7,000 recognized capital gain.

The law does include two nontaxable exchange provisions that apply to transactions involving corporate stock. Section 1036 authorizes a nontaxable exchange of common stock in a corporation for a different class of common stock in the same corporation. Similarly, preferred stock can be exchanged for preferred stock in the same corporation at no tax cost. Section 354 provides that no gain or loss is recognized when a taxpayer exchanges stock in one corporation for stock in a different corporation if both corporations are *parties to a reorganization.* The tax consequences of corporate reorganizations and the definition of that important term are the subject of Chapter 12.

Rollover of Capital Gains into SSBICs. Section 1044, enacted as part of the Revenue Reconciliation Act of 1993, allows the tax-free conversion of equity interests in one business into equity interest in another business in a very tightly controlled set of circumstances. Under Section 1044, regular corporations and individuals (but not partnerships, S corporations, or fiduciaries) may elect to defer the recognition of capital gain realized on the sale of publicly traded stocks or bonds by reinvesting the proceeds of the sale in a *specialized small-business investment company* (SSBIC). This reinvestment must occur within 60 days of the date of the sale. An SSBIC is a special-purpose venture capital firm authorized by the Small Business Administration to invest in businesses owned by minority groups and economically disadvantaged individuals.

The amount of gain individuals may elect to defer in any one year is limited to the lesser of $50,000 (an annual limitation) or $500,000 reduced by the gain deferred under Section 1044 in previous taxable years (a lifetime limitation). For corporations, the annual limitation and the lifetime limitation increase to $250,000 and $1 million, respectively. If only a portion of the proceeds of a securities sale is reinvested on a timely basis in an SSBIC, the amount not reinvested is treated as boot that triggers partial gain recognition. At this point in the chapter, the reader should be able to predict how the tax basis in the newly acquired SSBIC interest is computed—such basis equals the purchaser's cost of the interest reduced by unrecognized gain on the securities sale.

Wash Sales. Section 1091 is an atypical nontaxable exchange provision because it prevents only the recognition of *losses* realized on *wash sales* of marketable securities. A wash sale occurs when an investor sells securities at a loss and reaquires substantially the same securities within 30 days before or after the sale. This rule inhibits investors from selling securities for no other reason than to trigger a tax loss, then immediately buying the stock back to keep their original investment portfolio intact. If an investor is caught by the wash sale rule, the cost of the reacquired securities is increased by the amount of unrecognized loss realized on the sale of the original securities. Taxpayers can easily circumvent this nonrecognition provision by waiting for more than 30 days to reestablish their investment position. The risk of course, is that in the time between sale and repurchase, the market value of the securities has rebounded, and the taxpayer must pay a higher price for the same securities.

PROBLEMS AND CASES

1. In the current year, taxpayer Z entered into an arm's length transaction in which Z exchanged asset A (tax basis $10,000) for new asset B (fair market value $16,000). Under each of the following assumptions, apply the generic rules to compute Z's realized gain, recognized gain, and tax basis in the new asset.
   a. Asset A and asset B are not qualified property for nontaxable exchange purposes.
   b. Asset A and asset B are qualified property for nontaxable exchange purposes.
   c. Asset A and asset B are not qualified property for nontaxable exchange purposes. To equalize the values of the exchange properties, Z pays $800 cash to the transferor of asset B.
   d. Asset A and asset B are qualified property for nontaxable exchange purposes. To equalize the values of the exchanged properties, Z pays $800 cash to the transferor of asset B.
   e. Asset A and asset B are not qualified property for nontaxable exchange purposes. To equalize the values of the exchanged properties, Z receives $2,000 cash from the transferor of asset B.
   f. Asset A and asset B are qualified property for nontaxable exchange purposes. To equalize the values of the exchanged properties, Z receives $2,000 cash from the transferor of asset B.
2. In the current year, taxpayer S entered into an arm's length transaction in which S exchanged asset N (tax basis $75,000) for new asset O (fair market value $55,000). Under each of the following assumptions, apply the generic rules to compute S's realized loss, recognized loss, and tax basis in the new

asset. (Note that you do not have enough information to determine the extent to which taxpayer S may deduct any recognized loss in the current year.)

a. Asset N and asset O are not qualified property for nontaxable exchange purposes.

b. Asset N and asset O are qualified property for nontaxable exchange purposes.

c. Asset N and asset O are not qualified property for nontaxable exchange purposes. To equalize the values of the exchanged properties, S pays $4,500 cash to the transferor of asset O.

d. Asset N and asset O are qualified property for nontaxable exchange purposes. To equalize the values of the exchanged properties, S pays $4,500 cash to the transferor of asset O.

e. Asset N and asset O are not qualified property for nontaxable exchange purposes. To equalize the values of the exchanged properties, S receives $12,000 cash from the transferor of asset O.

f. Asset N and asset O are qualified property for nontaxable exchange purposes. To equalize the values of the exchanged properties, S receives $12,000 cash from the transferor of asset O.

3. Taxpayer J exchanged asset Y with a tax basis of $15,000 and a fair market value of $20,000 for asset Z worth $19,000 and $1,000 cash.

   a. If assets Y and Z are qualified assets so that the exchange is nontaxable to J, compute his realized and recognized gain on the exchange and his tax basis in asset Z.

   b. How would your answer to *a* change if asset Z were worth only $13,500 and J received $6,500 cash to equalize the value of the exchanged properties?

4. During the current year, ACE Inc. exchanged printing equipment used in its business for new equipment of a similar type. ACE's adjusted basis in its old equipment was $35,000, and its value was $43,000. ACE had claimed $16,000 of depreciation deductions with respect to this equipment. The value of the new equipment was $50,000; consequently, ACE had to pay $7,000 cash in addition to the old equipment to acquire the new equipment.

   a. If the old equipment and the new equipment do not qualify as like-kind within the meaning of Section 1031, what is the amount and character of gain recognized by ACE on the exchange, and what is the corporation's basis in the new equipment?

   b. If the old equipment and the new equipment do qualify as like-kind within the meaning of Section 1031, what is the amount and character of gain recognized by ACE on the exchange, and what is the corporation's tax basis in the new equipment?

5. Max Lind has agreed to transfer $25,000 cash and his title to a rental house to Sharon Baxter in exchange for her one-third interest in a commercial office building. The value of the rental house is $175,000, while the value of the

interest in the office building is $200,000. Both properties had been depreciated using the straight-line method.

a. If Max's adjusted basis in the rental house is $110,000, what is the amount and character of any gain recognized by Max on the exchange, and what is the tax basis in his interest in the office building?
b. If Max's adjusted basis in the rental house is $195,000, what is the amount and character of any loss recognized by Max on the exchange, and what is the tax basis in his interest in the office building?
c. If Sharon's adjusted basis in her one-third interest in the commercial office building is $153,500, what is the amount and character of any gain recognized by Sharon on the exchange, and what is the tax basis in her rental house?
d. If Sharon's adjusted basis in her one-third interest in the commercial office building is $187,500, what is the amount and character of any gain recognized by Sharon on the exchange, and what is the tax basis in her rental house?
e. If Sharon's adjusted basis in her one-third interest in the commercial office building is $214,000, what is the amount and character of any loss recognized by Sharon on the exchange, and what is the tax basis in her rental house?

6. In the current year, the DGK Partnership exchanged a Toyota automobile used exclusively in its business for a Ford automobile owned by Julie Benner. The partnership will use the Ford exclusively for business purposes. On the other hand, Julie used the Ford and intends to use the Toyota as her personal automobile. In answering the following, assume Toyotas and Fords are like-kind property within the meaning of Section 1031.

a. If the fair market value of the Ford is $24,000 and DGK's tax basis in the Toyota was $19,300, what is the amount and character of any gain recognized by DGK on the exchange, and what is the partnership's tax basis in the Ford?
b. If the fair market value of the Toyota is $24,000 and Julie's tax basis in the Ford was $20,000, what is the amount and character of any gain recognized by Julie on the exchange, and what is her tax basis in the Toyota?
c. If the fair market value of the Toyota is $24,000 and Julie's tax basis in the Ford was $25,000, what is the amount and character of any loss recognized by Julie on the exchange, and what is her tax basis in the Toyota?

7. The Lind Corporation owns investment land in Florida that is worth $200,000 and is subject to a $35,000 mortgage. Dampier Inc. owns a movie theater in Atlanta, Georgia, that is worth $440,000 and is subject to a $275,000 mortgage. By working through a broker that specializes in like-kind exchanges of real estate, the corporations have agreed to swap properties.

a. If Lind Corporation's basis in the Florida land is $185,000, what is the amount of any gain recognized by Lind on the exchange, and what is the corporation's basis in the movie theater?

b. If Dampier Inc.'s basis in the movie theater is $100,000, what is the amount of any gain recognized by Dampier on the exchange, and what is the corporation's basis in the Florida land?

8. Alpha and Omega want to exchange the following real estate properties:

	Alpha	*Omega*
FMV	$200,000	$150,000
Mortgage	45,000	–0–
Adjusted basis	90,000	60,000

a. How much cash should be paid and by whom for this transaction to make sense economically?
b. If the cash determined in *a* is paid, compute Alpha's realized gain, recognized gain, and basis in its new property.
c. If the cash determined in *a* is paid, compute Omega's realized gain, recognized gain, and basis in its new property.

9. Morton Inc. owned residential real estate with an adjusted tax basis of $569,000 that was condemned by the City of Cleveland because it was in the path of a new freeway the city plans to build. Morton received $1 million of condemnation proceeds for this real estate.

a. What are the tax consequences of the condemnation to Morton if it immediately used $200,000 of the proceeds to expand its inventory and the remaining $800,000 to purchase new residential real estate? What tax basis does Morton have in the new real estate?
b. How would your answer to *a* change if Morton's basis in the condemned property had been $1,150,000 rather than $569,000?
c. How would your answer to *a* change if Morton had used the entire amount of condemnation proceeds plus an additional $300,000 cash to purchase new residential real estate?

10. On June 12 of the current year, a thief broke into Jay Kwak's home and stole two personal items—a diamond ring that Jay purchased for $8,800 six years ago and a stereo system that he purchased for $4,500 just last month. The ring was insured for its current replacement cost of $10,000; the stereo was uninsured. Jay decided to use the $10,000 of insurance proceeds to purchase marketable securities. Based on these facts, explain the tax consequences of the theft to Jay.

11. On May 3, 1997, Paul and Pam Stein (ages 42 and 40) sold their principal residence for $146,000. They had purchased this home in 1980 for $87,500. Determine the amount of capital gain the Steins must recognize in 1997 because of the sale and the tax basis of their new home in each of the following cases:

a. The Steins purchased a new principal residence on January 13, 1997, for $175,000.
b. The Steins rented an apartment and did not purchase a new principal residence until August 16, 1999. The cost of the new home was $175,000.

c. The Steins purchased a new principal residence on March 31, 1998, for $115,000.
d. The Steins purchased a duplex for $160,000 on July 5, 1997. They use one unit of the duplex as their principal residence and lease the other unit to unrelated tenants.

12. Janet Munro, age 57, sold her principal residence on October 2 of the current year. The selling price was $255,000 and her tax basis in the residence was $200,000. Janet anticipates purchasing another home sometime in the future. However, for the next several years, she plans to travel extensively. In between trips, she will live in a rented apartment in New York City.

    a. What are the current year tax consequences to Janet if she makes a Section 121 election with respect to the $55,000 gain realized on the sale of her principal residence?
    b. Discuss with Janet the reasons she might not want to make a Section 121 election in the current year.

13. Bixby Inc. and Criola Inc. decided to become partners in a real estate development project. Bixby Inc. contributed land (fair market value $145,000, basis to Bixby of $25,000) in exchange for a one-third interest in the B&C Partnership, while Criola Inc. contributed land (fair market value $290,000, basis to Criola of $200,000) in exchange for a two-thirds interest.

    a. Determine the amount of gain recognized by the two corporations on this partnership formation, and compute the tax basis each has in its respective partnership interest.
    b. What tax basis does B&C Partnership have in the land contributed by its two partners?
    c. Two years after the partnership was formed, Bixby Inc. contributes certain business equipment (fair market value $65,000, basis to Bixby of $18,000). As a result of this contribution, Bixby's interest in B&C Partnership is increased to 44 percent. How much gain must Bixby Inc. recognize on the exchange of the equipment for an additional interest in the partnership?

14. Marty Bates owns 14,600 shares of Zeta Inc. common stock with a basis of $13 per share. This stock is currently selling on the New York Stock Exchange for $20 per share. Marty wants to diversify his investment portfolio by exchanging 8,000 shares of his Zeta stock for 4,000 shares of Delphi Inc. preferred stock, which are owned by a business associate of Marty's and are currently trading at $40 per share.

    a. Determine Marty's current year tax consequences if he makes this stock-for-stock exchange.
    b. What would be the tax consequences to Marty if he sells 8,000 Zeta shares for $160,000 cash and immediately reinvests the proceeds in a partnership that qualifies as an SSBIC? This would be Marty's first investment in an SSBIC.

15. Two years ago, Curtis Boyd purchased 1,345 shares of stock in Primat Corporation for $41,500. These shares are Section 1244 stock to Curtis. At the current time, the Primat shares are worth only $33,400, but Curtis believes the future of the corporation is bright, and he views the Primat shares as an excellent long-term investment. He would, however, like to trigger the unrealized loss accrued in the shares so he could deduct it against his current year salary income, which is high enough to put Curtis into the 39.6 percent marginal tax bracket.
    a. What are the tax consequences to Curtis if he sells the Primat stock on July 8 of the current year for $33,400 and repurchases it on July 12 for $33,950?
    b. What are the tax consequences to Curtis if he waits until August 12 to repurchase the Primat stock, but has to pay the current market price of $36,800 for the 1,345 shares? In this case, is Curtis financially better off because he managed to avoid the wash sale rule?

Case 8–1

Dick and Jane have decided to combine their two sole proprietorships into a new corporate entity, D&J Inc. Dick plans to transfer business assets worth $80,000 (adjusted basis $39,500) for 800 shares of stock, while Jane plans to transfer business assets worth $60,000 (adjusted basis $80,000) for 600 shares of stock. Dick, who is an attorney and CPA, will perform all the professional services necessary to complete the incorporation. In exchange for these services, he will receive an additional 50 shares of D&J stock.

a. Will Dick have to recognize any income or gain on this incorporation transaction? Explain briefly. Compute the tax basis in his 850 shares of B&J stock.

b. Will Jane be able to recognize a business loss on the exchange of her assets for B&J stock? Explain briefly. Can you suggest an alternative plan that might result in a better tax outcome to Jane?

c. Assuming the incorporation is completed based on Dick and Jane's original plan, what tax basis will B&J have in the transferred assets? What are the tax consequences to the corporation of paying Dick for his professional services with shares of stock rather than with cash?

Case 8–2

Fred Flatstone has been farming Flatstone Fields ever since he inherited it from his father 30 years ago. The value of the farmland as of the date of his father's death was $45,000. In recent years, civilization has been encroaching on the farm as more and more shopping centers and residential developments are built on the surrounding acreage. In addition to Flatstone Fields, Fred owns common stock in Dino Inc. with a value of $100,000 and a basis to Fred of $32,000.

Cliff Barnes is a local developer and real estate broker who routinely buys and sells both developed and undeveloped real estate. Cliff is eager to acquire Flatstone Fields and is willing to pay $900,000 cash to Fred for the land. Alternatively, Cliff is willing to transfer title to the Barnes Shopping Plaza to Fred in exchange for Flatstone Fields and the Dino stock. Cliff's adjusted basis in the shopping plaza is $500,000.

a. What amount and character of income must Fred recognize if he exchanges his farmland and stock for the shopping center? What basis would Fred have in the Barnes Shopping Plaza subsequent to this exchange?

b. Are there any immediate negative tax implications to Fred if he acquires the shopping center in a nontaxable exchange?

c. What amount and character of income must Cliff recognize if he exchanges the shopping center for the farm and stock? What basis would Cliff have in Flatstone Fields and the Dino Inc. stock?

CHAPTER 9

Special Limitations on Business and Passive-Activity Losses

To this point in the text, we have been operating under the premise that a business loss (an excess of business deductions over the gross income generated by a trade or business activity) is fully deductible against all other sources of a taxpayer's income. This premise is reflected by the fact that corporations with multiple lines of business can deduct a loss generated by one business against the income generated by another. If a corporation has an overall net operating loss for the year, that loss may be deducted against taxable income in other years through the mechanism of a net operating loss carryback or carryforward. If an affiliated group of corporations files a consolidated tax return, the net operating loss of one member corporation can be deducted against the taxable incomes of other members.

Business losses incurred by individual taxpayers enjoy a similar versatility. In marked contrast to investment losses and personal losses, business losses are fully deductible in computing an individual's adjusted gross income. In a year in which a person's business losses exceed his or her gross income, the excess loss can be carried back or forward as a net operating loss deduction. Business losses for individuals arise from a number of sources. The operation of a sole proprietorship or the rental of developed real estate can result in a business loss. Individuals who invest in business partnerships or S corporations may be allocated losses from the passthrough entity. Whatever its source, a business loss has the potential to offset current income recognized from other sources on an individual taxpayer's Form 1040.

In their purest form, business losses are attributable to an excess of annual operating expenses over revenues. From an economic perspective, the fact that a business loss may be deductible against other sources of income is only the silver lining on a dark and ominous cloud. Current deductibility can only minimize the after-tax cost of a business loss; it can't magically convert the loss into a financial benefit.

In this chapter we will explore a series of limitations on the deductibility of business losses. In the first half of the chapter, we'll look at the basis limitation rules applicable to losses generated by partnerships and S corporations. We'll move on to brief discussions of the phenomenon of tax-shelter losses, the origins of the tax-shelter industry, and the at-risk rules of Section 465. The second half of the chapter is devoted to a more thorough analysis of the passive-activity loss limitation of Section 469.

BASIS LIMITATIONS ON BUSINESS LOSSES

A taxpayer who makes a direct investment in an asset risks losing that investment if the asset is destroyed or becomes worthless. In other words, the amount of investment becomes the measure of the potential loss inherent in the asset. For tax purposes, the amount of the investment equates to the *adjusted basis* in the asset; the adjusted basis represents the maximum amount deductible if the taxpayer is unable to recoup his investment.

This same logic applies when a taxpayer invests in a business activity operated by a passthrough entity. The taxpayer's unrecovered investment, the amount she stands to lose if the business is unsuccessful, is reflected in the tax basis in her partnership interest (an intangible equity interest in a partnership) or her shares of stock in an S corporation. You may recall from Chapter 7 that the basis of an interest in a passthrough entity includes both the owner's direct investment of cash or property and any indirect investment in the form of the entity's undistributed income on which the owner has already paid tax.

When a passthrough entity incurs a business loss, the owner may deduct her allocated share of the loss but must reflect this indirect decrease in her investment by a negative basis adjustment. Negative adjustments can reduce the basis in a partnership interest or S corporation stock to zero, but cannot create a negative basis. Once basis has been reduced to zero, any additional losses allocated from the passthrough entity are nondeductible to the owner. These *suspended losses* are carried forward into future years and can be deducted if and when the owner increases the tax basis in her interest above zero. Conceptually, a zero basis in an interest in a passthrough entity indicates the owner has recovered her entire investment in the business in the form of tax deductions. The owner will not be entitled to further deductions until she is willing to make an additional investment in the business, or until the passthrough entity earns income that creates positive basis adjustments for its partners or shareholders.

To illustrate this loss limitation rule, let's assume Karen Wilson purchased one fourth of the outstanding stock in Summa Inc., a calendar year S corporation, for $25,000. During the first two years in which Karen was a shareholder, she was allocated $12,000 of Summa's business income and received no cash distributions, so at the beginning of the third year the adjusted tax basis in her Summa stock had increased to $37,000.

	Karen's Stock Basis
Initial cost basis	$25,000
Years 1 and 2:	
Allocated business income	12,000
Cash distributions	–0–
Tax basis at beginning of Year 3	$37,000
Year 3:	
Allocated business loss $40,600	
Currently deductible loss	(37,000)
Loss carryforward $3,600	
Tax basis at beginning of Year 4	–0–
Year 4:	
Allocated business income	$ 7,500
Deductible carryforward from Year 3	(3,600)
Tax basis at beginning of Year 5	$ 3,900

During the third year, Summa suffered a net operating loss, $40,600 of which was allocated to Karen. Karen can deduct $37,000 of this loss on her current year tax return; the $3,600 loss in excess of her stock basis can only be carried forward into future years. At the beginning of the fourth year, Karen's stock basis is zero. In the fourth year, Summa's business is again profitable and Karen is allocated $7,500 of taxable income. This income allocation increases Karen's stock basis to $7,500, enabling her to deduct her $3,600 loss carryforward from the previous year. Consequently, in the fourth year, Karen will pay tax on only $3,900 of net business income and will begin the fifth year with a positive $3,900 basis in her Summa stock.

The Inclusion of Debt as Investment Basis

Owners of passthrough entities have a strong incentive to maintain sufficient basis in their ownership interests to allow a current deduction for their allocated shares of the entity's business losses. The tax laws governing partnerships and S corporations are structured to help owners in this respect. Partners are entitled to include a proportionate amount of the partnership's debt in the basis of their partnership interests. As a simple illustration, suppose three individuals each contribute $10,000 cash to a newly created business partnership in which they are equal general partners. The partnership immediately borrows $24,000 from a local bank, which it uses to purchase equipment and supplies. Each partner's basis in his partnership interest is $18,000, the initial cash contribution plus a proportionate share of the partnership debt. While the mechanics for determining the precise amount of debt included in each partner's basis are technically complex, the theory underlying the inclusion is simple. Because of their unlimited liability, general partners may be required by law to make additional investments in the partnership business to satisfy creditor claims. Accordingly, the partners bear the potential risk of economic loss for every dollar borrowed by a partnership, and this risk is reflected as basis in their partnership interests.

Shareholders in S corporations enjoy limited liability; they are not responsible for debts incurred by the corporate entity. Consequently, the debts of an S corporation are not included in the basis of the stock held by the corporate shareholders. However, if a shareholder makes a direct loan to an S corporation, the amount of the loan is regarded as additional investment in the corporation against which the shareholder can deduct allocated business losses. Let's return for a moment to our example involving Karen Wilson and Summa Inc. At the beginning of the third taxable year, Karen's basis in her Summa stock was $37,000. During the year, Karen was allocated a $40,600 loss from Summa, only $37,000 of which was deductible because of the basis limitation. If Karen were willing to lend Summa $3,600 before the end of the year, she could deduct the remaining portion of her current year loss. This additional deduction would reduce the basis in her Summa debt to zero.

While this tax planning strategy seems appealing, Karen should carefully consider the risk inherent in her loan. If Summa's current year loss is a symptom of real financial distress, Karen's $3,600 loan may never be repaid. In such case, Karen would have committed the grievous error of spending $3,600 to secure a deduction worth, at most, $1,426 in tax savings. Karen should also understand that if Summa subsequently repays the debt (in which she has a zero tax basis), she must include the repayment in her gross income. Although her loan of the money to the corporation triggered a $3,000 tax deduction, its repayment will trigger $3,000 of income recognition. If Summa generates future taxable income before it repays its debt to Karen, the first $3,000 of income allocated to Karen will restore the basis in her debt to $3,000, and its subsequent repayment will be a nontaxable return of investment.

TAX-SHELTER LOSSES

If the stream of tax deductions generated over the life of a profitable business activity can in some way be divorced from actual cash flow and front-end loaded into the early years of the business operation, the result may be net operating losses deductible against other sources of the owner's income. Because of the acceleration of deductions, the recognition of taxable income is postponed and concentrated in the later years of the operation. As a result, the tax liability on this income is deferred and the present value of the cash flow from the business may be correspondingly increased.

A simple comparison of two business activities can demonstrate the relationship between tax deferral and cash flow. Assume two businesses, A and B, require an initial investment of $50,000 and will generate $21,000 of net business income over a three-year period. At the end of the three years, the $50,000 investment can be recovered intact. Business A generates $7,000 of taxable income and cash flow annually. If the owner of Business A is in a 39.6 percent marginal tax bracket, his after-tax cash flow from the business each year will be $4,228 and the present value of the cash flows at a 10 percent discount rate is $11,566.

Business A

Year	*Taxable Income*	*Cash Flow*	*Tax Savings or (Cost)*	*After-tax Cash Flow*	*Present Value of Cash Flow*
1	$ 7,000	$ 7,000	($2,772)	$ 4,228	$ 4,228
2	7,000	7,000	(2,772)	4,228	3,844
3	7,000	7,000	(2,772)	4,228	3,494
Total	$21,000	$21,000	($8,316)	$12,684	$11,566

Business B generates the same annual $7,000 cash flow; however, B's business operation is structured so that for tax purposes the first year of operations results in a $9,000 operating loss, while the second and third years' operations generate $12,000 and $18,000 of taxable income. The owner of Business B, also in a 39.6 percent tax bracket, can use his first-year loss to shelter other income and save $3,564 in taxes. Consequently, his cash flow from the business in the first year is $10,564. In the second and third years, the after-tax cash flow will equal $2,248 and ($128), respectively ($7,000 actual cash less tax liability on the taxable income). This pattern of cash flow has a present value of $12,502, a $936 improvement over the value of the cash flow from Business A.

			Business B		
Year	*Taxable Income*	*Cash Flow*	*Tax Savings or (Cost)*	*After-tax Cash Flow*	*Present Value of Cash Flow*
1	$(9,000)	$7,000	$3,564	$10,564	$10,564
2	12,000	7,000	(4,752)	2,248	2,044
3	18,000	7,000	(7,128)	(128)	(106)
Total	$21,000	$21,000	($8,316)	$12,684	$12,502

Tax Preference Deductions and Credits

The accrual method of accounting generally requires that revenues and all the expenses or costs incurred to generate such revenues be properly matched in the same year. As a result, taxpayers normally have little opportunity to mismatch by reporting deductions in an early year while deferring recognition of the related income until a later year. Congress, however, has long understood that it can affect the rate of return on investments in targeted businesses or industries by deliberately authorizing the acceleration of certain deductions or by creating artificial deductions and tax credits totally unrelated to negative cash flow or decline in asset value. These *tax preference* deductions and credits represent an indirect form of government subsidy; companies entitled to use preferences will inflate their rates of return on invested capital because of the current year tax savings attributable to the preference items. Investors will be attracted by this enhanced rate of return, and new sources of capital will flow into the targeted business or industry.

The oil and gas industry has been one of the most obvious beneficiaries of congressional largess in the tax preference area. The Internal Revenue Code provides that the intangible drilling and development costs of new oil and gas wells are deductible in the year incurred, even if such costs create a valuable asset (an oil well) with a productive life of many years. Similarly, certain oil and gas producers can deduct percentage depletion against their revenues from sales. The computation of percentage depletion was covered in Chapter 6; the characteristic of this deduction germane to our discussion of tax preference items is that percentage depletion is wholly independent of any economic cost incurred by the oil and gas producer.

Tax-Sheltered Investments

During the decades of the 1960s and 1970s, Congress enacted a number of tax preference items, which in turn gave birth to a wide variety of tax-favored or *tax-sheltered* investment opportunities. These investments were characterized by very attractive rates of return, which were primarily a function of the special tax benefits unique to the investment. Typically, the tax benefits resulted in artificial *paper losses* in the early years of the investment, losses that sheltered the investor's taxable income from other sources. The tax liability on the profit generated by the investment was deferred until the later years, so the effect of the tax cost on the investment's rate of return was minimized. Two key elements determined the rate of return on tax-sheltered investments:

the existence of other current income against which the investor could deduct tax-shelter losses and the marginal tax rate of the investor. The higher this tax rate, the greater the tax savings attributable to the shelter losses, and the higher the rate of return on the investment.

Investors who hastened to put their money into tax-sheltered business activities were behaving precisely as Congress intended. However, Congress soon observed that its use of the tax law to manipulate economic behavior was having undesirable side effects. Many enthusiastic high-income taxpayers sheltered so much current income that they ended up paying little or no federal tax. When these taxpayers realized that one generation of tax-sheltered investments was running out of front-end deductions and would soon begin to churn out large amounts of taxable income, they simply invested in another generation of shelters, thereby avoiding taxes year after year while their net wealth continued to increase. The adverse publicity concerning the hundreds of millionaires who paid no federal tax because of their ability to shelter their income certainly reinforced the public's belief that the tax system was inequitable and favored the rich over the middle and lower classes.

Unscrupulous tax-shelter promoters exploited the system by marketing *abusive tax shelters,* investments absolutely devoid of economic substance but larded with immediate tax write-offs. Bedazzled taxpayers who bought into these shelters often discovered that their original investments could never be recouped, and the Internal Revenue Service had no intention of allowing any of the spurious tax benefits to stand. The IRS mounted aggressive campaigns to stamp out the worst excesses in the shelter industry, asserting that many shelters lacked any semblance of a business purpose and should not be given effect for tax purposes. By the early 1980s, thousands of tax cases concerning the legitimacy of tax-sheltered investments had flooded into the legal system.

Because of the investment advantages associated with tax-favored industries, serious misallocations of national resources became apparent. A prime example of this misallocation occurred in the real estate industry. Real estate developers benefited enormously in 1981 when Congress enacted an accelerated system of cost recovery deductions for investments in depreciable real property. Under the original ACRS, the cost of buildings with productive lives of 40 to 50 years could be deducted over 15 years under a computational method accelerating almost 40 percent of the total deductions into the first four years. Developers plunged into a frenzy of construction as shelter-hungry taxpayers clamored for new investment opportunities, neither group paying much attention to the fact that the supply of commercial office space rapidly surpassed any reasonable expectation of future demand. Although Congress quickly tried to remedy the situation by extending the recovery period for real estate, the damage was done. By the mid-1980s, the real estate market had virtually collapsed under its own weight, forcing thousands of developers and investors alike into bankruptcy.

As the political and economic problems caused by the widespread availability of tax-sheltered investments started to surface, Congress began to see itself in the role of Dr. Frankenstein. Legislators debated the merits of a variety of proposals devised to somehow control the monster; some of these proposals eventually became law, while others were discarded. As we will discuss in Chapter 11, the alternative minimum tax was designed to ensure that both individual and corporate taxpayers who were sheltered from the regular income tax would pay at least some minimum amount into the federal coffers. The enactment of the at-risk rules was a second major attempt to tame the tax-shelter industry.

The At-Risk Rules

As we learned earlier in this chapter, partners in business partnerships can deduct their allocated losses only to the extent of the basis in their partnership interests. Also recall that any type of debt incurred by the partnership is included in the partners' bases. Because of this inclusion, partners in highly leveraged partnerships can deduct losses far in excess of the amount of cash they invest in the partnership business. In 1976, Congress tried to limit the deductibility of losses from tax-shelter partnerships to the amount of basis for which a partner bore a real economic risk of loss. Section 465 was enacted to disallow any loss in excess of a taxpayer's *at-risk amount.* Generally, the at-risk amount excludes any basis attributable to *nonrecourse debt,* debt secured only by partnership assets and for which no partner is personally liable.

The 1976 version of Section 465 was fatally flawed because it did not apply to investments in real estate, the industry in which nonrecourse financing was the most common. Although the section was revised a number of times, the at-risk rules have never lived up to congressional expectations. While these rules are still in effect, they have been eclipsed by still another deterrent against tax-shelter losses, the passive-activity loss limitation.

THE PASSIVE-ACTIVITY LOSS LIMITATION

Taxpayers reporting passive-activity losses may discover that these losses, like net capital losses, cannot be used to shelter taxable income from other sources, at least in the year in which they are first realized. Section 469, which disallows a current deduction for passive-activity losses, was introduced into the law in 1986 and was intended to discourage investment in tax shelters. Unfortunately, the provisions of Section 469 are worded so broadly that they may affect taxpayers in unintended ways. The complexity of this loss limitation will make self-compliance more difficult for anyone investing in a start-up trade or business that even temporarily loses money. In the remainder of this chapter, we will examine the basic provisions of Section 469, beginning with a broad overview and concluding with some tax planning considerations to help individuals cope with this important limitation.

A General Overview

Certain taxpayers who realize a business loss during the year may be unable to deduct the loss if it is generated by an interest in a passive activity. A passive-activity loss can be deducted against income generated by other passive activities, but not against portfolio income, compensation income, or income derived from an active business. To illustrate the fundamental impact of this limitation, assume an individual recognizes the following items of net income and loss during the year.

Source A	($20,000)
Source B	5,000
Source C	50,000
Total net income	$35,000

If source A is a passive activity, while sources B and C are not, this taxpayer would report net taxable income of $55,000. On the other hand, if source A is an active trade or business, this taxpayer would report net taxable income of only $35,000.

Even though net losses from passive activities cannot be deducted currently against other sources of income, they can be carried forward and offset against income from passive activities in subsequent years. Let's expand on our earlier example by adding information for the next two years, as follows:

	19x1	*19x2*	*19x3*	*Three-Year Total*
Passive activity	($20,000)	($ 5,000)	$ 30,000	$ 5,000
Portfolio source	5,000	7,000	10,000	22,000
Active business sources	50,000	63,000	70,000	183,000
Net income	$35,000	$65,000	$110,000	$210,000
Taxable income	$55,000	$70,000	$ 85,000	$210,000

This example shows that the Section 469 limitation is generally intended to delay rather than to deny the deduction for losses generated by passive activities. If a passive activity with front-end losses becomes profitable in its later years, the disallowed front-end losses can offset the income recognized in the later years. What happens if a taxpayer disposes of a passive activity before it has produced sufficient income to absorb all the losses carried forward from prior years? If the taxpayer's entire interest in the passive activity is disposed of in a taxable transaction, the taxpayer may report any loss carryforwards from the activity as fully deductible business losses in the year of disposition. A more thorough discussion of the tax consequences of passive-activity dispositions is included later in the chapter.

DEFINITIONS

The correct application of the Section 469 limitation depends on an understanding of a number of important definitional terms. A *passive-activity loss* is defined as the *net* loss from all passive activities in which a taxpayer engages during the year. It is this net loss that is nondeductible against portfolio income, compensation income, or income generated by an active business. It is important to appreciate the fact that a loss from one passive activity is fully deductible to the extent of income from another passive activity. Therefore, an investor who anticipates a loss from one passive activity has a strong incentive to acquire an interest in a profitable passive activity. By sanctioning the netting of passive-activity losses and income, Congress created a new type of tax-favored investment, *passive income generators,* affectionately nicknamed PIGs by the financial press.

A nondeductible passive-activity loss in the current year is suspended and carried forward into subsequent years when it may be deducted against future passive-activity income. Any portion of a suspended passive-activity loss attributable to a specific activity will be fully deductible against any source of income in a future year in which that entire activity is disposed of in a fully taxable transaction. To determine the portion of a suspended passive-activity loss attributable to each passive activity owned by the taxpayer, an allocation procedure is necessary.

Loss Allocation

Suppose a taxpayer is engaged in three passive activities with the following gains and losses in the current year.

Passive Activity	*Gain or Loss*
1	$15,000
2	(6,000)
3	(12,000)
Net passive-activity loss	($3,000)

We know that the current $3,000 passive-activity loss is suspended and carried forward. But to which activity is the disallowed loss attributable? The answer is to both of the losing activities. The $3,000 loss carryforward is allocated between activities 2 and 3 on a relative loss basis, as follows:

Activity 2: $ 6,000/$18,000 × $3,000 = $1,000
Activity 3: $12,000/$18,000 × $3,000 = $2,000

If the taxpayer sells activity 3 in the next year, the $2,000 suspended loss attributable to the activity will be "freed up"—fully deductible in that year as a business loss. The $1,000 suspended loss attributable to activity 2 continues to be subject to the passive-activity loss limitation.

Passive Activity

The Internal Revenue Code defines two types of passive activity. The first type is any trade or business in which the taxpayer does not materially participate. The second type is any rental activity, regardless of the level of participation of the taxpayer. Rental activities are generally characterized by payments from customers for the use of tangible property. However, activities in which substantial services are provided and customer payments are principally for such services rather than for the use of property are not considered rental activities. For example, the operation of a hotel is considered a business, not a rental activity. Similarly, businesses providing short-term use of property such as automobiles, tuxedos, or videocassettes are not rental activities.

Real estate professionals who devote more than 50 percent of their work efforts each year (a minimum of 750 hours annually) to a real property trade or business are considered to be engaged in business, rather than rental, activities. As a result, if such professionals meet the material participation requirement with respect to a real property trade or business that generates a loss, such loss is not subject to the Section 469 limitation. A *real property trade or business* is defined as any real estate development, redevelopment, construction, reconstruction, acquisition, conversion, rental, operation, management, leasing, or brokerage business.

Material Participation

When a taxpayer acquires an interest in a trade or business, the classification of that interest as either active or passive depends on the relationship between the taxpayer and the business. If the taxpayer *materially participates* in the business, the taxpayer's interest is active. If the taxpayer fails to meet this material participation standard, the interest is a passive activity. Clearly, the definition of material participation is crucial. The statute itself states that a taxpayer is materially participating only if he or she is involved in the operations of the business on a regular, continuous, and substantial basis. Material participation is determined independently for each taxable year (i.e., on an annual basis) and by reference to all relevant facts and circumstance. Factors to be considered could include (1) the frequency and regularity of the taxpayer's presence at the principal location from which business is conducted; (2) the nature of the work done by the taxpayer; (3) the significance of the taxpayer's efforts to the success of the overall business operation; and (4) the relationship between the taxpayer and the other individuals performing services in the business.

The Treasury has published regulations providing a number of reasonably objective tests for material participation. Under the first (and simplest) test, a taxpayer is presumed to materially participate in a business activity if he or she participates in the activity for more than 500 hours during the taxable year. Under the second text, material participation is established if the taxpayer's participation in the business activity constitutes substantially all of the participation of all individuals (including employees) for the taxable year. Thus, a sole proprietor who operates a business singlehandedly is materially participating in that business even if he or she only devotes 300 hours a year to its operation. On the other hand, if the sole proprietor turns over the day-to-day operations of the business to his employees and makes only an occasional management decision, neither the first nor second regulatory test for material participation is met. Our sole proprietor may have to rely on a subjective facts-and-circumstances argument to convince the Internal Revenue Service that material participation exists.

Activity

Given that the material participation requirement is applied to each separate *activity* in which a taxpayer has an interest, determining the scope of a single activity becomes necessary. To illustrate the importance of the activity concept, consider the following situation. Taxpayer Jerry Jones is a general partner in a partnership owning and operating a sporting goods store in Kansas City, Missouri. Jerry manages the store and devotes 1,500 hours during the taxable year to this business. During the current year, the partnership purchases a second sporting goods store in the same city. However, another partner manages this store, and Jerry is not involved in its daily operations. If the two stores are considered separate activities, Jerry Jones materially participates in one, but not the other. As a result, her interest in the first sporting goods store is an active business, while her interest in the second store is a passive activity. On the other hand, if the two stores are simply considered two divisions of a single activity, Jerry meets the material participation test with regards to this activity.

The definition of activity also becomes critical when a taxpayer disposes of a business interest. Assume an individual taxpayer owns two business interests with suspended passive-activity losses. In the current year, the taxpayer sells his interest in one business, but retains his interest in the second. If the two interests constitute a single passive activity, the taxpayer has failed to dispose of his *entire* interest in the activity, and no amount of suspended loss will be currently deductible. Alternatively, if the two interests are two separate passive activities, the sale of one activity will free up the suspended losses attributable to that activity.

The Senate Finance Committee Report (p. 739) accompanying the 1986 act explained the activity concept as follows:

> The determination of what constitutes a separate activity is intended to be made in a realistic economic sense. The question to be answered is what undertakings consist of an integrated and interrelated economic unit, conducted in coordination with or reliance upon each other, and constituting an appropriate unit for the measurement of gain or loss.

The Treasury regulations that define the term *activity* require taxpayers to combine separate business undertakings or rental undertakings into a single Section 469 activity if the undertakings represent an *appropriate economic unit.* The existence of an appropriate economic unit is based on all relevant facts and circumstances concerning the separate undertakings in question, including (1) similarities or differences in type or function of the undertakings, (2) the extent of common control, (3) the extent of common ownership, (4) the geographic locations, and (5) the interdependence of the undertakings. If we return to the situation involving Jerry Jones and evaluate the two sporting goods stores based on these criteria, the facts that the stores perform exactly the same function, are owned and controlled by one partnership, and are located in the same city strongly indicate they are an appropriate economic unit that must be regarded as a single business activity within the meaning of Section 469.

Portfolio, Compensation, and Active Business Income

The essence of the passive-activity loss limitation is that a passive-activity loss may not be used by a taxpayer to shelter his portfolio income, compensation income, or active business income. Portfolio income is produced by investment assets and includes interest, dividends, annuities, and royalties. Portfolio income also includes net gains recognized on the sale of investment assets. Compensation income includes wages, salaries, professional fees, and any income derived from the performances of personal services. Active business income is derived from a trade or business in which the taxpayer materially participates.

TAXPAYERS AFFECTED

The Section 469 limitation applies to all individual and fiduciary taxpayers as well as to closely held and personal service corporations. A corporation is closely held if at any time during the last half of its taxable year, 50 percent or more of the corporation's outstanding stock is owned by five or fewer individuals. A corporation is a personal service corporation if employees own more than 10 percent of the corporation's stock and if the principal corporate activity is the performance of personal services by the owner-employees. For corporate taxpayers subject to the passive-activity loss limitation, the determination of material participation is made with reference to the participation of the corporation's shareholders and employees.

A special statutory rule relaxes the passive-activity loss limitation to allow closely held corporations that are not personal service corporations to offset any passive-activity losses against active business income. Consequently, the limitation only forbids the deduction of passive-activity losses against a closely held corporation's portfolio income. This special rule means that closely held, profitable corporations can continue to use tax-shelter losses with minimal restriction. High-income taxpayers who own tax-sheltered investments generating passive-activity losses and profitable nonservice businesses should consider contributing both to a controlled corporate entity so the passive-activity losses can shelter the business income at the corporate level.

Passthrough Entities

The active, passive, or portfolio classification of any item of gross income or deduction recognized by a partnership or S corporation is determined by the relationship between the item and each partner or shareholder in the passthrough entity. Therefore, even if a partnership or S corporation is engaged in an active business, the net income or loss incurred in that business is not automatically deemed to be from an active source. That determination will be made with respect to each general partner or shareholder and will depend on whether that partner or shareholder materially participates in the entity's business. By legal definition, limited partners are not involved in the management or operations of a partnership; accordingly, the statute provides a presumption that limited partners do not materially participate in the partnership business.

To illustrate, assume three individual partners each own a one-third interest in the ABC partnership. During the current year, ABC recognizes a \$30,000 net business loss after paying \$25,000 to general partner A as compensation for services rendered. The partnership also earned \$5,100 of dividend income during the year and recognized a \$1,500 capital gain on the sale of marketable securities. While general partner A works full time for the partnership, general partner B participates only in occasional major business decisions, while partner C is a limited partner. The correct classification of ABC's income and loss for the year is shown on the next page.

Because of partner A's material participation in the partnership business, his interest in ABC is an active business interest. As a result, A will be able to deduct his allocated share of the business loss against his other sources of income for the year. However, partners B and C do not materially participate in the business. Their interests are passive activities, and their allocated shares of the partnership loss will be deductible only against income generated by other passive activities they may happen to own.

	Active	*Passive*	*Portfolio*
Partner A:			
Compensation	$25,000		
Net business loss	(10,000)		
Dividend income			$1,700
Capital gain			500
Partner B:			
Net business loss		($10,000)	
Dividend income			1,700
Capital gain			500
Partner C:			
Net business loss		(10,000)	
Dividend income			1,700
Capital gain			500

DISPOSITIONS OF PASSIVE ACTIVITIES

Any suspended loss attributable to a passive activity becomes fully deductible in the year in which the taxpayer disposes of his or her entire interest in the activity in a taxable transaction. Note that such a disposition is the final event in the life cycle of any business activity; at this point, all deferrals of income must come home to roost and all deferred losses must be acknowledged as true economic losses.

To illustrate these concepts, assume Bob Green invested in a business activity several years ago. Because Bob did not materially participate in the business and owned no interests in other passive activities, the $35,000 of ordinary losses allocated to him from the business were nondeductible passive-activity losses. In the current year, Bob sells his interest in the activity and recognizes a $75,000 gain, attributable to appreciation in the market value of the activity's business operation. At this point of final reckoning, it is clear that Bob made a wise economic decision when he invested in this particular business; over time his investment yielded a $40,000 net gain. Because Bob will include the $75,000 gain realized on sale in his current year gross income and deduct his $35,000 suspended passive-activity loss, his taxable income for the year will reflect this net gain. If Bob's sale of his passive-activity interest resulted in a $15,000 loss, the business investment has proven to be a disaster. Bob's total economic loss over time (the $35,000 suspended loss carryforward and the $15,000 loss realized on sale) is no longer subject to the Section 469 limitation, and Bob may report these losses on his current year return.[1]

Nontaxable and Partial Dispositions

Dispositions of passive activities in nontaxable transactions or dispositions of less than the taxpayer's entire interest in the activity do not free any suspended loss attributable to the activity. For example, if Bob Green transferred his interest in the passive activity to his closely held corporation in a nontaxable exchange, his $35,000 of suspended losses would remain subject to the passive-activity loss limitation even though Bob no longer directly owns the activity. Will the losses become deductible if Bob sells all his corporate stock? This and many other interesting questions concerning nontaxable and partial dispositions of passive activities have not yet been addressed in Treasury regulations.

Dispositions on Death or by Gift

If an individual owning a passive activity interest with suspended losses dies, the amount of the suspended loss that would have reduced taxable income if the owner had sold the interest for its fair market value immediately before death can be deducted on the decedent's final Form 1040. To explain this rule, let's consider a situation in which Elena Ruiz, an elderly widow, owns an interest in a passive activity (stock in an S corporation) with a $50,000 suspended loss. Elena's basis in the stock is $10,000 and its market value is $28,000. If Elena were to sell this stock (her entire interest in the passive activity), she would recognize an $18,000 gain and could deduct the entire $50,000 suspended loss. Thus, the net impact of the sale would be a $32,000 reduction in Elena's current year taxable income. If Elena dies, the S corporation stock passes to her estate and eventually to her heirs with a $28,000 basis (fair market value at the date of Elena's death). Section 469 requires that Elena's $50,000 suspended loss be reduced by the $18,000 tax-free basis step-up triggered by her death so that only $32,000 of loss is deductible on Elena's final Form 1040. Note that if the value of the S corporation stock exceeded $60,000, the tax-free basis step-up on Elena's death would be greater than $50,000 and no amount of the suspended passive-activity loss could be deducted in the year of her death.

If a taxpayer disposes of a passive activity by gift, any suspended losses are added to the carryover basis of the property in the hands of the donee. In this case, the donor will never derive any tax benefit from the suspended losses. Because these losses have been capitalized to the basis of the transferred interest, the donee will enjoy an indirect tax benefit from the suspended losses only if and when the interest in the passive activity is sold.

---

[1]The $35,000 ordinary business loss should be fully deductible in computing Bob's adjusted gross income. The $15,000 loss realized on sale of the interest may be a capital loss subject to the capital loss limitation discussed in Chapter 7.

SPECIALIZED APPLICATIONS OF THE PASSIVE-ACTIVITY RULES

Many specialized and detailed rules govern the correct application of the Section 469 limitation. This final section will discuss four of the more important specialized applications and will conclude with some thoughts concerning viable tax planning opportunities in the passive-activity area.

Passive-Activity Credits

If a passive activity generates a tax credit allocable to a taxpayer, the credit may only be used to reduce any portion of the taxpayer's current year tax liability attributable to net passive-activity income for the year. For example, if a taxpayer is allocated a $20,000 general business credit from a passive activity, has net passive-activity income for the year of $45,000, and is in a 36 percent marginal tax bracket, he may use $16,200 of the credit to offset the tax liability attributable to the passive-activity income. The unused credit of $3,800 is carried forward into future years. This example highlights the fact that a passive-activity credit may never reduce current tax liability in a year in which a taxpayer has a passive-activity *loss.* Unlike suspended passive-activity losses, a suspended credit attributable to an activity does not escape the Section 469 limitation in the year the entire activity is disposed of in a taxable transaction. However, the credit can still be carried forward to reduce tax liability on future passive-activity income.

De Minimis Rule for Rental Real Estate

Rental activities are automatically classified as passive activities, regardless of the extent of the owner's participation in the activity. Were it not for a special rule, many relatively low-income taxpayers who own one or two rental properties would be subject to the passive-activity limitation on their rental losses. To avoid catching these little fish in the Section 469 net, Congress carved out an exception so individual taxpayers can deduct up to $25,000 annually of any passive-activity loss attributable to rental real estate if they satisfy the following two conditions:

1. The taxpayer must actively participate in the rental activity. The *active participation* test is much less demanding than the material participation test applied to trade or business activities. It has just two requirements. First, the taxpayer must own at least a 10 percent interest in the rental real estate. Second, the taxpayer must be significantly involved in the management of the property; this requirement is satisfied if the taxpayer has the responsibility for approving tenants, setting lease terms, authorizing repairs, or even selecting a management service to care for the property.
2. The taxpayer's adjusted gross income (computed without regard to passive-activity losses, taxable Social Security benefits, or individual retirement account contributions) cannot exceed $100,000 for the year. The $25,000 loss allowance

must be reduced by 50 percent of any AGI in excess of $100,000. Thus, the special loss allowance is reduced to zero for any taxpayer with an AGI in excess of $150,000.

Application of the special exception for rental real estate losses is reasonably straightforward. Suppose George Evans owns two passive activities, one of which is a rental property in which George owns a 100 percent interest. In the current year, this property generates a $33,000 loss, while the other passive activity generates $12,000 of income. George's passive-activity loss for the year is $21,000, all of which is attributable to the rental property. If George is at all involved in the management of his property, he meets the active participation requirement. Consequently, if his AGI for the year is less than $100,000, the entire $21,000 passive-activity loss is fully deductible. If George's AGI were $114,000, the $25,000 loss allowance must be reduced by $7,000 (50 percent of George's AGI in excess of $100,000) and only $18,000 of his passive-activity loss is currently deductible. The $3,000 suspended loss is carried forward into the next year, when it again will be eligible for the rental real estate exception to the Section 469 limitation.

Working Interests in Oil and Gas Properties

A working interest in an oil or gas property is treated as an active business, regardless of the level of the owner's participation in the business. This exception to the passive-activity definition applies only if the owner's liability with respect to the working interest is unlimited; therefore, a limited partnership interest in an oil and gas property does not fall within this exception.

Publicly Traded Partnerships

By the year 1998, all publicly traded business partnerships (also known as master limited partnerships or MLPs) will be taxed as corporations, so income or loss generated by the partnership business will no longer flow through to the partners. However, in the interim, any income allocated to a partner from a publicly traded partnership cannot be offset against losses from other passive activities—in other words, an MLP cannot be a PIG! Similarly, any loss from an MLP can only be deducted against future income from that particular MLP. As with other passive activities, a taxable disposition of an MLP will result in the unlimited current deductibility of any suspended losses.

TAX PLANNING CONSIDERATIONS

Since its 1986 enactment, Section 469 has forestalled individual taxpayers from investing in business ventures offering little more than front-end tax write-offs. Unless such investors own interests in other profitable passive activities, any current year losses or tax credits from such business ventures no longer have tax-sheltering potential and cannot artificially enhance the value of the investment. Of course, even when a taxpayer chooses to invest in a business venture for solid economic reasons, and that business

TABLE 9–1 Comparison of Active Business and Passive-Activity Losses

	Active	*Passive*
Rule:	Net losses can be deducted against other sources of income.	Net losses cannot be deducted against other sources of income. However, they can be carried forward to offset income from passive sources in later years. Any aggregate remaining loss may be used to offset income from other sources in the year of a complete disposition.
General definition:	Taxpayer materially participates in the operations of the business activity on a regular, continuous, and substantial basis.	A trade or business in which the taxpayer does not materially participate, or any rental activity.
Examples:	Sole proprietorship run by the proprietor.	Secondary business activities in which the day-to-day efforts are managed by an employee or a management firm.
	Income and loss allocated to a partner or S corporation shareholder who materially participates in the active trade or business of the partnership or S corporation.	Income and loss allocated to a partner or S corporation shareholder who does not materially participate in the active trade or business of the partnership or S corporation.
	Working interests in oil and gas ventures.	Rental income or loss (subject to a *de minimis* rule for rental real estate).
		Income and loss from limited partnership interests.

happens to show a legitimate operating loss for the year, the passive-activity loss limitation is fully applicable, even if the venture has none of the characteristics of the classic tax shelter.

Investors who own interests in business activities with current or anticipated losses have a tremendous incentive to materially participate in the operation of the business. By keeping a careful record of the hours devoted to the business during the year, a taxpayer can demonstrate to the IRS that he or she meets one of the objective regulatory tests for material participation, thereby ensuring that the taxpayer's allocated share of the business loss is currently deductible.

Individuals who cannot meet the material participation standard with regards to losing businesses in which they own an interest are well advised to seek out investments in passive income generators so the PIG income can absorb the otherwise nondeductible passive-activity losses. When evaluating an investment in a business that promises passive activity income, individuals must decide if the investment makes economic sense. The PIG's after-tax rate of return (which reflects the tax savings attributable to the deduction of passive-activity losses) should be compared with the returns offered by other investment opportunities. If the PIG's after-tax rate of return is not competitive, individuals should find another investment, even if they must forego a current year deduction for their passive activity losses.

A summary of the basic rules governing the tax treatment of active business losses and passive-activity losses is contained in Table 9–1. Before turning to this table for guidance, readers should be reminded that the passive-activity loss limitation is a relatively new concept and the rules concerning its application are still evolving. The Treasury has yet to issue a complete set of regulations under Section 469, regulations that are sorely needed to provide direction in the area to taxpayers and tax professionals alike.

PROBLEMS AND CASES

1. Joyce Mellows owns a 40 percent interest as a general partner in MPT Partnership. Joyce contributed $20,000 cash for her interest. For its first taxable year, MPT recognized $32,000 of business income and a $10,000 capital loss. MPT made no cash distributions to its partners during the year. At the end of the year, MPT Partnership's debts total $8,000.
   a. Describe the current year tax consequences to Joyce of her investment in the MPT Partnership.
   b. Compute Joyce's basis in her partnership interest at the end of the partnership's first taxable year.
   c. How would your answers to *a* and *b* change if Joyce had received a $2,500 cash distribution from the partnership during the year?
2. Mel Santos owns 70 percent of the outstanding stock of Solana Inc., a calendar year S corporation. As president of Solana Inc., Mel materially participates in the corporate business. At the beginning of the current year, Mel's basis in his stock was $100,000. During the current year, Solana Inc. incurred a $200,000 net operating loss and earned $7,800 of dividend income. The corporation made no cash distributions to its shareholders during the year. At the end of the year, the corporation's debts to unrelated creditors totaled $330,000.
   a. Describe the current year tax consequences to Mel of his investment in Solana Inc.
   b. Compute Mel's basis in his Solana stock at the end of the current year.
   c. How would your answers to *a* and *b* change if Mel had contributed $15,000 cash to Solana Inc.'s capital during the year?
3. Refer to the original set of facts in problem 2. What are the tax consequences to Mel Santos if in the following year Solana Inc. generates $41,000 of business income and a $1,000 capital gain and makes no cash distributions to its shareholders?

4. Ben McShane owns 25 percent of the stock of McShane Inc., an S corporation. McShane Inc. operates a manufacturing business and is on a calendar year for tax purposes. Ben is employed by McShane Inc. on a full-time basis, drawing a $75,000 salary from the company. At the beginning of the current year, Ben's basis in his McShane stock was $310,000. The corporate treasurer has advised Ben that his allocable share of the corporation's net operating loss for the year will be $350,000. To be able to deduct this entire loss on his current year tax return, Ben is contemplating lending McShane Inc. $40,000 in return for a five-year note with an annual interest rate of 10 percent.
   a. As Ben's tax adviser, do you recommend that Ben adopt this planning strategy?
   b. How would your answer to *a* be affected if Ben is not employed by McShane Inc. and has nothing to do with the day-to-day operations of the corporation?
5. Tom Heaton makes an investment that will generate a $50,000 loss in 19x1 and 19x2, and $130,000 of income in 19x3. Tom is in the 31 percent tax bracket. Assume $100 of tax savings in 19x1 is worth $100 today; $100 of tax savings in 19x2 is worth $90 today; and $100 of tax savings in 19x3 is worth $81 today.
   a. What is the tax cost of this investment if it is an active business?
   b. What is the tax cost of this investment if it is a passive activity?
6. Bob and Mary Tidwell own and operate a grocery store. Their income (loss) from the grocery store and other activities is:

Grocery store	$40,000
Dividends from stocks	5,400
Loss from condominium that the Tidwells rent to students	(1,500)
Loss from investment in syndicated real estate partnership	(4,500)
Income from investment in cattle breeding partnership	3,000
Loss from investment in oil drilling partnership (working interest)	(3,500)

   Based on the above facts, compute the Tidwells' adjusted gross income.
7. In the current year, Susanne Doell recognized $60,000 of income from her own active business, $2,000 in portfolio income, and $10,000 loss from a passive activity.
   a. What is Susanne's adjusted gross income?
   b. If the above amounts had been earned by Doellco Inc., a closely held C corporation in a manufacturing business, what would its taxable income be?
8. Joe Katsuhara owns 40 percent of the outstanding stock of KLM Inc., a very profitable S corporation, and 15 percent of the outstanding stock of Shilo Inc., an S corporation that has been generating losses for several years. Joe's only other source of income is his annual salary from Morgan Productions Inc., a publicly held corporation. During the current year, Joe was allocated $39,700 of ordinary

business income from KLM Inc., a $24,600 ordinary business loss from Shilo Inc., and a $3,400 Section 1231 gain from Shilo Inc. Shilo recognized the Section 1231 gain on the sale of equipment used in its business.

a. If Joe materially participates in KLM's business, but does not materially participate in Shilo's business, what is the effect of the income and loss allocations from the two corporations on Joe's current year adjusted gross income?

b. How would your answer to *a* change if Joe does not materially participate in either KLM's or Shilo's business?

c. What fact in the problem strongly indicates that Joe does not materially participate in the business of either S corporation?

9. Rosa Sanchez owns three different partnership interests, all of which were purchased in 1987. She is a general partner in Partnership A and works approximately 1,100 hours every year in A's retail business. Rosa is also a general partner in Partnership B, which also operates a retail establishment. However, she spends only about 80 hours per year on B's business. Finally, Rosa owns a 7 percent general interest in C partnership, which owns and manages rental real estate. While partnership employees handle C's daily operations, the general partners make all major management decisions and approve all tenant applications.

   During the current year, Rosa is allocated the following amounts of income (loss) from each partnership.

Partnership A	$87,000
Partnership B	(43,000)
Partnership C	(12,000)

a. What is the net impact on Rosa's current year adjusted gross income of the above partnership allocations if partnerships A and B are considered separate business activities within the meaning of Section 469?

b. What is the net impact on Rosa's current year adjusted gross income of the above partnership allocations if partnerships A and B are considered a single business activity within the meaning of Section 469?

10. Ted and Jane Turner own a one-half interest in an apartment complex, the only passive activity the Turners own. The Turners are actively involved in managing the complex and routinely screen tenant applications. During the current year, the complex generated a $60,000 operating loss.

a. If the Turners' adjusted gross income for the year (before consideration of the rental loss) is $96,000, how much loss may they deduct on their current year return?

b. Would your answer to *a* change if the Turners' adjusted gross income for the year is $133,000?

c. Would your answer to *a* change if the Turners had $12,000 of current year passive-activity income from another source?

11. Lisa Futile owns a limited partnership interest with a $10,000 tax basis. Lisa has $30,000 of suspended passive-activity losses and $4,000 of suspended passive-activity credits with respect to this interest. Determine the tax consequences to Lisa of each of the following:

    a. She sells her interest to an unrelated party for $23,000.
    b. She gives her interest to her daughter Kara.
    c. She dies in the current year; at date of death the fair market value of the partnership interest is $23,000.

12. Lawrence Taylor owns an interest in two passive activities: 100 shares of stock in Sessa Inc., an S corporation, and a 15 percent interest in TTB Partnership. Lawrence has $6,000 of suspended Section 469 losses attributable to the Sessa investment and $4,500 of suspended Section 469 losses attributable to the TTB investment. An unrelated third party wants to purchase 75 of Lawrence's Sessa shares for $75,000. Lawrence's basis in these shares is $60,000. Describe the tax consequences to Lawrence if he decides to accept this offer.

13. Guy Bond, a single taxpayer, earns taxable income of $95,000 every year. He is also the sole shareholder of a C corporation that earns taxable business income of $150,000 per year. Guy is considering purchasing an interest in a passive activity that will generate a $5,000 loss in 1997 and 1998 and $15,000 of income in 1999. Neither Guy nor his corporation is involved in any other passive activities.

    a. Ignoring the time value of money, should Guy make this investment individually or through his corporation?
    b. Now assume $100 of tax savings in 1997 is worth $100 today; $100 of tax savings in 1998 is worth $90 today; and $100 of tax savings in 1999 is worth $81 today. (In other words, Guy has a discount rate of about 11 percent.) Should Guy make this investment individually or through his corporation?

Case 9–1

John C. Calhoun is an attorney in Owensville; his law firm owns the four-story Calhoun Building on Main Street. Two floors of the building are occupied by the law office, and two floors are rented to a group of doctors. John is so busy with his law practice that he is not involved in negotiating the leases with the tenants. The partners of the law firm selected a real estate agent to find tenants, negotiate leases, and manage the building.

John is one of 11 equal partners in the law firm. In the current year his share of the partnership's income and expense is:

Income	
Legal services fee revenue	$250,000
Rental income	65,000
Expenses	
Rental agent's commissions	$ 10,000 per year
Depreciation	100,000 per year
Maintenance	2,000 per month
Legal staff (payroll to nonpartners)	150,000 per year

The depreciation and maintenance amounts above are John's share of the total for the building. He has no other sources of income or expense and no carryforward items from other years.

a. What is John's adjusted gross income for the current year?

b. What tax planning suggestions do you have for John?

Case 9–2

Zonker Harris is considering three investments of $10,000. An investment in an active business will generate $700 of income and cash distributions in years one through three. An investment in an oil drilling partnership (working interest) will generate a $5,000 loss in years one and two and $11,900 of income and $1,900 of cash distributions in year three. An investment in a cattle breeding partnership (passive activity) will generate a $2,500 loss in years one and two and $7,300 of income and $2,300 of cash distributions in year three. Each investment will be worth $10,000 after three years.

a. If Zonker is in a 15 percent marginal tax bracket and has no passive activities, which investment should he choose?

b. If Zonker is in a 31 percent marginal tax bracket and has $20,000 of income from passive activities, which investment should he choose?

c. If the investment is being made by Zonkco, a closely held corporation in a 39 percent marginal tax bracket, which investment should it make? The corporation owns no other passive activities.

For each case, assume $100 of tax savings in year one is worth $100; $100 of tax savings in year two is worth $90; and $100 of tax savings in year three is worth $81.

CHAPTER 10

Compensation Planning

The most important (if not the only) item of gross income recognized by millions of individual taxpayers is the compensation they receive in their capacities as employees. An *employee* is a person who performs services on a regular basis for another party in exchange for a *salary* or *wage.* The employee/employer relationship is characterized by the employer's right to specify how, when, and where the employee's duties are to be performed. In contrast, an *independent contractor* who performs services for compensation retains control over the manner in which the work is to be performed. The independent contractor's clients can only accept or reject the final result of the contractor's efforts.

From a tax perspective, the distinction between an employee and an independent contractor is far from trivial. Employers must pay federal and state payroll taxes based on the amount of compensation paid to their employees during the year. Employers are required to withhold both federal income tax and employee payroll (FICA) tax from salary and wage payments. At the end of the year, employers must issue Forms W–2 to each employee. These forms provide detailed information as to gross compensation paid during the year as well as the various taxes withheld by the employer on the employee's behalf. When a business hires an independent contractor, the fees paid to the contractor are not subject to either employer/employee payroll taxes or income tax withholding. At the end of the year, the business must issue a Form 1099 to the independent contractor; this form simply states the total compensation paid during the year. As self-employed taxpayers, independent contractors must (1) report their total compensation received as gross income on a Schedule C, Form 1040, (2) make quarterly estimated payments of their current year tax liability, and (3) pay the federal self-employment tax.

Most low- or middle-income employees have little opportunity to initiate any tax planning with regard to their compensation. Their overriding financial goal is simply to command the highest wage or salary possible to maximize their after-tax disposable income. Rank and file employees typically have minimal control over the type of compensation package their employers offer. They can accept a job on the employer's terms or search for an alternative in the help-wanted section of the newspaper. On the other hand, highly paid employees can undertake some very effective tax planning. To the extent their current cash flow needs are less than their annual incomes, these individuals have the financial flexibility to convert taxable salary into nontaxable forms of compensatory fringe benefits. They can defer significant amounts of income into future years through employer-sponsored retirement savings plans. Moreover, highly paid employees tend to be in a stronger bargaining position vis-à-vis their employers and can negotiate employment contracts tailored to their own economic needs and preferences. An extreme example of employee leverage is when an employee is also a major stockholder in his or her corporate employer. Of course, when the employee is the *sole* corporate shareholder, the financial goals of the employee and the employer converge, and tax planning opportunities abound.

In this chapter, we will analyze the tax consequences of many popular compensation arrangements. These arrangements are, for the most part, available only to employees. Self-employed people—individuals operating as sole proprietors and general partners in partnerships—cannot take advantage of many of the compensation planning techniques discussed in the first sections of the chapter. Historically, this disparity provided a strong incentive for small-business owners to incorporate simply so they could become employees of the corporate business. As you will learn in the final section of this chapter, Congress has steadily worked to minimize the disparity in the compensation planning opportunities available to employees and self-employed individuals.

One meaningful way to classify and evaluate the wide variety of compensation arrangements is in terms of their tax effect on the employer and the employee. Few tax advisers would disagree with the following preference rankings for compensation arrangements.

Preference Ranking	*Tax Effect to Employer*	*Tax Effect to Employee*
1	Current deduction	No income recognition
2	Current deduction	Deferred income
3	Current deduction	Current income
4	Deferred deduction	Deferred income
5	No deduction	Income recognition

As you will learn in the following pages, each of these five categories of compensation arrangements is a viable possibility in today's business world.

TECHNIQUES PROVIDING A CURRENT DEDUCTION AND NO TAXABLE INCOME

Individuals are generally taxed on any economic benefits they receive for services rendered, no matter how indirect the benefits may be. In Chapter 2, we observed that the Internal Revenue Code provides a limited number of exceptions to this rule in the form of statutory exclusions from gross income for specific types of compensation. In Chapter 4, we noted that taxpayers may deduct all ordinary and necessary business expenses incurred in a trade or business, including any reasonable compensation paid to an employee. By carefully combining the exclusion and deduction provisions, it is possible to provide an employee with a real economic benefit that is never taxed and, at the same time, to provide the employer with an immediate deduction for the cost of the benefit.

Group Term Life Insurance

Section 79 allows employees to exclude from gross income the value of *group term life insurance premiums* paid by their employers to the extent the insurance coverage provided under this group term policy does not exceed $50,000. This exclusion is available only if the group term insurance plan does not discriminate in favor of corporate owners, officers, or highly compensated employees. If the life insurance coverage exceeds $50,000, the employee is taxed only on the cost of the premium for the excess; this cost is based on tables provided in Treasury regulations. Suffice it to note that the cost of coverage in excess of $50,000 is relatively inexpensive. An obvious economic advantage attaches to tax-free life insurance in comparison with insurance purchased with after-tax salary dollars.

In the case of life insurance, a double exclusion is actually possible. Note that the employee may exclude the value of the premiums paid by an employer on his behalf from gross income. Furthermore, if the employee dies and his beneficiaries collect insurance under the policy, they may exclude the policy proceeds from gross income.

Employee Death Benefits

Section 101 allows a taxpayer to receive up to $5,000 in excludable *death benefits* paid by a deceased employee's employer. The employer can deduct the amounts paid under such a death benefit plan. Although the dollar significance of this opportunity is obviously limited, any individual who takes the trouble to incorporate a business in order to obtain other employee tax benefits should also take the necessary action to ensure the right to this small additional benefit.

Health and Accident Plans

Section 106 provides an exclusion from an employee's gross income for the value of *health and accident insurance coverage* provided by an employer. This exclusion applies to the cost of the coverage—the insurance premiums paid on the employee's behalf. If an employee or family member suffers an illness or accident, the tax treatment of payments received from an employer-provided insurance plan depends on the nature of the payment. If the payment is a reimbursement for medical expenses, such as doctor or hospital bills, the payment is excludable from the employee's gross income. If the payment relates to a specific injury or loss of a body part or function, it is also excludable. However, insurance payments based on the length of time an employee is unable to work must be included in the employee's gross income. These payments, referred to as *sick pay,* are viewed as a replacement of the taxable salary or wage lost by the employee because of his or her absence from work.

It is important to appreciate the very real economic benefit of employer-provided health and accident insurance. If an employee had to purchase equivalent insurance coverage with after-tax salary, the employee would pay more for the same coverage; the exact amount of the increased cost depends on the employee's marginal tax bracket. Alternatively, the employee might be forced to purchase less desirable coverage for the same dollar cost.

Meals and Lodging

Section 119 permits an employee to exclude from gross income the value of *meals and lodging furnished on the employer's premises* if the provision of the food and lodging is for the convenience of the employer. In the case of lodging, the use of the lodging by the employee must be a condition of employment. To illustrate these concepts, consider the case of a corporate employer operating a large manufacturing facility 20 miles from the nearest public eating establishment. To minimize the time employees must be away from their jobs over the lunch hour, the employer might find it convenient to furnish a free noon meal in the company cafeteria. Although the employees are obviously receiving an employment-related economic benefit in the form of the free meal, the value of the meals consumed every year is excludable from the employees' gross incomes.

Examples of lodging provided to an employee for the convenience of the employer come easily to mind. A prison warden might be required to occupy a residence on the prison grounds as a condition of employment. Similarly, a headmaster of a boarding school might be required to live on campus. One of the most interesting cases involving the exclusion for the value of employer-provided lodging concerned beer magnates Adolph and Joseph Coors. Both individuals lived in homes located on the Coors brewery premises in Golden, Colorado. These homes were owned and maintained by the Coors corporation, but neither of the occupants paid any rent to the corporation for their use of the homes. The IRS argued that the rental value of the residences should be included in the income of the occupants. The Tax Court, however, concluded that Adolph Coors, as corporate treasurer, and Joseph Coors, as executive vice president, were required by the constant demands of their jobs to reside at the brewery. Because the lodging was provided for the convenience of the employer, the rental value of the homes was a nontaxable fringe benefit to Adolph and Joseph Coors.

Other Employee Benefits

If no specific statutory exclusion for a compensatory fringe benefit exists, Section 61 requires inclusion of the value of the benefit in the recipient's gross income unless the benefit can be placed into one of the four generic categories of excludable fringe benefits provided by Section 132. These four categories are:

1. No-additional-cost service.
2. Qualified employee discount.
3. Working condition fringe benefit.
4. *De minimis* fringe benefit.

To qualify as a *no-additional-cost service,* a fringe benefit must not add any substantial cost to a service already offered to the public in the ordinary course of the employer's business and must be offered to all employees on a nondiscriminatory basis. Thus, airline employees can travel tax-free on their employer's airline, so long as they fly on a space-available basis. Similarly, employees of a hotel corporation may occupy otherwise vacant rooms in their employer's hotel for little or no cost and avoid the recognition of any imputed income for the value received.

If an employee is given the opportunity of purchasing the employer's inventory or services at a discount and if this discount is extended to all employees, the employee generally need not report the bargain price element as gross income. In general, *qualified employee discounts* are limited to the employer's gross profit percent in the particular line of business in which the employee works; service discounts are limited to 20 percent of the price charged ordinary customers.

A *working condition fringe benefit* is any payment made by an employer on behalf of an employee to the extent the employee could have deducted the payment as a business expense if he had paid it out of his own pocket. For example, a CPA employed by a public accounting firm can exclude from gross income the dues paid by the firm for that employee's membership in state or national professional organizations, subscription costs for tax or auditing journals, and the annual state licensing fee to maintain the employee's CPA certificate. Note that if the CPA paid any of these expenses directly, she could deduct them as ordinary and necessary business expenses. Section 132 states that the value of employer-provided parking qualifies as a working condition fringe benefit; in 1996, the exclusion for the value of employer-provided parking is limited to $165 per month. The section also provides a special exclusion for the use of athletic facilities located on the employer's premises for the use of employees and their families.

Fringe benefits excluded under the *de minimis* rule are such items as cocktail parties and employer-provided coffee and doughnuts. These and other similar items are excluded solely because the value of the property or service given to the employee is so small that accounting for the item is simply unreasonable or administratively impracticable.

Some employers allow their employees to select the particular benefits they want to receive from a menu of fringe benefits. These programs are known as *cafeteria plans,* for obvious reasons. Section 125 makes it clear that no tax-free benefit will become taxable merely because it is part of a cafeteria plan or because some employees elect to receive cash or other taxable compensation. There is, however, an exception for plans that discriminate in favor of highly compensated employees; these plans do not qualify for tax-free status. Cafeteria plans must require employees to make their selections at the beginning of each year and not change the mix of benefits until the next year.

Employee Perquisites

One of the truisms of a capitalistic (or perhaps any) economic system is that rank has its privileges. As an employee climbs the corporate ladder, she can anticipate not only an increase in salary, but also any number of pleasurable improvements in her working environment. For example, a promotion to a vice presidency may entitle our employee to lunch with her clients in four-star restaurants. Her corporate employer may expect her to fly first-class when she travels for business reasons. She may even get to use the corporate country club membership for business entertainment purposes. Theoretically, these *employee perquisites* can be viewed as additional compensation earned by our new vice president. Practically, such perquisites may be impossible to value objectively in monetary terms and, as a result, cannot be captured as gross income to the recipient.

Congress is well aware of the opportunities for tax abuse in the area of employee perquisites. Nonetheless, Congress also understands that employers compete for top managerial talent by providing such perquisites, and the cost of the perquisites may be as vital to the success of the business as the cost of utilities, rent, supplies, or advertising. Consequently, the tax law generally treats the costs associated with employee perquisites as ordinary and necessary business expenses. However, as we discussed in Chapter 4, Section 274 imposes numerous (and very strict) limitations on the deductibility of business travel and entertainment. One of the more straightforward of these limitations is that only 50 percent of the cost of business meals and entertainment is deductible. So if a corporate employer encourages its officers and executives to entertain clients and customers, the corporation's after-tax cost of the entertainment will be higher than the after-tax cost of its other current operating expenses.

The use of a company car has become almost a traditional employee perquisite. In 1984, Congress decided to impose some restraints on the tax benefits associated with company cars by enacting Section 280F, the *luxury automobile* limitation. Under this section, a business that purchases a passenger automobile is limited as to the amount of annual depreciation deductions through which to recover the cost of the auto. Automobiles costing less than about $13,000 escape the limit; the cost of such vehicles can be recovered over a five-year period under the normal depreciation rules. For more expensive automobiles, the Section 280F limitation is quite harsh. For example, if a business buys a car with a $50,000 price tag, the recovery period over which this cost is depreciated is 31 years! Businesses that lease automobiles are subject to similar restrictions on the deductibility of their annual lease payments.

From an employee's perspective, the use of his employer's car exclusively for business purposes will not create gross income to the employee because such use qualifies as a working condition fringe benefit. But to the extent the employee also uses the company car for personal reasons (including routine commuting to and from work), he must recognize the imputed value of the personal use as additional income—noncash compensation that the employer must include on the employee's Form W–2 for the year. Moreover, the employee must be able to *subtantiate* his business usage of the company car. Without meticulous records, he runs the risk that the IRS will presume the entire usage of the company car was for personal (compensatory) reasons and tax him accordingly.

Interest-Free Loans

A fringe benefit that an employer might consider offering is an interest-free loan to an employee. For many years, the IRS and the courts debated the proper income tax consequences of such loans without reaching a satisfying conclusion. In 1984, Congress ended the debate with the enactment of Section 7872. This section requires that the amount of interest the employer forgoes by making an interest-free loan to an employee must be recognized by the employer as constructive income each year the loan is outstanding. On the other side of the transaction, the employee is considered to have constructively paid the interest. The statute then allows the employer to take a deduction for the compensation (the forgone interest) constructively paid to the employee, compensation that in turn must be included in the employee's gross income.

To illustrate this formidable sequence of imaginary transactions, assume Beta Inc. lends its chief executive officer $250,000 on an interest-free demand basis on January 1 of the current year. During the year, the applicable market rate of interest (as determined by the IRS) is 9 percent. Therefore, the CEO is considered to have paid $22,500 of interest to Beta in the current year. While Beta must include this amount in gross income, the corporation may also deduct $22,500 as salary expense. The CEO, in turn, must recognize $22,500 as additional compensation received in the current year. Note that none of these transactions involves any cash flow, and at the corporate level, the increased interest income is exactly offset by the additional salary deduction. The real impact of this elaborate schema is on the CEO. His gross income is increased by $22,500, an increase that will be offset only if his constructive interest payment is fully deductible. The deductibility of the interest will depend on the CEO's use of the borrowed funds. If he used the $250,000 for personal reasons—the worst-case scenario—no deduction is available and the CEO's taxable income for the year increases by $22,500.

TECHNIQUES PROVIDING A CURRENT DEDUCTION AND DEFERRED INCOME

Our second category of compensation arrangements includes those that provide for an immediate deduction to the employer and deferred income to the employee. The most common form of such arrangements is the employer-provided *qualified retirement plan,* which is described and defined in Section 401. Congress has bestowed a generous set of tax benefits on such plans which can be summarized as follows:

1. The employer can claim a current deduction for the amount of employee compensation paid into the employee trust created to administer the qualified retirement plan.
2. Employees are not taxed currently on the amount of compensation paid on their behalf into the employee trust. Employees will not recognize any gross income until they withdraw funds from the trust on retirement.
3. The employee trust is a tax-exempt entity. Consequently, the earnings generated by the funds in the trust are not subject to taxation, and the funds can grow and accumulate at a before-tax rate.

The dollar significance of these tax benefits to an employee who participates in a qualified retirement plan can hardly be overstated. The compounding effect of tax-deferred contributions and tax-deferred growth is phenomenal over the working life of an individual. To illustrate the power of this deferral, consider two individuals in the top 39.6 percent marginal tax bracket who each dedicate $15,000 of their annual gross compensation to a retirement plan that can earn an annual 9 percent yield on their investment for 30 years. The only difference in their situations is that taxpayer A participates in a nonqualified retirement program, while taxpayer B saves for retirement through a qualified plan.

	Taxpayer A	*Taxpayer B*
Before-tax compensation	$ 15,000	$ 15,000
Income tax on compensation	(5,940)	-0-
After-tax annual contribution to retirement plan	$ 9,060	$ 15,000
Before-tax yield on contributions	9%	9%
After-tax yield on contributions	5.44%	9%
Retirement fund balance after 30 years	$649,458	$2,044,613
Tax on withdrawal of balance	-0-	(809,667)
After-tax fund balance	$649,458	$1,234,946

After A pays the current tax on $15,000, his net savings for the year is reduced to $9,060. Moreover, the after-tax rate of growth on his annual investment is only 5.44 percent. Taxpayer B may save the entire $15,000 tax-sheltered amount of gross income, and her annual contribution will grow at a 9 percent rate. At the end of 30 years, A's retirement fund balance will be $649,458, while B's fund balance will be $2,044,613! Keep in mind that these balances do not represent a final comparison because A may withdraw and consume his retirement savings with no further imposition of income tax. By contrast, all withdrawals that B makes from her retirement plan will be fully includable in her gross income. However, even if B must pay tax at a 39.6 percent rate, her after-tax retirement fund balance is $1,234,946. Perhaps it is because the economic benefit of a tax-deferred qualified retirement plan is so impressive that requirements for qualification are so demanding.

Qualification of a Plan. An employer-sponsored retirement savings plan is qualified within the meaning of Section 401 unless it satisfies a formidable list of statutory requirements. Among the conditions necessary for qualification are the following:

1. The plan must be administered in trust form so plan assets are managed by an independent trustee for the exclusive benefit of the employees and/or their beneficiaries.
2. The plan must be a written, permanent plan and be communicated to the employees.
3. The plan must *not* discriminate in favor of corporate officers, stockholder-employees, or highly paid employees.
4. The plan must provide that employees have a nonforfeitable (vested) right to 100 percent of their retirement benefits after no more than seven years of service to the employer.
5. The plan must be funded—that is, the employer's annual contribution to the trust must be in the form of cash or other property.

For closely held corporations, the nondiscrimination requirement for qualified plans can be troublesome. The highly compensated shareholder-employees who manage the business might be eager to provide themselves with a tax-sheltered retirement plan, but may be reluctant to provide equivalent retirement benefits for other employees. In the past, business owners have tried to avoid the nondiscrimination rules by operating in a multicorporate form in which the owners were the sole employees of one corporation and the rank-and-file employees were hired by a second corporation. The first corporation could establish a generous retirement plan for the owner-employees, while the second corporation had no retirement plan at all. Congress eliminated this planning technique by requiring that for purposes of determining whether a retirement plan is discriminatory, a controlled group of corporations is regarded as a single employer.

Taxation of Employee Benefits. An employee covered by a qualified retirement plan need not report as taxable income any benefits under that plan until they are paid or otherwise made available. Usually, benefits are not distributed by a retirement trust fund until an employee terminates employment, retires, or dies. Often a qualified plan allows the employee to select from several options when deciding how to receive any accumulated benefits. He or she may be given a choice between (1) a lump-sum distribution, (2) a lifetime annuity for one life, or (3) a smaller lifetime annuity for as long as either the employee or the employee's spouse shall live.

Employees who elect to receive a lump-sum distribution must include the distribution—which may represent the entire amount of their retirement savings—in current year gross income. Fortunately, these employees are entitled to use a special method for calculating their current tax liability attributable to the distribution. The tax calculation is based on a complex 5-year or 10-year averaging method, the details of which are beyond the scope of our text. The important tax planning point is that the averaging method subjects the distribution to a much lower effective tax rate than may apply to the recipient's other income for the year.

When it bestowed such a liberal set of tax benefits on qualified retirement plans, Congress intended that such plans be used to provide retirement income. To discourage taxpayers from withdrawing funds before retirement, the law provides for a 10 percent penalty on any *premature withdrawal* from a qualified plan. Generally, any withdrawal is premature unless it is made by a taxpayer who has reached the age of 59½ or is permanently disabled, or unless the withdrawal is made by an employee's estate or beneficiary subsequent to the employee's death. Note that a withdrawal attributable to the employee's termination of employment is not exempt from this penalty. A taxpayer who wishes to avoid both the income tax and the 10 percent penalty on a premature withdrawal can *roll over* (recontribute) the withdrawn amount to a new employer's qualified plan or an individual retirement account (IRA). This rollover must be made within 60 days of the withdrawal.

Types of Qualified Retirement Plans

The term *qualified retirement plan* is a generic description for a variety of employer-provided plans with very different legal and financial characteristics. In this next segment, we will survey the common types of qualified plans.

Pension Plans. A pension plan has as its primary purpose the provision of a targeted amount of retirement benefits for covered employees; thus, pension plans can be described as *defined benefit* retirement plans. Once instituted, a pension plan becomes a fixed obligation of the employer who must make the contractual annual contribution to the plan without regard for the presence or absence of current business profits. Because of this financial commitment, new businesses with uncertain cash flows are typically reluctant to institute such a plan. Employees, especially middle-aged and older employees, strongly prefer the relative security of a fixed contractual arrangement. Because pension plans are intended to provide for retirement income, they seldom provide for any acceleration of benefits, even in cases of demonstrated need.

The maximum annual retirement benefit that can be provided under a qualified pension plan is the lesser of 100 percent of an employee's average compensation for his or her three highest compensation years or a $90,000 base amount, adjusted annually for inflation. In 1996, the base amount was $120,000. Thus, a corporate executive who has enjoyed an average annual salary of $300,000 before his retirement in 1996 can anticipate receiving no more than $120,000 a year as a pension from his employer's qualified plan. The maximum tax deduction an employer may claim for all contributions to a defined benefit plan is based on the actuarially determined cost of funding the future retirement benefits promised to the employer's current work force.

Profit-Sharing Plans

A profit-sharing plan is the most common example of a *defined contribution* retirement plan. As the name implies, a defined contribution plan specifies the amount of the annual payment to be made by the employer into each employee's retirement account. In a typical profit-sharing plan, this payment is defined in terms of a percentage of annual employer profits that will be contributed to the retirement plan. In a year in which the employer fails to generate a profit, there is no obligation to make a contribution. This feature makes profit-sharing plans especially appealing to new entrepreneurial businesses with highly volatile earnings and uncertain cash flows. From the employees' perspective, profit-sharing plans force them to share the risk associated with their employer's business; the benefit available to each employee on retirement is problematic and will depend in large part on the success of the business.

The annual contribution to an employee's profit-sharing account is limited to the lesser of 25 percent of the employee's annual compensation or $30,000. While this $30,000 ceiling will eventually be adjusted for inflation, no adjustment was required in 1996. To illustrate this limitation, assume a corporate employer has two employees who are participating in a qualified profit-sharing plan. One employee's base compensation is $45,000, while the second employee's base compensation is $150,000. The maximum contribution the employer may make to each employee's account is $11,250 (25 percent of $45,000) and $30,000, respectively. The tax deduction that an employer may claim for total contributions to a defined contribution plan is limited to 15 percent of total compensation paid to all participants during the current year. In our simple two-employee model, the maximum deduction to the corporation is $29,250 (15 percent of $195,000). Any excess of actual current contributions over this amount may be carried forward to be deducted in future years.

Other Defined Contribution Plans

A second popular type of defined contribution plan is the *money purchase pension plan.* The annual employer contribution to a money purchase pension plan is based on a formula (typically some percentage of base compensation) for each covered employee. These contributions, which are not discretionary with the employer but must be made every year, are used to purchase pension benefits for the covered employee. Employer contributions made to *stock bonus plans* and *employee stock ownership plans* (ESOPs) are invested in stock of the employer corporation. Consequently, the value of the employees' retirement savings is tied to the long-term financial success of the employer. In recent years, *Section 401(k) plans* (also described as *salary reduction plans* or *cash-or-deferred arrangements*) have become increasingly popular. Under this type of plan, each participating employee can define his or her own contribution by specifying some amount of current salary to be diverted into the retirement plan. To the extent of the specified amount, the employee is converting taxable compensation into tax-deferred retirement income. The maximum amount of compensation eligible for such conversion in 1996 is $9,500.

TECHNIQUES PROVIDING A CURRENT DEDUCTION AND CURRENT INCOME

The next category of compensation arrangements we will analyze includes the most common form of employee compensation—the routine wage or salary. This type of compensation offers no particular tax advantage; the employer claims a current deduction for its payment, while the recipient employee includes the compensation in current year gross income. The overwhelming popularity of compensation payable in hard currency is attributable to the maximum personal flexibility provided to employees who are free to spend their after-tax income in any way they desire.

Section 162 stipulates that only a reasonable amount of compensation for personal services rendered is deductible as an ordinary and necessary business expense. The question of reasonableness usually arises when a corporate employee is also a major shareholder in a closely held corporation, and facts and circumstances indicate that some amount of the purported salary payment to the owner/employee is, in reality, a disguised return on the owner's equity investment. As we discussed in Chapter 5, the consequence of such an unfortunate determination is that the corporate employer will lose a current deduction for the unreasonable portion of the salary payment (i.e., the constructive dividend).

Before 1994, the IRS had no firm basis for attacking the reasonableness of the astronomical salaries paid to the top executives of publicly held corporations. Such salaries are determined by independent corporate boards of directors and theoretically are ordained by the competitive marketplace. In the Revenue Reconciliation Act of 1993, Congress slapped a $1 million limit on the amount of executive compensation deductible by publicly held corporations. This limit applies only to the annual compensation paid to the corporation's chief executive officer and its four other most highly compensated officers. The $1 million limit is riddled with exceptions; for example, it does not apply to corporate contributions on behalf of its executives to qualified retirement plans. Nor does the limit apply to *performance-based compensation* paid because the executive attained a performance goal established by a compensation committee made up of outside directors. Both the amount of the performance-based compensation and the specific performance goal must be disclosed to and approved by corporate shareholders.

Restricted Property for Services

If an employer transfers property other than cash to an employee as compensation for services performed, the employee must recognize the fair market value of the property as current gross income, and the employer can claim the same amount as a current deduction. One type of property commonly used as compensation is equity stock in a corporate employer. This compensation technique gives the recipient a vested interest in the corporation's future and forges an additional bond of mutual self-interest between employer and employee. To prevent an employee from immediately selling newly received equity stock for cash, corporate employers typically require the employee to continue to work for the corporation for some stipulated time before unrestricted legal ownership in the shares is vested in the employee. If the employee quits before this time period has elapsed, the stock must be forfeited back to the corporation.

When property received as compensation is subject to a substantial risk of forfeiture, Section 83(a) states the recipient is not required to recognize the value of the *restricted property* as gross income until the year in which the risk of forfeiture lapses. However, under Section 83(b), the recipient may elect to include the value of the property in current year income, even though he may forfeit the property later. Why would an employee elect to accelerate the recognition of income that can legitimately be deferred? The sacrifice of deferral makes sense only if the employee believes the value of the stock will increase significantly during the restriction period. In this case, the acceleration of income means a smaller dollar amount will be subject to income tax.

To illustrate this tax planning dilemma, assume Beth Ramey receives 1,000 shares of her employer's newly issued common stock as compensation in the current year. The market value of the stock at date of issuance is $20,000. Beth's receipt of the stock is conditional; she must return the shares to the corporation if she leaves its employ on or before June 30, 2000. Beth is convinced that by this date, the 1,000 shares will have doubled in value. Beth can certainly choose to defer recognition of any income with respect to the restricted stock until 2000. In such case, she must include the stock's future value, perhaps as much as $40,000, in her 2000 gross income. If she makes a *Section 83(b) election,* she will include only $20,000 in her current year gross income. To make Beth's decision even more difficult, Section 83(b) warns that if she opts for current year income recognition, and then for some unforeseen reason quits her job before 2000, her forfeiture of the 1,000 shares will not give rise to a tax deduction! Moreover, Beth must make a Section 83(b) election within 30 days after the receipt of the restricted shares. Little wonder that Section 83(b) is referred to by tax advisers as the Las Vegas election.

And what of the tax consequences to Beth's employer? Section 83 requires only that the employer's deduction for Beth's compensation be matched against her recognition of income. In other words, if Beth elects current year recognition, the corporation will claim a current year deduction of $20,000. If Beth defers income recognition until 2000, her employer will claim a deduction in that year equal to the future value of the 1,000 shares. In the latter case, Beth's receipt of restricted property should more properly be included in our next category of compensation arrangements.

TECHNIQUES PROVIDING A DEFERRED DEDUCTION AND DEFERRED INCOME

Nonqualified Stock Options

Stock options as a form of employee compensation represent an opportunity for employees to acquire an equity interest in their corporate employers at a bargain price. To understand the tax planning implications of stock options, we must review some basic concepts.

A stock option is nothing more than a right to purchase a corporation's stock for a given period at a given price. If the option price is greater than or equal to the market price on the date the option is granted, the option itself has real economic value only if the period of the option is of some reasonable length. To illustrate, if someone were to offer you the guaranteed right to purchase General Motors common stock at today's market price, wouldn't you be willing to pay something for that option if it ran for, say, five years? Wouldn't you be willing to pay even more if it ran for 10 or 20 years? Under these conditions, the opportunity to make a substantial profit with a minimum investment is very real. An employee would simply hold the unexercised option as long as the value of the stock remained constant or decreased. If the market price decreased and remained depressed for the term of the option, the option would finally expire and prove to be worthless. On the other hand, if the value of the stock increased, the option would become as valuable as the excess of the market price over the option price multiplied by the number of shares authorized in the option.

At one time, the tax laws were interpreted so an employee was required to report as ordinary compensation income only the initial spread between an option price and the fair market value of the stock on the date the option was granted. Today, the rules that control the tax consequence of stock options are considerably more complex. At this juncture, we will consider the tax rules applicable to *nonqualified* options; the rules applicable to incentive stock options appear later in this chapter. The tax treatment of a nonqualified stock option depends on whether or not the fair market value of the option is *readily ascertainable* when the option is granted. If it is, the employee must immediately report that value, less anything he or she paid to acquire the option, as ordinary income; the same amount is immediately deductible by the employer corporation. If and when the employee exercises the option and acquires stock, there are no further tax consequences to employee or employer at that time.

As an example of the above set of rules, assume Ben Barnes is granted an option to acquire 1,000 shares of his corporate employer's stock for $50 per share at any time during the next five years. On the date Ben receives the option, the stock is selling on the open market for $60 per share. Clearly the option has a readily ascertainable value of $10,000 because immediate exercise of the option would allow Ben to acquire stock worth $60,000 at a cost of only $50,000. On receipt of the option, Ben must recognize $10,000 of compensation income and the corporation may deduct $10,000 as a business expense. Ben now has a $10,000 tax basis in the option; if he allows the option to lapse, he will be entitled to recognize a $10,000 capital loss. If he exercises the option and pays $50,000 to acquire 1,000 shares, his total basis in the shares will be $60,000—the basis in the option plus Ben's out-of-pocket cost. Ben will recognize no further gain until he sells the shares.

One of the major reasons stock options are used to compensate valued employees is to induce them to remain with the corporation. Consequently, options typically have no readily ascertainable value upon grant, so the recipient is encouraged to devote maximum effort to increasing the market price of the corporate stock so as to indirectly create value in the option. Using our above example, assume that on the day Ben's option was granted, his employer's stock was selling for only $48 per share. The option has no determinable value until the stock price climbs past $50 per share; therefore, Ben recognizes no income when he receives the option and has a zero tax basis in the option. Not until the year in which Ben exercises the option will he recognize ordinary compensation income in an amount equal to the excess of the market value over the option price of the stock. If Ben exercises the option when the market price is $68 per share, this excess, referred to as the *bargain element,* will be $18,000. The corporation will be entitled to its $18,000 deduction in the year of exercise. Ben's basis in the shares will be $68,000—his $50,000 out-of-pocket cost plus the income recognized upon option exercise.

From the above discussion, it should be obvious that the deferral of compensation income from the year in which a compensatory stock option is granted until the year the option is exercised is the primary tax advantage of a nonqualified stock option. The considerable nontax advantages of these options also deserve mention. They allow even a junior executive to acquire "a piece of the corporate action" at a bargain price. Second, the value of the option is tied to the value of the corporate stock, and thus the amount of compensation received by employees will be measured by the ultimate success of the employer's business. Finally, stock options represent a form of compensation that requires no cash outlay on the part of the corporate employer; in fact, upon exercise of the option, the corporation may actually receive an additional cash contribution to its own capital. If an employee acquires newly issued stock or treasury stock from the corporation upon option exercise, the real economic cost of the option is shifted to the existing corporate shareholders through a dilution of their equity interests.

Deferred Compensation Plans

As an alternative to qualified retirement plans, many corporate employers provide retirement benefits to their key employees through nonqualified plans. There are three primary benefits to these nonqualified *deferred compensation* arrangements. First, all the onerous and costly statutory requirements for plan qualification can be avoided. Second, deferred compensation plans can blatantly discriminate in favor of a corporation's highly paid executives. Finally, there are no limits on the amount of current compensation that can be deferred until retirement.

Given these benefits, what are the disadvantages of a deferred compensation arrangement? Quite clearly, the disadvantages relate to the risk assumed by an employee who participates in such an arrangement. When an employee agrees to defer the receipt of some amount of current compensation until retirement, the employer simply records a liability in the amount of the deferred compensation on the corporate books. In marked contrast to a qualified retirement plan, no corporate cash or assets are contributed to an independently administered trust for the employee's benefit. Instead, the employee becomes an unsecured creditor of the corporation. If the corporate business is financially secure, the employee's retirement will be equally secure. But if the corporation should fail and is unable to meet its financial obligations, the employee may discover that his or her deferred compensation arrangement is worthless.

In a typical unfunded plan, the employee has no vested property right in the deferred compensation; employees who leave the firm before retirement forfeit any claim to payment. As a result, employees will not recognize any income until the year in which payment under the deferred compensation plan is received. The employer will not have any tax deduction when the deferred compensation liability is accrued, but must wait to claim the deduction in the year in which the obligation is paid. Thus, both income recognition and expense deduction will occur in the same future year.

An employee who agrees to participate in a nonqualified retirement plan must carefully assess the risk inherent in the plan. One technique for minimizing the risk is for the employer to fund the deferred compensation arrangement by transferring assets into an independently administered trust for the employee's benefit. One of the first employers to request IRS sanction of this technique was a synagogue, and as a result, this type of trust has been labeled a *Rabbi trust.* Employer funds contributed to a Rabbi trust are segregated from the employer's other business assets and cannot legally be reclaimed by the employer. Nevertheless, if the employer gets into financial difficulties, the trust assets are subject to the claims of the employer's creditors. While a funded trust arrangement provides an additional measure of security for the employee, his or her rights in the trust remain forfeitable. For this reason, the tax consequences of a Rabbi trust are no different from the tax consequences of an unfunded deferred compensation plan.

TECHNIQUES PROVIDING NO DEDUCTION AND TAXABLE INCOME

A reader might question whether any arrangement that provides no deduction for an employer can be a viable compensation technique. Nevertheless, one such arrangement, the incentive stock option, is a common component of the compensation packages offered to corporate executives.

Incentive Stock Options

The tax law currently provides for only one type of qualified stock option labeled an *incentive stock option* (ISO). The qualification requirements for ISOs are numerous, complicated, and irrelevant to this text. Our interest in ISOs stems from the fact that owners of these options enjoy a singular tax benefit not available to the holders of nonqualified options: upon exercise of an ISO the bargain element is not recognized as current compensation income. To illustrate, let's return to the example involving Ben Barnes. Recall that Ben was granted a stock option allowing him to purchase 1,000 shares of his employer corporation's stock for $50,000. Assuming the option had no ascertainable value at date of grant, Ben recognized no ordinary income until he exercised the option. At that time, the market price of the stock was $68,000, and Ben recognized the $18,000 bargain element in the option as ordinary income. His basis in his newly acquired shares was $68,000.

If Ben's option had been an ISO, the $18,000 would not have been included in Ben's current year income, and his basis in the stock would be only its $50,000 cost. Note that the $18,000 bargain element is not permanently excluded from Ben's income. Instead, its recognition is deferred until Ben sells the stock. If Ben waits 15 years before selling the stock for its market value of $120,000, his taxable gain will be $70,000; in the nonqualified option example, this future gain would be only $52,000.

Several additional characteristics of ISOs deserve mention. Note that the ordinary compensation income represented by the bargain element in the option is converted to capital gain on sale of the stock. This conversion feature dramatically enhances the charm of ISOs. An employer never receives a tax deduction for the compensatory bargain element in an ISO. As a result, from the employer's perspective, an ISO is less desirable than a nonqualified stock option as a form of employee compensation. Finally, an individual who faces the prospect of paying an alternative minimum tax (the subject of Chapter 11) in the current year should take heed—the bargain element in an ISO is a positive adjustment in the computation of alternative minimum taxable income. Although this bargain element is not recognized as income for regular tax purposes, it is fully taxable for AMT purposes.

SPECIAL TAX CONSIDERATIONS FOR SELF-EMPLOYED INDIVIDUALS

As we mentioned at the beginning of this chapter, many tax-sheltered forms of employee compensation are denied to self-employed individuals. These taxpayers cannot enjoy nontaxable group term life insurance protection, qualified employee discounts, or free employer-provided coffee and doughnuts! Congress is aware of the value of employee fringe benefits and has taken steps in recent years to redress the tax imbalance between employees and self-employed persons. For example, self-employed individuals may claim a deduction for 30 percent of any amount paid during the year for health insurance for the individual, his or her spouse, and their dependents. The above-the-line deduction is intended to create a rough parity between self-employed persons who must pay for their own health insurance and employees who receive health insurance coverage as a nontaxable fringe benefit.

Keogh Plans

One of the most lucrative employee fringe benefits is participation in an employer-sponsored qualified retirement plan. Before 1962, self-employed individuals were barred from participating in any type of tax-sheltered retirement plan and, as a result, were under tremendous pressure to incorporate their businesses for the sole purpose of achieving employee status. In 1962, Congress enacted the original version of the *Keogh plan,* named after the congressman who sponsored the legislation. For the first time, self-employed taxpayers could make tax-deductible contributions out of their earnings to a tax-exempt retirement plan. While the 1962 legislation was a much-needed step in the right direction, the limits on the amount of annual Keogh contributions were much more restrictive than the corresponding limitations on contributions to employee retirement plans. Not until 1984 did Congress finally equalize the tax-sheltering potential of the two types of plans. Today, most self-employed taxpayers are content with their Keogh plans and no longer view employee status as the yellow-brick road to a tax-sheltered retirement.

The maximum deductible annual contribution that taxpayers can make to Keogh plans is the lesser of 20 percent of net earned income from self-employment or $30,000. (The current maximum employer contribution to an employee's qualified defined contribution plan is also $30,000.) From an entrepreneur's perspective, the most bothersome requirement for Keogh plan qualification is that the plan cannot be discriminatory; it must cover all full-time permanent employees of the taxpayer who establishes the plan. The economic value of the tax deferral available to a self-employed person through a Keogh plan can be quickly eroded by the additional cost of providing comparable retirement benefits to that person's employees. Clearly, the self-employed individual with a sizable income and no employees is the ideal candidate for a Keogh plan.

Individual Retirement Accounts and Simplified Employee Pensions

In 1974, Congress created the *individual retirement account* (IRA) to allow every employed taxpayer to accumulate some amount of tax-sheltered retirement income. Currently every taxpayer may contribute to an IRA; the maximum annual contribution is limited to the lesser of 100 percent of the taxpayer's earned income or $2,000 ($2,250 if the taxpayer also contributes to a spousal IRA for a husband or wife with no earned income). IRAs are tax-exempt accounts; any tax on the income earned by the IRA is deferred until the accumulated earnings are withdrawn at retirement.

Some amount of a taxpayer's annual contribution to an IRA may be currently deductible. To the extent of any allowable deduction, the contribution itself represents tax-deferred income to the taxpayer. If the taxpayer (or his spouse on a joint return) is not an *active participant* in any other qualified retirement plan, the entire annual contribution is deductible. If the taxpayer or spouse is an active participant, the deductibility of the contribution depends on the taxpayer's income level. If the adjusted gross income on a joint return is less than $40,000 ($25,000 on a single taxpayer's return), the entire amount of the IRA contribution for the year is deductible. If the adjusted gross income on a joint return is more than $50,000 ($35,000 on a single taxpayer's return), none of the contribution is deductible. If the adjusted gross income falls between $40,000 and $50,000 ($25,000 and $35,000 on a single taxpayer's return), the deduction is proportionally reduced as the adjusted gross income increases through this $10,000 "phaseout" range. To illustrate, suppose Mr. and Mrs. Evans have respective earned incomes of $25,000 and $21,700 on their joint return, and both taxpayers contribute the maximum $2,000 to their IRAs during the year. Mr. Evans is a participant in his employer's qualified profit-sharing plan. Because the Evans's $46,700 AGI is in the phaseout range, the nondeductible percentage of their $4,000 contribution equals $6,700/$10,000 or 67 percent. The Evanses may deduct only $1,320 (33 percent of $4,000) of their IRA contributions.

Many high-income taxpayers who are active participants in other qualified retirement plans are unable to deduct their IRA contributions. Even so, these taxpayers may continue to fund their IRAs to take advantage of the tax deferral on the on the earnings generated by the account. When a taxpayer retires and begins to withdraw funds from an IRA, he will include in gross income only that portion of the withdrawal attributable to his prior years' deductible contributions and tax-exempt earnings. Any portion of the withdrawal attributable to nondeductible contributions may be withdrawn tax-free.

The concept of a *simplified employee pension* (SEP) was added to the law in 1978 to provide employers with a way to avoid the complexities involved in establishing and maintaining a qualified pension or profit-sharing plan. The use of a SEP allows the employer to make contributions directly into each employee's IRA, thereby avoiding the necessity of a trust to administer the retirement plan. The annual limit on an employer's contribution under a SEP is the lesser of 15 percent of the employee's annual compensation or $30,000. The employer contribution is excludable from the employee's gross income and will not be subject to tax until withdrawn from IRA at retirement. The fact that an employer makes a SEP contribution to an employee's IRA does not preclude the employee from making his own personal contribution. Note, however, that because the employee is an active participant in the SEP, the deductibility of the personal contribution will depend on the employee's AGI level.

CONCLUSION

Compensation arrangements represent fertile soil out of which a wonderful variety of tax planning opportunities can grow. Virtually every employee and self-employed person, regardless of income level, can take advantage of at least one of the techniques discussed in this chapter. Of course, overly aggressive individuals who try to avoid current taxation of their earnings through questionable tactics are asking for trouble. Both the IRS and the courts have ways of dealing with taxpayers who are especially greedy. Compensation planning requires diligent compliance with both the letter and the spirit of the law. Consequently, the reader should temper any enthusiasm for the ideas suggested in this chapter with a clear appreciation of the need for expert tax advice before any of the ideas are implemented.

PROBLEMS AND CASES

1. To what extent do the following items represent a nontaxable fringe benefit to the recipient employee? You may assume that each of the benefits is offered to employees on a nondiscriminatory basis.

a. $80,000 of group term life insurance coverage. The annual cost of the insurance is $6.32 per $1,000 of coverage.
b. A 10 percent discount on all merchandise carried in the corporate employer's retail outlets. The employer's gross profit percentage on retail sales is 13 percent.
c. "Time-and-a-half" pay for every hour worked by an employee in excess of 50 hours per week.
d. Access to an employer-operated parking garage for $15 per month. Comparable parking facilities charge $50 per month.
e. Unlimited use of the employer's photocopying machine.
f. A $700 per month cash housing allowance for employees who work in Manhattan.
g. Payment of membership dues to the local YMCA or YWCA.
h. Payment of membership dues to the American Bar Association.

2. Bob Barker's corporate employer has transferred Bob from its Seattle office to its San Francisco office. To help Bob with the move, the employer has agreed to pay the $12,000 real estate commission on the sale of his Seattle home. Must Bob include this fringe benefit in his current year gross income?

3. Shannon Troy works for a corporate employer that recently adopted a cafeteria plan under which its employees can receive a $3,000 year-end cash bonus or enroll in the employer's qualified medical reimbursement plan that will pay up to $3,000 of any employee's annual medical bills. Shannon is in a 31 percent tax bracket and her annual medical bills average $2,300.

   a. Based on these facts, should Shannon choose the year-end bonus or the nontaxable fringe benefit?
   b. Would your answer change if Shannon were in a 15 percent marginal tax bracket?

4. David Wang has the full-time use of a car owned and maintained by David's employer. During the current year, David can substantiate that he drove the car 45,000 miles on business and 10,000 miles for pleasure. The employer has suggested to David that the entire value of one year's use of the automobile ($15,000) be included as compensation income on David's Form W–2 for the year, and that David simply claim the business portion of the usage as an employee business expense on his Form 1040. What would be the tax consequence to David if he accepted this suggestion? David estimates that his adjusted gross income for the year (including use of the company car) will be $130,000.

5. On July 1 of the current year, Maria Flores borrowed $20,000 from her corporate employer to use as a down payment to buy a personal residence. The employer required no collateral from Maria and charged her no interest on the loan. At the end of the year, the loan was still outstanding.

   a. Assuming the applicable market rate of interest is 7 percent, describe the tax consequences of this transaction to both the employer and to Maria.

   b. Would your answer change if Maria used the borrowed funds as a down payment to purchase investment real estate?

6. Explain the basic difference between a defined benefit retirement plan and a defined contribution retirement plan.

7. Jackson Lee retired in the current year. Jackson has determined he needs \$3,000 after-tax cash flow per month in addition to his Social Security benefits on which to live. Jackson will receive \$1,500 per month from his employer's qualified retirement plan, \$900 a month under a deferred compensation arrangement with his employer, and \$1,400 per month of investment income from his savings.

   a. Assuming Jackson is in a 28 percent marginal tax bracket, will his after-tax cash flow meet his budgeted needs?
   b. Would your answer change if the employer's retirement plan were nonqualified?

8. Rick Scarletti is a vice president of Sachem Inc. The corporation awarded year-end bonuses to all its executives in the form of 1,000 shares of Sachem common stock. However, the stock was restricted in that the executives must forfeit it back to the corporation if they leave Sachem's employ during the next two years. On the day the bonus was paid, Sachem shares were selling at \$26.50 per share on the New York Stock Exchange.

   a. What are Rick's choices concerning the recognition of gross income attributable to his year-end bonus?
   b. Based on a careful analysis of Sachem's business prospects, Rick estimates the stock should be selling at \$34 per share by the time his risk of forfeiture lapses. Rick is in a 39.6 percent marginal tax bracket. Based on this additional information, which choice would minimize Rick's tax cost of the bonus in present value terms? In making your computations, assume \$100 of tax paid in the current year costs \$100, while \$100 of tax paid in the year in which the risk of forfeiture lapses costs only \$81.

9. In the current year, Bertram Inc. granted a number of stock options to its executives. Kim Horikawa received an option to purchase 500 shares of Bertram common stock at \$20 per share at any time during the next four years. At date of grant, Bertram stock was trading at \$18 per share on the American Stock Exchange. Three years after receiving the option, Kim exercised the option on a day when Bertram's stock was trading at \$37 per share.

   a. If the stock option is nonqualified, how much income must Kim recognize in the year the option was granted?
   b. If the stock option is nonqualified, how much income must Kim recognize in the year the option was exercised?
   c. How much capital gain must Kim recognize in a subsequent year when she sells her 500 shares of Bertram stock for \$52 per share?
   d. In what year did Bertram Inc. receive a deduction for compensation paid to Kim in the form of the stock option? What is the amount of the deduction?

e. How would your answers to *a* through *d* change if the stock option had been an incentive stock option (ISO)?

10. Betty Furgeson operates a sole proprietorship; her average net income from the business is $95,000. Betty is very interested in providing herself with a tax-sheltered retirement plan and is considering establishing a defined contribution Keogh plan.

a. What is the maximum amount of income from her business that Betty can contribute to a Keogh plan?
b. What impact will the maximum contribution have on Betty's current year tax liability if she is in a 39.6 percent tax bracket?
c. What other factor must Betty consider before deciding to establish the Keogh plan?

11. Jim and Susan McMahon file a joint tax return. What maximum IRA contribution may they deduct in the following scenarios?

a. Jim earns a $55,000 annual salary and is covered by an employer-sponsored qualified retirement plan in which he is not yet vested. Susan works as a homemaker.
b. Same facts as in *a,* but Jim is not covered by a qualified retirement plan.
c. Jim earns a $35,000 annual salary and is covered by a qualified plan, Susan earns a $25,000 annual salary and is not covered.
d. Jim earns a $16,000 annual salary and Susan earns a $30,000 annual salary. Both are covered by qualified plans.
e. Jim earns a $55,000 annual salary and Susan earns a $75,000 annual salary. Neither is covered by a qualified plan.

12. Lyle Trezevant is a participant in both a qualified pension plan and a profit-sharing plan and has an adjusted gross income of over $70,000. Lyle understands that if he makes an annual contribution to an IRA, the contribution is nondeductible.

a. Is there any tax advantage associated with making nondeductible contributions to an IRA?
b. Is there any difference in the tax consequence of making a nondeductible IRA contribution and investing in tax-exempt municipal bonds?

13. Refer to the facts in problem 12. Assume Lyle established an IRA to which he made $22,000 of nondeductible contributions over an 11-year period. At the end of the period, Lyle withdraws his entire IRA balance of $31,700.

a. If Lyle is age 51, in perfect health, and in a 31 percent tax bracket in the year of withdrawal, compute his tax liability attributable to the withdrawal.
b. How would your computation change if Lyle is age 61 in the year of withdrawal?

14. Joe McVey is the CEO of one of the Fortune 500 companies. Ed McHone is the CEO of MC Space Industries, a family owned corporation. Both Joe and Ed draw an annual salary of $650,000. In addition, they participate in a qualified pension

plan and receive other executive perquisites common to many business executives.

a. Is it likely that an IRS agent auditing the corporate employer's tax return will disallow any amount of the salary paid to either Joe or Ed as unreasonable compensation? Explain briefly.

b. What factors would be considered in any dispute between the corporate employers and the IRS concerning the reasonableness of the salaries paid to their respective CEOs?

Case 10–1

Charley Huff and Walt Bratic are junior executives for two plumbing companies. Charley earns a $48,000 salary, but receives no fringe benefits; Walt earns a $40,000 salary and the following fringe benefits:

Benefit	*Value*
Group term life insurance ($40,000 coverage)	$ 200
Medical insurance coverage	2,200
Discount on plumbing services (15%)	120
Contribution to qualified profit-sharing plan	3,000
Total benefits received	$5,520

Both Charley and Walt are in the 31 percent marginal tax bracket; neither itemizes deductions. Assume the profit-sharing contribution will compound at a rate of 8 percent for 35 years, when it will be taxed at a rate of 31 percent. Neither man will make an IRA contribution or invest in a savings account. Which person is getting a better deal?

CHAPTER 11

The Alternative Minimum Tax

Congress enacted the *alternative minimum tax* (AMT) primarily for political reasons. Under the regular tax system, individuals and corporations with substantial amounts of economic income can take advantage of income-sheltering techniques that, in very extreme cases, reduce their tax liabilities to almost nothing. In past years, these extreme cases received a great deal of publicity and caused people to lose respect for a tax system so riddled with loopholes that millionaires and huge corporations could escape taxation altogether. In response to this embarrassing public perception, Congress decided to create a backup system to ensure that every person with significant income pays a "fair share" of the federal tax burden.

Conceptually, all taxpayers must calculate their annual tax liability under both the regular tax system and the backup alternative system. If the liability under the regular system is less than the liability under the alternative system, the alternative liability becomes the minimum tax due. As a practical matter, the average middle-class individual and the small corporate taxpayer will not bother with the alternative calculation because of the generous exemptions from the AMT. However, wealthy individuals who engage in complex business and investment transactions and large corporate enterprises must make both calculations every year.

This introduction to the alternative minimum tax is divided into three major parts. The first part explains general rules applicable to all taxpayers; the second part, those rules of special importance to corporate taxpayers; and the final part, rules unique to individual taxpayers.

FACTORS OF IMPORTANCE TO ALL TAXPAYERS

The alternative minimum tax is really a second income tax system, parallel to but separate from, the regular income tax described in all the other chapters of this text. The first version of the AMT, enacted in 1969, was largely intended to affect individuals; the current version seems clearly directed at large corporations. While most of the AMT provisions apply to all taxpayers, certain technical provisions are narrowly directed at a few specific targets. For example, one rule applies only to corporations that build merchant and fishing vessels; another applies only to certain Blue Cross, Blue Shield operations. Consistent with the philosophy of this book, we will consider only those provisions of widespread interest, and even those provisions will be discussed in conceptual terms.

Computing the Alternative Minimum Tax

Computation of the AMT begins with taxable income computed in the regular way, but before considering any net operating loss (NOL) deduction for the year. This amount is subject to various manipulations to derive a new tax base called *alternative minimum taxable income* (AMTI). AMTI in excess of a statutory exemption amount is multiplied by the AMT rate to determine the gross AMT liability. Finally, this amount may be reduced by two tax credits to determine the net AMT liability. This computation is diagramed in Figure 11–1.

Adjustments. Observe that the *AMT adjustments* identified in Figure 11–1 can be positive or negative and therefore can cause AMTI to be either larger or smaller than taxable income for the year. The set of adjustments includes items that are strictly a matter of timing; the same item of income or deduction is accounted for over different periods for regular tax and AMT purposes. For example, in the regular tax system, research experimentation expenses are fully deductible in the year incurred. For AMT purposes, such expenses incurred by individuals and passthrough entities must be capitalized and amortized over 10 years. In a year in which research and experimentation expenses are deducted in the computation of regular taxable income, 90 percent of the deduction must be added back as a positive adjustment in the computation of AMTI. Over the next nine years, this adjustment will reverse through a series of negative adjustments to regular taxable income.

The most common adjustment in the AMTI computation is the difference between the depreciation deductions allowable for regular tax and AMT purposes. In the

FIGURE 11–1 Calculating the Alternative Minimum Tax

	Taxable income for regular tax purposes
add back:	NOL deduction for regular tax purpose
plus/minus:	AMT adjustments (MACRS over ADS depreciation, etc.)
plus:	Preferences (certain tax-exempt interest, etc.)
less:	NOL deduction for AMT purposes
	Alternative minimum taxable income (AMTI)
less	AMT exemption (after any phaseout)
	AMT tax base
multiplied by:	AMT rate
	Precredit tentative AMT
less:	AMT credits
	Tentative AMT
less:	Regular tax
	AMT

computation of regular taxable income, fixed assets are generally depreciated using an accelerated system (MACRS). (This system is described in detail in Chapter 6.) However, an *alternative depreciation system* (ADS) must be used to calculate the AMTI depreciation deduction. The recovery periods under ADS are longer than the recovery periods under MACRS; for example, certain types of business equipment that can be depreciated over a 7-year recovery period for regular tax purposes must be depreciated over a 13-year recovery period for AMT purposes. Under MACRS, a 200 percent declining-balance method is used to compute depreciation for most business personalty. Under ADS, a slower 150 percent declining-balance method must be used. As a result of these differences, the MACRS depreciation deduction is greater than its ADS counterpart in the early years of an asset's life, and the excess deduction becomes a positive adjustment to regular taxable income. At some point in the asset's life, the situation will reverse and the annual ADS deduction will exceed the MACRS deduction. At this point, the annual AMT adjustment becomes negative. Over the life of the asset, the two systems result in the same total depreciation deduction, and the positive and negative adjustments in the AMTI calculation will zero out.

The following table identifies the various items requiring adjustment for AMT purposes:

	Adjustment Applies to—	
Adjust for—	*Corporation*	*Individual*
Depreciation of real and personal property	x	x
Mining exploration and development costs	x	x
Completed-contract method of accounting	x	x
Amortization of pollution control facilities	x	x
Certain itemized deductions		x
Circulation, research, and experimental expenses		x
Bargain element upon exercise of incentive stock options		x
Tax shelter farm activity losses		x
Adjusted current earnings	x	

Many of the adjustments on the preceding list are required of both corporate and individual taxpayers. Two important exceptions are the adjustments for certain itemized deductions and adjusted current earnings. Because these adjustments are of particular interest to individual and corporate taxpayers, respectively, they will be explained in greater detail later in this chapter. The computational details of the rest of the AMT adjustments are of limited interest to general business managers. The important thing for them to understand is that they may be required to keep three different sets of books: one for financial accounting purposes, a second for regular income tax purposes, and a third for alternative minimum tax purposes.

Preferences. *Preference items* are always positive additions to taxable income in the computation of AMTI. The list of preferences is shorter than the list of adjustments and includes the following:

Preferences	Preference Applies to— Corporation	Individual
Certain tax-exempt interest	x	x
Percentage depletion in excess of cost basis	x	x
Excess intangible drilling and development costs	x	x

Unlike many of the AMT adjustments described earlier, preferences will not zero out over time. In other words, preferences can only make AMTI a larger number than regular taxable income. For example, tax-exempt interest on most state and local bonds is excluded from gross income and consequently is not a component of regular taxable income. However, tax-exempt interest paid on certain *private activity bonds* issued by state and local governments after August 17, 1986, is a preference item that must be included in AMTI. This permanent difference between regular taxable income and AMTI will never reverse.

NOLs. The net operating loss deduction is computed differently for both regular and minimum tax purposes. The technical details of the different computations are of limited importance in the tax planning process. Every taxpayer, however, should know that an NOL deduction may not offset more than 90 percent of AMTI. As a consequence, businesses with very large NOL carryforwards may be required to pay a small amount of income tax because of the AMT.

Exemptions. Taxpayers with small amounts of taxable income and limited adjustment and preference items can generally ignore the AMT because of the exemptions allowed. The amount of the exemption varies by taxpayer.

Individuals—	
Married persons/joint return	$45,000
Married persons/separate returns and fiduciaries	22,500
Single persons and heads of households	33,750
Corporations	40,000

These exemptions are phased out by 25 percent of the taxpayer's AMTI in excess of a statutory threshold. The threshold amounts are:

	Threshold
Individuals—	
Married persons/joint return	$150,000
Married persons/separate returns and fiduciaries	75,000
Single persons and heads of households	112,500
Corporations	150,000

As a result of the phaseout, the AMT exemption for married persons filing jointly is reduced to zero if the couple's AMTI exceeds $300,000.

Exemption			$45,000
Phaseout:	AMTI	$330,000	
	Threshold	(150,000)	
	Excess AMTI	$180,000	
		25%	
		$ 45,000	
Reduction of exemption amount			(45,000)
Exemption after phaseout			–0–

For married persons filing separately and fiduciaries, the exemption is reduced to zero when AMTI exceeds $165,000, for single persons and heads of households when AMTI exceeds $247,500, and for corporations when AMTI exceeds $310,000.

Tax Rates. For individual and fiduciary taxpayers, the AMT rate consists of two brackets—26 percent on the first $175,000 ($87,500 for married persons filing separately) of AMTI in excess of the exemption amount and 28 percent on any additional AMTI. For corporate taxpayers, the AMT rate is a flat 20 percent of AMTI in excess of the exemption amount. The difference between the AMT rates and the top marginal rates for regular tax purposes is substantial. For individuals, the difference is 11.6 percentage points (28 percent compared to 39.6 percent) and for corporations the difference is 15 percentage points (20 percent compared to 35 percent). Consequently, taxpayers must have AMTI significantly greater than their regular taxable income before their tentative AMT will exceed their regular tax liability for the year.

Tax Credits. As a general rule, none of the tax credits available to individuals or corporations under the regular tax system can be used to reduce the AMT. The major exception is the foreign tax credit, which is described in detail in Chapter 13. However, taxpayers can offset no more than 90 percent of their tentative AMT with foreign tax credits. Consequently, taxpayers who avoid paying any regular tax because of large foreign tax credits may still owe 10 percent of their precredit AMT for the year.

Payment of the AMT

Technically, a taxpayer pays both the regular income tax and the alternative minimum tax imposed in the current year. The AMT is defined as any excess of the tentative alternative minimum tax over the regular tax liability. Consider the situation in which a corporation's taxable income and AMTI are $500,000 and $1 million, respectively, and no AMT tax credits are available. The corporation's regular tax is $170,000 ($500,000 × 34 percent), while its tentative AMT is $200,000 ($1 million × 20 percent). The corporation's AMT is $30,000, the excess of the tentative AMT over $170,000. The corporation will pay *both* the regular tax and the AMT for a total payment of $200,000. Practically, the corporation is paying the larger of its regular tax liability or its tentative AMT liability.

The discussion in the preceding paragraph may seem like a rather pointless semantic exercise—particularly from the perspective of the corporate officer in our example who writes the $200,000 check to the IRS. However, it is very important to quantify the precise amount of AMT paid in any given year. The current year's AMT liability is generally transformed into a Section 53 *minimum tax credit,* which is carried forward to subsequent taxable years. In a subsequent year, this credit will offset any amount of the taxpayer's regular tax liability in excess of tentative AMT.

To illustrate, refer to our example in which a corporation pays a regular tax of $170,000 and an AMT of $30,000. The $30,000 AMT becomes a $30,000 tax credit carried forward into the next year. Assume that in year 2 the corporation again pays both taxes—a regular tax of $210,000 and an AMT of $15,000. The Section 53 credit carried forward into year 3 is $45,000, the AMT liability for years 1 and 2. In year 3, our corporation's precredit regular tax liability is $250,000 while its tentative AMT is only $200,000. The corporation may use the entire Section 53 credit carryforward to reduce its regular tax to $205,000. A tabular presentation of this example emphasizes the important function of the minimum tax credit.

	Year 1	*Year 2*	*Year 3*	*Total*
Tentative AMT	$200,000	$225,000	$200,000	
Regular tax	170,000	210,000	250,000	$630,000
AMT (Section 53 credit)	30,000	15,000	(45,000)	
Total tax liability	$200,000	$225,000	$205,000	$630,000

Because our corporation could use its entire minimum tax credit in year 3, the total tax liability for the three-year period equals the total regular tax for the period. In this case the imposition of the AMT affected only the *timing* of the tax payments, causing an acceleration of the payments into the first two years of the example. Thus, the AMT prevented the corporate taxpayer from unduly minimizing tax liability in years 1 and 2 by deferring income into the future. However, when the deferral reversed in year 3, the Section 53 credit ensured that the taxpayer was not taxed a second time on the deferred income.

SPECIAL CORPORATE CONSIDERATIONS

The ACE Adjustment

The most troublesome adjustment in the computation of corporate AMTI is based on the corporation's *adjusted current earnings* (ACE) for the taxable year. The positive ACE adjustment equals 75 percent of any excess of adjusted current earnings over current year AMTI (before the ACE adjustment itself and any NOL deduction). The ACE adjustment can also be negative; current year AMTI may be reduced by 75 percent of the excess of AMTI over adjusted current earnings. However, the amount of a negative ACE adjustment for the year is limited to any positive cumulative total of prior years' ACE adjustments.

The computation of adjusted current earnings is roughly comparable to the computation of a corporation's economic income for the year. Specifically, many items of economic income excludable from regular taxable income must be included in adjusted current earnings. For example, key-man life insurance proceeds payable to a corporate beneficiary are excludable from gross income. Nevertheless the cash proceeds represent a very real economic benefit to the corporation and will increase adjusted current earnings accordingly. Similarly, dividend income not included in corporate taxable income because of the 70 percent dividends received deduction also becomes part of a corporation's adjusted current earnings for the year. As a result of the ACE adjustment, 75 percent of both the insurance proceeds and the dividends received deduction will be included in AMTI for the year even though neither the proceeds nor the deduction is an AMT adjustment or preference item per se.

Certain specialized accounting methods may not be used in the computation of adjusted current earnings. A corporation using the LIFO method for regular tax purposes must recompute its cost of goods sold for ACE purposes under the FIFO method. The installment sale method of reporting gain cannot be used in the ACE computation. Finally, amortization of corporate organizational costs is not permitted for ACE purposes.

To illustrate the insidious nature of the ACE adjustment, consider the situation of Delta Inc. The corporation has taxable income for the year of $1,800,000 and has no AMT adjustments or preference items so its AMTI before the ACE adjustment is also $1,800,000. Delta's adjusted current earnings for the year total $3,650,000.

Delta's taxable income		$1,800,000
AMT adjustments		–0–
Preferences		–0–
AMTI before ACE adjustment		$1,800,000
ACE	$3,650,000	
AMTI before ACE adjustment	(1,800,000)	
Excess ACE	$1,850,000	
	75%	
ACE adjustment	$1,387,500	1,387,500
AMTI		$3,187,500
		20%
Tentative AMT		$ 637,500
Regular tax (34% of $1,800,000)		(612,000)
AMT		$ 25,500

The addition of the $1,387,500 ACE adjustment results in a final AMTI of $3,187,500 and a tentative AMT of $637,500. Because Delta's regular tax liability is only $612,000, the corporation must pay an AMT of $25,500 in a year devoid of specific AMT adjustments or preference items.

The Environmental Tax

Corporations with AMTI (computed without any NOL deduction) in excess of $2 million must pay an *environmental tax* equal to 0.12 percent of the excess. As the name suggests, Congress has earmarked the revenues generated by this particular tax for environmental cleanup. Corporations may be liable for this tax even in years in which they owe no AMT.

DISALLOWED ITEMIZED DEDUCTIONS FOR INDIVIDUALS

Individual taxpayers who report sizable itemized deductions for the taxable year should be aware that many of these deductions may be disallowed for AMT purposes. In an AMT world, the following rules apply.

1. No deduction is allowed for miscellaneous itemized deductions (such as tax return preparation fees and employee business expenses) and state or local income and property taxes.
2. Medical expenses are deductible only to the extent they exceed 10 percent (rather than 7.5 percent) of the taxpayer's adjusted gross income.
3. While interest on a home mortgage incurred to acquire, construct, or substantially improve a personal residence is deductible for AMT purposes, interest on a home equity mortgage is not.
4. Investment interest expense is deductible to the extent of net investment income (including interest on state and local bonds) included in AMTI.
5. Any standard deduction or personal and dependency exemptions are disallowed.
6. The reduction of total itemized deductions based on 3 percent of excess AGI is not required in the calculation of AMTI.

To illustrate the impact of the AMT adjustment for itemized deductions, suppose Mrs. Clark, a single head of household with three dependents, has adjusted gross income of $100,000, itemized deductions totaling $40,000, four exemptions totaling $10,200, and taxable income of $49,800. Her regular tax liability for the year is $9,765. The itemized deductions consist of a $3,000 medical expense deduction (total medical expenses were $10,500), $11,000 of state and local taxes, $20,000 of interest on a home equity mortgage, and a $6,000 contribution to charity. As an investor in an equipment leasing partnership, Mrs. Clark was allocated a positive AMT depreciation adjustment of $16,000.

Based on these facts, Mrs. Clark's itemized deductions *for AMT purposes* consist of the $6,000 charitable contribution and the $500 of medical expenses in excess of 10 percent of AGI. Consequently, her AMTI for the year is $109,500 (regular taxable income plus disallowed itemized deductions, personal exemptions, and the AMT depreciation

Mrs. Clark's regular tax calculation	
Adjusted gross income	$100,000
Itemized deductions:	
Medical expenses ($10,500 – 7.5% AGI)	(3,000)
State and local taxes	(11,000)
Interest on home equity mortgage	(20,000)
Charitable contribution	(6,000)
Exemptions ($2,550 × 4)	(10,200)
Taxable income	$ 49,800
Regular tax	$ 9,765

Mrs. Clark's AMT calculation	
Taxable income	$ 49,800
Positive AMT depreciation adjustment	16,000
Disallowed itemized deductions:	
Medical expenses (only $500 allowed for AMT purposes)	2,500
State and local taxes	11,000
Interest on home equity mortgage	20,000
Disallowed exemptions	10,200
AMTI	$109,500
AMT exemption	(33,750)
AMT tax base	$ 75,750
	26%
Tentative AMT	$ 19,695
Regular tax	(9,765)
AMT	$ 9,930

adjustment). After deducting the $33,750 exemption for a head of household, Mrs. Clark's AMT base is $75,750, and her tentative AMT is $19,695. Consequently, Mrs. Clark must pay an AMT of $9,930 in addition to her regular income tax of $9,765.

CONCLUSION

The existence of the AMT system forces many taxpayers to make two separate sets of computations before they can file their tax returns for the year. The most likely candidates for payment of the AMT are:

1. Capital intensive businesses reporting little or no regular taxable income because of large MACRS depreciation deductions or NOL deductions.
2. Corporations reporting little or no regular taxable income but earning substantial amounts of economic income.
3. Individuals who report large itemized deductions.

While taxpayers in any of these three categories have obvious problems, many other unsuspecting individuals and corporations may find themselves victims of the AMT system. Even taxpayers with no apparent exposure to this tax must bear the cost of complying with its complex rules and record-keeping requirements and must consider the AMT implications of every tax planning maneuver. Unfortunately, in many situations, the interaction between the regular tax and the AMT is nearly impossible to predict and equally impossible to ignore.

PROBLEMS AND CASES

1. Manny Hernandez, a married individual who files a joint return, has taxable income of $90,000, $15,000 of positive AMT adjustments, $10,000 of tax preferences, and a $5,000 foreign tax credit.

   a. Compute Mr. Hernandez's tentative alternative minimum tax for the year.

b. How would your computation change if Mr. Hernandez had a $20,000 foreign tax credit for the year?

2. Robin Stone, a single taxpayer with two dependents, has adjusted gross income of $75,000, total itemized deductions of $40,000, three $2,550 exemptions, and taxable income of $27,350. Robin files her 1996 tax return as a head of household; her regular tax liability (after a $700 child care credit) is $3,403.

   Robin's itemized deductions consist of $8,800 of medical expenses, $9,000 of state and local taxes, $5,500 of charitable contributions, $13,800 of interest on the mortgage Robin took out to purchase her home, and miscellaneous itemized deductions of $2,900. During the year Robin earned $1,300 of tax-exempt interest from newly issued private activity bonds and $700 of tax-exempt interest from newly issued public utility city of Orlando bonds. Based on these facts, compute Robin's AMT for the current year.

3. During December, Bob Thomas deliberately prepaid certain real property taxes in order to accelerate the itemized deduction for the payment into the current year. What is the effect of this planning strategy if Mr. Thomas finds himself liable for the AMT in the current year?

4. Ginshu Knives, Inc., had $1 million in taxable income before any NOL deduction in the current year. Ginshu has no AMT adjustments or preference items. Ginshu has $2.5 million of NOL carryforwards into the year (for both AMT and regular tax purposes). What is Ginshu's current year tax liability?

5. What is a married couple's tentative alternative minimum tax if their AMTI before exemption is

   a. $100,000?
   b. $250,000?
   c. $400,000?

6. Le-Sung Ho's regular tax and AMT for 19x1–19x3 (before consideration of the AMT credit) are shown below.

Year	*Regular Tax*	*Tentative AMT*	*AMT*
19x1	$20,000	$45,000	$25,000
19x2	25,000	20,000	–0–
19x3	60,000	15,000	–0–

   The difference between the regular tax and AMT is due to Ho's use of the installment sale method of accounting for regular tax purposes. What is Mr. Ho's tax liability in each year? What is the effect of the alternative minimum tax in this situation?

7. Triad Inc. has current year taxable income of $500,000, which includes $60,000 of dividend income from other taxable domestic corporations. (Triad owns less than a 4 percent interest in any of these corporations.) Triad has excess MACRS depreciation over ADS depreciation of $120,000 and tax preference items of $29,000. During the year, Triad realized a $230,000 gain on the sale of

investment land; under the installment method of accounting, only $45,000 of the gain was included in current taxable income. Based on these facts, compute Triad's AMT for the year.

8. Longren Inc., a calendar year taxpayer, was incorporated in 19x0. For its first taxable year, Longren's AMTI before the ACE adjustment was $190,000 and its adjusted current earnings were $250,000. For 19x1, Longren's AMTI before the ACE adjustment was $460,000 and its adjusted current earnings were $511,000. For 19x2, Longren's AMTI before the ACE adjustment was $900,000, and its adjusted current earnings were $720,000. Based on these facts, compute Longren's 19x2 AMTI after the ACE adjustment.

9. Alex Grant, a married taxpayer, had the following items of income and expense from his widget business (a proprietorship) and personal activities in the current year:

Sales revenue	$1,250,000
Cost of goods sold	1,000,000
Operating expenses	150,000
MACRS depreciation	74,000 (ADS depreciation is $50,000)
Dividend income	50,000
Home acquisition mortgage interest	4,000
State income tax	2,000
Charitable contribution	3,000

Alex also received $20,000 in interest income from newly issued tax-exempt private activity bonds (face value $250,000, yielding 8 percent) and is entitled to two personal exemptions.

a. What is Alex's regular tax liability?
b. What is Alex's AMT liability?
c. What is Alex's after-tax rate of return on his municipal bonds?

10. Amazing Ronco Products, Inc., had the following items of income and expense for regular tax, AMT, and ACE purposes in the current year:

	Regular Tax	*AMT*	*Adjusted Current Earnings*
Sales revenue	$2,200,000	$2,200,000	$2,200,000
Cost of goods sold	1,700,000	1,700,000	1,700,000
Operating expenses	200,000	200,000	200,000
Depreciation	200,000	140,000	140,000
Tax-exempt interest	–0–	–0–	100,000
Key-man life insurance proceeds	–0–	–0–	75,000

The interest income is from a $1.25 million public activity municipal bond yielding 8 percent.

a. Compute Ronco's regular tax liability.
b. Compute Ronco's AMT liability.
c. What would Ronco's tax liability be if it did not have the interest income?
d. Compute Ronco's after-tax rate of return on the bond, assuming the bond price is constant.

Case 11–1

Unisynthesis, Inc. projects the following regular tax, AMT, and ACE amounts:

	Regular Tax	*AMT*	*Adjusted Current Earnings*
Sales revenue	$2,800,000	$2,800,000	$2,800,000
Cost of goods sold	2,200,000	2,200,000	2,200,000
Operating expenses	300,000	300,000	300,000
Depreciation	250,000	170,000	170,000

Unisynthesis is considering three investments: a $1 million corporate bond yielding 11 percent, a newly issued $1 million private use municipal bond yielding 9 percent, and a $1 million public use municipal bond yielding 8 percent. Rank these investments in terms of their after-tax yield.

CHAPTER 12

Corporate Acquisitions, Mergers, Divisions, and Liquidations

The last two decades witnessed an unprecedented number of transactions involving the purchase and sale of corporate businesses. Private companies went public, publicly traded corporations were taken private, and both successful and thwarted takeovers of multibillion dollar businesses made front-page news. During 1995 alone, 8,956 corporate mergers in which $458 billion changed hands were consummated. This chapter will explore the fascinating topic of corporate restructuring, beginning with a discussion of the key tax factors involved in acquisitions and mergers. We will introduce the basic concepts underlying nontaxable corporate reorganizations and summarize the esoteric provisions governing the taxation of corporate divisions. The chapter will conclude with a look at the tax consequences of the final event in the life of a corporation, the complete liquidation of the corporate business.

STRUCTURING THE CORPORATE ACQUISITION

Purchasing the Target's Assets

When one corporation decides to purchase an existing business operated by another corporation (the *target*), the purchaser must choose between an acquisition of the *business assets* or an acquisition of the *stock* of the target corporation. If the choice is an asset acquisition, the purchasing corporation may be selective, buying only certain business properties specified in a purchase contract for a negotiated price per asset. Alternatively, the corporate buyer and seller may contract to transfer the seller's business assets for a single lump-sum price. In both cases, the contract will specify which, if any, of the target corporation's liabilities will be legally assumed by the purchasing corporation as part of the acquisition. Any liabilities not assumed by the purchaser remain the responsibility of the target corporation and its shareholders. In a situation in which the acquiring corporation suspects that the target may have significant undisclosed or contingent liabilities, a contractual asset purchase makes good sense.

The acquiring corporation can indirectly purchase a target's assets by structuring a *merger* of the two corporations. A merger is the absorption of one corporate entity into another pursuant to controlling state law. Generally, state law requires the shareholders of both corporations involved in a merger to consent to the transaction. For example, in Texas a plan of merger must receive the affirmative votes of the holders of at least two thirds of the outstanding stock of each corporation. In a merger, ownership of all the target corporation's assets is transferred to the acquiring corporation by operation of state law, and the target corporation is legally dissolved. Subsequent to the merger, the acquiring corporation is responsible for all known and contingent liabilities of the merged target. If an acquiring corporation is concerned about its future exposure to unknown creditor claims against the dissolved target, it can require that some portion of the purchase price paid to the target's shareholders in the merger be held in escrow until expiration of the statutory period during which such claims are enforceable.

Purchasing the Target's Stock

A corporation might prefer to purchase a business indirectly by acquiring a controlling interest in the outstanding stock of the target corporation. Subsequent to the acquisition, the parent corporation will operate the business through its controlled subsidiary. If in the future the parent corporation decides to operate the business directly, it can simply liquidate the subsidiary. The acquisition of a controlling stock interest allows the buyer to purchase a business already neatly packaged in an existing legal corporate form. The purchase of this corporate package may offer many advantages. For example, the target may own nontransferable business assets such as copyrights, patents, licenses, or franchises. The target may be a party to favorable third-party leases or contracts that the purchaser does not want to renegotiate. There may be an established management structure in the target or a high level of employee loyalty that the purchaser wants to preserve. Finally, public recognition of the target corporation's name or other types of goodwill might be obtainable only through an acquisition of the legal entity itself rather than the entity's business assets.

One negative aspect of an entity acquisition is that the purchasing corporation is indirectly acquiring all the target corporation's disclosed, undisclosed, and contingent liabilities. Like any shareholder, a parent corporation has limited legal liability to the creditors of a subsidiary corporation. Therefore, the risk associated with undisclosed or contingent liabilities of a business is minimized if the business continues to operate in subsidiary form. However, if the parent decides to liquidate the subsidiary to obtain direct ownership of and control over the subsidiary's assets, it will become fully responsible for all liabilities of the business.

Taxable or Nontaxable Acquisitions

While a corporation is weighing the relative merits of an asset acquisition or a stock acquisition, it also must consider whether the acquisition should be structured in a taxable or a nontaxable form. The taxable or nontaxable distinction refers to the current income tax consequences of the transaction to the selling party—the target corporation that will sell its assets or the shareholders of the target who will sell their stock. From the acquiring corporation's perspective, a purchase of property is generally not a taxable event. Thus, the reader might ask why the acquiring corporation should care whether a proposed transaction will be taxable or nontaxable! The answer stems from the possibility that the seller will accept a lower price for the business if any realized gain on the sale does not have to be reported as current taxable income.

To illustrate this possibility, assume a target corporation is wholly owned by a corporate parent willing to sell Target's stock for $1 million cash. Parent has a $500,000 basis in the target stock, so the sale will result in a $500,000 realized gain. At a 34 percent tax rate, Parent will have to pay a $170,000 federal income tax on the gain and will pocket only $830,000 of the sales proceeds. If an acquiring corporation could somehow structure the purchase as a nontaxable acquisition, Parent should be willing to accept a reduced purchase price. To the extent the added incentive of a nontaxable transaction induces Parent to accept a lower price for Target's stock, the tax savings on the sale will be shared with the acquiring corporation.

As we will discuss later in this chapter, the dominant characteristic of a nontaxable acquisition is that a major portion of the purchase price consists of equity stock in the acquiring corporation. To the extent a corporation can use its own stock rather than cash or a debt instrument to acquire property, it is minimizing the current and future cash flow drain associated with the purchase. However, the use of equity as consideration certainly is not without cost; the existing shareholders of the acquiring corporation will suffer a dilution of their equity interest when new stock is issued to purchase a targeted business.

An Acquisitions Model

Both asset and entity acquisitions can be structured in taxable or nontaxable form. Therefore, the basic decision model for corporate acquisitions appears as diagrammed in Figure 12–1.

The selection of one of the four types of acquisitions is determined by the legal, financial, accounting, and tax considerations and constraints of both the acquiring and target corporations and their respective shareholders. In a *friendly takeover* of a business, the interests of the various parties may be in relative harmony so the acquisition may be accomplished with a minimum of negotiation and compromise. In a *hostile takeover,* the management of the target corporation spurns the unwelcomed advances of the potential purchaser and will often fight to prevent the acquisition from occurring. In either case, the corporations involved will incur legal, accounting,

Figure 12–1 Acquisitions Decision Model

Taxable asset acquisition	Taxable stock acquisition
Nontaxable asset acquisition (Type A or C reorganization)	Nontaxable stock acquisition (Type B reorganization)

and investment banking fees as well as other expenses attributable to the acquisition; the IRS and the courts have taken the position that these expenses cannot be deducted currently but must be capitalized for tax purposes. An extensive literature deals with the phenomenon of corporate acquisitions and the financial and economic ramifications of both friendly and hostile takeovers. The following sections will focus on the important tax aspects of acquisitions, beginning with the consequences of a taxable purchase of either the target corporation's business assets or the outstanding stock of the target corporation itself.

TAX CONSEQUENCES OF TAXABLE ACQUISITIONS

When a target corporation sells its business assets to an acquiring corporation, the target recognizes gain or loss based on the difference between the amount realized and the basis in the assets sold. If the sale of assets is structured as a merger of the target corporation into the acquiring corporation (after which the target no longer exists), the target must recognize gain or loss as if it had sold all its assets for their fair market value. The target's shareholders must also recognize gain or loss on the merger based on the difference between the value of the consideration received for their target stock and their basis in the stock.

For example, assume Lerner Inc., a publicly traded corporation, owns assets worth $5 million with an aggregate basis of $1.3 million. Lerner's shareholders have approved a merger of Lerner into Topco Inc. under Kentucky law; pursuant to the terms of the merger, Topco pays $45 for each share of outstanding Lerner stock. On its final tax return as a separate corporate entity, Lerner Inc. must report a $3.7 million gain on the sale of its assets. Each Lerner shareholder will report gain or loss based on the $45 amount realized on the sale of each share of Lerner stock.

The acquiring corporation takes a cost basis in the assets purchased in a taxable acquisition. The cost of depreciable or amortizable business assets will be recovered over time in the form of depreciation or amortization deductions. Similarly, the cost basis in purchased inventory will be recovered when the inventory is sold. When a corporation contracts to purchase business assets from a target, the buyer and seller can certainly negotiate the price of each specific asset. Alternatively, the parties can agree on a lump-sum purchase price for all the assets to be transferred. In the latter case, the acquiring corporation will want to allocate as much of the purchase price as possible to depreciable or amortizable assets and inventory to maximize its future cost recovery deductions.

The rules of this allocation game are found in Section 1060 of the Internal Revenue Code. The law requires that a lump-sum purchase price for the assets of a trade or business be allocated to each identifiable asset only to the extent of the fair market value of the asset. Furthermore, the allocation should be consistent between buyer and seller; the amount allocated to each asset will be the cost basis to the purchaser as well as the selling price of the asset to the target corporation. Naturally, the taxpayers have the burden of proof in establishing these values. If the lump-sum purchase price exceeds the total values of all identifiable business assets, the excess amount must be allocated to goodwill, which under Section 197 may be amortized over a 15-year period.

The Section 338 Election

In a taxable entity acquisition, the acquiring corporation buys the outstanding stock of the target corporation at the stock's current market value and takes a cost basis in the purchased shares. Normally, the stock acquisition has no effect on the basis of the business assets owned by the target. If the value of these assets is substantially higher than their tax basis, the acquiring corporation may certainly regret that the price paid for the target is reflected in the basis of the stock rather than in the basis of the business assets themselves.

In certain qualified stock purchases, the acquiring corporation can elect under Section 338 to treat the stock purchase as an asset purchase for tax purposes. This constructive asset purchase results in a new cost basis for the target corporation's assets, a basis equal to fair market value on the date of the qualified stock purchase. Before 1986, this artificial basis adjustment was essentially tax free and was therefore irresistible to many delighted corporations that bought controlling stock interests in target corporations with highly appreciated assets. Unfortunately, Congress sounded the death knell for Section 338 in 1986. The Tax Reform Act of that year revised the section to provide that the artificial basis adjustment to a target's assets would trigger full recognition of any unrealized gain or loss in those assets. Because of this revision, the tax-free step-up of basis to fair market value became a fully taxable event.

To illustrate the current effect of the Section 338 election, suppose Vega Inc. purchases 100 percent of Theta Corporation's stock for $2.5 million. Theta has no debt and its assets are worth $2.5 million, but the aggregate basis of the assets is only $1.1 million. If Vega elects to treat its stock purchase as a constructive asset purchase, Theta must immediately recognize the $1.4 million appreciation in its assets as taxable income and pay federal tax accordingly. Theta's basis in its assets will then be increased to $2.5 million.

Even the novice tax student should quickly appreciate the fact that Vega would be foolish to make a Section 338 election. The stepped-up basis in the Theta assets may generate future tax benefits in the form of cost recovery deductions or cost of goods sold. But Vega is paying for these future tax benefits with current tax dollars—the very antithesis of effective tax planning! In fact, today the Section 338 election is only beneficial in exactly the right set of unusual circumstances. If Theta had a net operating loss carryforward deduction to completely offset its $1.4 million recognized gain, Vega might seriously consider a Section 338 election to achieve a basis step-up in the assets at no tax cost. However, in the majority of taxable stock acquisitions, Section 338 is a section to be carefully avoided.

Leveraged Buy-Outs

Much of the recent publicity concerning corporate mergers and acquisitions has focused on a common acquisition technique, the *leveraged buy-out* (LBO). Although LBOs can be structured in many different ways, the defining characteristic of all LBOs is the high level of debt used as consideration in the transaction. The most spectacular LBO on record was the $24.7 billion buy-out of RJR Nabisco by Kohlberg Kravis Roberts and Company in 1988. The effect of the LBO on RJR Nabisco's financial statements was dramatic. The corporation's debt-to-equity ratio increased from approximately 1 to 1 to over 12 to 1, and its projected annual debt service payments increased sixfold.

A secondary characteristic of LBOs is the use of *junk bonds* to finance the acquisition. A junk bond is an unsecured corporate obligation bearing a very high yield and subordinated to various issues of senior debt. Because of their relatively high degree of risk, junk bonds are not considered investment grade by institutional investors. As part of the RJR Nabisco acquisition, $4 billion worth of junk bonds in the newly structured corporation were sold to the public.

LBOs can be structured as either taxable asset purchases or taxable stock purchases; we will use the latter to model a typical LBO. The first step in the buy-out is for a purchaser (or a consortium of purchasers) to identify a target corporation as a good candidate for an LBO. The characteristics of such a candidate include a history of very stable profitability, a solid market position, an established product, and little or no debt on the balance sheet. In this example, assume the identified Target has no outstanding long-term debt and the market value of its outstanding stock is $1 million. The purchaser creates a new corporation (Newco) to be used in the acquisition by transferring a relatively small amount of cash into Newco in exchange for 100 percent of Newco's equity stock. Newco then proceeds to purchase Target's outstanding stock, financing the acquisition primarily by the issuance of new debt (short-term notes, investment-grade bonds, and junk bonds). After Newco has acquired sufficient control, Target is liquidated into Newco and the LBO is complete.

Assume in our example that Newco used $100,000 cash and $900,000 of debt to acquire the $1 million worth of outstanding Target stock. In this case, $900,000 of equity in Target has been replaced by an equal amount of debt. Whereas the dividends Target had been paying on that equity were nondeductible in computing corporate taxable income, the interest payments on the new debt will be fully deductible. Thus, Target should enjoy a significant tax savings and a corresponding improvement in its cash flow subsequent to the LBO.

The popularity of LBOs has caused much anxiety to many financial and economic experts who deplore these major shifts from equity to debt financing. A corporation's exposure to cash flow problems, insolvency, and bankruptcy increases after an LBO. As yet, however, no substantial empirical evidence indicates that this increased risk has had a detrimental effect on the U.S. economy. Moreover, proponents of LBOs argue that some degree of leverage in a corporation's capital structure is healthy. Not only does the federal government subsidize debt through the interest expense deduction, but also the pressure to make the required debt service payments theoretically keeps corporate management on its toes.

Congress has been ambivalent as to whether federal tax laws should deliberately discourage the use of LBOs. While there has been much debate on the subject, little legislation has passed. Section 279, which dates to 1969, denies a deduction for interest paid on a corporation's *acquisition indebtedness* to the extent the interest exceeds $5 million. However, acquisition indebtedness is defined very narrowly and includes only debt that is convertible into the issuing corporation's stock. Corporations can avoid Section 279 quite easily by issuing nonconvertible debt; as a result, the section has had little impact in the LBO area.

In 1989, Congress enacted several new provisions aimed at LBOs. Section 163 was amended to disallow a deduction for interest paid on certain very high-yield junk bonds that more closely resemble equity in the issuing corporation than true debt. A second new rule disallows a carryback for any amount of a target corporation's net operating loss attributable to a leveraged buy-out of the target. This rule is triggered by any acquisition of 50 percent or more by vote or value of a target corporation's outstanding stock. Subsequent to the acquisition, the amount of interest paid on new debt issued to finance the acquisition is labeled *corporate equity reduction interest.* If this additional interest expense creates or increases a net operating loss for the target, the amount of the loss attributable to the interest cannot be carried back to a taxable year before the LBO. The rule applies to any net operating loss for the year in which the acquisition occurs and for the two succeeding taxable years. Note that this new rule does not restrict the carryforward of losses attributable to the increased interest burden caused by an LBO. However, it does sharply curtail the availability of a quick refund of income taxes paid by the target in years before the LBO.

Tax Aspects of Hostile Takeovers

In a hostile takeover, the board of directors and the existing management of the target corporation object to the proposed acquisition. They may believe the potential buyers are interested only in a quick profit and have no long-term interest in the target's business and that their own strategic plans for the corporation's future will offer the shareholders a superior return on invested capital. The entrenched management may have self-preservation in mind; the new owners might decide to clean house by replacing the target's management team with new people. Whatever the motive for management's resistance, a hostile takeover attempt can certainly result in high financial drama as the defenders battle the *corporate raider* for control of the target.

Certain defense tactics that have developed in the hostile takeover arena have resulted in intriguing new tax rules. One of management's more popular tactics has been the *golden parachute,* a huge severance bonus for corporate executives who lose their jobs as a result of a takeover. Not only should the target's contractual liability for golden parachutes increase the cost of a hostile takeover, but also, if worse comes to worst and the old management team is fired, the lucrative golden parachute payments will soften the blow. Apparently, Congress is not particularly sympathetic to this tactic. In 1984, Congress enacted legislation that disallowed any corporate deduction for excess parachute payments and slapped the recipients with a 20 percent excise tax in addition to the regular income tax imposed on the payment.

The tax laws can be equally harsh on the corporate raider. After a raider has signaled an intention to acquire a target by purchasing a sizable block of the target's publicly traded stock, the threatened target may try to buy the raider off by paying an inflated price to redeem the stock. In 1987, Congress expressed its distaste for such *greenmail* payments by enacting a 50 percent excise tax in addition to the regular income tax on any gain enjoyed by the raider on the stock redemption.

Many potential target corporations wanting to discourage future takeover attempts have issued contingent stock purchase rights to their existing shareholders. These rights, described as *poison pills,* allow the shareholders to purchase additional target stock at a price substantially less than the market price. The rights can be exercised only on the occurrence of a specified event, such as the acquisition of a certain percentage of the target's outstanding stock by a corporate raider. This defensive strategy will cause a significant increase in the number of outstanding shares the raider must purchase to gain control of the target; thus, the poison pill could make the cost of the takeover prohibitively high. In Revenue Ruling 90–11, the Internal Revenue Service announced that adoption of a poison pill plan to discourage hostile takeovers is a nontaxable event. The stock purchase rights issued to shareholders under the plan are not subject to current valuation and do not represent a taxable dividend to the recipient shareholders.

TAX CONSEQUENCES OF CORPORATE REORGANIZATIONS

The decision model in Figure 12–1 labels the nontaxable acquisitions as *reorganizations*. For federal tax purposes, the term *reorganization* refers to a wide variety of corporate transactions that accomplish very different business objectives. However, any reorganization, regardless of its function, is treated as a nontaxable exchange (or a series of nontaxable exchanges) among the various parties to the reorganization.

Our discussion of the tax consequences of acquisitive reorganizations will be based on prototypes of both an asset acquisition and a stock acquisition. A prototype asset acquisition can be diagramed as shown in Figure 12–2. Note that in this reorganization, the business assets of the target corporation are transferred from the target to the acquiring corporation, subsequent to which Target no longer exists as a viable business entity. The shareholders of Target surrender their ownership of Target and receive an equity interest in the acquiring corporation.

Figure 12–3 depicts a prototype acquisition of the target as a controlled subsidiary. In this reorganization, the shareholders of Target directly exchange their target stock for stock in the acquiring corporation; the target itself does not participate in the transaction. After the reorganization, the original target shareholders own an equity interest in the acquiring corporation, which in turn owns the stock of Target.

Figure 12–2 Nontaxable Asset Acquisition

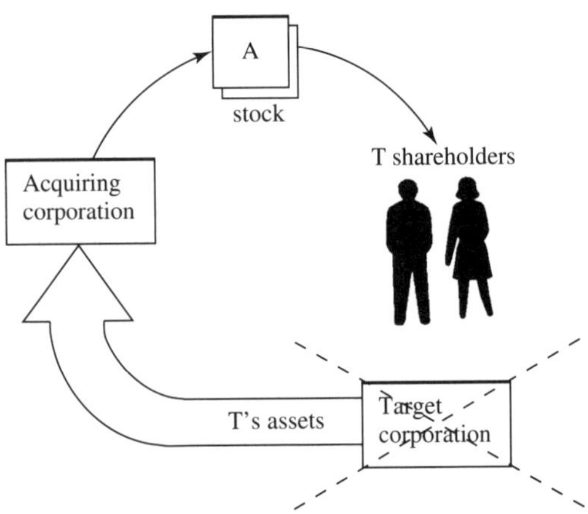

Figure 12–3 Nontaxable Stock Acquisition

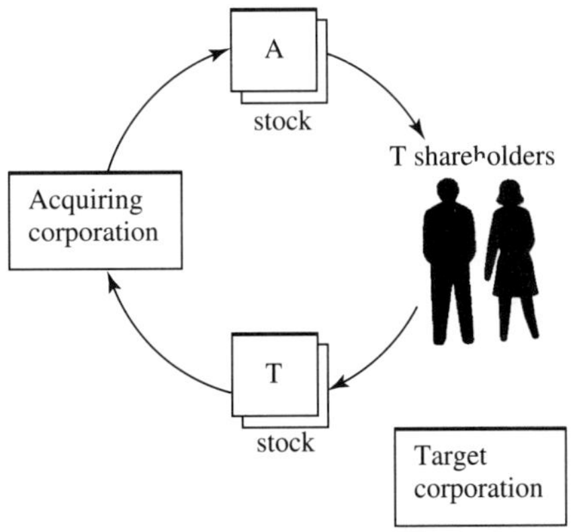

Judicial Requirements for a Reorganization

During the early history of the income tax, the federal courts were called on many times to determine the appropriate circumstances in which a corporate acquisition should be nontaxable to the various participants. Gradually, three basic requirements of tax-free corporate reorganizations evolved. These broad judicial requirements have been supplemented with more exacting statutory tests for reorganization status. Nonetheless, a brief examination of the judicial requirements can provide valuable insight into the nature of a tax-free reorganization.

The first requirement is that the original owners of the target corporation maintain a *continuity of proprietary interest* in the corporate business. In other words, in our prototype reorganizations, Target's shareholders have not simply cashed out their investment in Target. Instead, they have changed the form of their investment and continue to own an indirect interest in Target's business subsequent to the reorganization. This continuity of interest is achieved to the extent that the shareholders exchange their target stock for an equity interest in the acquiring corporation. However, each shareholder in the target corporation need not maintain a continuity of interest; the Internal Revenue Service will issue a favorable ruling as to this requirement for acquisitions in which at least 50 percent of the consideration paid to all target shareholders consists of stock in the acquiring corporation. To illustrate, assume Eaton Inc. is owned by three shareholders who hold 55 percent, 25 percent, and 20 percent of the corporation's outstanding stock. An acquisition of Eaton Inc., in which the majority shareholder receives only stock in the acquiring corporation while the two minority shareholders receive cash, meets the continuity of interest requirement. Moreover, any type of equity interest in the acquiring corporation will do. In our example, the additional fact that our majority shareholder exchanged voting common stock in Eaton Inc. for nonvoting preferred stock in the acquiring corporation would not present a problem.

The second judicial requirement for a reorganization is *continuity of business enterprise.* The acquiring corporation must either continue the historic business of the target or use a significant portion of the target's assets in an ongoing business.

The third requirement is a valid *business purpose* driving the acquisition. Clearly, Congress did not intend to bestow reorganization status on transactions with no purpose other than that of tax avoidance. If the various taxpayers involved can't demonstrate a persuasive legal, financial, or accounting reason for a corporate reorganization, they run the risk that the Internal Revenue Service will refuse to grant the transaction nontaxable status.

These judicial requirements have a common theme that is neatly summarized in Treasury regulations: "The purpose of the reorganization provisions of the Code is to except from the general rule (or taxability) certain specifically described exchanges incident to such readjustments of corporate structures . . . as are required by business exigencies and which effect only a readjustment of continuing interest in property under modified corporate forms."

Consequences to the Acquiring Corporation

In both our prototype reorganizations, the acquiring corporation uses its own stock to buy either Target's assets or the outstanding stock in Target. Section 1032 provides that a corporation never recognizes gain or loss when it uses its own stock to acquire any type of property in any type of transaction. This broad nonrecognition rule applies to the use of newly issued stock as well as Treasury stock held by a corporation.

In a reorganization, the acquiring corporation does not take a cost basis in the assets or stock purchased. Instead, the tax basis of the assets or stock in the hands of the seller(s) becomes the acquiring corporation's basis. To illustrate this important *carryover basis* rule, suppose a potential target corporation owns business assets with an adjusted tax basis of $2 million and a value of $10 million. If an acquiring corporation wants to buy the assets, it will open negotiations by offering consideration worth approximately $10 million. However, if the acquisition is ultimately structured as a reorganization, the acquiring corporation will have only a $2 million basis in the business assets. From the acquiring corporation's perspective, this carryover basis requirement is often a negative aspect of a nontaxable acquisition.

The carryover basis rule may cause a very practical problem in an acquisition of stock when the target corporation is publicly traded or has a large number of shareholders. While each shareholder's tax basis in each share of target stock technically should carry over to the acquiring corporation, this information may be impossible to obtain with any degree of accuracy. In recognition of this problem, the Internal Revenue Service will allow the acquiring corporation to use a statistical sampling technique to estimate a reasonable carryover basis in the target's stock.

Consequences to the Target Corporation's Shareholders

The target corporation's shareholders who participate in the reorganization by exchanging target stock for the acquiring corporation's stock do not recognize any gain or loss on the exchange. The tax basis in their surrendered shares will simply become the tax basis in their new shares in the acquiring corporation. Because of this substituted basis rule, the exchange really should be described as tax deferred rather than nontaxable. If and when a shareholder disposes of his new shares in a taxable transaction, the original amount of gain or loss on the exchange will be recognized. Say Jeff Gaines surrenders 200 shares of stock in Barto Inc. for 125 shares of stock in Wheeler Inc. as part of Wheeler's acquisition of Barto. If Jeff's basis in his Barto shares is $39,000 and the Wheeler shares he receives are worth $75,000, his realized gain on the exchange is $36,000. If the acquisition qualifies as a reorganization, Jeff does not have to pay tax currently on any part of the gain. However, his basis in the Wheeler shares is only $39,000. If Jeff eventually sells these 125 shares for $80,000 cash, his taxable gain will be $41,000—the $36,000 deferred gain on the reorganization exchange plus the $5,000 appreciation in the value of the Wheeler shares that occurred subsequent to the exchange.

If some amount of the consideration paid to target shareholders in a reorganization consists of cash or property other than the acquiring corporation's stock, the shareholders who receive cash or property will have to recognize taxable gain. Remember our earlier example in which Eaton Inc. was owned by three shareholders who surrendered their stock to an acquiring corporation. The 55 percent shareholder received only stock in the acquiring corporation while the two minority shareholders received cash. This acquisition could qualify as a reorganization and, as a result, the majority shareholder would have a nontaxable exchange. Even in a reorganization, however, the two minority shareholders who received only cash must recognize any gain or loss realized on the sale of their shares. If a target shareholder receives both stock in the acquiring corporation and cash or other property, any *gain* (not loss) realized on the exchange must be recognized to the extent of the cash or the value of the other property. Assume that Jeff Gaines, introduced in the previous paragraph, received only 100 shares of Wheeler stock worth $60,000 and $15,000 cash in exchange for his Barto shares. Because he received cash, Jeff must recognize $15,000 of his $36,000 realized gain.

Consequences to the Target Corporation

If an asset acquisition can be classified as a reorganization, the target corporation will not recognize any gain or loss on the disposition of its assets. As our prototype diagram illustrates, after the target transfers its business properties to the acquiring corporation, it simply goes out of existence. In a stock acquisition, the target corporation is not directly involved in the transaction, so no gain or loss occurs at the target corporation level.

TYPES OF ACQUISITIVE REORGANIZATIONS

Section 368(a)(1) of the Internal Revenue Code defines seven different types of corporate reorganizations. In the jargon of the tax professional, these reorganizations are conveniently labeled by reference to the subparagraph describing each one. Section 368(a)(1)(A) describes a type A reorganization, Section 368(a)(1)(B) describes a type B reorganization, and so on. Only the first three of these seven types of reorganizations involve the acquisition of a target corporation's assets or stock by another corporation. The first of these is the type A reorganization, a *statutory merger* or *consolidation.*

Statutory Mergers and Consolidations as Type A Reorganizations

As we discussed earlier in the chapter, one corporation can acquire the assets of another through a merger of the two corporations. In a corporate *merger,* the acquiring corporation is the surviving legal entity; in a corporate *consolidation,* the acquiring and the target corporations combine to form a new legal entity. The statutory law of the state or states in which the participants are incorporated furnishes the prerequisites for and legal characteristics of both mergers and consolidations. If a merger or consolidation has a business purpose and satisfies the continuity of proprietary interest and continuity of business enterprise tests, it qualifies as a tax-free type A reorganization. If a merger or consolidation fails to meet any of these requirements, it is a fully taxable transaction at both the corporate and shareholder levels.

You may recall from our earlier discussion that the shareholders of both the acquiring and target corporations must approve a merger between the two. In cases where one or both of the corporations are publicly held, meeting this requirement can be both time-consuming and costly. As a result of this problem, a variation on the basic type A reorganization, the *forward triangular merger,* has become very popular. In a triangular merger, a publicly held acquiring corporation forms a new subsidiary corporation into which the target corporation is merged. Because the acquiring corporation is the sole shareholder of the corporate subsidiary actually participating in the merger, consent of the shareholders of the acquiring corporation does not have to be obtained. After the triangular merger is completed, the parent corporation may simply liquidate the subsidiary to gain direct ownership and control of the target assets.

A type A reorganization gives the acquiring corporation the greatest flexibility in the type of consideration that may be offered to the shareholders of the target corporation. To achieve the requisite continuity of proprietary interest, at least half the consideration must consist of equity stock in the acquiring corporation. The rest of the consideration can consist of any mixture of cash, other property, or debt. A negative characteristic of a type A reorganization is that under state law the acquiring corporation in a merger or the new corporation formed in a consolidation assumes all known and contingent liabilities of the target. This unwelcome exposure to creditor claims can create a preference on the part of the acquiring corporation for the second type of nontaxable asset acquisition, the type C reorganization.

Practical Mergers

A type C reorganization is often referred to as a *practical merger.* Both type A and type C reorganizations allow one corporation to acquire the business assets of a target; in a type C reorganization, however, the acquisition is based on a legal contract executed between the two corporations rather than by operation of state law. This contract will specify the assets to be purchased as well as the liabilities of the target to be assumed by the acquiring corporation. In a type C reorganization, the acquiring corporation must obtain substantially all the assets of the target *solely* in exchange for the acquiring corporation's *voting* stock. Therefore, while a practical merger allows the acquiring corporation to limit its exposure to liabilities, it also is very inflexible as to the type of consideration the acquiring corporation may use. Another requirement is that the target corporation must liquidate by distributing the stock of the acquiring corporation received in the exchange (as well as any assets retained) to its shareholders. In a type C reorganization, the target shareholders do not have the option of keeping their corporation alive after the sale of its business assets.

Stock-for-Stock Exchanges

A type B reorganization is used when a corporation wants to acquire a controlling interest in the stock of a target corporation. This reorganization involves the exchange of the target's outstanding stock *solely* for *voting* stock in the acquiring corporation. Immediately after this exchange, the acquiring corporation must own at least 80 percent voting control of the target as well as 80 percent of the total number of shares of each nonvoting class of stock. This *stock-for-stock exchange* is between the acquiring corporation and the target shareholders; the target corporation itself is not involved in the transaction. Note that 80 percent control does not have to be acquired in the exchange; the requirement is satisfied as long as control exists subsequent to the exchange. To illustrate this subtle distinction, assume that Alpha Inc. exchanges its voting stock for 55 percent of the outstanding stock in Target Inc. Clearly this is not a type B reorganization and the exchange will be taxable to the participating target shareholders. Five years later, Alpha exchanges its voting stock for another 40 percent stock interest in Target. Immediately after this second exchange Alpha owns 95 percent of Target; consequently, the exchange constitutes a type B reorganization and is nontaxable to the target shareholders.

The fact that the only consideration permitted to be used in a type B reorganization is voting stock in the acquiring corporation makes this type of reorganization dangerously inflexible. The disastrous attempt of International Telephone and Telegraph (ITT) to acquire Hartford Fire Insurance Co. in a type B reorganization exemplifies the rigid nature of the form. In 1970, ITT offered to exchange its newly issued voting preferred stock for Hartford's common stock, representing to the Hartford shareholders that their exchanges would be nontaxable. In this transaction, ITT acquired more than 95 percent of the Hartford stock outstanding immediately before the exchange. Unfortunately, two years earlier ITT had acquired 8 percent of the outstanding Hartford stock for cash. The Internal Revenue Service determined that the cash-for-stock and the stock-for-stock exchanges were components of a single plan of acquisition, a plan that violated the solely for voting stock requirement of a type B reorganization. As a result, thousands of infuriated Hartford shareholders were informed that their exchanges of Hartford shares for ITT shares were fully taxable events. Various shareholder groups, financed by ITT, promptly litigated the issue. Their primary argument was that the cash acquisition of only 8 percent was irrelevant to the transaction and should be ignored because ITT had actually acquired the requisite 80 percent control of Hartford in the stock-for-stock exchange. The appellate courts refused to bend the statutory language in the slightest to accommodate this interpretation of a type B reorganization. After defeats in the First and Third Circuit Courts of Appeal, ITT threw in the towel and settled with the Internal Revenue Service on behalf of the Hartford shareholders for $18.5 million.

PRESERVATION OF THE TARGET'S TAX ATTRIBUTES

One important consideration in a corporate acquisition is the extent to which the tax attributes of the target corporation will survive the transaction. Tax attributes are the various features associated with the corporation as a taxpaying entity; common tax attributes include the corporation's earnings and profits account and the numerous accounting methods or conventions used to compute taxable income. Usually the most important tax attributes as far as the acquiring corporation is concerned are the various loss or credit carryforwards of the target corporation. These carryforwards represent future tax benefits, and their preservation may be an important goal in structuring the corporate acquisition.

To demonstrate the current value of a loss carryforward, suppose a target corporation has business assets with an independently appraised value of $6 million and a $1 million net operating loss carryforward. An acquiring corporation that believes it can earn a competitive rate of return by investing in Target's assets will pay $6 million for the assets alone. If the acquiring corporation projects that Target's business will generate $500,000 of taxable income in the two years subsequent to the acquisition, the acquiring corporation has a strong incentive to preserve the loss carryforward to shield this projected income from federal taxation. The potential tax savings at a 34 percent rate is $170,000 per year, and the present value of the savings at a 10 percent discount rate is $295,040. Therefore, the acquiring corporation theoretically should be willing to bid as much as $6,295,040 for the target's business if the loss carryforward is included in the deal!

Survival of Tax Attributes in Certain Acquisitions

If we refer back to Figure 12–1, we can easily analyze the status of a target corporation's tax attributes in each of the four quadrants of our acquisitions decision model. In the two quadrants in which the target's stock is acquired, the preservation of the target's tax attributes is essentially a nonissue. In an entity acquisition, the legal identity of the target corporation is undisturbed and the target's tax attributes clearly survive the transaction.

In a taxable acquisition of assets, it is also easy to reach the correct conclusion that a corporate purchaser cannot buy the tax attributes of another corporation in the same manner in which it can buy tangible or intangible business properties. It is only when we turn to the fourth quadrant, the nontaxable acquisition of assets through a type A or a type C reorganization, that the question of the preservation of the target's tax attributes requires some thought. Remember that these reorganizations are viewed as corporate restructurings involving a continuity of both the shareholders' proprietary interest and the business enterprise of the target. This viewpoint suggests the tax attributes of the target should survive the reorganization, even if the legal identity of the target does not. This is exactly the logic reflected in Section 381. This very useful code section states that in a type A or a type C reorganization the acquiring corporation "shall succeed to and take into account" the tax attributes of the target corporation as of the date of the transfer of assets. Accordingly, when a corporation purchases the business assets of a target corporation in a nontaxable acquisition, the target's earnings and profits, accounting methods, and loss and credit carryforwards all follow the assets and become the tax attributes of the acquiring corporation.

The Section 382 Limitation

The fact that loss carryforwards of a target corporation survive in three out of the four types of corporate acquisitions has worried Congress for decades. The congressional concern has always been that an acquiring corporation might find a target attractive *only* because of the target's substantial loss carryforwards. In such a case, the acquisition might be motivated solely by a desire to minimize income taxes rather than by any legitimate business, legal, or financial reason. As an extreme example of this undesirable situation, assume Mega Inc., a very profitable manufacturing business with several independently operated divisions, decides to purchase a controlling stock interest in Luma Inc. For the past several years, Luma has operated a string of retail clothing stores and has accumulated net operating loss carryforwards in excess of $15 million. Immediately after the stock acquisition, Mega's management closes all the retail stores, sells all the assets used in Luma's historic business, and fires all the Luma employees. Mega then transfers one of its own operating divisions into Luma and proceeds to deduct the loss carryforwards that were generated by the now-defunct retail business against the income generated by the manufacturing division operating within the Luma corporate shell.

In 1943, Congress responded to its concern by enacting the original version of Section 269. This section applies to acquisitions of corporations with loss or credit carryforwards if the *principal purpose* of the acquisition is evasion or avoidance of federal income tax. In such a case, Section 269 gives the Internal Revenue Service the broad authority to simply disallow the loss or credit carryforwards. While Section 269 might seem a very powerful weapon in the congressional crusade against tax-motivated acquisitions, it has its limitations. The section is applied subjectively, requiring a determination of taxpayer motive and intent underlying an acquisition. As a result, when the Internal Revenue Service has chosen to invoke Section 269, the taxpayer response has invariably been to litigate the issue. The success of many taxpayers in convincing the courts that the primary motivation for a corporate acquisition was not tax evasion or avoidance led Congress to conclude that Section 269 has been ineffectual in combating the undesirable traffic in loss corporations.

In 1986, Congress tried a new approach to the problem of tax-motivated acquisitions by revising Section 382. This section establishes an annual limitation on the amount of loss carryforwards deductible against taxable income for any year following a significant change in the ownership of the loss corporation. A technical discussion of the statutory definition of a change in ownership is well beyond the scope of this text. Suffice it to say that all the types of corporate acquisitions discussed in this chapter clearly constitute an ownership change within the meaning of Section 382.

The Section 382 limitation equals the current long-term tax-exempt federal rate (an interest rate published monthly by the Internal Revenue Service) multiplied by the fair market value of the loss corporation's outstanding stock on the date of the ownership change. However, if the historic business of the loss corporation is discontinued during the two-year period following the ownership change, the limitation drops to zero. A simple example can highlight the essentials of this calculation. Suppose Beta Inc. pays $1 million to acquire 100 percent of the stock in Trion Inc. Beta projects that after an infusion of working capital and some much-needed changes in management, Trion's historic business should begin to show a profit of approximately $200,000 a year. On the date of purchase, the long-term tax-exempt rate is 7 percent. Subsequent to the acquisition, the Section 382 limitation on Trion is $70,000—only $70,000 of Trion's net operating loss carryforwards can be deducted annually against Trion's future taxable income. If Trion had a net operating loss carryforward of only $50,000, the limitation is no problem; if Beta's projections are accurate and Trion's annual income is $200,000, the entire carryforward can be deducted in one year. In contrast, if Trion has a loss carryforward of $500,000, only $70,000 of this loss can be deducted against the $200,000 income every year, and it will take eight years for Beta to reap the full tax benefit of the loss carryforward.

The congressional logic behind the Section 382 limitation is quite interesting and can be explained by reference to the above example. Because Trion's stock was worth $1 million, presumably the net value of Trion's business assets is also $1 million. If Trion were to convert these assets into $1 million of long-term Treasury bills, it could absorb its own loss carryforwards against the annual taxable interest income from the bills. If the Treasury bill rate were 9 percent, Trion's annual income would be $90,000, and any loss carryforward could be used at a rate of $90,000 per year. However, when Beta purchases Trion, the usage rate of the carryforward will be based on a *tax-exempt* rate of return, which will always be lower than the market rate of return on taxable investments. Theoretically, the use of the lower interest rate in the calculation of the Section 382 limitation ensures that the value of any loss carryforward to Beta cannot be more than its value to Trion. Therefore, Beta has no tax incentive to acquire Trion only because of the availability of loss carryforwards.

CORPORATE RESTRUCTURINGS

Corporations and their shareholders can engage in a number of transactions that change the structure of the corporate ownership but do not involve the acquisition of another business. This section will explore the tax consequences of these transactions, beginning with corporate divisions.

Corporate Divisions

It is common for a parent corporation to operate different businesses through controlled corporate subsidiaries. If the shareholders of the parent corporation decide they would prefer to own a subsidiary corporation directly, the parent can simply distribute a controlling stock interest in the subsidiary to its shareholders. After this distribution (which in tax jargon is labeled a *spin-off*), the former parent and subsidiary have become brother-sister corporations owned by the same group of shareholders (see Figure 12–4).

A variation of this transaction often occurs when the shareholders of the parent corporation no longer agree on corporate policy and decide to go their separate ways. In this case, a controlling interest in a subsidiary can be distributed to one group of shareholders in exchange for their stock in the parent corporation. After this *split-off,* one group of shareholders directly owns the former subsidiary, and the remaining shareholders are left in sole possession of the parent corporation (see Figure 12–5).

Without a special rule, the spin-off and split-off described above would be taxable transactions to both the parent corporation and the shareholders. In both transactions, the parent corporation would have to recognize a taxable gain to the extent the value of

Figure 12–4 Corporate Spin-off

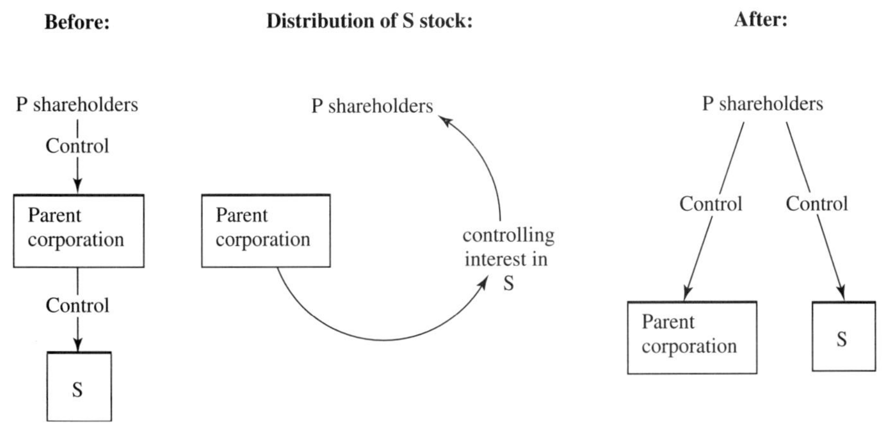

Figure 12–5 Corporate Split-off

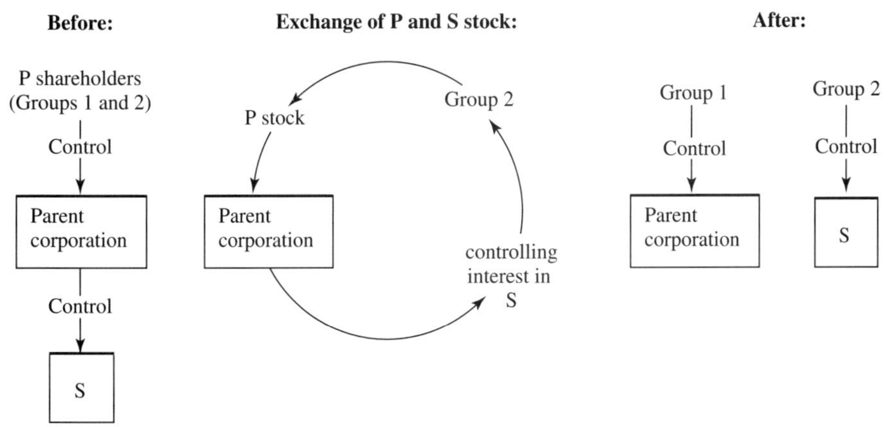

the distributed subsidiary stock exceeded its tax basis. In the case of the spin-off, the recipient shareholders would have to recognize the value of the distributed stock as a dividend from the parent. In the case of the split-off, the exchange would generally be treated as a redemption of the parent corporation's stock; as a result, the participating shareholders would recognize capital gain equal to any excess in value of the subsidiary stock received over their tax basis in the parent stock surrendered.

Because both a spin-off and a split-off are essentially readjustments of corporate ownership rather than transactions in which the shareholders are cashing in their corporate investments, Congress enacted a special provision, Section 355, to make these transactions nontaxable to both the parent corporation and the participating shareholders. Unfortunately, Section 355 is fearsome in its complexity, laden with a number of stringent requirements, all of which must be met before a spin-off or split-off is granted nontaxable status. For example, Section 355 demands that the division of the parent and subsidiary must be motivated by a corporate business purpose; a shareholder business purpose will not suffice. Example 6 in the Treasury regulation interpreting this requirement illustrates the subtle distinction between a corporate and a shareholder business purpose in the following situation: Corporation X owns all the stock in corporation Y, which is distributed pro rata to X's five individual shareholders. The sole purpose of the distribution is to enable the shareholders to elect subchapter S status for corporation Y. (Remember that an S corporation may not have corporate shareholders.) The example concludes that the distribution does not have a *corporate* business purpose, so the distribution of the Y stock is a taxable dividend to the recipients. Because of this type of technical nuance, Section 355 must be approached with extreme caution; its successful application absolutely requires the services of an expert on corporate divisions.

Other Reorganizations

In addition to the type A, B, and C acquisitive reorganizations discussed earlier in the chapter, Section 368 defines four other reorganizations, all of which involve nontaxable exchanges between corporations and their owners. A type D reorganization occurs when one corporation transfers a portion of its assets into a newly created subsidiary immediately before a spin-off or split-off of the subsidiary under Section 355. A type E reorganization involves the *recapitalization* of a single corporation. As an example of a recapitalization, suppose the owners of a corporation exchange their original shares of voting common stock for a mixture of newly issued voting common, nonvoting common, and nonvoting preferred stock. Because this change in the capital structure of the corporation qualifies as a reorganization, the exchange is nontaxable. A type F reorganization involves a mere change in the identity, form, or state of incorporation. If the shareholders in Green Inc. of Ohio want to reincorporate their business in Illinois, the exchange of stock necessary to accomplish the change in the state of incorporation is nontaxable. Finally, a type G reorganization occurs when the shareholders and creditors of a bankrupt corporation exchange their interests for stock in a successor corporation under a plan approved by a bankruptcy court.

CORPORATE LIQUIDATIONS

The final event in the life of a corporation is its complete liquidation. Transactionally, a liquidation is quite straightforward. After all existing corporate liabilities are discharged, any remaining cash and property are distributed to the shareholders according to the liquidation rights of their various preferred and common stock interests. This sequence of events is just the reverse of an incorporation, in which shareholders transfer cash and property to a newly created corporate entity. As we discussed in Chapter 8, the formation of a corporation is nontaxable to both the shareholders and the corporation itself. Thus, it would be logical for shareholders to expect consistent nontaxable treatment when the corporation is liquidated. Unhappily, this expectation is wrong. While a corporation can be created at no tax cost, liquidating that corporation can result in a significant tax liability, both to the corporation and to the shareholders. A cynic might conclude a corporation is very much like a marriage—cheap to get into and expensive to get out of.

To focus on the tax consequences of a liquidation, let's use Gamma Inc., a calendar year corporate taxpayer owned by sole shareholder Martin Dobbs. Martin decided to shut down the corporate business as of December 31, 1997. After all the corporate debts were paid, Gamma had $50,000 cash and two assets, business equipment worth $80,000 with a corporate tax basis of $15,000 and inventory worth $25,000 with a basis of $30,000. On January 10, 1998, legal title to the assets was transferred to Martin and the corporation was dissolved under state law. Section 336 requires that a liquidating corporation recognize gain or loss on the distribution of property to its shareholders as if the property were sold for its fair market value. Thus, Gamma must recognize a $65,000 gain on the distribution of the equipment and a $5,000 loss on the distribution of the inventory. Although Gamma had no operating income for 1998, it did have $60,000 of taxable income and a $10,000 income tax liability.

Martin Dobbs received $50,000 cash and property worth $105,000 as a liquidating distribution from Gamma Inc. He also assumed legal responsibility for paying the corporation's $10,000 final tax bill. Martin must treat the $145,000 *net* distribution as an amount realized from the sale of his stock. If his tax basis in his shares is $20,000, he must recognize and pay tax on a $125,000 capital gain. His tax basis in the equipment and inventory will be the assets' fair market value. If Gamma Inc. had any loss or credit carryforwards from prior years, Martin will not be entitled to use them. A liquidating corporation's tax attributes die with the corporation.

Liquidation of a Controlled Subsidiary

The single exception to the rule that a corporate liquidation is a completely taxable event applies when a parent corporation liquidates a subsidiary in which it owns an 80 percent or more interest. In this situation, the parent and controlled subsidiary can legitimately be regarded as a single economic unit under the control of the parent's shareholders. As a result, Congress is willing to view the liquidation as a change in form rather than of substance. The law provides that neither the subsidiary nor the parent will recognize any gain or loss on the distribution of the subsidiary's assets to the parent. Both the tax basis of the assets to the subsidiary and all the subsidiary's tax attributes will carry over to the parent corporation.

Refer back to our example involving the liquidation of Gamma Inc. If another corporation owned 100 percent of Gamma Inc.'s stock, Gamma would not recognize any gain or loss on the distribution of its assets to its controlling parent. The parent corporation's receipt of $155,000 worth of cash and assets from its liquidated subsidiary would also be a nontaxable event, and the parent's tax basis in its Gamma stock would disappear. The parent's tax basis in the Gamma equipment would be $15,000, and the basis of the inventory would be $30,000. Finally, the parent corporation would inherit all Gamma's corporate tax attributes.

PROBLEMS AND CASES

1. John Stewart owns 100 percent of the outstanding stock in Stewart Inc. Martel Industries Inc. has several very good business reasons for acquiring Stewart Inc. and has offered to pay $2 million cash for John's stock. Alternatively, Martel is

willing to exchange 35,000 shares of its voting preferred stock with a current market value of $1.6 million for John's stock.

a. Will the stock-for-stock exchange described in the facts above qualify as a corporate reorganization?
b. Assume the exchange does qualify as a reorganization. If John as a basis of $500,000 in his Stewart stock, which offer (cash or stock) would result in the greater after-tax value of the consideration John will receive? Would your answer change if John's basis were $1.2 million rather than $500,000?
c. Assume John's basis in his Stewart stock is $500,000. What additional factors should John consider before deciding which offer to accept?

2. Beta Inc. wants to acquire the business operated by Thompson Inc., an unrelated corporation with the balance sheet shown below.

a. Assume Beta Inc. and Thompson Inc. agree to a lump-sum purchase price for the entire business (all Thompson's assets) of $3,650,000 cash and Beta's assumption of Thompson's $200,000 business debt. Subsequent to the sale, Thompson's sole shareholder, Carla Thompson, does not plan to liquidate the corporation. Describe the tax consequences of this transaction to both corporations.
b. Assume Beta Inc. and Thompson Inc. agree to a lump-sum purchase price for the entire business (all Thompson's assets) of $2,400,000 cash, 40,000 shares of Beta Inc. common stock worth $1,250,000, and Beta's assumption of Thompson's $200,000 business debt. How does this change in facts affect the tax consequences of the transaction to both corporations?

	Adjusted Tax Basis	*Fair Market Value*
Accounts receivable	$ 55,000	$ 60,000
Inventory	425,000	640,000
Plant and equipment	1,000,000	500,000
Accumulated depreciation	(730,000)	—
Investment land	400,000	2,000,000
	$1,150,000	$3,200,000
Business debt	$ 200,000	$ 200,000
Owners' equity	950,000	3,000,000
	$1,150,000	$3,200,000

c. Assume Beta Inc. and Thompson Inc. agree to a lump-sum purchase price for the entire business (all Thompson's assets) of $2,500,000 cash and Beta's assumption of Thompson's $200,000 business debt. How does this change in facts affect the tax consequences of the transaction to both corporations?

3. Refer to the facts in problem 2. Assume Beta Inc. negotiates with Carla Thompson to purchase 100 percent of Thompson Inc.'s outstanding stock for $3,650,000 cash. Carla's basis in this stock is $1,400,000.

a. What are the tax consequences of this acquisition to Beta Inc., Thompson Inc., and Carla Thompson if Beta does not make a timely Section 338 election with regards to the acquisition?
b. What are the tax consequences of this acquisition to Beta Inc., Thompson Inc., and Carla Thompson if Beta does make a timely Section 338 election with regards to the acquisition?
c. What factors not mentioned in the problem might prompt Beta Inc. to make the Section 338 election?

4. In the current year, Rowen Inc. purchased 12 percent of the publicly traded stock of Alt Inc. for $8 million. Alt's board of directors were concerned that this purchase marked the beginning of a hostile takeover attempt and immediately offered to redeem Rowen's stock for $10 million. If Rowen Inc. accepts this greenmail payment, what will be the tax liability on the corporation's taxable gain if Rowen is in a 35 percent marginal tax bracket?
5. In the current year, Bender Inc. purchased Nalco Industries Inc. in a leveraged buy-out. As a result of the acquisition, Nalco increased its outstanding debt by $50 million; the annual interest payable on this new debt will be $6.5 million. In the first year subsequent to the LBO, Nalco generated a net operating loss of $9 million. If Nalco's taxable income for each of the three preceding years was $7 million, what amount of income tax refund can the corporation expect to receive because of any carryback of the current year loss?
6. Lincoln Inc. and Washington Inc. are planning to consolidate into a new corporation, WashLin Inc., under the laws of the state of Michigan. According to the plan of consolidation approved by the shareholders of both corporations, the shareholders will receive total consideration consisting of $500,000 cash, $1 million of short-term notes, and $5 million worth of newly issued common stock in WashLin in exchange for their Lincoln or Washington stock. Discuss to what extent the participating shareholders must recognize any gain or loss realized on their exchanges.
7. During the current year, Alolo Inc. was merged into Byron Inc. under Hawaiian law. Byron Inc. had an excellent business reason for the merger and intends to continue to operate Alolo's historic business. As of the date of the merger, Alolo's assets had a fair market value of $750,000 and a basis of $510,000. Pursuant to the merger agreement, Mrs. Abby Ling, the sole shareholder in Alolo, received $500,000 of consideration in exchange for her Alolo shares. Her basis in the shares was $179,000.

   a. What are the tax consequences of the merger to Byron Inc., Alolo Inc., and Mrs. Ling if the consideration paid to Mrs. Ling consisted of $350,000 cash and Byron short-term notes with $150,000?
   b. What are the tax consequences of the merger to Byron Inc., Alolo Inc., and Mrs. Ling if the consideration paid to Mrs. Ling consisted of $350,000 worth of Byron nonvoting preferred stock and Byron short-term notes worth $150,000?
8. During the current year, Max Conway surrendered his 500 shares of Bentley stock (basis $25,000) upon Bentley's merger into Tellco Inc. The merger was a

type A reorganization for federal tax purposes. What are the tax consequences to Max in each of the following independent situations and what basis will Max have in the assets received?

a. Max received 200 shares of Tellco common stock worth $60,000 in exchange for his Bentley stock.
b. Max received 150 shares of Tellco common stock worth $45,000 and $15,000 cash in exchange for his Bentley stock.
c. Max received 150 shares of Tellco common stock worth $45,000 and marketable securities in an unrelated publicly traded corporation worth $15,000 in exchange for his Bentley stock.

9. In the current year, Jumbo Inc. acquired 100 percent of the outstanding stock of Little Inc. in exchange for $7.5 million worth of Jumbo voting common stock and $2.5 million cash. After the acquisition, Little Inc. continued to operate as a controlled subsidiary of Jumbo Inc.

   a. Was the stock-for-stock exchange a nontaxable event to the participating Little shareholders?
   b. Would your answer change if the consideration had been $9.9 million worth of Jumbo voting common stock and only $100,000 cash?

10. White Inc. would like to acquire ownership of the business operated by Black Inc. The officers of White fear that Black Inc. may have major undisclosed and contingent liabilities. The owners of Black Inc. have stipulated they are willing to sell their corporation only if the transaction will be nontaxable. Discuss which type of reorganization seems to be required in this situation.

11. Acmex Inc. wants to acquire an exclusive beer distributorship held by Moore Inc. The contract between Moore and the brewery provides that the distributorship is nontransferable. Acmex Inc. made a tender offer of four shares of its voting common stock for each share of Moore stock outstanding. Generally, this was considered to be a very favorable exchange. However, two minority Moore shareholders disagreed; neither Mr. Chang (who owns 12 percent of Moore) nor Ms. Lenz (who owns 10 percent) was interested in receiving Acmex stock in exchange for their Moore stock. The president of Acmex is willing to buy Ms. Lenz's stock for cash and then exchange it for Acmex stock. Accordingly, Acmex would acquire 88 percent of the outstanding Moore stock in the proposed exchange transaction.

    a. What type of reorganization is Acmex trying to arrange? Why can't Acmex structure the reorganization as a simple statutory merger between Acmex and Moore? Explain briefly.
    b. Will the proposed transaction qualify as a reorganization? Explain briefly.

12. Waylon Inc. owns 100 percent of the stock of three operating subsidiaries. During the current year, Waylon made a pro rata distribution of all its stock in one subsidiary to its 15 individual shareholders. The total value of the stock at date of distribution was $900,000; Waylon's basis in the stock was only

$440,000. At the date of distribution, Waylon had earnings and profits in excess of $4 million.

a. If the distribution qualifies as a Section 355 spin-off, what are the tax consequences to Waylon Inc. and the recipient shareholders?
b. If the distribution fails to qualify as a Section 355 spin-off, what are the tax consequences to Waylon Inc. and the recipient shareholders?

13. Kim and Dan Rosemund each inherited 50 percent of the stock in Thorn Corporation when their parents were killed in an airplane crash. Although this sister-brother duo tried to get along for three years after their parents' death, it became increasingly obvious to everyone that their strong disagreements over company policy would soon ruin what had been a financially successful enterprise. Although the value of the stock in Thorn Corporation was estimated to be $1 million on the date Mr. and Mrs. Thorn died, it is worth no more than $650,000 today. Based on recent appraisals, the total value of the corporate assets is within $50,000 of their aggregate tax basis. Kim and Dan have decided to split the old family corporation into two new corporations—one owned by each of them. Would you recommend that they structure this corporate split-up as a type D reorganization or as a taxable liquidation of Thorn Corporation? Explain briefly.

14. During the current year, Zeron Inc. was merged into Parton Inc. in a merger pursuant to Ohio law. This merger did not represent an ownership change within the meaning of Section 382. At the date of the merger, Zeron Inc. had a net operating loss carryforward of $200,000. For the first taxable year subsequent to the merger, Parton Inc. had $300,000 of taxable income before any net operating loss deduction.

    a. Compute Parton Inc.'s taxable income for its first taxable year subsequent to the merger if the merger was a taxable acquisition.
    b. Compute Parton Inc.'s taxable income for its first taxable year subsequent to the merger if the merger was a type A reorganization.

15. In 1997, 90 percent of the outstanding stock in Brio Inc. was acquired in a transaction that triggered application of Section 382. The acquisition price of the stock was $1,800,000. On the date of acquisition, Brio had a net operating loss carryforward of $1,250,000 and the long-term tax-exempt federal interest rate was 6.5 percent.

    a. Determine Brio's taxable income for 1998 if its operating income for the year is $680,000.
    b. How would your answer to *a* change if the new owners of Brio sold all the existing corporate assets in 1998 and began a new business enterprise in Brio?

16. Smithville Inc. is an S corporation with a single class of voting stock outstanding. The current Smithville shareholders, all members of the Smith family, want to bring several grandchildren into the ownership group. However, the current shareholders don't want to give these immature youngsters any

control over the management of the corporate business. The shareholders decide to surrender their old voting stock (aggregate basis $175,000 in exchange for two new issues of Smithville voting and nonvoting common stock. The nonvoting stock will be transferred as gifts to the various grandchildren. If the value of the corporation on the date of the exchange is $1 million, what are the tax consequences of the exchange to the Smithville shareholders?

17. The shareholders of Duco Chemicals and Pesticides, Inc. are convinced that the name of their corporation is generating considerable public animosity toward the corporation's products. They want to reincorporate the business into Environment Unlimited, Inc. Will the shareholders be required to recognize a taxable gain or loss on their exchange of their Duco stock for the newly issued stock in Environment Unlimited? Briefly explain.

18. Walt Thomas, the sole shareholder in Thomas Enterprises Inc., has decided to liquidate his corporation on March 31 of the current year. The balance sheet of the calendar year corporation as of that date is as follows:

	Adjusted Tax Basis	*Fair Market Value*
Cash	$ 30,000	$ 30,000
Inventory	70,000	78,000
Furniture and fixtures	250,000	50,000
Accumulated depreciation	(230,000)	—
Marketable securities	40,000	49,000
	$160,000	$207,000
Owners' equity	160,000	207,000
	$160,000	$207,000

For the period from January 1 through March 31, Thomas Enterprises Inc. generated an $18,000 operating loss.

a. Based on the above facts, compute Thomas Enterprises Inc.'s income tax liability for its final taxable year ending March 31.
b. What are the tax consequences of the liquidation to Walt Thomas if he has a $50,000 tax basis in his Thomas Enterprises Inc. stock?
c. What tax basis will Walt Thomas have in the various corporate assets he received in the liquidation?

19. Refer to the facts in problem 18. How would your answers change if the sole shareholder in Thomas Enterprises Inc. were Centex Operations Inc. rather than Walt Thomas?

20. Weedon Inc. has only two shareholders: David Inc., which owns 88 percent of Weedon's outstanding stock, and Bright Inc., which owns the remaining 12 percent. The shareholders have agreed to liquidate their corporation. As of the date of liquidation, Weedon owns $780,000 cash and investment land worth $240,000 with a basis of $100,000. Weedon also has a capital loss carryforward of $165,000.

a. David Inc. has a basis of $600,000 in its Weedon stock. What are the tax consequences to David Inc. and Weedon Inc. if Weedon distributes $686,400 cash and an 88 percent undivided interest in the land as a liquidating distribution to David Inc.?

b. Bright Inc. has a basis of $130,000 in its Weedon stock. What are the tax consequences to Bright Inc. and Weedon Inc. if Weedon distributes $93,000 cash and a 12 percent undivided interest in the land as a liquidating distribution to Bright Inc.?

Case 12–1

On January 1, 1992, Mr. and Mrs. George incorporated George Foods Inc. to operate a grocery business. The Georges invested their life savings of $200,000 in the corporation; the money was used to purchase a building and provide initial working capital for the corporation. Unfortunately, by late 1997 the Georges realized that because of their lack of business acumen and experience, their grocery was a failure.

Because of the construction of a nearby shopping mall, the real property owned by the corporation has increased considerably in value. As a result, Megafoods Inc. has approached the Georges to negotiate a purchase of the property. Megafoods has formulated two different acquisition strategies: buy the property for $400,000 cash or exchange its own stock worth $375,000 for 100 percent of the George Foods Inc. stock. To analyze the financial consequences of the two strategies, Megafoods has determined the following:

1. If Megafoods purchases the property, it will allocate $320,000 of the purchase price to the building and $80,000 of the purchase price to the land.
2. If Megafoods purchases the corporation, the annual depreciation deduction on the building will continue to be $3,800 a year for the next 25.5 years. (The recovery period for commercial buildings placed in service in 1992 was 31.5 years.)
3. As of the proposed transaction date, George Foods Inc. has a net operating loss carryforward of $75,000. The long-term tax-exempt federal interest rate on the proposed date will be 7 percent.
4. Megafoods anticipates it can revive the grocery business operated by George Foods Inc. and generate substantial operating revenues almost immediately. Before consideration of any depreciation or net operating loss carryforward deductions, the marginal tax rate on this income is expected to be 34 percent.

Based on the above set of facts, which strategy would Megafoods prefer? Assume a 10 percent discount rate in making the necessary calculations to support your conclusion.

CHAPTER 13

Jurisdictional Issues in International and Interstate Taxation

The United States has a global system of taxation under which every U.S. citizen and domestic corporation is taxed on *worldwide* income. Conversely, individuals who are citizens of other countries and foreign corporations may be subject to our federal tax system to the extent they earn income attributable to U.S. sources. In this chapter, we will consider both the opportunities and problems arising under a global system of taxation as we expand our discussion to include international business transactions.

For the first time in this text, we must consider the fact that other nations have their own unique systems of taxation under which they may claim jurisdiction to tax not only the worldwide income earned by their citizens but also any income earned within their national borders by noncitizens. Foreign income tax systems may differ dramatically from our own federal system, not only in terms of rate structure but also in their definition of taxable income. In addition, the reader should understand that many industrialized nations are less dependent on income taxes than the United States. For example, the *value-added tax* (VAT), a sales tax levied at each stage of the manufacture and sale of goods, is a major source of governmental revenue in European countries.

At this stage in our country's economic history, multinational business operations are rapidly becoming the rule rather than the exception. Increasing globalization is creating exciting opportunities for U.S. businesses to expand into the emerging markets of Eastern Europe, Africa, Asia, and South America. These opportunities are coupled with a new set of formidable obstacles; business managers with international aspirations must learn to cope with differences in currencies, language, technological sophistication, and cultural and political traditions. Managers should also be aware of the fiscal complications that inevitably occur when a single stream of business income is subject to the taxing authority of two or more countries. The most obvious complication is the potential burden of double taxation; the cumulative effect of a series of modest income taxes imposed by several jurisdictions on the same income base could be overwhelming.

Tax Treaties

National governments generally operate on the assumption that it is in their self-interest to promote the growth and development of international business operations. These governments understand that if they fail to accommodate their tax systems to the needs of the international business community, their economies will be at a serious competitive disadvantage in the global marketplace. Consequently, the nations of the world have created a network of bilateral and multilateral *tax treaties* designed to minimize the frictions between their respective tax systems and to reduce the impact of the double taxation of international business income. The United States currently has tax treaties with more than 40 countries, ranging from the tiny economies of Iceland and Malta to such industrialized giants as Japan and Germany.

While tax treaties certainly facilitate and encourage international business, they also add an extra dimension to international tax planning. A U.S. company trying to determine the tax consequences of conducting business in a particular foreign locale must consider the general provisions of the Internal Revenue Code dealing with international transactions, the applicable tax laws of the foreign country, and the unique terms of any existing tax treaty between the United States and that country. Little wonder that tax advisers with an expertise in the international area are in enormous demand!

Implications of U.S. International Tax Policy

As the 20th century draws toward its close, the United States no longer enjoys its post-World War II domination of the world economy. U.S. multinational corporations are currently locked in a struggle with determined competitors from Europe and the Pacific Rim. If U.S. businesses hope to continue as serious contenders, our federal government cannot ignore the global implications of its tax policies and must be willing to discard any traditional attitudes that undermine our international competitiveness.

Tax policies designed to encourage U.S. investment in developing nations not only create new markets for American goods and services but also indirectly promote economic and political stability in the Third World. Should tax policy also encourage U.S. investment in the developed nations of Europe and Asia? Political economists who argue against foreign investment by U.S. businesses usually emphasize the short-term flow of capital out of the United States, as well as the loss of American jobs to foreign labor markets. Proponents of foreign investment cite the long-term return of profits back to U.S. investors, as well as empirical data suggesting that overseas investment expands, rather than shrinks, the market for U.S. exports.

Legislators must also grapple with the issue of whether our tax system should provide incentives or disincentives for foreign investment in the United States. Currently, the aggregate amount of such investment is well over $1 *trillion.* The sheer size of the U.S. market, its skilled work force, and the stability of our political and financial systems will undoubtedly continue to attract investors from other countries. Policy makers who believe that inflows of foreign capital stimulate local economies and create employment for American workers are in favor of tax incentives designed to entice such investment to our shores. Those voices raised in opposition to such incentives denounce the "selling of America" and equate foreign investment with a surrender of control and ownership of our natural resources and productive capacities.

This brief synopsis of international tax policy can only suggest the complexities of the issues involved. Nonetheless, one point should be clear. The United States must confront these issues with the understanding that in the global village of the 21st century an isolationist attitude is no longer a realistic option.

In the remainder of this chapter, we will examine some of the more important tax rules affecting U.S. individuals who receive income from foreign sources and U.S. corporations doing business abroad. We will also consider the tax consequences to foreign investors who conduct business in this country. The final section of the chapter will compare the jurisdictional issues inherent in the international tax area with similar issues arising in the context of multistate taxation within the United States.

U.S. TAXPAYERS WITH FOREIGN SOURCE INCOME

U.S. citizens, resident aliens, and domestic corporations (corporations organized under the laws of one of the 50 states or the District of Columbia) are subject to U.S. tax on their worldwide incomes. A resident alien is a citizen of another country who has established permanent residency in the United States; resident aliens file the same tax forms and are taxed in exactly the same manner as U.S. citizens. (The special rules applying to nonresident aliens are discussed later in the chapter.) Individuals and corporations earning income from foreign sources face certain unique tax problems for which Congress has devised interesting solutions. The first of these problems we will explore concerns individual taxpayers who live and work in a foreign country.

The Foreign Earned Income Exclusion

U.S. citizens who live and work abroad, referred to as *expatriates* for tax purposes, often must contend with a much higher cost of living than their counterparts who reside in the United States. Generally, differentials in the cost of living between individual taxpayers are of no concern to the Treasury; as we learned in Chapter 3, personal living expenses are nondeductible. If a person decides to accept employment in New York City rather than Tulsa, Oklahoma, it is up to her to negotiate with her employer for additional compensation to offset the higher cost of living. In the international arena, companies that need to station personnel in countries with excessively high costs of living must either pay a premium to attract a U.S. employee or hire a local (foreign) employee to fill the position. In the latter case, the salary paid by the U.S. business to the foreign employee may escape U.S. taxation.

To help multinational businesses compete in the U.S. labor market and to encourage them to employ U.S. citizens in their foreign operations, Section 911 provides a *foreign earned income exclusion* for expatriates who have established tax homes in other countries. This exclusion applies to self-employment income of compensation earned in a foreign country and is limited to $70,000 per year. Expatriates may also exclude any *housing cost amount,* defined as actual housing expenses in excess of a statutory base amount. (For 1996, the statutory base is $9,426.) If the expatriate resides overseas for only a portion of a year, these exclusions must be prorated on a daily basis. The Section 911 exclusions are not available to U.S. government employees, such as embassy officials or military personnel. However, special rules allow the expatriates to reduce their tax burdens on foreign earned income by other means.

To illustrate the effect of the Section 911 exclusions, assume Marie Yamaguro, a U.S. citizen and executive of a multinational corporation, has lived and worked in Japan for the past eight years. Marie's annual compensation consists of a $140,000 salary plus a $12,000 housing allowance. Marie's monthly rent on her apartment in Osaka is $1,500 per month. If Marie qualifies as an expatriate for all of 1996, she can exclude $78,574 of her compensation from 1996 gross income. This exclusion equals $70,000 plus $8,574 ($18,000 actual housing cost in excess of $9,426). If Marie decides to return to her native California and leaves Japan at the end of August, her current year exclusion is reduced to $52,383 (244 days/366 days multiplied by $78,574).

The Foreign Tax Credit

While the foreign earned income exclusion is very useful to U.S. citizens who live and work abroad, it does nothing to solve the double taxation problem for thousands of U.S. taxpayers who receive income subject to foreign taxation yet never set foot outside this country. As we learned in Chapter 3, our federal law allows a deduction for foreign income taxes paid or accrued during the year. Unfortunately, a deduction for foreign income taxes is, at best, an imperfect remedy. Consider a case in which a taxpayer in a 36 percent marginal tax bracket earns $10,000 of gross income out of which a foreign jurisdiction has already collected $2,500 of tax computed at a 25 percent marginal rate. If this tax is claimed as a deduction, the $7,500 of net income generates a U.S. tax liability of $2,700. Accordingly, our taxpayer pockets only $4,800 of the original $10,000, and is paying an effective rate of tax of 52 percent.

Section 901 provides a more effective mechanism to mitigate the double taxation of income in the form of *foreign tax credit.* This credit is available to U.S. citizens, resident aliens, and domestic corporations and is based on any income taxes paid or accrued during the year to any foreign country. Taxpayers incurring such taxes may either deduct them in the computation of taxable income or credit them against their U.S. income tax liability for the year. Note that the credit is only for income taxes—foreign excise taxes, value-added taxes, sales taxes, property taxes, and transfer taxes are not creditable. The law also prohibits any credit for foreign income taxes paid on earned income excluded from gross income under Section 911.

If we refer back to our earlier example, the economic impact of the foreign tax credit should be immediately apparent. If our taxpayer elects to claim a credit rather than a deduction for the $2,500 foreign tax paid on $10,000 of gross income, he will recognize the entire $10,000 as taxable income on which his precredit U.S. tax liability is $3,600. However, this liability is reduced by the entire $2,500 paid to the foreign jurisdiction, so his final U.S. tax liability is only $1,100 and his effective worldwide tax rate on the $10,000 of income is just 36 percent.

The foreign tax credit is subject to a very important limitation. The amount of the current year credit cannot exceed a specific percentage of the total U.S. precredit tax for the year. This percentage is calculated by dividing the taxpayer's *foreign source income* for the year by total taxable income. To illustrate, suppose the $10,000 of gross income in our example qualifies as foreign source income and represents 10 percent of our taxpayer's total taxable income of $100,000. Let's also assume the total precredit U.S. tax on this income is $36,000. The foreign tax credit under this set of facts is limited to $3,600 (10 percent of the total precredit tax). Because the $2,500 foreign tax actually paid is less than the limit, the full amount is creditable. But now let's modify the example by increasing the foreign tax rate to 40 percent rate (rather than 25 percent) so the foreign tax liability is $4,000. In this case, only $3,600 of the foreign tax may be claimed as a current year credit. While this credit reduces the U.S. tax attributable to the foreign source income to zero, the $400 of excess foreign tax paid has no effect on the U.S. tax burden imposed on U.S. source income.

This limitation on the foreign tax credit results in a total tax burden on foreign source income computed at the highest rate of any jurisdiction in which the income is subject to tax. In our initial example (in which the foreign tax rate was only 25 percent), the $3,600 total tax burden on the $10,000 of foreign source income ($2,500 of foreign tax and $1,100 of U.S. tax) reflected the 36 percent U.S. rate. In our modified example (in which the foreign tax rate was increased to 40 percent), the $4,000 tax burden ($4,000 of foreign tax and zero U.S. tax) reflected the foreign rate. Remember that for alternative minimum tax purposes, the foreign tax credit can offset only 90 percent of a taxpayer's alternative minimum tax. In such case, the effective tax rate on foreign source income will exceed the statutory rate of either jurisdiction.

In a year in which the foreign tax credit limitation prevents a taxpayer from crediting the entire amount of foreign taxes paid, the excess foreign tax payment can be carried back two years and forward five for inclusion in the foreign tax credit computation for those years. To complete the earlier example in which our taxpayer could claim only $3,600 of his $4,000 foreign tax liability as a current year credit, assume that in the next year the taxpayer pays only $2,700 of foreign income tax and reports $90,000 of total taxable income of which $18,000 (20 percent) is foreign source income. His total precredit U.S. income tax liability is $32,400, and his foreign tax credit limitation is $6,480 (20 percent of $32,400). Consequently, our taxpayer can claim both his $2,700 current-year foreign tax payment and his $400 excess payment from the previous year as a foreign tax credit against his $32,400 U.S. liability.

Income Sourcing Rules

Because the foreign tax credit limitation is based on the amount of foreign source income included in total taxable income, the determination of whether a particular income item is attributable to a source within or without the United States is critical. As you might expect, the Internal Revenue Code contains an elaborate and lengthy set of *sourcing rules.* For our purposes, a quick look at some of the more widely applicable of these rules will suffice.

The source of compensation for services rendered is based on the geographic location where the services are physically performed. For example, the salary of a U.S. citizen who resides and works in Germany for a U.S. corporation is foreign source income, while the salary of the U.S. citizen who resides and works in San Diego for a Mexican corporation is U.S. source income. The source of income derived from the manufacture of goods is based on the location of the manufacturing facility. In contrast, the source of income derived from the sale of purchased inventory (wholesaling and retailing) depends on the jurisdiction in which title to the inventory passes from seller to buyer. If a business manufactures goods in the United States and sells them abroad, the net income from the entire operation is usually considered half U.S. source and half foreign source income. The source of interest income is determined by the residence of the debtor, while the source of dividend income is determined by the country of incorporation of the payor. Finally, the source of rental income is based on the physical location of the rental property.

U.S. CORPORATIONS DOING BUSINESS ABROAD

The increasing importance of international operations to domestic corporations cannot be overemphasized. The accounting firm of Price Waterhouse estimates that foreign affiliates currently account for 30 percent of worldwide sales and 43 percent of reported worldwide profits of U.S. multinational corporations. When a domestic corporation decides to expand its operations into a foreign jurisdiction, it must consider any number of legal, accounting, and financial implications, not the least of which are the tax consequences of the expansion.

A U.S. corporation with multinational aspirations must decide on the legal form in which to operate its foreign affiliates. One option is for the corporation to simply open a branch office in a foreign or *host* country. This *branch operation* is not a legal entity in its own right, but is merely an extension of the domestic corporation. Any income or loss generated by the foreign branch operation is commingled with the income and losses of all other corporate business operations. To the extent foreign branch income is included in corporate taxable income, it will be subject to the U.S. income tax. To the extent this branch income is also subject to income taxes imposed by the host country, the corporation will be entitled to a credit for the foreign taxes paid.

A second option is for a U.S. corporation to create a controlled corporate subsidiary to house the foreign business operation. Because of the corporate parent's limited liability as a shareholder, this option effectively isolates any risk inherent in the foreign operation. A second advantage is that a controlled subsidiary can have an independent management structure specifically tailored to any special needs of the foreign operation.

If the controlled subsidiary is organized as a U.S. corporation, it can file a consolidated U.S. corporate income tax return with its parent, so the income and losses from the foreign operation are commingled with those of the parent and other domestic subsidiaries. The consolidated group can claim a foreign tax credit (computed on a consolidated basis) for income taxes paid by its domestic subsidiaries to foreign jurisdictions. Alternatively, the controlled subsidiary can be incorporated under the laws of the foreign country; in this case, the subsidiary will be a foreign, rather than a domestic, corporation even though it is wholly owned by a U.S. parent. Multinational corporations frequently have cogent political and legal reasons for using foreign subsidiaries, such as the public image of the corporate business or local prohibitions against foreign ownership of real property located within the host country.

Income Deferral through the Use of a Foreign Subsidiary

When a U.S. corporation conducts a foreign business operation through a foreign subsidiary, rather than as a branch operation or through a domestic subsidiary, the foreign subsidiary's income or losses cannot be commingled with those of its parent. (You may recall from Chapter 5 that only domestic corporations may file consolidated tax returns.) Operating losses incurred by a foreign subsidiary cannot offset the current income of the domestic parent corporation. Depending on the tax laws of the host country in which the subsidiary is incorporated, it is possible that the loss may be carried back or forward as a net operating loss deduction.

Income from the overseas operations of a foreign subsidiary is subject to any income tax imposed by its home country, but generally escapes U.S. taxation as long as the income is not *repatriated* (i.e., returned to this country in the form of dividend distributions to the U.S. parent). The deferral of U.S. taxation can be an incentive for U.S. multinational corporations to avoid repatriation of the earnings of foreign subsidiaries by reinvesting those earnings in the subsidiaries' business operations or in other foreign investments. If a U.S. parent has no pressing need for cash distributions from its foreign subsidiaries, U.S. taxation of the subsidiaries' income can be postponed indefinitely.

When a foreign subsidiary does pay dividends to its U.S. parent, the problem of double taxation again takes center stage. Remember that such dividends already represent after-tax income to the extent the foreign subsidiary paid a corporate income tax to its home country in the year the income was earned. The dividend distribution itself represents gross income to the recipient shareholder, and the home country typically levies a second income tax on this dividend at the shareholder level. Most jurisdictions try to guarantee the payment of this tax by requiring the distributing corporation to withhold the tax from any dividend paid to a foreign shareholder (the U.S. parent in this discussion).

Let's use a simple numerical example to illustrate this complicated situation. In the first four years of its operations, a foreign subsidiary of a U.S. corporation earned a total of \$500,000 of taxable income and paid \$110,000 of foreign income tax, computed at a 22 percent rate. No dividends were paid during the first three years, so no U.S. tax was imposed on the subsidiary's income. At the end of the fourth year, the subsidiary declared a \$130,000 dividend (one third of its \$390,000 after-tax income) to its sole shareholder, the U.S. parent corporation. The subsidiary's home country imposed a 10 percent tax on the U.S. parent with respect to this dividend and required the subsidiary to withhold the tax and remit it to the home country. As a result, the U.S. parent received a net cash distribution of only \$117,000.

Total income earned by the foreign subsidiary	\$500,000
Foreign income tax paid by the subsidiary (22%)	(110,000)
After-tax income	\$390,000
One third of the after-tax income paid as dividend to U.S. parent	\$130,000
Foreign tax imposed on the parent and withheld by the subsidiary (10%)	(13,000)
Net cash received by the U.S. parent	\$117,000

How does the United States tax this dividend when it is received by the parent corporation? Because no dividends received deduction is available for dividends paid from foreign corporations out of their foreign source income, the entire $130,000 dividend is included in the parent's taxable income. The parent is entitled to a $13,000 foreign tax credit for the tax it paid with respect to the dividend. However, another $36,667 of foreign taxes (one third of $110,000) has been paid *by the subsidiary* with respect to the business earnings represented by the dividend. In acknowledgment of this fact, Section 902 provides a *deemed paid foreign tax credit* to any domestic corporation owning at least 10 percent of the voting stock of a foreign corporation from which it receives dividends during the taxable year.

To compute its deemed paid credit, a qualifying corporate shareholder must *gross up* the amount of the foreign dividend received by any foreign income taxes paid with respect to the dividend. In our example, the U.S. parent grosses up the $130,000 foreign dividend by $36,667 and includes $166,667 in its current year income.

Dividend received by the U.S. parent	$130,000
Gross up by foreign income tax paid by the subsidiary with respect to dividend	36,667
Dividend included in parent's gross income	$166,667
	35%
Precredit U.S. tax on dividend	$ 58,333
Foreign tax credit:	
Tax paid by the parent on dividend	(13,000)
Section 902 deemed paid credit	(36,667)
U.S. tax liability	$ 8,666

The precredit tax on the dividend at a 35 percent rate is $58,333. The parent may claim a credit for the $13,000 tax withheld from the dividend and a deemed paid credit of $36,667, thereby reducing the actual U.S. tax liability on the repatriated business income to only $8,666. In this example, the effective foreign tax rate imposed on the business income is less than the 35 percent U.S. rate. If the situation were reversed so that the foreign rate exceeded the U.S. rate, the total foreign tax credit would be limited to the amount of U.S. tax attributable to the grossed-up foreign dividend.

Controlled Foreign Corporations

Domestic corporations owning foreign subsidiaries that operate in jurisdictions with low corporate tax rates are motivated to shift as much income as possible to those subsidiaries. Before 1962, U.S. companies routinely located subsidiaries in *tax haven* jurisdictions, countries with minimal or no corporate income tax. In many cases, the tax haven subsidiary existed only on paper, performing no function other than to provide tax shelter for the company's business income. Suppose a U.S. furniture manufacturer wanted to export its goods to a Belgian subsidiary for retail sale in the European market. If the manufacturer sold directly to its Belgian operation, it would pay U.S. tax on its manufacturing profits. Furthermore, the Belgian subsidiary would pay Belgian tax on the profits derived from the retail sale of the furniture. If, however, the U.S. parent also owned a subsidiary incorporated in the Cayman Islands, a tiny Caribbean nation with no corporate income tax, the parent could sell its furniture to this subsidiary for an artificially low price. The Cayman subsidiary could then immediately resell the furniture to the Belgian subsidiary for an artificially high price.

Understand that, in the above scenario, the furniture manufactured in the United States was shipped directly to the company's warehouse in Brussels; the Cayman subsidiary was not involved in the actual production process. Nevertheless, the subsidiary's momentary legal title to the goods shifted most of the profit derived from the entire business operation to the Cayman subsidiary. Until such time as the subsidiary repatriated income by paying a dividend to its U.S. parent, no income taxes were levied on the business income.

The tax avoidance scheme involving the Cayman Island corporation is just one example of dozens of creative strategies used by multinational businesses to divert income to tax haven subsidiaries. In 1962, Congress ended the most abusive of these strategies by enacting a set of rules applying to *controlled foreign corporations* (CFCs). A CFC can be loosely defined as any foreign corporation in which U.S. shareholders (including a corporate parent) own more than 50 percent of the combined voting power or stock value. If a CFC earns certain types of income during the year, such income is *constructively* repatriated to any U.S. shareholder owning a 10 percent or more interest in the CFC. Consequently, these shareholders must pay current U.S. tax on their pro rata share of the foreign income deemed to be repatriated, even though no cash or property is actually received from the CFC. The shareholders are entitled to increase the basis in their CFC stock by the amount of this constructive income. If in subsequent years, the CFC makes actual distributions to its U.S. shareholders, the shareholders may treat these distributions as tax-free returns of capital to the extent of the CFC income deemed repatriated in prior taxable years.

Subpart F Income

Not all the income earned by a CFC must be constructively repatriated to its U.S. shareholders. Only certain categories of tainted income (labeled *Subpart F income* in the Internal Revenue Code) are subject to this treatment. Subpart F income has many different and complex components, one of the more important of which is income derived from the sale of property if (1) the CFC either buys the property from or sells the property to a related party, and (2) the property is neither manufactured nor sold for use within the CFC's home country. In our Cayman Island example, the Cayman CFC is related to both the U.S. manufacturer from which it purchased the furniture and the Belgian retailer to which the furniture was sold. Moreover, the furniture was neither manufactured nor sold for consumption in the Cayman Islands. Quite clearly, the profit derived from the sale of the furniture is Subpart F income, which will be deemed to be repatriated to the U.S. parent and taxed currently at a 34 or 35 percent tax rate.

Transfer Pricing and Section 482

While the Subpart F income rules are potent, they do not extend to many types of foreign source income earned by foreign subsidiaries of U.S. multinational corporations. Accordingly, U.S. parents continue to benefit by shifting business income to foreign subsidiaries facing a marginal tax rate lower than that of the parent and its domestic subsidiaries. Of course, if a U.S. parent has subsidiaries incorporated in countries with corporate tax rates *higher* than the U.S. rates (such as France, Germany, Japan, or the United Kingdom), the basic tax planning strategy is reversed, and business income is shifted away from the high-tax foreign subsidiaries and into domestic affiliates.

One obvious way to shift income among the members of a controlled corporate group is through the pricing structure for intercompany transactions between the members. Consider the possibilities for income shifting if a U.S. corporation owns an Irish subsidiary that is actively engaged in the manufacture of consumer goods for sale in Europe. Although the Irish subsidiary is a CFC, the income it derives from sales of goods manufactured in Ireland and sold to *unrelated* purchasers is not Subpart F income. Consequently, this income is subject only to the modest Irish corporate income tax until such time as it s repatriated to the U.S. parent.

If the U.S. parent (or any of its domestic subsidiaries) sells raw materials to the Irish affiliate, the lower the price charged for the materials, the greater the amount of income shifted to Ireland. If the U.S. parent provides administrative, marketing, or financial services to the Irish business operation, the parent will further inflate the subsidiary's profits (and diminish its own) by charging the subsidiary only a nominal amount for the services rendered. Similarly, if the U.S. parent owns patents, copyrights, licenses, or other intangible assets utilized in the Irish manufacturing process, the parent could forgo any royalty payment for the use of the intangible asset.

All the above pricing strategies could result in a shift of corporate income to the Irish subsidiary. Not surprisingly, the United States and most other foreign jurisdictions, mindful of the income distortion resulting from artificially rigged transfer prices, insist that related corporations deal with each other in the same arm's-length manner as they would deal with unrelated parties. In our system, Section 482 gives the Internal Revenue Service the authority to apportion or allocate gross income, deductions, or credits between or among two or more related businesses "in order to prevent evasion of taxes or to clearly reflect the income" of any of the related businesses.

While the language of Section 482 is broad enough to apply to any type of business transaction between related parties, the section really comes into its own in the international arena. The IRS has enjoyed some success in using its Section 482 authority to ensure that domestic corporations report and pay U.S. tax on an appropriate amount of income attributable to any intercompany transactions involving foreign subsidiaries. One reason for this success is the prevailing judicial attitude that the IRS's determination of an arm's-length pricing standard should be upheld unless the taxpayer can demonstrate that the determination is "arbitrary, capricious, or unreasonable." Clearly, multinational corporations are in a weak defensive position in disputes concerning their transfer pricing practices and must be constantly aware of any Section 482 exposure created by their intercompany transactions.

Foreign Sales Corporations

The U.S. tax system provides preferential treatment for domestic corporations that conduct their export activities through marketing subsidiaries qualifying as *foreign sales corporations* (FSCs). The FSC provisions are intended to stimulate sales of domestically produced goods in the international market, thereby creating more jobs for U.S. workers. For a marketing subsidiary of a U.S. parent to qualify as an FSC, the subsidiary must be incorporated in one of a specified group of foreign countries and must maintain a business office, accounting records, and a bank account in that country.

Although an FSC is technically a foreign corporation, it is generally subject to current U.S. taxation on its *foreign trade income.* However, to the extent a U.S. parent routes its export sales through an FSC, 15 percent of the net profit from such sales is exempt from U.S. tax. (This exemption percentage can vary under certain circumstances.) As a result, the effective corporate tax rate on such foreign trade income is reduced from 34 or 35 percent to 28.9 or 29.75 percent (85 percent net profit times the applicable U.S. rate percent). When the FSC repatriates its after-tax profits by distributing a dividend to its U.S. parent, the parent may claim a special 100 percent dividend received deduction, thereby eliminating any double taxation on the FSC's foreign trade income.

TAXATION OF U.S. SOURCE INCOME TO FOREIGN INVESTORS

In the previous sections of this chapter, we concentrated on the tax rules applying to U.S. citizens and domestic corporations with foreign source income. In this next section, we will reverse our perspective and consider the U.S. tax consequences to nonresident aliens (individuals who are both citizens and residents of a foreign jurisdiction) and foreign corporations when they earn income from sources within the United States. The tax treatment of U.S. source income to foreign recipients depends on the classification of the income as either nonbusiness income or income effectively connected with a U.S. trade or business.

Nonbusiness U.S. Source Income

Our federal tax law imposes a 30 percent flat rate tax on any *fixed or determinable, annual or periodic* U.S. source income received by any nonresident alien or foreign corporation during the taxable year. This broad category consists primarily of investment income such as interest, dividends, and annuities. The 30 percent tax has two notable features. First, it is levied on gross income; the recipient cannot claim a deduction for any expenses incurred in the production of the income. Second, the *payor* of the income is required to withhold the tax at the time of payment and remit the withheld amount of the U.S. Treasury on behalf of the foreign recipient. This withholding requirement is extremely practical. Not only does it ensure that the U.S. tax is collected before the income "crosses the water," but is also eliminates the need for the foreign recipient to file any type of U.S. tax return.

The Internal Revenue Code exempts certain types of investment income paid to foreign investors from the 30 percent withholding tax. For example, interest income generated by deposits in U.S. financial institutions as well as interest paid on certain corporate bonds is not subject to U.S. taxation. Foreign investors are also not required to pay U.S. tax on capital gains realized on the sale of U.S. securities.

The statutory 30 percent rate on U.S. source nonbusiness income is routinely modified under the terms of any tax treaty in effect between the United States and the home country of the investor. For example, the tax treaty between the United States and the United Kingdom provides for a withholding tax on U.S. source dividends of only 15 percent (or 5 percent if the dividend is paid to a parent U.K. corporation) and no withholding tax on U.S. source interest income.

Income Effectively Connected with a U.S. Business

If a nonresident alien or foreign corporation engages in business within the United States, any net income *effectively connected* with the conduct of such business is subject to U.S. taxation at the rates applicable to domestic taxpayers. The crucial determination of whether a specific item of income is effectively connected with a U.S. business is based on facts and circumstances and can be extremely subjective. To provide a bit more objectivity, tax treaties between the United States and foreign jurisdictions typically provide that income earned by a foreign entity is not effectively connected with the conduct of a U.S. business unless the entity maintains a *permanent establishment* within the United States. For example, if an Italian footwear manufacturer uses an independent agent to market its shoes in the United States, the income from sales to U.S. customers is not effectively connected with the conduct of a U.S. business and therefore escapes U.S. taxation. In contrast, if the Italian company sets up an office in New York City (i.e., a permanent establishment) to manage its U.S. sales operation, the income attributable to the operation is subject to U.S. taxation.

Nonresident aliens subject to federal tax on their effectively connected U.S. business income must file a Form 1040NR, reflecting both gross income and all related business deductions. Nonresident aliens may not claim a standard deduction and are generally limited to only one personal exemption. Unmarried individuals compute their tax liabilities using the rates applicable to single taxpayers, while married individuals use the rates for married taxpayers filing separate returns. Foreign corporations must report any effectively connected U.S. business gross income and related business deductions on Form 1120F. The U.S. corporate tax on the net business income is computed under the same rules and at the same rates applicable to domestic corporations.

Income from Real Property

As a general rule, U.S. source rents are classified as investment income, subject to the statutory 30 percent withholding tax. The law allows foreign taxpayers to elect to treat rent income from real property located in the United States as income effectively connected with the conduct of a U.S. business. The primary reason for the election is to secure a deduction for the various expenses attributable to the rent property. For example, suppose a Venezuelan corporation owns an apartment complex in Miami, Florida, that generates $1 million of annual gross revenues and has annual operating expenses of $600,000. If the foreign corporation fails to make the election to treat the apartment complex as a U.S. business, it must pay $300,000 of tax (30 percent of $1 million gross income) to the U.S. government. If the election is made, the U.S. tax liability drops to $136,000 (34 percent of $400,000 net income).

You may recall from our earlier discussion that capital gains realized by foreign investors are not subject to U.S. tax. This lenient rule suggests that foreign investors in U.S. real estate could sell their investment and avoid any U.S. tax liability on their profit. To prevent such a result, a specific statutory rule mandates that gain realized on the disposition of an interest in U.S. real property is always classified as effectively connected U.S. business income. Consequently, such gain is taxed at the regular federal rates.

STATE TAX ISSUES

This final section introduces a new topic—multistate taxation of business income. Including this topic in a chapter devoted primarily to international taxation may strike the reader as incongruous. However, the jurisdictional conflicts arising when two or more nations claim authority to tax the business income of a multinational corporation are virtually identical to the conflicts suggested when two or more states impose an income tax on a company engaged in interstate commerce. In the following paragraphs, we will first briefly examine the characteristics of the tax systems of the 50 states. We will then focus on the omnipresent problem of double taxation and compare the way the problem is addressed at the interstate level to the way it is handled in the international arena.

State Tax Bases

While the federal government's primary sources of tax revenue are the employer/employee payroll taxes and the individual and corporate income taxes, states and subdivisions thereof depend most heavily on various types of nonincome taxes to fund their governments. According to recent data, *general sales taxes* levied on retail sales of goods and services, *excise taxes* levied on sales of specific items such as tobacco and alcohol, and *property taxes* levied on both real and personal assets account for approximately 65 percent of aggregate state tax revenues.

In addition to these nonincome taxes, the majority of states have both an individual and a corporate income tax. Because of the text's emphasis on business transactions, our discussion of state taxes will be limited to the taxation of income earned by corporations. Most state tax systems *piggyback* on the federal system in their computation of corporate taxable income. In other words, corporate taxable income as reported on the federal Form 1120 is the initial reference point for calculating the state income tax base. Each state system requires various modifications to the federal income number. For example, many states require interest income from state and local bonds (tax-exempt for federal purposes) to be included in taxable income for state purposes; conversely, interest income from federal obligations such as Treasury bills (fully taxable at the federal level) is exempt from state income taxation. A second common modification to federal taxable income is the add-back of any deduction for state income taxes paid by the corporation during the year.

The chief benefits of piggyback systems are their simplicity and administrative ease. But perhaps the most important characteristic of these systems is their sensitivity to decisions made in Washington D.C. Each time Congress decides to redefine corporate taxable income at the national level, state tax revenues are indirectly affected. When Congress enacts a new provision increasing the corporate income tax base, states piggybacking on this base enjoy a tax windfall. But when a legislative change to the Internal Revenue Code reduces the tax base, these states suffer an automatic decline in tax revenues.

About half the states with a corporate income tax have a flat tax rate; the other half use a progressive rate schedule with several income brackets. The rates are relatively modest; the highest marginal rates are usually less than 10 percent of corporate taxable income. Interestingly, one third of the states, including California, New York, and Florida, impose some version of a minimum tax in addition to the regular corporate income tax.

Double Taxation of Corporate Income by U.S. Jurisdictions

Domestic corporations must accept as a fact of economic life that both the federal government and any number of state governments may have jurisdiction to tax their annual incomes. The deduction for state income taxes paid allowed in the computation of federal taxable income provides some relief. Suppose a corporation with $500,000 of operating income (before any deduction for state taxes) conducts its business in a state with an 8 percent income tax. The corporation must pay $40,000 to the state, a payment that reduces taxable income on its Form 1120 to $460,000. The federal tax on this income at a 34 percent rate is $156,400. Consequently, the corporation's combined income tax bill for the year is $196,400, and its overall effective tax rate is 39.2 percent.

Our corporation's problem with double taxation is exacerbated if more than one state has the authority to tax its income. The *home state* in which a corporation is legally organized generally has the right to tax any and all income earned by the corporation. On the other hand, any state within which the corporation conducts business (a *host state*) has the right to tax that portion of the corporation's income attributable to such business activity. Given that thousands of U.S. corporations conduct business in more than one, if not all 50 states, some degree of national coordination of state tax systems is plainly necessary to avoid fiscal anarchy.

The federal government's constitutional authority to regulate commerce among the states has allowed Congress and the federal courts to establish some basic ground rules. For a state corporate income tax to be constitutional, it must not discriminate against interstate commerce and must apply only to those corporate activities sufficiently connected to the state to justify taxation. In addition, a corporation's total taxable income must be apportioned among the various states claiming jurisdiction. The states themselves have taken collective action to enhance the fairness and uniformity of their respective tax systems. Many states model their income tax statutes after the Uniform Division of Income for Tax Purposes Act (UDITPA), drafted in 1957 by the National Conference of Commissioners on Uniform State Laws. These states send representatives to the Multistate Tax Commission, which periodically issues guidance on the implementation of UDITPA.

Apportionment of Income among States

The threshold question in multistate taxation concerns the minimum level of corporate business activity within a state that will trigger the imposition of that state's income tax. Generally, a corporation can avoid creating a *nexus* (i.e., a connection justifying taxation) if its activities within a state are strictly limited to soliciting sales of the corporation's product. Activities directly related to solicitation, such as advertising, are permissible. If, however, a corporation's activities within the state extend beyond mere solicitation and include, for example, installation of the product for the customer and the subsequent repair and maintenance of the product, a nexus for taxation may be established.

Corporations subject to income taxation in one or more host states, as well as their home state, must *apportion* their total taxable income among the states. Only the amount of income apportioned to each state is subject to that state's income tax. Observe that under an apportionment system, the home state of incorporation is surrendering its right to tax corporate income earned outside the state. To illustrate, assume that Midwest Inc. is an Illinois corporation conducting business in Illinois and Missouri. During the current year, 70 percent of Midwest's $100,000 taxable income is apportioned to Illinois, while 30 percent is apportioned to Missouri. If the Illinois tax rate is 9 percent, while the Missouri rate is only 6 percent, Midwest's state income tax burden totals $8,100 (9 percent of $70,000 plus 6 percent of $30,000). Although the home state's tax rate is higher than the host state, the home state does not impose an incremental tax on the income apportioned to the host state.

An apportionment system for avoiding double taxation is fundamentally different from the credit system used at the international level. If the jurisdictions involved in the above example were the United States (the home country) and a foreign host country with a corporate tax rate of 20 percent, the United States would impose a precredit tax of $34,000 on the entire $100,000 of Midwest Inc.'s worldwide income. Midwest could then claim a $6,000 credit for the foreign tax levied on the $30,000 of foreign source income. As a result the United States would collect a 14 percent tax (the excess of the U.S. rate over the foreign rate) on the foreign source income.

The apportionment of corporate income among states is based on a formula that typically consists of three factors: the amount of sales, payroll, and corporate property attributable to each state. Most state statutes accord these factors equal weight in the formula. As an example, let's examine the following data for Midwest Inc., our corporation doing business in Illinois and Missouri:

	Illinois	*Missouri*	*Total*
Sales revenues	$220,000 (55%)	$180,000 (45%)	$400,000
Payroll expenses	$198,000 (90%)	$22,000 (10%)	$220,000
Property values	$650,000 (65%)	$350,000 (35%)	$1,000,000

Under an equally weighted three-factor formula, Midwest's apportionment percentages are determined as follows:

	Illinois	*Missouri*
Sales revenues factor	55%	45%
+ Payroll expense factor	90%	10%
+ Property value factor	65%	35%
Apportionment percentage	$\frac{210\%}{3} = 70\%$	$\frac{90\%}{3} = 30\%$

Based on the apportionment percentages, $70,000 of Midwest's $100,000 taxable income for the current year is apportioned to and taxed by Illinois, while $30,000 is apportioned to and taxed by Missouri.

In the international area, the characterization of U.S. source or foreign source income requires an inquiry into the origin of each income item recognized during the taxable year. In contrast, the formula apportionment of income to various state jurisdictions ignores the actual source of any particular item of business income. In certain circumstances, this approach can lead to peculiar results. Suppose Midwest Inc. keeps two separate sets of books and records for its Illinois and Missouri operations. Even if the accounting records indicate that the net incomes for each operation were $45,000 and $55,000, respectively, the total income would still be apportioned according to the three-factor formula for state tax purposes.

One final feature of the apportionment system deserves our attention. If each state used the same formula and defined the sales, payroll, and property factors in exactly the same manner, not one dollar of corporate business income would be doubly taxed at the state level. Not surprisingly, such perfect consistency does not exist. Because of any number of anomalies in the apportionment formulas used by the different states, some amount of corporate income is invariably either taxed twice or not taxed at all.

Multistate Tax Planning

Corporations planning to minimize their state income tax burdens can adopt two strategies. First, they can avoid establishing a nexus for taxation in any state with a high tax rate. Second, they can attempt to manipulate the factor values in the apportionment formula to skew the results. For example, if a corporation deliberately locates its highly compensated employees in a low-tax jurisdiction, the heavier value for the payroll factor will shift taxable income to that jurisdiction. Conceptually, these strategies make perfect sense. However, state income taxes represent a single cost of conducting business, and corporations should never adopt a planning strategy to minimize this cost if that strategy has a negative impact on more significant aspects of the corporation's business.

CONCLUSION

In earlier chapters, we discussed tax implications of selecting a particular type of business entity. In this chapter, we have added a new tax planning variable—the impact of the tax jurisdiction in which the business entity will operate. To the extent that taxpayers can manipulate this variable by deliberately locating their business operations in a low-tax jurisdiction, the rate of return on their investment will be increased.

If a business operation spans more than one jurisdiction, the owners run the risk that double taxation will erode the profitability of their investment. If the competing jurisdictions are two nations, the availability of a foreign tax credit may soften the blow. If the competing taxing authorities are our national government and a state government, a federal deduction for state taxes paid offers partial relief. And if more than one state claims the right to tax a single stream of business income, the apportionment of that income among the claimants can hold the total state tax bill to a tolerable amount.

PROBLEMS AND CASES

1. Jon Crier, a single taxpayer and U.S. citizen, has lived in Copenhagen, Denmark, for the last three years. Jon is an employee of the Danish Tourism Bureau and earns an annual salary of $94,000, his only source of gross income. In 1996, Jon paid $35,000 of income tax to Denmark. Based on this data, compute Jon's U.S. tax liability. In making your calculation, assume Jon has no dependents, does not itemize deductions, and had housing expenses of less than $8,000 for the year.
2. Darla Wood, a single taxpayer and U.S. citizen, has lived in Singapore for the last five years. Darla works for a U.S. corporation that pays her an annual salary of $130,000 plus a $20,000 housing allowance. Darla rents an apartment in Singapore for $3,000 per month. If Darla has no other sources of gross income in 1996, compute her adjusted gross income for the year.
3. Easley Inc., a U.S. corporation, engages in both domestic and foreign business activities. All its foreign activities are conducted through branch offices. During the current year, Easley earned $2 million of taxable income, $398,000 of which is foreign source income. During the year, Easley Inc. paid $295,000 of foreign income taxes. Based on these facts, compute Easley Inc.'s U.S. income tax liability.
4. Connors Inc., a U.S. corporation, conducts its business activities in the United States. Connors owns two controlled domestic subsidiaries (A and B) that conduct business in two different foreign jurisdictions. For the current year, the three corporations report the following:

	Foreign Source Income	*U.S. Source Income*	*Foreign Income Taxes Paid*
Connors Inc.	$ -0-	$600,000	$ -0-
Subsidiary A	350,000	15,000	38,000
Subsidiary B	470,000	41,000	235,000
	$820,000	$656,000	$273,000

   a. Assuming Connors Inc. and its two subsidiaries file a consolidated tax return, compute the current year consolidated tax liability.
   b. How would the aggregate tax liability of the group change if each of the three corporations filed its own separate tax return?
   c. Can you explain the difference in the tax liabilities calculated in *a* and *b*?
5. Varnum Inc., a calendar year U.S. corporation, began operations in 19x1. For its first taxable year, Varnum reported $500,000 of taxable income, $200,000 of which was foreign source. During 19x1, Varnum paid $82,000 of foreign income taxes. In 19x2, Varnum's taxable income was $900,000, $630,000 of which was foreign source. During 19x2, Varnum paid $151,000 of foreign income taxes. Based on these figures, compute Varnum's 19x1 and 19x2 U.S. income tax liability.
6. Jordan Enterprises Inc. (JE), a U.S. corporation, wants to expand its business operations into a foreign host country that imposes a 20 percent tax on corporate

income earned within its borders. Jordan anticipates its new foreign operation will generate losses for three years. After the initial loss period, the corporation should be extremely profitable. Discuss any tax advantages and disadvantages if JE decides to:

a. Operate the foreign business through a U.S. (domestic) corporate subsidiary.
b. Operate the foreign business through a corporation created under the laws of the host country.

7. Casis Inc., a U.S. corporation, owns 100 percent of the outstanding stock in Damien Inc., a foreign corporation. All of Damien's income is attributable to its business activities in Europe, and its marginal rate (for foreign income tax purposes) is 18 percent. During the current year, Damien Inc. distributed a $50,000 dividend to Casis Inc. Because the country in which Damien is incorporated does not levy a tax on dividends paid to foreign shareholders, Damien was not required to withhold any tax from the $50,000 payment.

   a. If Casis Inc. is in a 34 percent tax bracket and has no foreign tax credit carryforward into the current year, compute the corporation's current U.S. tax liability on the dividend received from Damien Inc.
   b. How would your answer to *a* change if Casis Inc. has a $20,000 foreign tax credit carryforward into the current year?

8. JMT Inc., a U.S. corporation in a 34 percent tax bracket, owns 35 percent of the stock of Lydo Inc., a Swiss corporation meeting the definition of a controlled foreign corporation (CFC). At the beginning of the current year, JMT's basis in its Lydo stock is $660,000. During the year, Lydo Inc. has total taxable income of $1 million, $300,000 of which is Subpart F income. The Swiss income tax on this total income is only $100,000. Lydo pays no dividends during the year. Describe the current U.S. tax consequences of JMT's investment in Lydo Inc.

9. Manuel Lopes, a citizen and resident of Portugal, owns 1,000 shares of stock in Tempaco Inc., a U.S. corporation. During the current year, Tempaco declared a cash dividend of $25 per share on its outstanding stock. The dividend was paid to shareholders of record on July 1. In November of the current year, Manuel realized a $7,300 gain on the sale of 600 Tempaco shares. What are the U.S. tax consequences of these transactions to Mr. Lopes? The United States and Portugal do not have a tax treaty in effect.

10. Aren Assadi, a citizen and resident of Turkey, is a partner in Byron Mining and Development, a U.S. partnership doing business in Colorado, Nevada, and Utah. During the current year, Mr. Assadi was allocated $4,600 of business income from the partnership. Mr. Assadi is also a 10 percent owner of an apartment complex in downtown Los Angeles. During the year, the partnership generated $800,000 of gross rents and incurred $680,000 of deductible expenses. The United States and Turkey do not have a tax treaty in effect.

    a. Is Mr. Assadi required to file a U.S. individual income tax return for the current year?

b. What options does Mr. Assadi have with regards to paying tax on the income generated by his investment in the Los Angeles real estate? Compute his U.S. tax liability under each option.

11. Benari Inc., a German corporation, has current operating income of $2 million, $1.3 million of which is effectively connected with the conduct of a U.S. business. Benari also earned $49,000 of interest income on its cash deposits in various U.S. banks. Benari's marginal German corporate income tax rate is 50 percent.

    a. To what extent must Benari Inc. pay U.S. tax on its U.S. source income?

    b. Is Benari entitled to any foreign tax credit against its U.S. tax liability for the year?

Case 13–1

Colpath Inc. is a Florida corporation conducting business in both Florida and Georgia. All of Colpath's business assets are located in Tallahassee, Florida. For the current year, Colpath's accounting records show the following (in thousands of dollars):

	Florida	*Georgia*
Sales revenues	$600	$390
Cost of sales	(400)	(260)
Gross profit	$200	$130
Payroll expenses	$ 40	$ 20
Mortgage interest	15	—
Operating expenses	45	51
Depreciation	31	—
Pretax income	$ 69	$ 59

a. Assuming that both Florida and Georgia use the equally weighted three-factor formula to apportion corporate income for state income tax purposes, how much of Colpath Inc.'s $128,000 current income will be included on each of the corporation's two state income tax returns?

b. How would your answer change if Florida uses the equally weighted three-factor formula, but Georgia uses a formula in which the sales revenue factor is double weighted (i.e., given twice as much weight as the other factors)?

CHAPTER 14

Family Tax Planning

Family tax planning centers on the tax consequences of intrafamily transfers of wealth, either by gift or on the death of a family member. The federal taxes imposed on these transfers were originally enacted to redistribute some portion of the vast private fortunes owned by the nation's wealthiest families to the public domain. As a result, the federal gift, estate, and generation-skipping transfer taxes affect only a tiny fraction of the population, those individuals fortunate enough to have accumulated significant personal wealth. A second consequence of the narrow focus of the transfer taxes is that they are not an important source of federal revenue; transfer taxes represent less than 1 percent of the total federal revenues collected every year. Clearly, from a macroeconomic perspective, the federal transfer tax system plays a very small role in our national economy. However, from the point of view of wealthy individuals desirous of preserving accumulated capital and passing it on to children and grandchildren at the least tax cost, a basic understanding of this tax system is critical.

In this chapter, we will consider the rules governing the computation of the federal gift and estate taxes, as well as possible methods for minimizing these taxes. A third type of federal tax, the generation-skipping transfer tax, is so complex and so specialized in its application that we may safely omit any discussion of its esoteric provisions.

FEDERAL TAXATION OF GIFTS

The federal gift tax is imposed on certain gratuitous transfers of property by individuals. The tax is a liability of the *donor*, the person making the gift, not the *donee*, the person receiving the gift. The tax applies to all forms of property: realty and personalty; business, investment, and personal-use property; tangible and intangible property; and present and future interests in property. In other words, if a taxpayer today makes an irrevocable transfer of a future interest in a property to a person not yet born, the transfer may be subject to an immediate gift tax, even though the full economic impact of the transfer of property rights may not occur for many years.

A transfer must be irrevocable before the gift tax will apply. If a person prepares a last will and testament or names a beneficiary to a life insurance policy, such action does not constitute a gift so long as the taxpayer retains the right to modify his present intention at any time. Finally, the reader should understand that the gift tax has essentially nothing to do with the income tax. For example, the interest on state and local government bonds is exempt from the federal income tax. A gift of a state or local bond is wholly subject to the federal gift tax. Similarly, a gift of cash paid out of a salary already reduced by the income tax is nonetheless a taxable gift.

The Gift Tax Calculation

The gift tax liability is based on the following formula:

	Fair market value of total gifts made during the calendar year
less:	Annual exclusions and deductions
	Current year taxable gifts
plus:	Prior year taxable gifts
	Cumulative taxable gifts
	Transfer tax rate
	Tax on cumulative gifts
less:	Tax computed on prior year gifts
	Precredit gift tax
less:	Unified credit
	Gift tax payable

This formula has some unique characteristics that we will discuss in order. To begin, let's turn our attention to the definition of a *gift* within the meaning of the tax law.

Gifts. The Internal Revenue Code provides that any transfer of property for less than adequate and full consideration in money or money's worth shall be considered a gift. The application of this seemingly straightforward rule can be surprisingly difficult. If a person makes a foolish deal—if the person, for instance, sells a property worth $500,000 for $400,000—the law implies that the person has made a $100,000 gift to the purchaser. Instead of trying to apply the law literally, the IRS usually tries to determine the intent of the taxpayer. If he or she entered into an arm's-length transaction in the ordinary course of business, the transaction will not be subject to a gift tax. If the transaction is one between related parties or if the IRS has any other reason to suspect the transaction is not a bona fide sale or exchange, it may tax as a gift the difference between the fair market value given and the consideration received.

The assumption that a gift must be motivated by love, affection, or at least generosity does not necessarily apply for federal tax purposes. Treasury regulations specify that *donative intent* on the part of the individual transferring property for insufficient consideration need not exist for the transfer to be a taxable gift. The classic example of a lack of donative intent involved a father who promised his son a sizable cash reward if the son would complete an undergraduate college degree. During the son's college years, he and his father became estranged, and on the son's graduation the father refused to honor his promise. The son sued the father for breach of oral contract and won his case. Imagine the father's reaction when he not only was legally forced to pay his son the promised cash, but also was informed by the IRS that this transfer for less than full and adequate *monetary* consideration was a taxable gift.

The dollar amount subject to the gift tax is measured by the fair market value of the property transferred less the value of any consideration received by the transferor. Determining fair market value of gifted property may be the most difficult aspect of computing a gift tax liability. If no established market exists for the property, valuation becomes extremely subjective and must be based on all relevant facts and circumstance. For properties of significant or controversial worth, donors may require the services of an independent appraiser to ascertain the value reported on the gift tax return.

If a donor transfers less than a total interest in a property, even more difficult problems of valuation are encountered. For example, a taxpayer may make a gift of the income from a property to person A for her lifetime; a gift of the same income stream to person B for his lifetime, but to take effect only after the death of person A; and finally a gift of the remainder interest in the property to person C. Before the gift tax consequences can be determined, we must know the value of the gifts made to persons A, B, and C. Obviously, such valuations can only be made with certain presumptions about the size of the income stream over a period of years, a discount rate, and a mortality table of expected human lives. Any attempt to investigate problems of valuation would lead us far afield of the objectives of this book. We will therefore assume that such valuation problems can be solved and proceed with the more direct tax consequences.

Exclusions and Deductions. After all potentially taxable gifts of property during the year have been identified and valued, the donor may exclude up to $10,000 of the value of the gifts made to each donee during the year. The donor may then deduct the remaining value of any gift made to his or her spouse, a qualified charity, or a public institution.

The *annual exclusion* for the first $10,000 of gifts made to each donee renders the vast majority of gifts nontaxable. Any individual can give an unlimited amount of property away without a gift tax if he or she is willing to give it to enough different people. Over a lifetime, a large sum can be given tax free to any one individual if the donor begins making gifts at an early age. Over 50 years, for example, a person could transfer $500,000 to one child without incurring a gift tax, if the taxpayer would but make the maximum $10,000 tax-free gift each year. If a husband and wife each make gifts in that amount, the total that can be transferred tax free is doubled.

Although gifts to religious, literary, scientific, educational, and other charitable organizations are generally not subject to gift tax, these gifts must be reported and then deducted on the gift tax return if they exceed $10,000 to any one organization in any one year. This unlimited charitable deduction may seem surprisingly generous until we recall that the primary purpose of the gift tax is the redistribution of private wealth to the public sector. The fact that a wealthy individual initiates the redistribution by donating to public charities simply eliminates any need for government intervention.

Finally, any taxpayer can give his or her spouse an unlimited amount of property without incurring any gift tax because of the *marital deduction*. Additional details and planning suggestions relating to the marital deduction are explained later in this chapter.

Tax Rates. The steeply progressive tax rates applied to the total of taxable gifts made during a calendar year are provided in Table 14–1. These donative transfer tax rates are, for a wealthy few, only the apparent tax rates because the benefits of the lower marginal rates are phased out by a 5 percent surtax on taxable donative transfers in excess of $10 million. As a result of this surtax, all taxable transfers in excess of $21.04 million are now taxed at a flat rate of 55 percent.

The computation of the gift tax is very different from that of the income tax. Although the gift tax is computed and paid every year, it is not really an annual tax. Instead, the tax is imposed on the cumulative value of gifts that an individual makes over a lifetime. To illustrate this unique computation, assume a donor makes his first taxable gift of $100,000 in 1990. From Table 14–1, the precredit tax on this gift is $23,800. In the current year, our donor makes his second taxable gift of $90,000. To compute the tax, the amount of the current gift must be added to the total of prior year taxable gifts and the tax on this cumulative amount calculated. In our example, the tax on cumulative gifts of $190,000 is $51,600. The amount of tax calculated on prior year gifts is then subtracted to result in the precredit tax on the current year gift. In our donor's case, subtracting the $23,800 tax on the 1990 gift from $51,600 results in a current year gift tax of $27,800. The fact that the first $100,000 gift created a smaller tax liability than the second $90,000 gift highlights the effect of the cumulative nature of the gift tax computation. Because each successive gift will be boosted higher into the

Table 14–1 Unified Estate and Gift Tax Rates

For Taxable Transfer Equal to or More than —	*But Less than—*	*The Tax is Equal to—*	*Plus the Following Rate Times Any Amount in Excess of that in Column 1:*
$ 0	$ 10,000	$ 0	18%
10,000	20,000	1,800	20
20,000	40,000	3,800	22
40,000	60,000	8,200	24
60,000	80,000	13,000	26
80,000	100,000	18,200	28
100,000	150,000	23,800	30
150,000	250,000	38,800	32
250,000	500,000	70,800	34
500,000	750,000	155,800	37
750,000	1,000,000	248,300	39
1,000,000	1,250,000	345,800	41
1,250,000	1,500,000	448,300	43
1,500,000	2,000,000	555,800	45
2,000,000	2,500,000	780,800	49
2,500,000	3,000,000	1,025,800	53
3,000,000	—	1,290,800	55

progressive rate schedule and taxed at an increased marginal rate, each gift will be more expensive to the donor in terms of the federal gift tax.

The Unified Credit. There is a single *unified credit* that reduces a donor's gift tax liability. The credit equals $192,800 reduced by any amount of credit used in prior years. The effect of this credit is to shelter an individual's first $600,000 of taxable gifts from any gift tax liability.

A Comprehensive Illustration

To pull together the various elements of the gift tax calculation, assume Margaret Leeds, a single taxpayer, makes the three following gifts in the current year:

To daughter Kay	$150,000 cash
To friend Michael	$5,000 cash
To First Baptist Church	$20,000 (securities at market value)

Because of the availability of the $10,000 annual exclusion, the gift to Michael is totally excludable and the taxable gift to Kay is only $140,000. The gift to charity is fully deductible. Therefore, Margaret's total taxable gifts for the current year are $140,000, and her tax liability on this amount is $35,800. However, the unified credit will reduce her actual tax liability to zero.

In the next year, Margaret makes the following gifts:

To daughter Kay	$500,000 (real estate at market value)
To granddaughter Kim	$50,000 (value of new automobile)

Margaret's taxable gifts for the year are $530,000 ($550,000 less two exclusions), and her cumulative gifts total $670,000. The tax on this total is $218,700; the tax on this year's gifts is $182,800 ($218,700 less $35,800 tax computed on prior year's gifts). Margaret may reduce this tax by her remaining unified credit of $157,000 ($192,800 less $35,800 credit used in prior years). Therefore, her tax liability for the year is $25,900. Note that if Margaret continues to make taxable gifts in future years, she no longer has any unified credit to offset future tax liability.

Planning Considerations

The gift tax is exceedingly easy to avoid. A taxpayer who does not want to incur this tax merely has to suppress any generous impulses. In practice, tax planning relative to the gift tax usually relates to determining the lesser of two evils. The taxpayer will accept the need to pay a gift tax whenever doing so reduces some other tax by an amount greater than the gift tax incurred. The general constraints to be considered in making such a determination will be discussed in the final section of this chapter.

Systematic Giving. Taxpayers with substantial amounts of property should begin a systematic pattern of giving as early in life as possible if they want to minimize the aggregate tax they or their heirs must pay. In some situations, a taxpayer may believe nontax considerations are more important than tax savings, and the actions of such a taxpayer should be guided accordingly. A taxpayer who believes childhood wealth leads to laziness, unhappiness, or family strife would be well advised to forgo any tax savings in the interest of a better quality of human existence. For those who do not believe early wealth contributes to a less meaningful existence, systematic giving can be beneficial.

Only systematic patterns of giving can assure a taxpayer that she has taken maximum advantage of the $10,000 annual exclusion. This tax-minimizing provision is applicable to every taxpayer. Thus, if a husband and wife want to maximize their gift tax opportunities, they should make all gifts jointly. If both parties consent to this special treatment, even if the property given belongs entirely to one spouse, the annual exclusion for the couple increases from $10,000 to $20,000 per donee. A consent to make gifts jointly must be in writing and filed on a timely basis with the IRS.

To demonstrate the importance of systematic giving, observe that if a couple has two married children and if each child has two children, that couple can transfer more than $3 million tax free to family members in just 20 years. If each parent gives each child, child's spouse, and grandchild $10,000 per year, the total—$20,000 × 8 × 20 years—amounts to $3,200,000!

Serial Gifts. Under certain circumstances, a taxpayer may desire to transfer a particular property to a donee, but the transfer of the entire property at one time may be expensive because of the gift tax rules. Suppose, for example, that, after exhausting their unified credit, a couple jointly desired to transfer a specific property worth $120,000 to their daughter. If they made the complete transfer in a single year, the transfer would be subject to a gift tax on $100,000. Instead of arranging the transfer as a gift, the couple might consider selling the property to the daughter, with the initial payment to be made in the form of six $20,000 promissory notes, with one note maturing in each of the next six years. Each year, the couple might forgive the daughter the $20,000 note due that year and thus avoid any gift tax on the transfer. This possibility raises several interesting tax questions for both the parents and the daughter. For example, the IRS might disregard the form of the initial transfer and treat the transfer as a gift rather than a sale under the substance-over-form doctrine. If the form of the transaction is sustained, the sale could create taxable gain for the parents, even though they will never receive any cash. The tax basis of the property to the daughter, for income tax purposes, would depend on how she is deemed to have acquired it; one set of basis rules applies to property acquired by gift and another set to purchased property. Although this serial gift notion creates several interesting tax problems, it has been used successfully in minimizing gift taxes.

FEDERAL TAXATION OF ESTATES

The federal estate tax is levied on the transfer of the ownership, possession, or enjoyment of property occasioned by the death of an individual. This tax is a liability of the decedent's estate and must be paid by the executor before the decedent's property can be distributed to the beneficiaries of the estate.

The Estate Tax Calculation

The estate tax liability is based on the following formula:

	Fair market value of gross estate
less:	Deductions
	Taxable estate
plus:	Cumulative taxable gifts
	Cumulative taxable transfers
	Transfer tax rate
	Precredit estate tax
less:	Gift taxes paid
less:	Estate tax credits
	Estate tax payable

Gross Estate. Each and every property interest owned by an individual at the moment of death must be included in that individual's gross estate. This rule applies to both tangible and intangible assets and to real and personal property, regardless of where the property is located. If a property right is identified as part of a decedent's gross estate, the fair market value of the right must be determined. Many property rights, such as capital stock in a closely held family corporation, have no readily ascertainable market value. Fortunately, Treasury regulations provide detailed guidance concerning the valuation of numerous types of assets.

Property interests owned by an individual at death generally constitute the decedent's *probate estate*. The disposition of the probate estate is controlled by the decedent's will; if an individual dies *intestate*—without leaving a valid will—the intestacy laws of the state in which he or she resided will control the disposition of the assets in the probate estate. Although the specifics vary from state to state, a decedent's assets will generally pass in order to a surviving spouse, surviving children or grandchildren, surviving parents, surviving siblings, and so on. If no surviving heirs can be located, the assets will become the property of the state of residence.

The gross estate for federal tax purposes may include the value of property the decedent did not legally own at date of death—property not included in the decedent's probate estate. If an individual owned property as a *joint tenant with right of survivorship*, the ownership of the property will automatically shift to the surviving joint tenants, regardless of the terms of the individual's will. Nonetheless, a percentage of the value of the property based on the individual's original contribution to the acquisition of the property will be included in his or her gross estate. For example, if an individual contributed $10,000 of the original $40,000 purchase price of jointly owned property and the property was worth $200,000 on the date of the individual's death, $50,000 of the value of the property is includable in the gross estate.

A decedent's rights in a retirement annuity, pension or profit-sharing plan, or an IRA are usually paid to the beneficiaries named in the retirement plan or contract rather than to the decedent's estate. The value of these rights, however, is includable in the gross estate. Another common asset that may be so included is life insurance proceeds payable because of the decedent's death. Typically, such proceeds are paid to those beneficiaries named in the insurance contract and are not subject to probate. Unfortunately, if the decedent owned the insurance policy on his or her own life, the proceeds will be in the gross estate and may be subject to the federal estate tax. A simple technique to avoid this needlessly expensive outcome is for the individual to transfer the ownership of the policy into an insurance trust before death. The beneficiaries will still receive the proceeds on the individual's death, but the proceeds will escape inclusion in the gross estate.

The scope of the federal estate tax is broad enough to encompass not only transfers of legal ownership but also transfers of the possession or enjoyment of property occurring on an individual's death. The classic example of this latter type of transfer involves a wealthy individual who surrenders the legal title to property to an irrevocable trust. The terms of the trust provide that the income from the property will be paid to the transferor for his lifetime. Only upon the transferor's death will the trust property be distributed to family members or friends. From a strictly legal perspective, the transferor no longer is the owner of the property, and no portion of the trust assets will be included in the transferor's probate estate at death. Nevertheless, the possession and enjoyment of the trust property will not pass to the other beneficiaries of the trust until the transferor dies. Because the transferor retained the right to the income from the property given away during life, the value of the trust property determined at the date of death must be included in his or her gross estate.

The above example illustrates several basic principles concerning the computation of the federal gross estate. First, the fact that an individual gives away the legal ownership of property during life does not necessarily ensure that the value of that property will not be in the individual's future gross estate. If an individual makes a gift with any type of "string attached," the retained control or enjoyment represented by that string is usually sufficient to pull the date-of-death value of the gifted property back into the individual's gross estate. If a gift tax was paid on the original transfer, it will simply be credited against the decedent's final estate tax liability. Second, because of the tendency of property to appreciate in value over time, including previously gifted property in a gross estate can result in a dramatic increase in total tax liability. In our example developed in the preceding paragraph, let's assume the property placed into trust was worth $500,000 at the date of transfer. Although the transferor gave away only the *remainder interest* in the property placed in trust (the ownership of the property after the transferor's death), the tax law requires that the full $500,000 value of the property be recognized as a current year gift. In this example, assume the transferor paid a tax on this particular gift of $90,000. Now assume the property appreciated handsomely in value during the years it was held in trust so that when the transferor finally dies, the property is worth $2.5 million. It is this date-of-death value that will be included in the transferor's gross estate and subjected to the federal estate tax. The gift tax paid on that early gift will, of course, reduce this estate tax, but a sizable tax liability will remain.

One of the more common misconceptions regarding the federal estate tax is that an individual's probate estate for legal purposes must necessarily equal his gross estate for tax purposes. We have discussed only a few types of valuable assets that are not part of the probate estate but that are most certainly includable in the gross estate. Hopefully, the lesson is clear. An individual who anticipates accumulating a minimal probate estate and therefore decides that any family tax planning is unnecessary may be courting economic disaster.

Deductions. The tax law authorizes four major deductions against the gross estate in the computation of a decedent's taxable estate. The first deduction is for all outstanding debts of the decedent and any creditor claims against the estate. For example, if a tract of real estate worth $8 million is included in a decedent's gross estate and that real estate is subject to a $2 million mortgage, the mortgage may be deducted so that only the decedent's $6 million equity is included in the taxable estate. Because of this deduction, the estate tax is imposed on the net (rather than the gross) value of properties transferred at death.

The second deduction against the gross estate is for the decedent's funeral expenses and any administrative expenses of settling the estate. The latter includes legal, accounting, and appraisal fees, commissions paid to the executor of the estate, and the various costs of maintaining and preserving the decedent's property during the probate period. The deduction for these expenditures reduces the potential taxable estate to the net dollar amount that the decedent's heirs will actually receive when the estate is finally closed.

Current law provides an unlimited estate tax marital deduction. This important deduction shields most small estates from the federal estate tax so long as there is a surviving spouse. Under the law existing before 1982, only a complete transfer of all property rights qualified for a marital deduction. Since 1981, an executor may elect to treat a bequest of an income interest for life to a surviving spouse as a qualifying marital bequest. For example, a husband can now leave a life interest in all his assets to a spouse, pass all remainder interests to his children, and still have this bequest qualify for the unlimited marital deduction. In that event, however, the total value of the remainder interest must be included in the gross estate of the wife when she dies.

Finally, the law authorizes a deduction for property transferred to a nonprofit government, religious, charitable, scientific, literary, or educational organization. In this case, the fact that an individual voluntarily redistributes his accumulated wealth at death to public organizations of his or her own choosing negates the need for any federal estate tax.

The Addition of Taxable Gifts. The fact that gifts and estates are subject to a single, unified tax is implicit in the formula on page 273. Observe that cumulative taxable gifts are added back to the taxable estate to determine the tax base. The progressive transfer tax rates (Table 14 –1) are then applied to compute a tax on this base. All gift taxes paid are subtracted out to leave the amount of tax levied on the taxable estate. This computation emphasizes that the taxable estate can be regarded as the unavoidable final transfer in the series of taxable transfers made during an individual's life. The cumulative nature of the federal transfer tax ensures that the taxable estate will be stacked on top of all the decedent's lifetime gifts and as a result will be subject to the highest marginal tax rate.

Tax Credits. The federal estate tax system provides tax credits for (1) state inheritance taxes, (2) death taxes paid to foreign countries, (3) prior federal estate taxes paid on properties included in more than one estate within a 10-year period, and (4) the unified credit. Each of the first three tax credits is intended to reduce the multiple taxation of a single tax base.

The tax credit allowed against the federal estate tax for taxes paid as state inheritance taxes provides all states with a minimum revenue from inheritance taxes. If a state did not impose such a tax, its residents would obtain no personal benefit since the federal estate tax would be increased accordingly. On the other hand, if a state attempted to increase its own state inheritance tax substantially above the maximum federal tax credit, it would stand a real chance of losing its wealthier citizens to another state. The few states that have attempted to impose significantly higher inheritance taxes have found that state residency can easily be changed, especially for the wealthiest taxpayers.

The tax credit allowed for successive federal estate taxes on specific properties included as part of more than one taxable estate within a single 10-year period is intended to reduce the potential cumulative effect of the estate tax. The amount of this credit is directly related to the time interval that has elapsed between the deaths of the various owners. If 2 years or less have elapsed since the property last passed through a taxable estate, the tax credit is 100 percent of the prior tax; if 2 to 4 years have elapsed, the credit is equal to 80 percent of the prior tax; if 4 to 6 years, it is 60 percent; if 6 to 8 years, 40 percent; and if 8 to 10 years, 20 percent. No tax credit is allowed if the property passed through a taxable estate more than 10 years earlier. As a practical matter, this tax credit is of limited importance because most people with substantial property try to arrange their personal affairs to ensure that property will not pass through a taxable estate in such a short period.

The full $192,800 unified credit is subtracted from the estate tax liability to compute the net tax payable. It may appear that this amount of credit can be used twice—once to reduce any gift tax liability during an individual's life and again to reduce any gift tax at death. However, this apparent double usage is illusory. Note that in the computation of the estate tax, only the amount of gift tax *paid* on cumulative gifts rather than the gift tax *computed* on these gifts is subtracted from the gross tax liability. To illustrate the significance of this point, assume an individual made exactly $600,000 of taxable gifts during his lifetime. Because of the use of the unified credit, no actual gift tax was paid on these gifts. At death, the individual has a taxable estate of $150,000 and a tax base of $750,000 (taxable estate plus taxable gifts). The gross tax on this base is $248,300, and since no gift tax was paid, the estate tax before credits is also $248,300. Subtracting the $192,800 credit results in a net tax payable of $55,500. This tax equals the applicable marginal rate of 37 percent on the taxable estate of $150,000. Thus, the unified credit sheltered only $600,000 of our individual's wealth from transfer taxation.

Planning Considerations

When an individual earns income or receives valuable property from some external source, that individual really has only two choices: spend it or save it! To the extent the individual chooses current consumption, he or she is indirectly planning to avoid ever paying a federal transfer tax. If the individual chooses to save some portion of his income or property, sooner or later this accumulated wealth will be transferred to other individuals or organizations. The individual may voluntarily decide to transfer his wealth during his lifetime; in such a case, the federal gift tax implications of the transfer must be addressed. Even if the individual has no desire to give away any amount of property during life, the individual's death will trigger a final, unavoidable transfer of wealth, the federal estate tax consequences of which will have to be determined.

Any person who has already accumulated a considerable amount of property or who plans to do so in the future should be aware of certain basic estate planning considerations. A complete inventory at market value of the various property interests potentially includable in an individual's gross estate must be the first step in any estate plan. The second step is to determine the disposition of these interests on the individual's death. The terms of the individual's will should be carefully reviewed to establish the disposition of the probate estate. Beneficiaries of any interests included in the gross estate but not included in the probate estate should be identified. At this point, the amount of federal, state, or foreign death taxes for which the individual's estate would be liable can be estimated, and viable techniques for minimizing that liability can be considered.

The optimal use of the unlimited marital deduction is a central feature of many estate plans. If a decedent's entire net estate passes outright to a surviving spouse, the taxable estate is reduced to zero. This simple technique, however, may not be the optimal use of the marital deduction if the tax shelter provided by the decedent's $192,800 unified credit is wasted. To illustrate, assume Mr. Barker would like to bequeath property to certain relatives and friends, as well as to his spouse. Any nonmarital bequests will result in a taxable estate on Mr. Barker's death. However, if Mr. Barker has not made any taxable gifts during his life, his unified credit will offset the tax liability on a $600,000 taxable estate. To fully use his credit, many estate plans provide for *bypass* bequests of $600,000. These bequests can be made directly or in trust to beneficiaries other than the surviving spouse.

The primary benefit of the marital deduction is the deferral of payment of the federal estate tax on marital wealth until the death of the second spouse. Assume Mr. Barker, the taxpayer introduced in the previous paragraph, has a projected net estate of $5 million, is age 70, and has been a resident of Ohio, a common law state, his entire life. His wife, age 64, has no substantial property of her own. On Mr. Barker's death, $600,000 of his assets go to a bypass trust for the benefit of the couple's grandchildren. The $4.4 million balance of the estate goes to Mrs. Barker. Mr. Barker's taxable estate is $600,000 and no estate tax is payable. If the marital deduction had not been used, the current tax liability on a $5 million estate would have been $2,205,200. If Mrs. Barker outlives her husband by 10 years and leaves her $4.4 million taxable estate to her children and grandchildren, the tax liability 10 years hence will be $1,875,200, which at a 10 percent discount rate represents a present tax cost of only $722,971. Note that this example also illustrates a secondary benefit of the marital deduction. Because Mrs. Barker inherited property from her husband, the $192,800 unified credit available to Mrs. Barker can be used on her death to shelter a second $600,000 of family wealth from the federal estate tax.

Unfortunately, use of the marital deduction can have a detrimental effect in situations in which the marital bequest will be subject to a higher marginal tax rate in the estate of the second spouse to die. This problem can be demonstrated by changing the facts in the Barker example. Assume Mr. and Mrs. Barker are residents of California, a community property state, and Mr. Barker's $5 million net estate represents his half interest in the couple's total $10 million of community assets. If a $2,205,200 federal estate tax were imposed on Mr. Barker's estate, the effective tax rate would be 44 percent ($2,205,200/$5,000,000). However, if $4.4 million of Mr. Barker's assets are bequeathed to his wife as a marital deduction, this amount of wealth will be added to Mrs. Barker's $5 million interest in the community property and will increase her potential taxable estate to $9,440,000. In this case, the entire amount of property inherited from Mr. Barker will be taxed at both a marginal and an effective tax rate of 55 percent. A second negative consequence of the marital deduction occurs when the property bequeathed to a surviving spouse increases dramatically in value in the time period between the deaths of the spouses. If the property left to Mrs. Barker by her husband is worth considerably more than $4.4 million when Mrs. Barker dies, the tax savings from the deferral may be counterbalanced by the increased tax cost on the appreciation.

As the above discussion indicates, the optimal use of the marital deduction in any given family situation may not be immediately obvious. Instead, the family and the estate planner must consider many uncertain variables such as the relative life expectancies of the spouses, the tax rates that would apply to the estates of each, the appropriate discount rate for comparing present tax costs and benefits, and the potential appreciation in the marital assets before a tax planning strategy is finally adopted.

INTERACTION BETWEEN THE TRANSFER TAXES AND THE INCOME TAX

Successful family tax planning requires consideration of both the transfer tax and the income tax consequences of any given transaction. Sometimes the two sets of consequences are compatible, but in certain situations a planning strategy that minimizes one type of tax increases the other type of tax. The next section of this chapter will explore the interaction of these two types of federal taxes in several common planning contexts.

When a wealthy taxpayer decides to make a gift to a family member who owns a relatively small amount of property, the particular asset selected for the gift becomes important. Generally, an asset generating a high level of income is a good candidate. The future after-tax income from the donated property can create new wealth for the donee, wealth that will not be accumulating in the estate of the donor. Moreover, the donee may face a lower marginal income tax rate than the donor, so the tax paid on the income stream will be reduced subsequent to the gift.

Consider the case of a father in the 39.6 percent marginal income tax bracket who gives an investment asset generating $20,000 of annual income to his two single adult daughters as co-owners. If each child has less than $20,000 of other gross income for the year, her marginal tax rate on the $10,000 of incremental income will be only 15 percent, and the annual tax liability on the income will decrease from $7,920 (39.6 percent of $20,000) to $3,000 (15 percent of $10,000 times two). Consequently, the family has saved $4,920 of income tax because of the father's gift. The amount of income tax savings inherent in any intrafamily income shift depends on the comparative tax rates of the persons involved. If the two daughters in this example each have $30,000 of other gross income, their marginal tax rate on the incremental income would jump to 28 percent and the family's tax savings on the income shift would drop to $2,320 ($7,920 less $5,600). Of course, if the daughters in this example were under the age of 14, the *kiddie tax* discussed in Chapter 5 would impose the father's 39.6 percent marginal rate on most of the investment income, and no tax savings would result from the income shift.

While the kiddie tax certainly constrains the tax benefit resulting from gifts of income-producing assets to young children, several planning techniques can minimize its impact. If the gifted property consists of stock in growth corporations that pay minimal or no dividends, the annual increase in the value of the stock represents deferred income that will not be subject to tax until the stock is sold—at some point after the little shareholder celebrates his or her 14th birthday. Similarly, children under the age of 14 can be given Series E or EE savings bonds, the interest income on which will not be recognized until the bond is redeemed.

Transfers of Appreciated or Depreciated Assets

From a transfer tax planning perspective, a gift of property that is rapidly appreciating in value is an excellent idea. Both the current value of the property and the future appreciation will be removed from the donor's potential taxable estate. If the intention of the family is to sell the property in the foreseeable future, the income tax consequences of the transfer are favorable. The donor's basis in the property will carry over to the donee so that if the donee sells the property, any appreciation that occurred while the donor owned the property as well as any postgift appreciation will be taxed at the donee's tax rate.

If the family intends to hold the property as a long-term investment, tax planning is complicated by the fact that if the original owner retains the property until death, the income tax basis of the property will be stepped up to the property's fair market value at date of death. As a result, the entire amount of predeath appreciation in the asset permanently escapes income taxation. However, this same amount of appreciated value would be included in the owner's taxable estate and subject to the federal estate tax. Now the goals of transfer tax minimization and income tax minimization are in direct conflict. Important considerations in resolving the conflict are the comparative estate and income tax rates the family will face. For example, if the estate tax rate on the appreciated value is expected to be the maximum 55 percent, while the potential income tax rate on the same appreciation will be 39.6 percent, the wiser action would seem to be a gift of the property during the owner's life.

If an individual owns an asset that has depreciated in value, tax planning with regards to the asset is fairly straightforward. The asset should not be given away because the basis of gifted property for purposes of determining a loss on subsequent sale is the *lesser* of the donor's basis or the value of the property at date of gift. Therefore, any decline in value that occurred before the date of gift will be nondeductible when the donee eventually sells the property. Similarly, if the original owner retains the depreciated property until death, the basis will be reduced to fair market value, and the predeath decline in value will never be recognized for tax purposes. The best strategy is for the owners to sell any deprecated asset before death, recognize the tax loss, and use the sale proceeds to make a more promising investment.

Tax Planning with Charitable Contributions

Many wealthy taxpayers are inclined to make substantial transfers of property to their favorite charitable organizations, and the federal tax laws encourage them to act on their generous inclinations. A gift to charity made during the taxpayer's life or a bequest to charity under the terms of the taxpayer's will are both fully deductible for transfer tax purposes. The fact that a gift to charity will also result in an income tax deduction for the donor makes the gift option more attractive. There are limits on the amount of the charitable contribution income tax deduction—very broad limits, but limits nonetheless. In general, a taxpayer's annual deduction for contributions to public charities may not exceed 50 percent of his or her adjusted gross income. To the extent a taxpayer's contributions consist of certain appreciated capital assets, the limit drops to 30 percent of adjusted gross income. There are additional limits on contributions to private foundations. Any amount of a current year contribution in excess of the applicable limit may be carried forward by the taxpayer for five years.

In choosing an asset to donate to charity, an individual should be aware that a gift of an appreciated capital asset offers a substantial income tax benefit—the amount of the deduction equals the fair market value of the asset rather than the donor's tax basis in the asset. As a consequence, the donor will enjoy a tax deduction computed with reference to appreciation that will never be included in the donor's taxable income. To illustrate the economics of this situation, consider the individual in a 39.6 percent marginal tax bracket who owns a capital asset with a current value of $100,000 and a tax basis of only $25,000. If the individual sells the asset for cash with the intention of donating the after-tax proceeds to her favorite charity, she will recognize a $75,000 capital gain on sale, pay a 28 percent capital gains tax of $21,000, and receive a charitable contribution deduction of only $79,000 ($100,000 proceeds less $21,000 tax liability). The deduction will reduce her tax bill by $31,284. Thus, her charitable contribution has resulted in a net tax savings of $10,284. If, on the other hand, our taxpayer donated the capital asset directly to charity, her charitable contribution deduction (subject to the 30 percent AGI limitation mentioned above) would be $100,000, and her tax savings would be $39,600! Clearly, the tax law encourages the direct contribution of the appreciated asset to charity. However, a caveat is in order. Remember that the favorable outcome in the above illustration occurs only if the donated property is a capital asset. If an individual donates an asset that would generate ordinary income on its sale, the charitable contribution deduction is limited to the donor's adjusted tax basis in the property.

CONCLUSION

Successful family tax planning involves the careful consideration of personal objectives as well as income, gift, and estate tax provisions. Most successful tax plans involve a substantial lead time if they are to be implemented properly. The careful integration of the many pertinent considerations involves full cooperation on the part of all parties. Any individual who has accumulated over $600,000 worth of property should give serious consideration to discussing his or her personal situation with a qualified tax adviser.

PROBLEMS AND CASES

1. Mr. and Mrs. Burns have a net worth of $6 million, most of which is invested in securities yielding 9 percent. Although they live very comfortably, they do not spend all their earnings from their investments. They have four children, ages 15 to 25, who are all in school and have low incomes.
   a. If Mr. and Mrs. Burns live for 10 more years, how much estate tax will they save if they give each of their children $20,000 this year?
   b. What are some other tax-motivated reasons for making such gifts?
2. Laura Weber desires to give common stock with a tax basis of $10,000 and a fair market value of $60,000 to charity. If Laura is in the 39.6 percent marginal tax bracket, what is the amount of her (regular) income tax savings?
3. Grandmother Ewing owns a large ranch in West Texas (tax basis, $75,000). Although people say the ranch is worth $1 million, it provides Mrs. Ewing with an income of only $60,000 (more or less) each year. Since Mrs. Ewing has adequate income from other sources, this low rate of return on the ranch does not bother her. She loves the family ranch and hopes it will stay in her family for many years, remaining in essentially the same undeveloped condition it is in today. Mrs. Ewing has already decided to pass title to the ranch to her son, R.J., but she is uncertain whether to do it now (before she dies) or to wait, letting the ranch be part of her estate. Mrs. Ewing fully understands that she could guarantee the ranch would remain in the family for many years if she would place the property in trust, with appropriate instructions to the trustee not to sell the land. She also knows that trustees charge management fees and that financial conditions sometimes change so ideas that seem good now turn out to be unsatisfactory in the future. Because of her strong feelings on these matters, she has clearly ruled out the use of a trust as far as the ranch is concerned. Her only remaining decision is whether to give it away now or let it pass through her estate. Given the strength of Mrs. Ewing's feelings on this matter, what do you recommend that she do? Explain.
4. Mr. and Mrs. Carver would like to make a sizable gift to their alma mater, the University of Alabama. The Carvers own property worth several million dollars, so their only real problem is deciding what to give the university. Among the options they are considering are the following:
   (1) Cash of $100,000.
   (2) Marketable securities (basis, $60,000; value, $100,000), which Mr. Carver purchased as an investment eight years ago.

(3) Part of this year's bumper cotton crop (basis, \$0; value, \$100,000). (One of the Carvers' many trades and businesses is raising cotton. The cotton has no basis because, like all other farmers and ranchers, the Carvers immediately deduct the cost of seed, fertilizers, etc.)

a. From the income tax point of view, which of these properties would make the best gift, assuming the Carvers are in the 39.6 percent marginal tax bracket? Explain briefly.
b. From the gift tax point of view, which of these properties would make the best gift? Explain briefly.

5. Martin Harvard strongly believes that three properties he owns will increase significantly in value within the next 24 to 36 months. Those three properties can be described as follows:

   EFG stock: basis, \$160,000; current value, \$162,000.

   FGH stock: basis, \$2,000; current value, \$162,000.

   GHI stock: basis, \$260,000; current value, \$162,000.

   Mr. Harvard is thinking seriously about making a gift of one of these three properties to his only child, Mervin. Given his premonition about the next two or three years, which property do you recommend that he give? (Assume Martin and Mervin are in approximately the same marginal tax brackets.) Explain briefly.

6. A wealth couple made the following gifts in years 19x1 through 19x4.

Year	*Gifts to Daughter*	*Gifts to Son*	*Gifts to Charity*
19x1	\$ 80,000	\$ 50,000	\$ 55,000
19x2	100,000	120,000	60,000
19x3	120,000	100,000	60,000
19x4	200,000	230,000	90,000

   Assuming these were the first taxable gifts ever made by this couple and all gifts were considered to be made jointly by husband and wife, determine the following:

   a. The current taxable gifts in each year, 19x1 through 19x4.
   b. The current net gift tax liability in each year, 19x1 through 19x4.

7. When Hal Owen died this year, the title to all his property passed to the Owen Trust under the terms of a will giving Mrs. Owen a mere "life interest" in the property. Hal Owen's will further stipulated that, on the death of his wife, the remainder interest in any trust property should pass to their two children, Suzzie and Brad.

   a. Describe in simple terms what is meant by Mrs. Owen's "life interest" in the property previously owned by her deceased husband.

b. Would the terminable interest left by Hal to his wife qualify for the marital deduction?

c. What valid nontax reasons might Hal have for leaving his property in trust rather than leaving it directly to his wife and/or their children?

d. What good tax reasons might Hal have had for leaving all his property in trust even if Mrs. Owen owned a substantial amount of property in her own name and clearly had no need for additional assets during her remaining lifetime?

8. Mike Davis, a bachelor, recently changed the terms of his will, bequeathing his entire probate estate to a lifelong friend. Mr. Davis owns several insurance policies on his own life; under the terms of the policies, Mr. Davis's niece Susan will receive $350,000 on Mr. Davis's death. Mr. Davis also named Susan as his beneficiary under his employer's qualified retirement plan. Currently Mr. Davis has an account balance in the plan of $400,000. Because Mr. Davis has never made a taxable gift and because the estimated value of his probate estate is only $500,000, Mr. Davis is assuming there will be no federal estate tax liability when he dies. Discuss the validity of Mr. Davis's assumption.

9. In 1967, Mrs. Lennon transferred $500,000 worth of assets into an irrevocable trust for the exclusive benefit of her children. Under the terms of the trust instrument, annual income will be distributed among the children according to Mrs. Lennon's exclusive direction. When the youngest child attains the age of 25 years, the trust assets will be distributed equally among the living children. In 1967, Mrs. Lennon paid a $42,000 gift tax attributable to the creation of the trust. What are the estate tax consequences of this trust arrangement if Mrs. Lennon dies in the current year when the value of the trust assets is $1.2 million?

10. Sam Simpson dies in the current year, leaving a net estate of $2.5 million. After specific bequests of $100,000 to Sam's favorite public charity and $1.5 million to his surviving wife Claire, the residue of the estate was bequeathed to Sam's grandson Walter. During his lifetime, Sam made adjusted taxable gifts of $300,000; because of the unified credit, however, Sam never paid a gift tax. Compute the federal estate tax payable by Sam's estate.

Case 14–1

Grandfather Howell, age 74 and in rapidly failing health, owns a valuable tract of land near a growing metropolitan area. The land has a current value of $5 million and a tax basis of $1.2 million. Mr. Howell has already received several offers to buy the land, and although he is in no immediate need of cash, he is inclined to sell before the real estate market declines. Mr. Howell's current will provides that all his property, including the land, will go to Grandmother Howell, age 64 and in excellent health. However, the Howells really would like their wealth ultimately to pass to their orphaned grandchild, Jenny. Consequently, Mrs. Howell's will leaves all her property to Jenny. The Howells have never made any taxable gifts.

a. Discuss the tax consequences if Mr. Howell makes a current gift of the land to Jenny, who then sells the land as quickly as possible.

b. Discuss the tax consequences if Mr. Howell redrafts his will and leaves the land to Jenny rather than Mrs. Howell. In this case, Jenny will sell the land as soon as possible after the grandfather's death.

c. Is either of the above two planning strategies superior to the Howells' current plan regarding the land?

CHAPTER 15

The Tax Compliance Process

The federal income, gift, and estate taxes are all self-compliance taxes. The Internal Revenue Code explicitly requires persons liable for any of these taxes to compute the amount of tax due, file the proper return, and maintain adequate records to support the calculations presented on such return. As a practical mater, the tax laws are so complex that a majority of individuals engage a tax professional to assist in the preparation of their returns. Nevertheless, even individuals who rely entirely on professional help remain personally responsible for complying with the law and must bear the consequences of failure to comply.

The first segment of this final chapter of the text is an overview of the income tax compliance system. The procedural rules governing payment of tax and filing of returns and the Internal Revenue Service's audit process are explained. Your rights as a taxpayer in dealing with the IRS, as well as the penalties the IRS may impose during the audit process, are described. The segment closes with a discussion of the judicial process by which taxpayers may challenge the results of an IRS audit in federal court.

The second segment of the chapter focuses on the future of the federal tax system. In this segment, the author revisits the basic tax policy issues introduced in Chapter 1 and reexamines the perceived shortcomings of the existing tax system. The chapter concludes with a discussion of alternative tax systems currently in vogue as potential replacements for our federal income tax.

FILING AND PAYMENT REQUIREMENTS

Most individual taxpayers report their income on the basis of a calendar year and must file their returns for the current year by April 15 of the following year. The few individuals who have adopted a fiscal year must file their returns by the 15th day of the fourth month following the close of the taxable year. Corporations, which report on the basis of either a calendar year or a fiscal year, just file their returns by the 15th day of the third month following the close of their taxable year. The various extensions of the filing deadlines available to individuals and corporations were discussed in Chapter 5.

As a general rule, both individuals and corporations must pay the entire tax due for the year by the *unextended* filing date of the return for such year. From the government's perspective, taxpayers who are late in paying any amount of tax have received a loan from Uncle Sam. Consequently, the IRS automatically bills these taxpayers for *interest* based on the period of time from the required payment date to the date the delinquent tax is actually paid to the IRS. The annual interest rate charged by the government equals the federal short-term rate plus three percentage points. Interest is compounded daily and the rate is adjusted quarterly.

Millions of taxpayers overpay their annual income tax in the form of excess withholding or estimated tax payments. Conceptually, these individuals have made a loan to the federal government. However, the Internal Revenue Code states that the government is not required to pay interest on any overpayment of tax refunded within 45 days after the filing date for the return on which the refund is requested or the date such return is actually filed, whichever is later. As a result, taxpayers who routinely receive their refund checks within this statutory grace period do not earn interest on the refund. In the rare case when the IRS fails to mail a refund check on a timely basis, the government must pay interest to the taxpayer. The annual interest rate paid by the government equals the federal short-term rate plus only two percentage points.

Late-Filing and Late-Payment Penalty

If a taxpayer fails to file an income tax return on a timely basis, the IRS may impose a *late-fling and late-payment penalty,* the calculation of which is quite complicated. Basically, this penalty equals 5 percent of the balance of tax due with the return for each month (or portion thereof) that the return is delinquent. The 5 percent penalty runs only for five months (i.e., until the penalty equals 25 percent of the balance due). After five months, the penalty rate drops to one-half percent of the balance of tax due with the return. This reduced penalty can run for an additional 45 months.

To illustrate this calculation, assume that Mr. Tripp failed to request an extension of time to file his 1996 return and didn't mail his return to the IRS until July 29, 1997. The return showed a 1996 tax liability of $45,890 and $42,000 of tax withheld during the year by Mr. Tripp's employer. Mr. Tripp enclosed a check for the $3,890 balance due with his late return. Because the tax due was not paid by April 15, the IRS will charge Mr. Tripp interest on $3,890 for the period of time form April 16 through July 28. Because Mr. Tripp's return was not filed on a timely basis, the IRS may assess a penalty of $778 ($3,890 multiplied by 5 percent for each of the three full months and the part of a fourth month that the return was late). The IRS may agree to waive this penalty (but not the interest) if Mr. Tripp can show reasonable cause for his tardiness.

One interesting feature of the late-filing penalty deserves mention. The amount of the penalty is a function of the balance of tax due with a delinquent return. If a taxpayer has overpaid his income tax for the year, his return will show a refund due instead of a balance due. In this case, the government cannot assess any penalty if such return is filed after the due date. Of course for as long as the return is delinquent, the government is enjoying an interest-free loan from the taxpayer that does not have to be repaid until the taxpayer finally decides to file.

Return Processing

Each year, approximately 125 million income tax returns are filed with the IRS by individuals, corporations, partnerships, and fiduciaries. These returns pour into the 10 IRS service centers located throughout the country. These centers are information processing facilities where each tax return is checked for mathematical accuracy and logged into the IRS's massive computer system. This system enables the IRS to cross-check each tax return against other types of information returns filed with respect to the taxpayer, such as a Form W–2 filed by the taxpayer's employer or Form 1099s filed by payors of interest, dividend, rents, or other types of income to the taxpayer.

If a return reflects a math error or a discrepancy between the return and a corresponding information return, the service center mails a letter to the taxpayer explaining the problem and indicating that the taxpayer must pay additional tax or can expect to receive an additional refund. The service centers are responsible for depositing personal checks or money orders attached to tax returns with the U.S. Treasury and for authorizing refund checks to be prepared and mailed.

Many people place unjustified significance on the fact that the government promptly cashed the check included with their return for the balance of tax due or that they received their refund check on a punctual basis. While these events prove that their tax return was processed, they do not in any way mean that the IRS has accepted the accuracy of the return as filed. The IRS has three years from the later of the statutory due date (April 15 for calendar-year individuals) or the date the return was actually filed to examine that return for mistakes and to assess any additional tax for the year. For example, if a taxpayer files her 1997 tax return on the extended due date of August 15, 1998, the IRS has until August 15, 2001, to audit the return and assess additional tax.

The normal three-year *statute of limitations* is extended to six years if the return contains material errors. If the IRS determines that a return is *fraudulent* (a concept discussed later in this chapter), the return remains open (subject to audit) indefinitely. Because of the possibility of audit, taxpayers should keep all supporting paperwork such as receipts and canceled checks on which the return is based for at least three years after the return is filed. Any legal documents containing information pertinent to the return (closing statement on a property sale, divorce decree, etc.) and a copy of the return itself should be retained as permanent records.

THE AUDIT PROCESS

The IRS selects corporate tax returns for audit primarily on the basis of the magnitude of the corporation's business operations, measured in terms of taxable income and net worth as reported on the Form 1120. Individual returns are usually selected by a highly classified computer program that analyzes the contents of each return and assigns the return a DIF (*discriminate function*) score. The score is a theoretic measure of the return's potential for generating additional tax revenue on audit. The higher the score, the greater the likelihood that the return contains an error that resulted in an understatement of tax liability for the year. Obviously, those returns with the highest DIF scores are chosen for examination. Although the details of the DIF selection process are a closely guarded secret, it seems reasonable to assume that highly speculative investment activities, itemized deductions that are unusually high for a person in a certain income bracket, and deductions that are prone to manipulation or abuse (travel and entertainment expenses, nonbusiness bad debts, losses generated by a secondary business, etc.) inflate a return's DIF score. Similarly, returns reflecting large amounts of income are much more likely to be selected for audit than returns reflecting modest incomes.

Routine audits are conducted by personnel working out of one of the 63 IRS district offices scattered throughout the United States. The simplest audits, called *correspondence examinations,* may be handled entirely by telephone or through the mail. More complex audits take place at an IRS office (an *office examination* conducted by a tax auditor), or at the taxpayer's place of business (a *field examination* conducted by a revenue agent). Office audits tend to focus on a few questionable items on a return. Field audits are broader in scope and involve a complete examination of the taxpayer's books and records for the year or years under investigation.

If the IRS requests a personal interview with a taxpayer, or if the taxpayer requests an interview during the course of an audit, the IRS must schedule the interview at a reasonable time and a location convenient for the taxpayer. Individuals who must deal with the IRS can represent themselves or authorize an attorney, certified public accountant, or *enrolled agent* to represent them. While attorneys and CPAs are licensed to practice by state boards or agencies, *enrolled agents* receive certification to practice before the IRS by passing an exam on tax law written and administered by the IRS itself.

Taxpayers who are notified that their tax returns are under audit may panic unnecessarily. Any person who made a good faith effort to comply with the laws in preparing the return and has maintained adequate records has nothing to fear. In a best case scenario, the audit will be concluded promptly with no change in the tax liability for the year, or even with a refund (plus interest) due to the taxpayer. Of course, the return was selected for audit in the first place because of its high probability of error in the taxpayer's favor. Consequently, the more probable outcome is that the office auditor or revenue agent will decide that the return contains a mistake that resulted in an understatement of the correct tax liability. In this case, the taxpayer is assessed a *deficiency* (the amount of additional tax owed), plus interest based on the number of days between the time the return was originally filed and the date the deficiency is finally remitted to the government.

Corporations may deduct the interest paid on federal income tax deficiencies as a business expense. Currently, the IRS and the Tax Court are in disagreement as to whether interest paid by an individual on an income tax deficiency relating to that individual's unincorporated business is deductible. Treasury regulations specifically state that interest paid by an individual on a federal income tax deficiency is nondeductible personal interest "regardless of the source of the income generating the tax liability." In a recent decision, the Tax Court concluded that this regulation is invalid.[1] The court held that to the extent an income tax deficiency relates to the operation of an individual's trade or business, the interest is fully deductible above-the-line as an ordinary and necessary business expense.

---

[1] *Redlark,* 106 T.C. No. 2 (1996).

Your Rights as a Taxpayer

In 1989, Congress enacted *The Taxpayer Bill of Rights*, which requires the IRS to deal with every citizen and resident in a fair, professional, prompt, and courteous manner. The bill stipulates that the IRS must provide the technical help needed by taxpayers to comply with the law. Currently, the IRS publishes over 100 free information booklets, one of which, Publication 910 *Guide to Free Tax Services,* is a catalog describing the many types of assistance offered. Taxpayers can order booklets, as well as tax forms and instructions, by calling the IRS toll-free at 1-800 TAX-FORM (829-3676).

The Taxpayer Bill of Rights ensures personal and financial confidentiality. If the IRS requests information from a taxpayer, the taxpayer has the right to know why the IRS is asking for the information, exactly how the information will be used, and the nature of any consequences if the taxpayer refuses to provide the information. However, the bill contains an important disclaimer: the IRS can share tax return information with state tax agencies, and under strict legal guidelines, the Department of Justice, other federal agencies, and foreign governments under tax treaty provisions.

Noncompliance Penalties

Negligence. Occasionally during the course of an audit, a revenue agent will conclude that the taxpayer did not make a good faith effort in computing a correct tax liability for the year under examination. In such case, the IRS may impose an administrative penalty on the taxpayer. The Internal Revenue Code provides for dozens of different penalties, each one designed to discourage a particular type of misconduct. One of the more frequently imposed is the *negligence* penalty, which equals 20 percent of any underpayment of tax attributable to the taxpayer's failure to make a prudent attempt to comply with the law, or the taxpayer's intentional disregard of tax rules and regulations.

For example, suppose that the IRS agent who audited Ned Lyon's 1995 Form 1040 discovered three errors that collectively resulted in a $45,000 understatement of Ned's 1995 tax liability. The agent believed that two of the errors were attributable to Ned's sincere misunderstanding of the law, but that Ned had no legitimate excuse for the third error. The amount of the understatement attributable to the third error was $13,000. If the agent decides to impose a negligence penalty on Ned, the amount of the penalty would be $2,600 (20 percent of $13,000). Ned would be required to pay this penalty in addition to the $45,000 deficiency and the interest thereon.

The distinction between an honest mistake and negligence is certainly nebulous. A taxpayer's exposure to the negligence penalty depends on subjective factors such as the complexity of the issue in question, the taxpayer's level of education and business experience, the existence of supporting documentation, and the taxpayer's degree of cooperation during the course of the audit. When the IRS determines that a taxpayer's actions justify a negligence penalty and the taxpayer wants to challenge this determination, the burden of proof in the dispute rests on the taxpayer. In other words, the taxpayer must prove by a *preponderance of evidence* that the agent's finding of negligence is incorrect. Individuals who follow the advice of tax professionals in preparing their returns are much less likely to incur a negligence penalty than individuals who personally prepare their returns, although reliance on professional advice is not a guaranteed defense.

Civil Fraud. The harshest administrative penalty that the IRS may impose is the *civil fraud* penalty, which equals 75 percent of the portion of an underpayment of tax attributable to fraud. Fraud can be defined as a person's willful attempt to cheat the government by deliberately understating tax liability. Fraud is characterized by the systematic omission of substantial amounts of income from the tax return or by the deduction of nonexistent expenses or losses. Revenue agents often assess a fraud penalty when they discover that a taxpayer keeps two sets of financial records—one for tax purposes and one reflecting the taxpayer's true income. The fact that a taxpayer has altered or destroyed business records and documents, concealed assets, or cannot account for large cash receipts or deposits is a strong indication of fraud. Because of the severity of the penalty, the burden of proof in establishing fraud falls on the IRS. To sustain a fraud penalty, the IRS must have more than just a preponderance of evidence; it must show by *clear and convincing evidence* that the fraud occurred.

Criminal Fraud. If a revenue agent uncovers a particularly egregious incident of fraud, the IRS may decide to turn the matter over to its Criminal Investigation Division. This division will assign a *special agent* to gather evidence to determine if the government has a strong enough case to indict the taxpayer for *criminal fraud,* also known as *tax evasion.* Tax evasion is a felony offense, punishable by severe monetary fines (up to $100,000 in the case of an individual and $500,000 in the case of a corporation) and by imprisonment in a federal penitentiary. An individual must be convicted of tax evasion in a court of law, and the prosecution must establish the individual's guilt *beyond a reasonable doubt.* If the Criminal Investigation Division decides that the case against the taxpayer does not meet this strict evidential standard and is therefore too weak to prosecute, the IRS may have to settle for the civil fraud penalty.

Tax Return Preparer Penalties

The Internal Revenue Code imposes penalties on income tax return preparers who fail to comply with certain statutory rules of professional conduct. The term *income tax return preparer* refers to any person who prepares returns (or who employs other people to prepare returns) for compensation, regardless of whether such person is a licensed attorney, certified public accountant, or enrolled agent. Preparers are required to sign the tax returns they fill out for their clients, include their identifying number on such returns, furnish clients with copies of the completed returns, and retain copies of all returns or a list of the names and identifying numbers of all clients. Preparers are prohibited from endorsing or negotiating any tax refund checks paid to their clients. Violation of any of these procedural rules without reasonable cause results in a monetary penalty. For example, a preparer who fails to sign a tax return may be assessed $50 for each failure. The maximum amount of this penalty with respect to returns filed during any calendar year is limited to $25,000.

If a preparer takes a position on an income return that results in an understatement of tax liability, and the preparer knows (or should know) that such position has no realistic possibility of being sustained on its merit, the IRS may assess a $250 penalty with respect to the return. If the understatement is the result of a willful attempt by the preparer to understate the tax liability, or if the position represents an intentional disregard of rules and regulations, the penalty increases to $1,000. Obviously, these penalties are intended to discourage tax advisors from taking overly aggressive positions in order to reduce their clients' tax liabilities. Even though the monetary amount of the penalties is modest, they can result in adverse publicity that may seriously damage an income tax return preparer's professional reputation.

CONTESTING THE RESULT OF AN AUDIT

Taxpayers who disagree with all or any part of the results on an audit (including the imposition of administrative penalties) may appeal the disputed issues to a regional Appeals Office of the IRS. An appeal leads to an administrative conference between the taxpayer (or more typically, the taxpayer's representative) and a specially trained IRS appeals officer. The purpose of the conference is to resolve the controversy in a manner that is fair and impartial to both the government and the taxpayer. Appeal officers have broad latitude in settling disputes and may negotiate a compromise between the taxpayer's and the government's position on questionable issues. IRS Publication 5 *Appeal Rights and Preparation of Protest for Unagreed Cases* explains a taxpayer's appeal rights and the appeals procedure in detail.

Litigation

When a taxpayer and the government cannot resolve their differences in an administrative conference, the taxpayer has the right to take the case to federal court for judicial review. In federal tax matters, one of three *trial courts* has original jurisdiction. A taxpayer may refuse to pay the deficiency determined by the IRS and instead file a petition with the U.S. *Tax Court* to hear the case. Alternatively, the taxpayer may pay the deficiency, then immediately sue the government for a refund in either the local U.S. *District Court* or the *Court of Federal Claims* located in Washington D.C.

The selection of the appropriate judicial forum is an important matter of strategy to be determined by the taxpayer's legal counsel. Each of the courts is quite different in operation, and one might be more advantageous than the others, depending on the nature of the tax controversy to be settled. The Tax Court adjudicates only federal income, gift, and estate tax issues and is comprised of judges who are acknowledged experts in the tax law. In contrast, District Court and Court of Federal Claims judges preside over cases involving a wide variety of legal issues and may have no special expertise in the tax area.

Taxpayers who want a jury trial must take their case to the District Court. In both the Tax Court or Court of Federal Claims, a single judge or a panel of judges tries the case and renders a verdict. If the controversy to be resolved is one of fact rather than the technical application of the law, the taxpayer's attorney may recommend that the matter be put to a jury in the hope that the jury panel (who, after all, are taxpayers themselves) may be naturally sympathetic. Of course, the viability of this strategy depends on the particular issue at hand. For example, if the parent of a chronically ill child is arguing that the cost of a nontraditional treatment program

Figure 15–1 The Tax Litigation Process

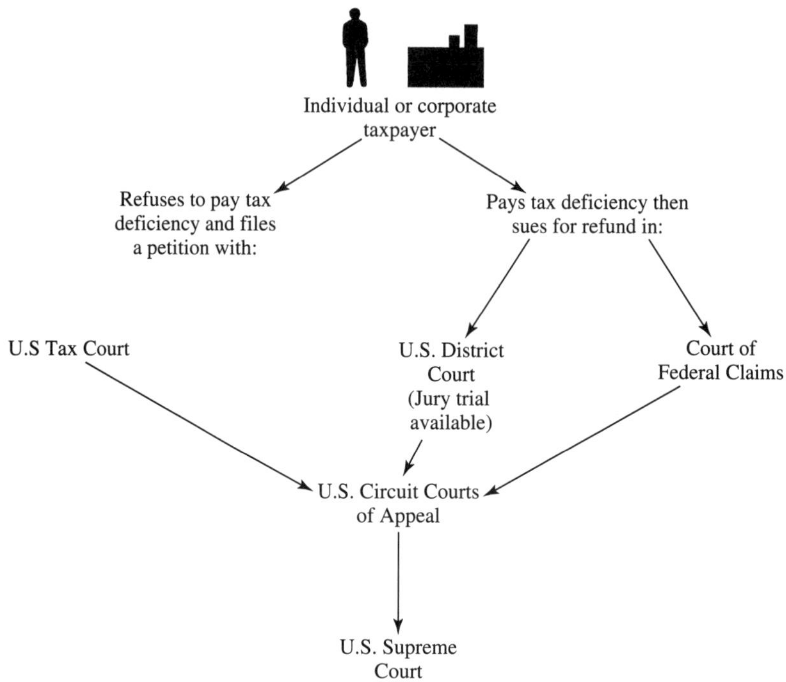

should qualify as a deductible medical expense, a jury trial seems a wise choice. However, if a businessman is trying to prove that a $750,000 salary from his closely held corporation is reasonable compensation, he may be much better off pleading his case before a Tax Court judge.

The party to the litigation that loses at the trial court level (taxpayer or government) may appeal the verdict to one of the 13 U.S. *Circuit Courts of Appeal.* The geographic location of the trial court proceeding determines which appellate court has jurisdiction. These courts generally do not review findings of fact by a lower court, but they will consider if the lower court properly applied the relevant law to the facts. After the appellate court has either affirmed or reversed the trial court's decision, the losing party may appeal the case to the U.S. *Supreme Court.* This Court may agree to hear the case (*grant certiorari*) or refuse to hear it (*deny certiorari*). When the Supreme Court denies certiorari, the decision of the appellate court is final. During an average term, the Supreme Court agrees to hear no more than a dozen federal tax cases, which are selected either because the Court believes that the case involves a significant and unresolved principle of law or because two or more appellate courts have rendered conflicting opinions on the proper resolution of a tax issue.

While it is true that every taxpayer who disagrees with the IRS concerning the correct amount of tax liability for a year has a right to his day in court, many people are reluctant to bear the emotional and financial cost of litigation. In order to make the legal system a bit more accessible to the average person, Congress established a *Small Cases* division of the Tax Court. A taxpayer who is disputing a deficiency of $10,000 or less for any one taxable year may request an informal hearing presided over by an officer of the court. The current filing fee for such hearing is only $60, and the taxpayer may plead his own case without the necessity of an attorney. After the presiding officer has heard the taxpayer's side of the story and rendered judgment, the matter is settled—neither taxpayer nor government may appeal the case to any other court.

Taxpayers who prevail in their litigation with the IRS may be entitled to recover litigation expenses from the government. Such expenses include court costs, attorney fees not in excess of $75 per hour, fees paid to expert witnesses, and payments for technical studies, analyses, tests, and reports that the court agrees were necessary for the preparation of the taxpayer's case. Taxpayers requesting recovery of their litigation expenses must convince the court that the IRS's position in the case was not substantially justified. A factor that the courts consider in determining whether an IRS position was justifiable is whether the government pursued the litigation in order to harass or embarrass the taxpayer or out of political motivation.

The existence of the Small Cases division of the Tax Court and the right of taxpayers to recover litigation costs from the government reflect congressional sympathy for individuals who sincerely believe that they are right and the IRS is wrong. On the other hand, Congress has little tolerance for people who waste the government's time and money by initiating foolish lawsuits against the IRS. Section 6673 of the Internal Revenue Code authorizes the Tax Court to impose a monetary penalty up to $25,000 on a taxpayer who takes a frivolous or groundless position in a proceeding before the court or institutes a proceeding primarily for delay.

IRS Collection Procedures

Taxpayers who have exhausted every avenue of appeal without success must finally pay the amount of tax deficiency (including interest and penalties) to the government. The IRS has the authority to collect the amount owed by whatever means necessary, including seizing the taxpayer's assets and selling them at auction, levying bank accounts, and garnishing the taxpayer's salary or wage. The IRS, however, knows full well it can't get blood out of a stone. If a taxpayer has insufficient financial means to pay a tax deficiency and is willing to cooperate, the IRS may negotiate a settlement (referred to as an *offer in compromise*) for some lesser amount. Alternatively, the IRS may allow the taxpayer to pay off the debt over time on an installment basis.

A question sometimes arises as to which person is legally responsible for the payment of an income tax deficiency. If the taxpayer is a corporation, the deficiency must be satisfied out of corporate assets; typically, shareholders are not liable for their corporation's unpaid taxes. A major exception to this limited shareholder liability arises when the corporation is no longer in existence. In this circumstance, the shareholders have *transferee liability* for the corporation's unsatisfied debts, including federal taxes, to the extent of the value of any assets they received upon liquidation of the corporation.

The Innocent Spouse Rule

When individuals sign their Form 1040s each year, they become liable for any future tax deficiency with respect to that return. In the case of a joint return, both husband and wife must sign the return, thereby becoming *joint and severally liable*. This means that the IRS may assess either person for the entire amount of any deficiency determined on subsequent audit of the return. Occasionally, this rule can work a real hardship on a person who is liable for substantial back taxes attributable to a joint tax return that he or she signed without any knowledge of the information included therein. Such a person may be relieved of liability for the tax deficiency under the *innocent spouse rule.*

Such relief is dependent on three conditions. First, the deficiency must be attributable to the omission of gross income or the claim of a bogus deduction or credit by the person's spouse. Second, the person must establish that in signing the return he or she did not know, and had no reason to know, that the return understated the correct tax liability. Third, taking into account all the facts and circumstances, it is inequitable to hold the person liable for the deficiency. One factor that the courts weigh very heavily in analyzing this third condition is whether the person significantly benefited, directly or indirectly, from any gross income omitted from the return. If a court concludes that a significant benefit existed, innocent spouse relief is generally denied, even if the person seeking relief was clearly ignorant of the omission. Normal spousal support is not considered a significant benefit, but an unusually lavish or extravagant lifestyle may indicate that both spouses were profiting from the omitted income. Another factor that the courts consider is whether the person seeking relief has been deserted by or is divorced from his or her spouse.

THE CURRENT TAX SYSTEM: A STATUS REPORT

In recent years, dissatisfaction with the federal tax system has become a chronic public condition. A major aspect of this dissatisfaction is the system's failure to generate sufficient revenues to pay for the goods and services that we as citizens and voters collectively demand from our government. Because of the revenue shortfall, the federal government operates at a tremendous deficit and must borrow billions of dollars in the capital markets to pay its bills. This profligacy has resulted in a national debt of roughly $5 trillion. In 1997, Uncle Sam will pay more than $240 billion of interest on this debt, a payment representing 17 percent of the federal budget.

Many critics condemn the current tax system as inefficient in macroeconomic terms. These critics contend that a progressive income tax levied on the profit derived from labor and capital inhibits entrepreneurial initiative. In addition, the tax discourages individuals from investing their after-tax earnings because the financial return on investments (interest, dividends, capital appreciation, etc.) is again subject to taxation. In this respect, the tax is biased against saving and in favor of personal consumption. This bias may partially account for this country's relatively low personal savings rate (approximately 4 percent in contrast to Germany's 12 percent rate and Japan's 15 percent rate).

The most widespread complaint against the income tax system is that it is unfair. Of course, no government has been or ever will be capable of designing a tax that people enjoy paying. As Edmund Burke, the English parliamentarian and social scientist, observed, "To tax and to please, no more than to love and be wise, is not given to man." Nevertheless, the public perception that the federal income tax is unfair has increased dramatically in recent decades.

This perception of inequity has many negative consequences. Research has shown that individuals who are convinced that the income tax system is inherently unfair are more likely to deliberately underreport their taxable incomes than individuals who believe the system is fair. This result suggests that as public confidence in the equity of the federal tax system erodes, the level of compliance will decline. As greater numbers of citizens regard tax evasion as acceptable, and even rational, behavior, the tax system will place an increasingly unfair burden on the honest remainder who continue to comply with the law.

> Taxpayer morale ultimately depends on the belief that taxes are fair. If the basis for this belief comes under suspicion, voluntary compliance with the tax laws is jeopardized. Thus, the perceived lack of fairness of the income tax may be as important as actual complexities, economic distortions, and inequities.[2]

Many individuals base their belief that the federal income tax system is unfair on the fact that the system is so complicated. They are convinced that the system is full of exotic loopholes that benefit only high-income taxpayers who can afford expert legal advice. Hopefully, readers of this text understand that this conviction is unfounded. Many of the complexities of the income tax law discussed in previous chapters, such as the depreciation recapture rules, passive activity loss limitation, and alternative minimum tax, were designed to ensure that high-income taxpayers could not manipulate the system to unwarranted advantage. Affluent individuals undeniably use the tax planning techniques discussed throughout this text on a routine basis to maximize their after-tax rate of return on investments and business activities. However, the majority of these techniques derive from simple, commonplace features of the law rather from any closely guarded, esoteric secrets known only to tax professionals.

Is the federal income tax system really that complicated for the average middle-class American? In 1993, 114 million individual income tax returns were filed. Forty-nine million of these returns were filed on either a Form 1040A or a Form 1040EZ, both of which are short, simple forms. Half of the remaining 65 million taxpayers filed Form 1040s on which they claimed a standard deduction, rather than itemized deductions. Arguably, the majority of these returns contained only a few numeric entries. Granted, almost two thirds of all taxpayers who filed a From 1040 paid a return preparer to do the work for them; however, this fact does not necessarily mean that the tax system is fatally flawed. As one commentator observed:

> Specialization is an aspect of a highly developed economy. We no longer grind our own flour, cut our own hair, or repair our own automobiles. There is no more

[2]Department of the Treasury, *Tax Reform for Fairness, Simplicity, and Economic Growth* 1 (Washington, D.C.: U.S. Government Printing Office, 1984), p. 9.

reason to expect that everyone should do his own tax return than that everyone should be his own cardiologist.[3]

Alternatives to an Income Tax

Almost every year, Congress enacts legislation to modify the existing tax system. Regardless of the details of the legislation, lawmakers invariably praise the changes as much needed improvements to the efficiency and equity of the law. Periodically, Congress engages in serious discussions of wholesale tax return that would result in a complete overhaul of the existing system. The most ambitious reformers want to replace the income tax with a superior method of generating federal revenues.

The Flat Tax

A much publicized alternative to the current system is the so-called *flat tax.* The different versions of the flat tax that have been introduced over the past years have certain common characteristics. The defining characteristic is an individual rate structure consisting of a zero rate on a base amount of taxable income and a single rate on all income in excess of the base. For example, Representative Dick Armey (R-Texas) has proposed a system in which the first $33,300 of annual income earned by a married couple with two children would be exempt from tax, while any income in excess of the exemption amount would be taxed at a 17 percent rate. Technically, this flat tax is not a proportionate tax, but a progressive tax with only two rate brackets.

Mr. Armey's current version of the flat tax makes a number of major changes in the computation of an individual's tax base. For example, interest income, dividends, and investment gains would be excluded from taxable income. Most itemized deductions, such as medical expenses, home mortgage interest, and charitable contributions, would be eliminated. Clearly, the implementation of the flat tax would radically alter both the tax base and the tax rate. Consequently, it is hard to generalize as to whether such implementation would result in an increase or decrease in any one person's federal tax liability.

Politicians who champion the flat tax apparently have convinced themselves and a significant segment of the general public that it would be both simpler and fairer than the current income tax. Most tax experts scoff at the notion that a reduction in the number of brackets in the tax rate structure in and of itself is a meaningful simplification in the law. They also point out that a rate structure with only two brackets is not innately more or less fair than a rate structure with six brackets. Finally, any observer of the political scene must question whether Americans would ever embrace a tax system under which the rich and super-rich face exactly the same marginal tax rate as the average, middle-class citizen.

Consumption Taxes

Many economists advocate replacing the federal income tax system with some type of *consumption tax.* A consumption tax is levied on the amount of wealth that a person consumes. In other words, you don't pay the tax if you don't spend your money.

---

[3]Herbert Stein, "If It Ain't Broke . . . " *The Washington Post* (September 10, 1995), p. C3.

Sales taxes imposed on retail purchases of most goods and *excise taxes* imposed on the retail purchase of a few specific items (gasoline, cigarettes, liquor, etc.) are familiar example of *transaction-based* consumption taxes. Each time a consumer buys a retail good, a tax is imposed on the transaction and collected by the vendor to be remitted to the taxing jurisdiction.

Sales taxes are criticized as being regressive, bearing most heavily on people with the least financial ability to pay. To illustrate this problem, assume that State P has a 5 percent sales tax on all retail purchases of goods and services. Individual I earns $20,000 of annual disposable income and spends this entire amount on consumable items. In contrast, Individual J earns $100,000 of annual disposable income; J spends only $75,000 on consumables and invests $25,000. Individual I pays $1,000 of sales tax annually, and his average tax rate (with respect to disposable income) is 5 percent. Individual J pays $3,750 of sales tax annually, and his average tax rate is 3.750 percent ($3,750 ÷ $100,000 disposable income).

A 1988 study concluded that "sales and excise taxes everywhere are regressive, often shockingly so; they can create unconscionable hardships for people living in poverty, they represent real financial burdens for middle-income families, and they let the rich, particularly the super-rich, off the hook almost entirely."[4] The majority of states have attempted to mitigate the inherent regressivity of sales taxes by legislating broad exemptions for groceries purchased for home consumption, prescription medicines, and residential utilities.

Cash Flow Tax. A consumption tax may be *time period-based* rather than transaction-based. A person's consumption for a year is generally measured as the amount of cash received during that year less any amount of cash spent on nonconsumable items, such as business and investment expenditures. The person's consumption tax liability equals the amount of annual consumption multiplied by the applicable tax rate. Because of its emphasis on cash receipts and disbursements, this version of a consumption tax has been labeled a *cash flow tax.*

To illustrate the structural difference between a cash flow and an income tax, let's develop a three-year model involving two taxpayers, Mr. Smith and Mr. Jones. Both individuals earn a $50,000 salary in Year 1, which is their only source of taxable income. Mr. Smith spends every penny of his income on consumer goods and services (food, rent, clothing, entertainment, etc.), while Mr. Jones spends only $40,000 on consumer goods and services and invests the remaining $10,000 in interest-bearing bonds. Under an income tax system, Mr. Smith and Mr. Jones have the same tax base (recognized income) and would pay the same amount of tax. Under a cash flow tax system, the tax base equals the amount of cash spent on consumption. Consequently, Mr. Smith's tax base would be $50,000, while Mr. Jones's tax base would be only $40,000, and Mr. Smith would pay a larger consumption tax than the more frugal Mr. Jones.

---

[4]Citizens for Tax Justice, "Nickels and Dimes: How Sales and Excise Taxes Add Up in the 50 States," March, 1988.

	Mr. Smith	*Mr. Jones*
Year 1:		
Salary/**taxable income**	**$50,000**	**$50,000**
Savings	-0-	(10,000)
Consumption	**$50,000**	**$40,000**
Year 2:		
Salary	$51,000	$50,000
Interest income	-0-	1,000
Taxable income	**$51,000**	**$51,000**
Savings	-0-	(9,000)
Consumption	**$51,000**	**$42,000**
Year 3:		
Salary	$51,000	$50,000
Interest income	-0-	1,500
Taxable income	**$51,000**	**$51,500**
Withdrawn savings	-0-	6,000
Consumption	**$51,000**	**$57,500**

In Year 2, Mr. Smith's salary increases to $51,000, all of which he spends during the year. Mr. Jones's salary remains at $50,000. However, he also earns $1,000 of interest income. Mr. Jones uses this interest plus $8,000 of his salary to buy additional bonds. Under an income tax system, both taxpayers have recognized $51,000 of taxable income and would pay the amount of tax. Under a cash flow tax system, Mr. Smith would be taxed on $51,000 of consumption, while Mr. Jones would be taxed on $42,000 of consumption.

In Year 3, Mr. Smith's taxable income and consumption remain at $51,000. Mr. Jones receives a $50,000 salary and earns $1,500 of interest income. Instead of adding to his savings during the year, Mr. Jones *dissaves* by cashing in $6,000 worth of bonds and spending the proceeds. While Mr. Jones's taxable income in Year 3 is $51,500, his taxable consumption for the year is $57,200.

As the three-year model demonstrates, a cash flow tax is biased against current consumption and in favor of deferred consumption (i.e., savings). Theoretically, the tax should encourage individual taxpayers to save a greater portion of their financial resources in order to reduce their current tax bill. On a macroeconomic level, this taxpayer behavior should result in a higher national rate of investment and capital formation.

While a cash flow tax may be more economically efficient than an income tax, nothing in its structure makes it inherently fairer or simpler than an income tax. Both systems require taxpayers to measure an annual base (taxable income or taxable consumption) on which their tax is computed. The equity of either system depends on the precision with which the statutory definition of taxable income or taxable consumption reflects economic reality. And under either system, Congress must design a rate structure (whether proportionate or progressive) that distributes the tax burden across citizens with different amounts of taxable income or taxable consumption.

Value-Added Tax. A third variety of consumption tax is a *value-added tax* (VAT). Conceptually, a VAT is levied on businesses engaged in any phase of the manufacturing or distribution of goods and services. The tax equals a percentage of the value added to the overall production process by the business. To illustrate the concept of value added, assume that Firm M manufactures a certain small appliance. M's cost per unit for materials, labor, and overhead is $40; and M sells each unit to Firm W, a regional wholesaler, for $46. M's $6 profit represents the incremental value that M added to the production process. If M is subject to a 5 percent VAT, M must pay a 30 cent tax (5 percent of $6) for each unit sold. Now assume that Firm W sells appliances purchased from M to various unrelated retailers for $50 per unit. Firm W's $4 profit on the sale of each unit represents the incremental value that W added to the production process by providing distributional services. Consequently, Firm W must pay a 20 cent VAT (5 percent of $4) for each unit sold.

The above example is extremely simplistic in that it ignores the possibility that both Firm M and Firm W could shift the economic incidence of any VAT for which they are liable by increasing the price at which they sell their product to the next business in the production sequence. To the extent that a VAT is shifted along the entire production sequence to the final purchaser (the customer who buys the product or service for personal consumption), the VAT resembles a retail sales tax.

Because a VAT is imposed on business organizations rather than individuals, it has the advantage of being eminently enforceable. Major industrial nations such as the United Kingdom, France, Canada, Germany, and Japan have used some form of VAT for decades to raise enormous amounts of tax dollars. In this country, conservative politicians have opposed a VAT precisely because it has such potential to increase federal revenues, which in turn could be used to expand, rather than shrink, the size and scope of the federal government. Many conservatives' worst fear is that the current deficit crisis may compel Congress to enact a VAT in addition to (rather than as a replacement for) the federal income tax. Another source of concern is that a VAT tends to be invisible—a tax that people hardly realize they are paying. Consequently, the tax will not be subject to public scrutiny and may fail to inspire healthy debate concerning its merits or shortcomings.

THE FUTURE OF THE FEDERAL TAX SYSTEM

Not even the experts have a crystal ball that allows them to predict the future of our federal tax system. The author is sure of only two things. First, for as long as the United States exists, there will be a federal tax system. Second, that system, whatever its form, will be the subject of perennial and unrelenting controversy. After all, tax reform is hardly a novel idea. In 1977, the Treasury published *Blueprints for Basic Tax Reform,* which proposed eliminating the existing tax structure and replacing it with either a comprehensive-based income tax or a cash flow consumption tax. Politicians, tax practitioners, and academics alike bestowed effusive praise on *Blueprints* and then promptly forgot about it. In 1982, the Senate Finance Committee held hearings on a flat tax, and in 1985, several flat tax bills were actually introduced in Congress. The Tax Reform Act of 1986 was hailed as a sweeping piece of bipartisan reform legislation that created a two-bracket rate structure for individuals and eliminated any preferential treatment of capital gains. Just seven years later in the Revenue Reconciliation Act of 1993, Congress undid much of the reform inherent in the 1986 act by expanding the rate structure to five brackets and reinstating a 28 percent maximum rate on capital gain.

Is meaningful reform of the federal tax system an impossible dream? Of course not. However, permanent reform is best achieved gradually, through incremental and evolutionary change. Zealots who advocate tearing out the current system by its roots and supplanting it with a utopian alternative are forgetting that "the enemy of better is best."[5] The perfect federal tax system will no doubt continue to elude us. Nonetheless, our task as a democratic society is to comply with the current law in a responsible manner as we continually work toward improvement.

PROBLEMS

1. Ms. Cooper did not request an extension of time to file her 1996 income tax return and did not mail the completed return to the IRS until July 2, 1997. She enclosed a check for $2,380, the correct balance of tax due with the return.
   a. Assuming that Ms. Cooper cannot show reasonable cause for filing a delinquent return, compute the late-filing and late-payment penalty for which she is liable.
   b. How would your answer *to a* change if Ms. Cooper did not mail her return until November 21, 1997?
   c. How would your answer to *a* change if Ms. Cooper return showed a request for a $750 refund rather than a balance of tax due?
2. Don Dittmar filed a delinquent 1996 tax return on July 3, 1997. The return reflected total tax liability of $3,700, withholding of $4,000, and a $300 refund due. Based on these facts, compute the late-filing penalty for which Don is liable.
3. Laranzo Inc. uses a fiscal year ending November 30 for purposes of filing its federal income tax return. The corporate controller filed Laranzo's Form 1120 for its taxable year ending November 30, 1996, on December 23, 1996.
   a. Based on these facts, what is the last day on which the IRS may assess the corporation for additional tax relating to this fiscal year?
   b. How would your answer to *a* change if Laranzo's income tax return for its fiscal year ending November 30, 1996, was timely filed on its extended due date of August 15, 1997?
4. Statistically, about 1 percent of the individual Form 1040s filed for a taxable year are subject to IRS audit. Discuss why a Form 1040 reflecting an adjusted gross income of $31,000 and a standard deduction has much less than a 1 percent chance of audit, while a Form 1040 reflecting adjusted gross income of

[5]Sheldon S. Cohen, "Taming the Tax Code," *Tax Notes* (September 18, 1995). Mr. Cohen was IRS Commissioner from 1965 to 1969.

$235,000 and itemized deductions of $85,790 has a much greater than 1 percent chance of audit.

5. During the course of an IRS audit of her 1995 income tax return, Beth Helm provided the revenue agent with a meticulous set of records substantiating every numeric entry on the return. The agent actually complimented Beth on the quality of her return preparation. Nevertheless, in computing her tax liability, Beth did make a $435 error in her favor. When Beth received formal notification that she owned an additional $435 of 1995 tax, she was dismayed to learn that the IRS was also billing her for $92 of interest on the deficiency. Beth doesn't understand why she must pay interest when she obviously made a good faith effort to comply with the tax law. Can you explain why?
6. Barrett Holt has an M.B.A. degree from Stanford University and has been in business for himself for 18 years. The revenue agent who audited Barrett's 1995 Form 1040 discovered a glaring error that resulted in a $16,200 understatement of tax for the year. When the agent questioned him about the error, Barrett just shrugged his shoulders and could offer no reasonable explanation.
   a. If the revenue agent decides that the error resulted from Barrett's intentional disregard of a tax rule, compute the amount of the negligence penalty the agent may impose on Barrett.
   b. Should the fact of Barrett's education and business experience influence the agent's decision to impose the negligence penalty?
7. During the course of her audit of Mr. and Mrs. Jacob's individual tax returns for 1995 and 1996, revenue agent Amelia Sui learned that the couple kept two sets of books and records for their sole proprietorship. The Jacobs presented her with one set that substantiated the amount of net business income reported on their returns for the two-year period. Amelia discovered the second set during a routine examination of the business's computer files. This second set indicates that the Jacobs earned over $80,000 during 1995 and 1996 that they omitted from gross income. The tax deficiency attributable to the omission was $32,000.
   a. If Amelia concludes that the Jacobs committed fraud by deliberately omitting income from their tax returns, compute the amount of the civil fraud penalty the IRS may impose.
   b. Describe the procedural steps the IRS must take if it wants to charge the Jacobs for criminal fraud.
   c. Why might the IRS decide to impose a civil fraud penalty on the Jacobs but not charge them with criminal fraud?
8. Explain the legal concept of "burden of proof" as it relates to the taxpayer penalties for:
   a. Negligence
   b. Civil fraud
   c. Criminal fraud
9. During a field examination of Gentech Inc.'s corporate income tax returns for 1995 and 1996, the revenue agent discovered that the corporation's treasurer had

deliberately and systematically omitted substantial amounts of income and inflated deductions to minimize the corporation's tax liability. The agent suspects that the treasurer adopted this course of action with respect to the corporation's tax returns as early as 1989. Can the IRS initiate an audit of Gentech's tax returns all the way back to 1989? Explain briefly.

10. Mr. Jay, a very successful commercial artist, engaged Darla Evans, a local attorney, to prepare his 1996 income tax return. Mr. Jay provided the attorney with his check records, deposit slips, receipts, and financial documents pertaining to 1996 and carefully read through the completed return before signing it.

    In 1998, Mr. Jay's 1996 return was selected for audit. The IRS agent discovered that Ms. Evans incorrectly deducted certain of Mr. Jay's personal living expenses. Consequently, the tax liability shown on the return was understated by $8,900. The agent decided that the deduction represented an unrealistic position, with no reasonable basis in the law.

    a. Based on the above facts, is Mr. Jay liable for payment of the $8,900 tax deficiency plus interest?
    b. Could the IRS impose a negligence penalty on Mr. Jay?
    c. Could Ms. Evans be subject to penalty because of the error she made in preparing Mr. Jay's income tax return?
    d. Would your answer to *c* change if Ms. Evans were Mr. Jay's sister, and she prepared his return as a favor rather than for compensation?

11. Janet and Mike Black filed a joint 1995 tax return on which they reported $24,000 of adjusted gross income. During the year, Mike was extremely ill and was hospitalized for four months. Janet, desperate for additional cash to pay her husband's mounting medical bills, took a night job as a bartender at a local club. She earned approximately $7,000 of tips from this second job, none of which she reported on the 1995 return. Mike had no idea his wife had gone to such lengths on his behalf.

    In 1996, Mike and Janet divorced. In 1997, Mike was notified by the IRS that he owed a $1,100 deficiency plus interest attributable to the unreported tips that had been omitted from the 1995 joint return. Based on these facts, should Mike be able to avoid paying this deficiency because he qualifies as an "innocent spouse"? Explain your conclusion.

12. Brenda Bradley has decided to contest a $28,650 tax deficiency that the IRS assessed with respect to her 1995 Form 1040. She understands that she can initiate the litigation in U.S. District Court or the U.S. Tax Court. State any reasons why Brenda might prefer one trial court over the other.

Index